D1617335

PATRIARCHY AND ECONOMIC DEVELOPMENT

UNU/WIDER

Studies in Development Economics embody the output of the research programmes of the World Institute for Development Economics Research, which was established by the United Nations University as its first research and training centre in 1984 and started work in Helsinki, Finland, in 1985. The principal purpose of the Institute is policy-oriented research on the main strategic issues of development and international co-operation, as well as on the interaction between domestic and global changes.

PATRIARCHY AND ECONOMIC DEVELOPMENT

Women's Positions at the End of the Twentieth Century

Edited by

VALENTINE M. MOGHADAM

A study prepared for the World Institute for Development Economics Research of the United Nations University (UNU/WIDER)

CLARENDON PRESS · OXFORD
1996

Oxford University Press, Walton Street, Oxford OX2 6DP
Oxford New York
Athens Auckland Bangkok Bombay
Calcutta Cape Town Dar es Salaam Delhi
Florence Hong Kong Istanbul Karachi
Kuala Lumpur Madras Madrid Melbourne
Mexico City Nairobi Paris Singapore
Taipei Tokyo Toronto
and associated companies in
Berlin Ibadan

Oxford is a trade mark of Oxford University Press

Published in the United States
by Oxford University Press Inc., New York

UNU/WIDER: World Institute for Development Economics
Research of the United Nations University, Katajanokanlaituri 6B
FIN-00160 Helsinki, Finland

British Library Cataloguing in Publication Data
Data available

Library of Congress Cataloging in Publication Data
Data available
ISBN 0–19–829023–3

1 3 5 7 9 10 8 6 4 2

Typeset by Graphicraft Typesetters Ltd, Hong Kong
Printed in Great Britain
on acid-free paper by
Bookcraft (Bath) Ltd., Midsomer Norton, Avon

PREFACE

The main objective of this volume has been the analysis of interrelations between patriarchy and the development process. Fundamental questions have been raised by the authors. What has been the effect of the development process on gender relations? Did the patriarchal structure of the societies reproduce existing inequalities, resulting in further deterioration in the social position of women? Could the social struggles and the institutional changes moderate, or even eliminate, certain traditional characteristics of the societies influencing gender relations? These links between patriarchy and development have not been previously studied, documented, discussed, and analysed, in such a systematic way. Nor have they been treated in the comparative and multi-dimensional perspective offered by this volume.

As is well known, patriarchy, the concept of which has been widely used in literature, has a narrower and a broader meaning. In its narrower sense, it is the rule by the father within the family and the consequent subordination of both his wife and children. In the broader concept, patriarchy is used as a term for characterizing the society which is dominated by men, within the family and outside. It characterizes a society that reproduces male dominance in all areas of its life, in education, work, and in its socio-political institutions. The authors of this volume—internationally recognized experts in gender and development studies—offer an interesting combination of theoretical, historical, and empirical approaches from different parts of the world, including the Nordic welfare states, and the former socialist countries (the transition economies). They focus, however, on the problems of the developing countries. In certain parts of the developing world patriarchy has changed very little, and still assumes cruel forms. The studies in this volume prove not only that the functioning of patriarchal societies has varied significantly over time, and in different parts of the world depending on the cultures and the socio-economic formations, but they also reveal the great differences which exist between certain countries and regions at the end of the twentieth century. The trajectories of patriarchy and development have not been linear, but have had different impacts on the various groups of the societies. They point, however, to the main similarities from the perspectives of the issues raised, that in spite of the improvements in the social and economic position of women, some of the fundamental characteristics of the patriarchal societies have a major influence on the possibilities for full participation in, and on the outcomes of, the development process.

The research programme of UNU/WIDER, on which this volume is based, is an integral part of the studies on the human dimension of development. The issues raised by the authors and the responses are also of key importance for the United Nations system, which has become the most important global institution dealing with the improvement of the position of women. I express my sincere thanks and appreciation to the authors of this book for their scholarly contributions, and particularly to Dr Valentine Moghadam who directed this important project for her high-level intellectual and managerial work. I recommend the volume to all those who are interested in gender issues embedded in the overall human aspects of the development process.

MIHÁLY SIMAI
Director, UNU/WIDER

Helsinki
June 1995

CONTENTS

LIST OF CONTRIBUTORS

TUOVI ALLÉN is Senior Researcher at the Labour Institute for Economic Research, Helsinki, Finland.

SHEILA CARAPICO is Associate Professor in the Department of Political Science, University of Richmond, Virginia, USA.

ELIZABETH DORE is Senior Lecturer at the School of Languages and Area Studies, University of Portsmouth, UK.

RITA S. GALLIN is Director of the Women and International Development Program at Michigan State University and co-editor of *The Women in Development Annual Review.*

LEELA KASTURI is a consultant at the Centre for Women's Development Studies in New Delhi, and Associate Editor of the *Indian Journal of Gender Studies.*

JOHN LIE is Associate Professor in the Department of Sociology, University of Illinois, Urbana-Champaign.

VALENTINE M. MOGHADAM is Senior Research Fellow at the World Institute for Development Economics Research (WIDER) of the United Nations University, based in Helsinki.

JANE L. PARPART is Professor of History, Women's Studies, and Development Studies at Dalhousie University, Halifax, Nova Scotia, Canada.

RUTH PEARSON is Senior Lecturer in Economics at the School of Development Studies, University of East Anglia, Norwich, UK.

HELEN I. SAFA is Professor in the Department of Anthropology and the Center for Latin American Studies, University of Florida, Gainesville, USA.

GUY STANDING is Director of Labour Market Policies in the International Labour Office in Geneva. He was formerly Director of the ILO's Central and Eastern European Team.

SYLVIA WALBY is Professor of Sociology, University of Leeds, UK.

Introduction and Overview

Valentine M. Moghadam

What has been the impact of economic development on the lives and status of women? What effect does development have on gender relations, and how do patriarchal structures affect the development process? At the end of the twentieth century, and after four world conferences on women, is patriarchy on the decline, or is it only its form that is changing? The chapters in this book address these questions through theoretical, historical, and empirical approaches, and by providing critical analysis and macro- and micro-level data for east Asia, the Middle East and North Africa, Latin America and the Caribbean, sub-Saharan Africa, the Indian subcontinent, the Nordic countries, and Eastern Europe and the former Soviet Union.

Before turning to the chapters themselves, let us first look at some contradictory evidence of the development process and women's positions. Around the world, women's life expectancy, literacy, educational attainment, labour-force participation, contraceptive use, and political participation have all increased. In all but a few countries, women's life expectancy exceeds men's; in some former state-socialist countries, more women than men attained university degrees; around the world the working class and professional-managerial class are now female as well as male; family planning programmes, women's advancement, and the women's movement have led to postponement of marriage and increased control over fertility; and more women are seeking major roles in national and international decision-making. Another achievement is that more and more women have entered the field of law, pushing for legal reforms and working to extend legal literacy to women. Women are also the new proletariat worldwide. This phenomenon has been termed the 'globalization of female labour' and, in a somewhat different vein, the 'feminization of labour' (Joekes, 1987; Standing, 1989). The role of women in manufacturing has been receiving considerable attention from scholars—if not always from planners and policy-makers. The industrial performance of the newly industrialized economies suggests an important mutual relationship between women's employment and overall development and industrial growth.

And yet, major gaps continue between men's and women's advancement. In industrial countries, gender discrimination continues in employment and wages, with women often getting less than two-thirds of the employment opportunities and about half the earnings of men. In developing countries, the great disparities, besides those in the job market, are in health care, nutritional support, and education. For example, women make up two-thirds of the illiterate population in developing countries. And south and east Asia, defying the normal biological result that women live longer than men, have a disturbing adverse sex ratio.[1] An annual report of the United Nations Development Programme, the *Human Development Report*, ranks countries by a composite index consisting of longevity (life expectancy at birth), knowledge (adult literacy and mean years of schooling), and income (real purchasing power). The 1993 report found that when the human development index is adjusted for gender disparity, no country improves its HDI value—another way of confirming that no country treats its women as well as it treats its men (UNDP, 1993: 16). However, three countries improve their HDI ranking: Sweden (from 5 to 1), Denmark (from 12 to 4), and New Zealand (from 16 to 7).

REGIONAL TRENDS

A recent publication by the United Nations, *The World's Women 1970–1990: Trends and Statistics*, describes global trends in women's status and compares their situation across regions and countries. The report contains six broad themes: (1) women, families, and households—which includes indicators on formation, duration, size, and structure of families/households, as well as a discussion of domestic violence; (2) public life and leadership; (3) education and training; (4) health and child-bearing, which includes data on life expectancy, causes of death, the health of girls, and fertility; (5) housing, human settlements and the environment, which includes indicators on migration and women's access to basic utilities; and (6) women's work and the economy. As the report shows, since 1970 there have been important changes in what women do—out of choice or necessity, depending on the hardships and the opportunities they face. The following summary of regional trends in women's status and social positions is from the report (UN, 1991: 1–2).

In *Latin America and the Caribbean*, women in urban areas made some significant gains according to indicators of health, child-bearing, education, and economic, social and political participation. But there was little change in rural areas, and the serious macro-economic deterioration of many Latin American countries in the 1980s undercut even the urban gains as the decade progressed.

In *sub-Saharan Africa*, there was some improvement for women in health and education, but indicators in these fields are still far from even minimally

[1] UNDP, *Human Development Report 1993* (New York: Oxford University Press, 1993), 17; Amartya Sen, 'More than 100 Million Women are Missing', *New York Review of Books*, 37/20 (1993), 61–6. The reasons for the adverse sex ratio are high maternal mortality, infanticide, and nutritional neglect of the girl-child, which derive from concepts of gender that devalue females and privilege males.

acceptable levels in most countries. Fertility remains very high, and there are signs that serious economic decline, coupled with rapid population growth, is undermining even the modest gains in health and education. Women's economic and social participation and contribution is high in sub-Saharan Africa, but there remain large differences between men and women in most economic, social, and political indicators.

In *northern Africa and western Asia*, women made gains in health and education. Fertility declined slightly but remains very high: 5.5 children in northern Africa and 5.3 in western Asia. Women in these regions continue to lag far behind in their economic participation and in social participation and decision-making. The rise of fundamentalist movements could affect the progress women have made in the past twenty years, by insisting on domestic roles for women.[2]

In *southern Asia*, women's health and education improved somewhat. But as in Africa, indicators are still far from minimally acceptable levels and are still very far from men's. Nor has economic growth, when it has occurred, helped women—apparently because of their low social, political, and economic participation in both urban and rural areas.

In much of *eastern and south-eastern Asia*, women's levels of living improved steadily in the 1970s and 1980s. Many of the inequalities between men and women—in health, education, and employment—were reduced in both urban and rural areas and fertility also declined considerably. Even so, considerable political and economic inequalities persist in much of the region because women are confined to the lowest-paid and lowest-status jobs and sectors and because they are excluded form decision-making.

Throughout the *developed regions*, the health of women is generally good and their fertility is low. But in other fields, indicators of the status of women show mixed results. Women's economic participation is high in northern Europe, North America, and, until marketization, in eastern Europe and the USSR. It is lower in Australia, Japan, New Zealand, and southern and western Europe. Everywhere occupational segregation and discrimination in wages and training work very much in favour of men. In political participation and decision-making in 1992, women were relatively well represented only in northern Europe.

The picture, then, is a mixed one, as the chapters in this book also show. (For descriptive data on selected developing and industrial countries, including countries covered in this book, see the tables and figures in the Appendix.)

[2] Some fundamentalist movements exhibit flexibility on the question of women. In Iran and Turkey, Islamist movements have many educated women supporters. See Valentine M. Moghadam, *Modernizing Women: Gender and Social Change in the Middle East* (Boulder, Colo.: Lynne Rienner Publishers), esp. ch. 5.

SCOPE OF THE BOOK

This book comes in two main parts, reflecting the two concerns that motivated the UNU/WIDER research conference for which most of the papers were written.[3] Those concerns pertained to the concept of patriarchy and its relevance to contemporary gender relations, and the impact of development broadly defined—but especially industrialization and female wage labour—on women's status and women's lives. Both issues have been the subject of considerable debate in the sociological, feminist, and development literatures, and several of the contributors to this volume have been actively engaged in those debates. For example, the concept of patriarchy had been criticized by some feminists following its early popularity (Barrett, 1980, esp. ch. 1), but Sylvia Walby's theoretical work has in more recent years salvaged 'patriarchy' as a conceptual tool and inspired many feminist researchers perplexed by the intractability of gender subordination, including, in this book, Liz Dore on pre- and post-colonial Nicaragua and Tuovi Allén on contemporary Nordic welfare states. With respect to industrialization and women in the Third World, Ruth Pearson (along with Diane Elson) was influential in drawing attention to the exploitative nature of women's integration into wage work and the significance of cheap female labour for multinational corporations. Helen Safa's writings have also been highly critical of the way female labour has been incorporated into multinational networks in Latin America and the Caribbean. Guy Standing's feminization-of-labour thesis notes that the increasing utilization of female labour has coincided with the deterioration of work conditions.

Yet some researchers, including myself, have been concerned that the emphasis on industrial exploitation—like Walby's argument that the system of patriarchy is highly stable, pervades all social structures, and is responsible for the negative aspects of women's engagement in paid work—has obscured not only some of the positive changes effected by certain aspects of the development process (principally education and employment for women), but, more crucially, women's *agency*. That is, it seemed important to test the hypothesis that patriarchy could be resisted and undermined by both development processes and women's activities. Equally important was the task of investigating the ways that industrialization and wage employment have afforded women the opportunity to become autonomous human beings and to contribute to social development beyond household responsibilities. These theoretical possibilities and research agendas seemed especially important to me, a student of the Middle East and North Africa.

[3] The conference took place at UNU/WIDER in Helsinki in July 1992.

PATRIARCHY AND ECONOMIC DEVELOPMENT

Part I, on Historical and Theoretical Perspectives, begins with Sylvia Walby's chapter on patriarchy. It will be recalled that in *Origin of the Family, Private Property and the State,* Engels stated that the 'world-historical defeat of the female sex' occurred with the rise of the ancient Near Eastern state, the agricultural revolution, and ownership over land and people. It is here where, as historian Gerda Lerner put it, patriarchy originated. Demographer John Caldwell has designated Asia—south, west, and east—as the 'patriarchal belt', and feminist Deniz Kandiyoti has termed it 'the belt of classic patriarchy'—a region where patriarchal structures remain most resilient. With this understanding, some have hypothesized that patriarchal structures weaken as development proceeds—development defined sociologically as industrialization, urbanization, and proletarianization. Walby considers this position, but argues against it. Echoing the concern of a recent book on race in the United States (Wilson, 1980), Walby asks whether patriarchy has declined historically as a central organizing principle of societies and social relations, and argues that it has not. Defining patriarchy as 'a system of social structures and practices in which men dominate, oppress, and exploit women', Walby distinguishes 'private' and 'public' forms of patriarchy and delineates six dimensions and sites of patriarchy: household work, paid work, the state, male violence, sexuality, and cultural institutions. Her premise that 'systematically structured gender inequality' is a key element of the definition of patriarchy leads her to conclude that patriarchy is not eliminated but rather changes form when women move from one socio-economic and political system to another. On the issue of whether there is a positive relationship between changes in paid work and changes in other dimensions of women's lives, her response is to reject the 'base–superstructure model in which the economic base determines the superstructure of such things as political participation and sexual autonomy'.[4]

John Lie examines a case of peripheral industrialization, that of Korea, and implicitly takes issue with Walby's theory of patriarchy, for he argues that gender becomes operational with the emergence of industrialization. For example, the 'cheapness' of female labour is a product, an invention, of the newly differentiated gender roles that pits the norm—male work—against other deviations, such as 'female'. At the same time, the trajectory from agrarian patriarchy to patriarchal capitalism in Korea shows that the dissolution of agrarian patriarchal households and the incorporation of women in the process of industrialization provides both social and epistemological bases for gender-based politics and consciousness.

[4] See Walby in this volume.

Lie's chapter shows that seclusion of upper-class women was practised in Korean pre-capitalist agrarian patriarchy, suggesting a rigid differentiation of sex roles similar to that of the 'classic patriarchy' of south and west Asia. Similarly, Elizabeth Dore's chapter shows that prior to the commercialization of land in Nicaragua—and contrary to certain notions of a gender-egalitarian 'golden age' prior to colonialism—indigenous and poor Ladino women did not share men's right to use of common land. It is interesting that in the case Dore describes, it was the privatization of land that allowed women to appear as landholders. But, she argues, endorsing Walby's theory, a new form of patriarchy emerged: (*a*) family contract labour in which the man was designated head of the household and given the cash advance, and he allocated the family members' labour; (*b*) women-headed households whose cash advances and remuneration were invariably lower than men's; (*c*) sexual abuse of women by the *patron.*

A theoretical point stressed in Dore's chapter concerns the importance of class relations in rural Nicaragua before the commercialization of the economy and the society were differentiated by gender. That is, property rights—or social relations of production—are elaborated by both class and gender, and where relevant, by race and caste as well. Likewise, Sheila Carapico's essay on Yemen shows that the impact of the development process on women's lives depends very much on factors such as status, class, political regime, and resource endowment. Carapico's chapter examines changes in women's roles in the context of recent modernization of tribal society, and finds that class inequalities intersect with longer-standing status distinctions among women. Yemen is an extreme case of late development and this may help to explain why at the present (early) stage of socio-economic development it is not wage employment but housewifery that confers status on women in Yemen. Carapico also draws attention to the importance of the state in definitions of status and of the possibilities open to women. During the years of Marxist rule in South Yemen, significant constitutional changes were enacted and women were encouraged to seek education and employment, whereas such policies were not found in more conservative North Yemen.

Leela Kasturi's chapter on India combines a riveting account of truly progressive legislative efforts to weaken patriarchal structures put forward by the women's movement over a period of fifty years, with a denunciation of distorted development in India and its implications for the status of women. Participation in the independence movement, educational attainment, and access to the new leadership gave India's élite women an opportunity to present demands for the advancement of women in the immediate post-independence period. Women activists have consistently sought to change the direction of socio-economic development in favour of greater social and gender equality. Kasturi's verdict, however, is that their efforts have been stymied not only by government inertia (if not hostility) but by the very nature of the development process, 'which has affected women far more adversely than men. . . . Male bias in development thinking, planning and implementation has affected women's position in the family, the community, and society.' She draws attention to crimes against women such as rape, dowry murder, female foeticide, and child prostitution, and ends by stressing the importance of women's *political* activity for gender equality and for national development.

Like Kasturi, Jane Parpart discusses the importance of the law. Her chapter focuses on use of the law in Zimbabwe to challenge patriarchal authority and control, particularly at the community and household levels, and describes a number of case studies of women's struggles over property. This is done from within a postmodernist feminist perspective that is highly critical of the development process, and a methodological stance that emphasizes attention to micro-level dynamics and women's own voices. The macro-economic data paint a rather grim picture, and social indicators pertaining to women suggest 'little improvement over patriarchal domination during the colonial era'. She concludes that patriarchy remains a formidable obstacle to women's advancement and to progressive legislation aimed at assisting women, and that this 'explains the continued underfunding of the Women's Ministry' and other issues.

INDUSTRIALIZATION, STATE POLICIES, AND WOMEN

Part II takes up issues of industrialization, state policies, and female labour. The simple empirical fact of the increase in female industrial labour has apparently resolved an earlier debate in the WID literature that industrialization and foreign investment in a capitalist framework had the effect of marginalizing female labour.[5] The emphasis on the exploitative nature of manufacturing work for women (Fernandez-Kelly, 1983; Elson and Pearson, 1981) begged the question of whether exploitation was unique to women workers, and whether women from poor or low-income households were better off without paid work (Lim, 1990; Moghadam, 1990). More recent studies focus not on the relations of exploitation—which, after all, are a *sine qua non* of the capitalist enterprise, national and multinational alike—but on the centrality of female labour to the export sector, and hence to national development and growth, and on the relationship between women's industrial work and the growth of a gender or social/class consciousness. In a recent study commissioned by the UN regional commission for Asia and the Pacific, Frances Perkins explored the effects of outward-oriented economic policies on the economic position of women

[5] For an excellent summary of the debate, see Susan Tiano, 'Gender, Work, and World Capitalism: Third World Women's Role in Development', in Beth Hess and Myra Marx Ferree (eds.), *Analyzing Gender* (Beverly Hills, Calif.: Sage Publications, 1987).

and found that women were better off in outward-oriented trade regimes than in closed economies, in terms of level of female labour-force participation, trends in employment, and other indicators of economic and social welfare of women, such as ratios of female to male earnings and numbers of hours worked in the economies of Asia and the Pacific over the past fifteen to twenty years. She finds major differences in these indicators pertaining to women between the outward-oriented east and south-east Asian ESCAP countries, on the one hand, and the south Asian economies of India, Pakistan, Bangladesh, and Nepal, on the other (Perkins, 1993).

Statistics showing increases in female labour-force participation do not reveal very much about labour-market dynamics and conditions of labour, however. As many of the chapters in this book show, not only are women still disadvantaged in the new labour markets (in terms of wages, training, and occupational segregation), but they form a large part of 'non-regular' labour. Moreover, working conditions vary considerably across the export manufacturing sector. Electronics factories are usually large, modern operations that use up-to-date machinery and have amentities such as cafeterias and free transportation for their workers. Apparel factories are more diverse, ranging from clean, modern facilities to poorly ventilated, dingy 'sweatshops'. In general, though, and as the early WID literature stressed, many jobs in the export sector are deskilled, monotonous, dead-end positions that offer few benefits. An important issue for policy-oriented research, therefore, is working conditions and labour standards in the export manufacturing sector.

Ruth Pearson's chapter beings with a re-examination of her earlier arguments, with Diane Elson, regarding the increasing employment of women in the export manufacturing industries of various Third World countries. More than ten years later, she finds no uniform pattern of utilization and spread of female labour, and takes issue with Standing's feminization-of-labour thesis. She emphasizes the importance of extending the discussion to women's extensive and changing role in industrial production and processing in the informal sector. She concludes on two notes. First, the gendered nature of the workforce reveals the variety of forms of industrial organization, formal and informal alike, suggesting the fallacy of notions of linear paths of economic development. Secondly, a complete understanding of the implications of industrialization for women requires an examination of micro-level issues such as women's attitudes to employment, intra-household decision-making, women's aspirations, and so on.

This second point is taken up by Helen Safa, whose chapter discusses profound changes in women's roles in production and in the family, and focuses on women in export-processing zones (EPZ) in the Dominican Republic, a country which is both politically and culturally very conservative. Safa begins with the analytic point that there are three crucial sites of women's subordination—the family, the workplace, and the polity—and that 'patriarchy is manifest' at all three levels. Like Walby, she notes the changing forms of patriarchy with the development of capitalism in industrial countries, and then turns her attention to Latin America and the Caribbean, where she finds evidence that women's engagement in wage labour has improved their position within the household. Her central argument is that there have been more gains to women in the family than in the labour market and the polity. The latter institutions are characterized by an authorization state, lack of union activity, and government complicity in the exploitation of labour, and especially the super-exploitation of female labour.

Safa stresses the connection between the rise of cheap female labour and export-led growth, as others have done. One of her many interesting points concerns the context within which export-led industrialization (ELI) became the development strategy. She notes that ELI was a matter of domestic policy in south-east Asia, and occurred earlier, whereas in Latin America and the Caribbean many countries were forced to adopt it by IMF/World Bank policies. Advocates of internally oriented growth argue that national sovereignty and the establishment of a national market are at stake, and this is difficult to dispute. But the available evidence indicates that ELI tends to encourage more female employment, and Safa's chapter confirms this.

We know that economic development affects not only women's work but women's fertility and role in the family. Change in patterns of decision-making in the household is an important indicator of change in gender relations. Safa's chapter provides strong support for the view that employment enhances women's bargaining power within the household. In terms of fertility, most of the EPZ workers Safa interviewed had four children. This may appear to be a large number, but the women themselves came from families of ten, and were now considering contraception or sterilization, mainly because of the high cost of living. Certainly one of the most interesting of Safa's findings is the change in women's consciousness; the women she interviewed expressed the desire for stable but egalitarian marital relationships.

Safa's findings have been confirmed by other studies of women workers in the export manufacturing sector and their gender and class consciousness. Much of the early literature emphasized their structurally and culturally induced docility; in this early view, women were the preferred workforce in assembly plants in the export sector not only because they are less expensive than men to employ, but because they are easier to manage. Yet Susan Tiano has challenged this stereotype through her interviews with women electronics and apparel workers in the Mexican maquiladora industry, who, she argues, display not only acquiescence and accommodation, but alienation and resistance to exploitation (Tiano, 1993). Thus, though poorly paid and offering few chances of upward mobility, jobs in export manufacturing have provided women workers in some areas the means by which they can improve their position within the household and the family—as well as contribute to household welfare and national development. As working women become major economic contributors to the household, they tend to share household decisions with their husbands or elder family members.

Issues of consciousness and the gender division of labour are also taken up in Rita Gallin's chapter. In many developing countries the salaried labour force is largely male, and much of the female economically active population engages in unpaid family labour. Gallin examines women and work in small- and medium-sized businesses in Taiwan, and finds that women who worked without wages in family businesses frequently voiced dissatisfaction with the arrangement. They were also resentful of their dual burden—responsibility for housework as well as involvement in the family business. Her chapter reveals how the family business—be it a farm or a firm—not only perpetuates the gender division of labour but also reproduces the social division of labour: the 'capitalist' (owner, decision-maker, and manager) is the male, while the 'worker' (and unpaid, at that) is the woman. In the workplace, men's and women's earnings are unequal. How is this gendered division of labour maintained? Gallin shows how the articulation of the Chinese family system with state policy and managerial practices gives women unequal access to education, capital, and connections.

Several chapters in this book stress that not all the manufacturing jobs women take on are in the formal sector, and not all female manufacturing workers receive salaries and benefits. Tunisia is a case in point, where in 1985 labour-force statistics indicate a 55 per cent female share of manufacturing, much of which is home-based work. My own chapter on Iran, Turkey, and Tunisia shows that although more and more women are being drawn into salaried employment—with important positive effects on gender relations and women's autonomy—non-regular employment is increasing at the same time, the informal sector expanding, and there are also cultural backlashes against women's visibility in the public sphere and in labour markets.

'National development' in what used to be called the Third World has been largely a state project, inasmuch as governments and bureaucracies, in concert with their international allies, have defined the goals of development (commercialization of agriculture, establishment of industries, sectoral growth rates, building of infrastructure, provision of health care, education, and social services) and implemented these with various degrees of commitment and success. State policies—macro-economic and social—and the legal code shape women's access to economic resources, their position in labour markets, and possibilities for advancement. As Jean Pyle has shown for Ireland, and as I have shown for countries of the

Middle East and North Africa, some governments set an upper limit to the female share of employment in line with patriarchal imperatives (Pyle, 1990; Moghadam, 1993, ch. 2). In the Middle East educational attainment is still limited, employment even more so, and female illiteracy is widespread. This is a failure of public policy, the failure of Middle Eastern states to translate oil wealth into human development and the advancement of women. In the current global environment of economic restructuring, however, state autonomy and the capacity of states to define and pursue development on their own terms has been severely circumscribed. The implications for women in the Middle East and North Africa are mixed, for although neo-patriarchal states may have to forgo culturally derived prescriptions on women's activities, the feminization of labour is still predicated on the 'cheap female labour' calculation.

Women's position in the manufacturing labour force is the subject of Standing's chapter. His detailed study of Malaysia and the Philippines reveals that women workers are still concentrated in textiles and electronics and 'other manufacturing'; the men are concentrated in metals, minerals, and chemicals. However, some data suggest that sex segregation may be declining in the food processing, wood products, paper products, and chemicals sectors. Among managers there is a stated preference for men as production workers; women seem to have easier access to technical and professional categories. Women are better off in large firms than in small ones. Export orientation and female employment are positively correlated. Pay is higher in foreign firms for both men and women. The smaller the firm the larger the male–female wage differential. In larger firms the greater pay differential may be due to the absence of women in the high-income high-status managerial and administrative posts. In Malaysia, the presence of a trade union is associated with higher relative wages of women, in all three skill categories. Certainly for countries like Malaysia and the Philippines, flexible labour markets and ELI will continue to rely on women workers, but women workers continue to face many barriers to equality within those labour markets.

What of the labour-market position of women workers in more industrial countries? Tuovi Allén asks how the Nordic model of gender equality in the society and in the labour market affects patriarchy. Is it strengthened—in perhaps a new form—or is it undermined? Although the emergence of female employment in Nordic countries has been 'rapid and irreversible', the Nordic labour market has always been highly dependent on female labour, diverging from the European pattern of the family wage and the ideology of the male provider. In recent decades, universal welfare policies and high public spending on social services have led to more social equality and more gender equality. This has occurred even though women were not specific targets of equality measures. Rather, social corporatism, centralized wage bargaining, and strong government involvement are behind gender equity. Further, this has created a political culture in which the state is regarded 'as a tool to be used', rather than something to be feared or respected or worshipped. Thus, the state can be used to ease the burden on women and allow them to exercise their citizenship rights.

Characteristics of the Nordic female labour force, of 'state feminism', and of the welfare state support the widely held view that the status of women is highest in these countries. Allén notes, however, that women are still the majority of those engaged in part-time work, and occupations remain very sex-typed. On the other hand, she suggests provocatively, occupational sex-typing may have been beneficial for women, because it seems to have guaranteed growth and stability of women's employment.

Allén's chapter also underscores the connection between the high level of public spending and the high level of female employment in the public sector. The Nordic countries provide support for the argument that women benefit from public spending and large public sectors. As my chapter on the Middle East also demonstrates, the public sector provides job security, salaries, social insurance, child care and maternity leave, as well as, at times, 'affirmative action' opportunities, whereas the private sector does not. And in the United States, the so-called glass ceiling is higher in the public sector than in the private sector, allowing women more room for promotion and advancement. A great deal of evidence supports the view that almost everywhere the public sector is a better employer.[6] However, structural adjustment policies in developing countries and responses to economic recession in developed countries target public spending and the public sector. Will women in the Nordic countries lose their relatively privileged economic status as their economies are restructured? Will they—like women workers in the former state-socialist countries—have to settle for less?

Tuovi Allén's point that women are better off in countries with strong trade union traditions, especially as regards wage equality, is consistent with Standing's findings for Malaysia and the Philippines. But her chapter ends on the disconcerting note that women's dependence has shifted from husbands to the state—in Walby's terms, from private to public patriarchy—and that this dependence is risky at a time of recession and restructuring. This point has also been made in connection with women in the former state-socialist countries (Einhorn, 1993).

Part II ends with my examination of the trajectory of socialist development

[6] See OECD, *Women and Structural Change in the 1990s* (Paris: OECD, 1993), especially the chapter on women in the public sector, which concludes that 'evidence collected so far suggests that gender differentials are smaller in the public than in the private one'. The report also notes that given that women generally earn more in the public than in the private sector (at least at the higher institutional levels of government) and that women's rate of entry into the public sector is higher than that of men, public-sector employment seems to have caused the average female wage to rise relative to the average male wage.

and women's status in eastern Europe and the former Soviet Union. Events since the fall of communism and during the transition to a market economy attest to the non-linearity of social change, including the advancement of women. In many former socialist countries, not only have women lost jobs in larger numbers and faster rates than have men in the context of economic restructuring, but their previously high parliamentary representation has plummeted since democratization. In seeking to understand why women are not better off after decades of education and employment, I suggest that the answer lies in both the structure of gender relations of the socialist era and in inherent features of (emergent) capitalism and the new labour markets. The double burden of women meant that they continued to be identified with family roles, while the capitalist market creates an environment of competition in which vulnerable groups and women with child-care needs lose out. The inability of women to organize themselves politically and mobilize around gender interests has further emboldened those with patriarchal agendas.

SOME CONCLUSIONS AND FORWARD-LOOKING STRATEGIES

Clearly, the trajectories of patriarchy and development have been far from linear. Many of the benefits of the development process have accrued to élites or to the middle classes, while the women and men of the working classes have been jobs disappear and wages fall. In transition economies, even middle-class professionals have seen drastic declines in living standards, and too many women are resorting to prostitution. Patriarchal models of development and of transition account for this. In this book, chapters tell us of the workings of patriarchy in feudal societies (Lie), in pre-colonial and post-colonial societies (Dore, Kasturi, Parpart), in the Middle East and North Africa (Carapico, Moghadam), and indeed even in the advanced industrial world (Walby). Patriarchal models of social transformation, such as current models of transition from state socialism to capitalism, are responsible for the setbacks women have suffered in their status in Eastern Europe and the former Soviet Union, while patriarchal models of economic development and industrialization result in the exploitative work conditions and gender inequalities described by Pearson, Gallin, Standing, Safa, Moghadam, and Allén.

What all this suggests is the need for a new definition of development, and alternative development strategies. A useful understanding of the objectives of development is contained in the concept of *human development* —the enlargement of people's choices. Where people's choices are narrowed or eliminated, this is distorted development, or maldevelopment. Where development enhances people's lives, life options, and choices, this is human development. This concept is especially pertinent to women, who historically have been the most disadvantaged in terms of autonomy and advancement. Education, employment, and good work conditions and remuneration are among the necessary conditions for autonomy and choice, and should be considered basic human entitlements. At a more strategic level, however, we need to strive for egalitarian gender relations within the family and cultural changes in the sphere of reproduction such that tasks previously considered exclusively feminine—especially child rearing, care providing, and housework—will be distributed more equally among men, women, the community, and the state. That is to say, strategies are needed not only to improve women's access to economic, political, legal, and cultural resources, but ultimately to transform the institutions and relations that sustain inequalities.

REFERENCES

BARRETT, MICHÈLE (1980, 1988), *Women's Oppression Today: The Marxist/Feminist Encounter* (London: Verso).

EINHORN, BARBARA (1993), 'Democratization and Women's Movements in East Central Europe: Concepts of Women's Rights', in V. M. Moghadam (ed.), *Democratic Reform and the Position of Women in Transitional Economies* (Oxford: Clarendon Press).

ELSON, DIANE and PEARSON, RUTH (1981), 'Nimble Fingers Make Cheap Workers: An Analysis of Women's Employment in Third World Export Manufacturing', *Feminist Review*, spring: 87–107.

FERNANDEZ-KELLY, MARIA PATRICIA (1983), 'Mexican Border Industrialization, Female Labor Force Participation, and Migration', in June Nash and Maria Patricia Fernandez-Kelly (eds.), *Women, Men and the International Division of Labor* (Albany, NY: SUNY Press).

JOEKES, SUSAN (1987), *Women in the World Economy: An INSTRAW Study* (New York: Oxford University Press).

LIM, LINDA Y. C. (1990), 'Women in Export Factories: The Politics of a Cause', in Irene Tinker (ed.), *Persistent Inequalities: Women and World Development* (New York: Oxford University Press).

MOGHADAM, VALENTINE M. (1990), 'Gender, Development and Policy: Toward Equity and Empowerment', UNU/WIDER Research for Action Series (Helsinki: UNU/WIDER), Nov.

—— (1993), *Modernizing Women: Gender and Social Change in the Middle East* (Boulder, Colo.: Lynne Rienner Publishers).

OECD (1993), *Women and Structural Change in the 1990s* (Paris: OECD).

PERKINS, FRANCES (1993), 'Integration of Women's Concerns into Development Planning: Market Interventions', in ESCAP, *Integration of Women's Concerns into Development Planning in Asia and the Pacific* (New York: United Nations).

PYLE, JEAN (1990), 'Female Employment and Export-Led Development in Ireland: Labour Market Impact of State-Reinforced Gender Inequality in the

Household', in Jane Parpart and Sharon Stichter (eds.), *Women, Employment and the Family in the International Division of Labour* (London: Macmillan).

SEN, AMARTYA (1993), 'More than 100 Million Women are Missing', *New York Review of Books*, 37/20: 61–6.

STANDING, GUY (1989), 'Global Feminisation through Flexible Labour', *World Development*, 17/7: 1077–95.

TIANO, SUSAN (1987), 'Gender, Work, and World Capitalism: Third World Women's Role in Development', in Beth Hess and Myra Marx Ferree (eds.), *Analyzing Gender* (Beverly Hill, Calif.: Sage Publications).

—— (1993), 'Acquiescence, Accommodation, Alienation, and Resistance: Maquila Employment and Women's Consciousness', paper prepared for the Conference on *Engendering Wealth and Well-Being*, University of California, San Diego, 17–20 Feb.

UNDP (1993), *Human Development Report 1993* (New York: Oxford University Press).

United Nations (1991), *The World's Women: Trends and Statistics 1970–1990* (New York: United Nations).

WILSON, WILLIAM JULIUS (1980), *The Declining Significance of Race: Blacks and Changing American Institutions* (Chicago: University of Chicago Press, 2nd ed.).

PART I

HISTORICAL AND THEORETICAL PERSPECTIVES

The 'Declining Significance' or the 'Changing Forms' of Patriarchy?

Sylvia Walby

INTRODUCTION

Is patriarchy in decline? Or has it merely changed form? Whether the development process decreases patriarchy is the question underlying this chapter. The answer to this question depends not only on the empirical evidence, which is being addressed in other chapters, but on the definition and theorization of 'patriarchy' itself. This chapter will address these theoretical questions on 'patriarchy' in the context of the trajectories of development and patriarchy.

The significance of gender relations in macro-historical trajectories of development is now widely recognized (Boserup, 1970; Elson and Pearson, 1981; Leacock and Safa, 1986; Jayawardena, 1986; Mitter, 1986; Moghadam, 1992; Sen, 1984, 1987). There is now a wealth of data on how gender relations have been changing, although the picture is still far from complete. The task of adequately theorizing these changes in gender relations at a macro-level necessitates adapting, refining, and building appropriate concepts. Existing concepts in other mainstream analyses typically insufficiently address the specificity of gender, leaving it as an empirical question rather than a theorized phenomenon. Many of the problems which have been identified with the use of the concept of patriarchy are related to contingent rather than necessary features of the concept. However, critics have frequently attempted to dismiss the concept of patriarchy for problems which they incorrectly suggest are intrinsic.

Many of the attempts at global understanding of development do not deal with the gender dimension (e.g. Wallerstein, 1974; Frank, 1967). There have been a few significant attempts within the development, historical, sociological, and women's studies literature to begin to make sense of global patterns of gender relations (Boserup, 1970; Kelly, 1984; Lerner, 1986; Mies, 1986).

The substantive question of whether the processes of development and of industrialization have increased or decreased gender inequality is highly contested. On the one hand, economic development was seen to go along with increased educational, economic, and political participation of women as part of the process of modernization. The suggestion that economic development emancipates women finds a wide resonance in the literature on gender across the range of social science disciplines; across many and various conceptions of development, economic development, modernization, and industrialization; across time and space from contemporary Western changes to industrialization in the West to historical and contemporary changes in newly industrializing countries.

On the other hand there has been scepticism about the extent to which women have been able to control the proceeds of their waged labour, and concern about issues such as the conditions under which women work, about decreases in women's property rights, about increased sexual exploitation and effective political voice (Agarwal, 1988; Rogers, 1980; Brydon and Chant, 1989). The issue of a backlash is relevant to both newly industrializing countries (Afshar, 1989) and to the West (Faludi, 1992), and the possibility of reverse is historically clear (see Koonz, 1987 on Nazi Germany). Within Western feminist and gender theory the question of whether this century is seeing advances has often divided between theoretical perspectives. There has also been an awareness that language of progress and regress risks ethnocentric bias. Indeed so much so, that many would reject the question as inherently value laden.

My concern here is to examine the different ways in which the concept of patriarchy has been developed to address the diverse empirical issues. The concept of 'patriarchy' has a long, complicated, and contested history. I shall be arguing that in revised form the concept of patriarchy is indispensable. However, addressing the problems that have been raised about some of the ways the term has been used is essential. The first issues are those of definition.

THE DEFINITION OF 'PATRIARCHY'

The concept of patriarchy has been defined in a number of different ways, but usually with two similar core elements. Firstly, there is the core notion of gender inequality. Secondly, that there is a degree of systematicity, in that the different aspects of gender relations are connected in some way.

In order to take the debate forward it is necessary to consider the divergences in usage and to assess the merits of the different definitions. There are three main sources of divergence and debate.

First, whether the notion of gender inequality is expressed as men's domination over women, using the biological categories (e.g. Firestone, 1974), or whether the reference is to social structures and practices (e.g. Hartmann, 1979). If the definition refers only to biological categories, then the danger of biological reductionism is very strong. Since most analysts reject the notion that biology determines gender, it is important that the definition of patriarchy itself makes reference to the social dimension. However, it is important not to lose sight of the importance of the biological signifier. My preferred definition of patriarchy as a system of social structures and practices in which men dominate, oppress, and exploit women, attempts to capture the middle ground here.

A second major issue is whether the definition of patriarchy is tied to the household or not. One strand of thought defines patriarchy in terms of men's domination over women through the household, often including a generational aspect in which the oldest man in a household dominates all household members including young men (Hartmann, 1979; Moghadam, 1992; Weber, 1947). Other writers have preferred not to tie the definition of patriarchy to any particular household form, and have left open the question as to the relationship of the household to gender inequality (Mies, 1986). Mies argues that we need to go beyond the old usage of the term 'patriarchy' which refers to the rule of the father, since, she argues, many other categories of men (for example, male bosses) are involved in the subordination of women. This is a key contested issue which will emerge crucially through the debates on changes in patriarchy which I shall discuss below. I shall argue that the household form of domination is a contingent, not necessary, part of patriarchy, and hence should not be included in its definition.

A third major divergence in the definition of patriarchy lies in the extent to which writers include a theory of patriarchy within the definition. For instance, Hartmann (1979) states that the chief way in which patriarchal control is maintained is through the appropriation of women's labour. Her definition of patriarchy thus includes a theoretical relationship in which labour is the base and other aspects of society constitute a superstructure. (However, the base–superstructure model is softened in later work by Hartmann.) Other theorists have variously suggested male violence (Brownmiller, 1976), sexuality (MacKinnon, 1989) and reproduction (Firestone, 1974), and various other areas as the basic structure. However, while MacKinnon sees sexuality as definitive of gender, not all the others find it necessary to build the base of patriarchy into its definition.

It is not theoretically useful to tie the concept of patriarchy to anything other than gender inequality. It is unnecessarily restricting, and at times highly misleading, to tie it to either a specific household form, or to a dominant structure, such as the economic. One of the major problems which stems from this is the difficulty of theorizing changes in gender relations. Yet it is vital to be able to do this. These issues are central to the debate on patriarchy and will be discussed in detail below.

SEPARATE OR FUSED SYSTEM

Since patriarchy both pre-dates and post-dates capitalism it cannot be derivative from it. Patriarchal relations exist in feudal societies (Middleton, 1981; Lie, this volume) and they existed in pre-1989 and post-1989 Eastern

Europe (Einhorn, 1993). That development of capitalism affected patriarchal relations is clearly the case, but a change in the form of patriarchy is not the same as its demise or creation.

There have been various ways of analysing the relationship between patriarchy and capitalism, depending on the degree and form of their engagement.

First, they can be considered to be so closely intertwined that they become not merely symbiotic, but fused into one system, Eisenstein (1979) took this position, arguing that patriarchy provides a system of control and law and order, while capitalism provides a system of economy, in the pursuit of profit. However, there are some logical problems here. If the two are fused into one system it is only one, yet Eisenstein does speak of their interrelationship as if they were two.

Second, patriarchy and capitalism can be regarded as analytically distinct (Hartmann, 1979; Mitchell, 1975). Writers differ in their mode of separation of patriarchy and capitalism. Some allocate different structures to the different systems, while others do not. Mitchell (1975) allocates the economic level to capitalism and the unconscious and culture to patriarchy. Hartmann (1979) sees patriarchal relations as crucially located in the expropriation of women's labour by men in the two key sites, the household and paid work. These two forms of appropriation reinforce each other, since women's disadvantaged position in paid work makes them vulnerable in negotiations over the domestic division of labour, while their position in the family disadvantages them in paid work. Thus she sees patriarchy and capitalism as ultimately mutually reinforcing systems, even if there are moments of tension.

Mies takes a mid-way position on the separation and integration of patriarchy and capitalism. She notes that patriarchy long pre-dated capitalism, and is usually in combination with another social system, for instance feudalism. Patriarchy and capitalism are seen as very closely connected, but ultimately capitalism is merely another form of patriarchy. Patriarchy, like capitalism, is a world system. Patriarchy is maintained by a series of structures and practices including the family, systematic violence, and the expropriation of women's labour. Mies uses the term 'capitalist-patriarchy' to refer to the current system which maintains women's oppression. Capitalism, for Mies, is the latest form that patriarchy takes. Thus she reverses the more conventional hierarchy between the two systems and argues that patriarchy pre-dates capitalism and has analytic priority. She resolves the dilemma of dual-systems theory, as to how systems of 'patriarchy' and 'capitalism' might interrelate, by theorizing capitalism as an expression of patriarchy.

Mies argues that the dependency of women in the industrialized countries is only possible because of the exploitation of women in non-industrialized countries. Mies argues that the domestication or, as she calls it, the housewifization of women in the metropolitan capitalist nations is dependent upon the exploitation of the Third World. The first stage is the process of forcible colonization and the development of the luxury trade. The second stage is the development of an internal colony, in which women are colonized by men in Europe. The relations within the industrialized countries is only half the account, the other is that in the colonies and ex-colonies.

Mies argues that there has been a shift in the international division of labour from the old one in which raw materials were exported from the colonies for processing in the industrialized world and then marketed world wide, to a new international division of labour. In the new division, industrial production is transferred to the developing countries, producing unemployment in the industrialized countries. It is women who are the new industrial producers in the Third World, and it is women who, Mies claims, are the consumers of these items in the First World. Women are the cheaper labour force in the Third World since their designation as dependent housewives enables them to be paid low wages. Women in the First World, fired from their jobs as a result of the transfer of industry, are the consumers.

The weakness in the account stems from problems in some of the supporting evidence and from theoretical silences—not unexpectedly, given the scope of the project. First, her argument that women in the First World are currently subject to housewifization following the transfer of industry to the Third World is empirically incorrect. Women are entering paid employment in greater proportions than ever before, despite having higher unemployment rates than men in almost all Western countries bar Britain (OECD, 1980). To be sympathetic one could note that this process is not complete, but nevertheless the direction of change is the opposite from that argued by Mies. Secondly, the nuclear family form was not unique to modern capitalism. Laslett (1977) and McFarland (1978) have shown that it is not unique and that it pre-dated the rise of capitalism, so could not have been caused by it. Even the more intensely domesticated version in which the women are not allowed to take outside employment is not unique to the Victorian middle classes since it can be found among Islamic societies, especially among their traditional urban middle and upper classes (also, this is changing). In short, Mies places too much explanatory emphasis upon changes in capitalism, despite her stated interest in a world system of patriarchy.

RELATIONS BETWEEN THE DIFFERENT ASPECTS OF PATRIARCHY

Many writers have argued that the concept of patriarchy has insuperable problems because it is inherently essentialist. There are considered to be related problems of ahistoricism, reductionism, and inability to deal with cultural diversity (Barrett, 1980, though see Barrett, 1990; Rowbotham, 1981; Segal, 1987). This criticism has been levelled especially against the use of the concept of patriarchy by radical feminists, particularly those who have focused on the issues of reproduction, sexuality, and violence, such as Brownmiller (1976), Daly (1978), and Firestone (1974). Here the critique has argued that these accounts reduce women's oppression to one base and ultimately one which is biology, and hence that they are essentialist (see Segal, 1987).

Thus there are doubts as to whether 'patriarchy' is an appropriate term to grasp the complexity and diversity of patterns of gender relations (see Alcoff, 1988; Barrett and Phillips, 1992; Walby, 1992). There is an argument that the patterns of gender relations are too varied to justify attempts at grasping global patterns. This reaches its peak amongst writers of postmodernist tendency who have sometimes suggested that even the term 'woman', let alone 'patriarchy', can be inappropriately over-homogenous. One important dimension of this criticism has come from those who argue that cultural difference is insufficiently grasped by the term patriarchy, in that it tends to suggest that patriarchal relations are similar across ethnic groups (Carby, 1982; Hooks, 1984; Yuval-Davis and Anthias, 1989).

However, these problems only arise if patriarchy is conceptualized in the following ways. First, it is a problem if the definition refers to biological categories as the unit of analysis. As we have seen this is not the case in some definitions, though it is in others. Second, it is a problem if a simple base–superstructure model is used in which one dimension of social life determines all other aspects of gender relations. This is only true of certain usages of the concept. In those theories which have more complex internal models of patriarchy this problem need not occur. In these latter cases there is no simple reduction. If these two problems are avoided then there is no need for the concept and theory of patriarchy to be essentialist.

The solution to this problem is for the system of patriarchy to be conceptualized as being composed of several interrelated structures. At a lower level of abstraction, within each of these structures specific patriarchal practices can be identified which are less deeply sedimented. Structures are emergent properties of practices. Any specific empirical instance will embody the effects not only of patriarchal structures, but also of capitalism and racism (Walby, 1990).

I have argued that the system of patriarchy over the last 150 years in the UK should be considered to be composed of six structures: patriarchal relations in household work, patriarchal relations in paid work, a patriarchal state, male violence, patriarchal relations in sexuality, and patriarchal relations in cultural institutions.

Patriarchal relations in the household are my first structure. It is through these that women's household labour is expropriated by their husbands, fathers, or cohabitees. The woman may receive her maintenance in exchange for her labour, especially when she is not also engaged in wage labour. Of course, the nature and extent of this work varies, especially, but not necessarily, with the wealth and income of the woman and her husband.

The second patriarchal structure within the economic level is that of patriarchal relations within paid work. A complex of forms of patriarchal closure within waged work excludes women from the better forms of work and segregates them into worse jobs which are deemed less skilled.

The state is patriarchal as well as being capitalist and racist. While being a site of struggle and not a monolithic entity, the state has a systematic bias towards patriarchal interests in its policies and actions.

Male violence constitutes a further structure, despite its apparently individualist and diverse form. It is behaviour routinely experienced by women from men, generating fear which has restrictive effects upon the actions of most women. Male violence against women is effectively condoned by the lack of state intervention against it except in extreme circumstances, although interpersonal violence is usually technically illegal.

Patriarchal relations in sexuality constitute a fifth structure. The sexual double standard, prostitution, and pornography are examples of practices here.

Patriarchal cultural institutions complete the array of structures. These are significant for the generation of a variety of gender-differentiated forms of subjectivity. This structure is composed of a set of institutions which create the representation of women within a patriarchal gaze in a variety of arenas, such as religion, education, and the media.

While this model was developed within the context of the last 150 years of UK history, with some modifications, the main features are globally relevant. These would include the reconceptualization of the boundary between the structures of patriarchal relations in paid work and in the household in the context of agricultural and peasant economies where such a boundary is not so clearly discernible.

CONCEPTUALIZING CHANGE

There are serious disagreements as to whether or not women's position has been improving with economic development. In the light of the foregoing discussion these can be divided into three types. First, there are disagreements over the same empirical issues. Second, there are disagreements over which empirical issues are important and how changes in different dimensions of women's lives are to be weighted in order to give an overall statement as to whether there has been an increase or decrease in gender inequality. Third, there is disagreement over how changes in gender relations are to be conceptualized.

An example of the first type of disagreement over empirical issues is over whether the workload of women in a particular society had decreased or increased. This is obviously made difficult if the statistics are inadequate, but more importantly there may be disagreements over what may be contained within the concept 'work': for instance, whether 'work' includes unpaid housework, or is restricted to work which enters the money economy. The work that women do in the domestic and informal sectors of the economy is notoriously undercounted in official statistics (see Thomas, 1992), in local understandings of what counts as significant work (Agarwal, 1988), as well as divergent views among development 'experts' (Rogers, 1980). Futher, there are very considerable differences in the extent to which women engage in housework, depending on class and income. But, none the less, this is more of an empirical than a theoretical question, even though the boundaries of such concepts are heavily theory laden.

The second type of disagreement is over the question of which aspects of women's lives count most towards an overall index of gender equity. Here there is profound disagreement. A key focus is over whether paid work intrinsically enhances a woman's emancipation. One aspect of this is the question of whether paid work is more or less alienating than work in the household. Can one aspect be balanced against another? For instance, some writers have argued that the development of commercialized sex in pornography and institutionalized prostitution is more likely with the development of a market economy; indeed some have argued that a sexual counter-revolution has historically been a feature of the backlash against women's gains in the political and economic arenas (e.g. Jeffreys, 1985; Millett, 1970; Faderman, 1981). (However, prostitution has long predated capitalism.) Whether or not there has been progress then depends upon the ranking of the significance of the different dimensions of women's lives.

EXPLAINING CHANGES

In many ways the question of whether paid employment liberates women is central to many of the debates about trajectories of development and patriarchy. The conceptual and theoretical underpinnings to the thesis that it does liberate women are interesting and all highly contested. First, there is the proposition that paid work is more advantageous to the woman than unpaid work. This often includes a second proposition, that women are able to control the wages they obtain in paid work. A third and related presumption is that the presumed advantages that a woman gains in employment increase the control she has in other areas of her life, such as the domestic division of labour, and in other social relations, such as access to political decision-making arenas.

There is thus an implicit, if not explicit, theory of patriarchy within this proposition that women benefit from increased paid employment. It presumes the connectedness of the different aspects of gender relations, that is, a degree of systematicity. It further presumes that these operate consistently in the same direction (rather than having an adverse impact).

Yet each of these propositions has been challenged, these challenges in turn drawing on implicit or explicit theories of gender relations.

Is paid work better than unpaid work? Much of the recent literature on 'race', ethnicity, and gender has queried this presumption. If the paid work that women do is terrible, as is often the case of those women in vulnerable positions, then it may be that domestic work is more fulfilling, allowing greater autonomy (Hooks, 1984).

Can women control the rewards from their work? Do they get paid themselves, or are their wages given to or controlled by dominant family men? There are a significant number of examples of men retaining control of the wages of women in their families (Mark-Lawson and Witz, 1990).

Standing (1989: 1090–1) has suggested that there are seven areas where the degree of control that women have over the rewards for paid work need to be considered, and advocates the collection of better data. First, control over self; for instance, as bonded labourers. Second, control over the hours of work, such as not working longer than they would wish. Third, control over the means of production. Fourth, control over raw materials. Fifth, control over output, such as whether the woman is allowed to sell her wares herself. Sixth, control over proceeds of output, especially over whether the woman worker controls the wages which are paid, or whether male kin or intermediaries prevent this. Seventh, control over labour reproduction, especially over the ability to renew and enhance their own skills.

Is there a positive relationship between changes in paid work and changes in other dimensions of women's lives? The conventional position implicitly presumes a base–superstructure model in which the economic base determines the superstructure of such things as political participation and sexual autonomy. Such base–superstructure models have been widely criticized when used in relation to class as well as in relation to gender, as oversimplifying complex causal interactions. Indeed some writers have argued that we should not exclude an inverse relationship: for instance, the backlash against women's successes in both first-wave and second-wave Western feminism in the arena of political and economic rights which took place at the sexual level (Jeffreys, 1985; Millett, 1977, Faderman, 1981; Faludi, 1992).

There is a question as to what are the circumstances under which paid work emancipates women. Historically in the West this has occurred at those moments when women have also been gaining political rights. When women won political citizenship as the result of the turn of the century women's movement, this was used to ensure that waged work provided wider, not merely burdensome, opportunities for women (Walby, 1988).

The third and final question involves the very definition of patriarchy. If patriarchy is defined narrowly, then changes in some dimensions of gender inequality will be considered irrelevant, while changes in the element defined as key may be sufficient to justify a claim that patriarchy has ended. This is the problem with definitions of patriarchy which focus too narrowly on men's domination of women through the household, such as Mann (1986).

THE END OF PATRIARCHY?

Mann (1986) has argued that patriarchy no longer exists, although there is still gender inequality (presumably within the UK). This is because he defines a patriarchal society as 'one in which power is held by male heads of households' and where there is a 'clear separation between the "public" and the "private" spheres of life' (Mann, 1986: 41), and these conditions no longer hold. He suggests that there are three reasons for this: the erosion of the public/private boundary, employment trends, and the nation state's welfare interventions into the household/family (Mann, 1986: 55). Yet he is not suggesting that there is not gender inequality, indeed he suggests that it should be taken more seriously in that stratification should be regarded as gendered. Neither is he suggesting that there are not key 'stratification nuclei' (p. 56), nor that there are not significant commonalities by gender—'child-rearing unites almost all women' (p. 54).

In short Mann is arguing that there is still a significant amount of gender inequality but, because it is not centrally determined by a male-dominated household, it is not patriarchy.

I think this is not a helpful theorization of the issues. The key element of a definition of patriarchy is that there is systematically structured gender inequality. Mann accepts that this is empirically the case, but denies the application of the concept. He does this because he has defined patriarchy as centrally linked to a male-dominated household. I think this is a mistake.

FORM AND DEGREE OF PATRIARCHY

The separation of the degree of patriarchy from its form is a crucially necessary theoretical development. On each dimension of gender relations it is often possible to specify the degree of inequality between the sexes, but much more difficult to do this at the level of the system as a whole because of the inherently value-laden decision as to the significance of different aspects of gender relations. For instance, it is possible to state whether the gap in the hourly wage rates for men and women is greater or lesser. However, the relative balance of oppression in household work and paid work is a more problematic question.

It is possible for there to be a change in the form of patriarchy without a change in its degree and vice versa.

PUBLIC AND PRIVATE PATRIARCHY

There have been two major forms of patriarchy in the West over the last couple of centuries: public and private. They differ on a variety of levels: first, in terms of the relations between the structures, and second, in the institutional form of each structure. Further, they are differentiated by the main form of patriarchal strategy: exclusionary in private patriarchy and segregationist in public patriarchy. Private patriarchy is based upon household production, with a patriarch controlling women individually and directly in the relatively private sphere of the home. Public patriarchy is based on structures other than the household, although this may still be a significant patriarchal site. Rather, institutions conventionally regarded as part of the public domain are central in the maintenance of patriarchy.

In private patriarchy it is a man in his position as husband or father who is the direct oppressor and beneficiary, individually and directly, of the subordination of women. This does not mean that household production is the sole patriarchal structure. Indeed it is importantly maintained by the active exclusion of women from these public arenas by other structures. The exclusion of women from these other spheres could not be perpetuated without patriarchal activity at these levels.

Public patriarchy is a form in which women have access to both public and private arenas. They are not barred from the public arenas, but are none the less subordinated within them. The expropriation of women is performed more collectively than by individual patriarchs. The household may remain a site of patriarchal oppression, but is no longer the main place where women are present.

In each type of patriarchy the six structures are present, but the relationship between them and their relative significance is different. For instance, I am not arguing that in private patriarchy the only significant site is that of the household. In the different forms there are different relations between the structures to maintain the system of patriarchy.

In the private system of patriarchy the exploitation of women in the household is maintained by their non-admission to the public sphere. In a sense the term 'private' for this form of patriarchy might be misleading, in that it is the exclusion from the public which is the central causal mechanism. Patriarchal relations outside the household are crucial in shaping patriarchal relations within it. However, the effect is to make women's experience of patriarchy privatized, and the immediate beneficiaries are also located there.

In the public form of patriarchy the exploitation of women takes place at all levels, but women are not formally excluded from any. In each institution women are disadvantaged.

The second aspect of the difference between private and public patriarchy is the institutional form of each of the structures. This is a movement from an individual to a more collective form of appropriation of women. There has also been a shift in patriarchal strategy from exclusionary to segregationist and subordinating.

In the context of the UK over the last 150 years the change within each structure has been as follows. Within paid work there was a shift from an exclusionary strategy to a segregationist one, which was a movement from attempting to exclude women from paid work to accepting their presence but confining them to jobs which were segregated from and graded lower than those of men. In the household there was reduction in the confinement of women to this sphere over a lifetime and a shift towards the state in the main locus of control over reproduction. The major cultural institutions ceased to exclude women, while subordinating women within them. Sexual controls over women significantly shifted from the specific control of the husband to that of a broader public arena; women were no longer excluded from sexual relations to the same extent, but subordinated within them. Women's exclusion from the state was replaced by their subordination within it. There are, of course, variations by class and ethnicity within the UK, in these changes.

The cause of this change was feminist activity at the turn of the century in the context of the increasing demand for female labour in an expanding capitalist economy.

EASTERN EUROPE

There are sub-systems within this: for instance, pre-1989 eastern Europe had a state-led form of public patriarchy, while the USA had a labour-market led form of public patriarchy, with Western Europe in between with its welfare state and female employment participation rates. However, as is becoming clear, it would be unwise to declare that women in Eastern Europe suffered a lesser degree of patriarchy than those in the West despite their greater participation in paid work, since the degree of inequality in the household and the size of the burden of household work appears to have been greater.

The current trajectory in Eastern Europe appears to be unhappily poised between a shift to a market-led form of public patriarchy, and a return to more private forms, as suggested by Moghadam's chapter in this volume.

It may be that a backlash against the exploitation of state-led public patriarchy will lead to a more private form of patriarchy. However, the economic shock treatment advocated by US economists may lead these countries simply into a market-led form of public patriarchy.

CONCLUSION

The concept of patriarchy is indispensable to the macro-level analysis of changes in gender relations. The concept needs to be developed in the light of the legitimate criticisms of some of the early formulations. In particular, the internal differentiation of structures within the system, and their various combinations into different forms of patriarchal system, is crucial if the concept is to be able to deal appropriately with historical, spatial, cultural, and ethnic diversity. Systematically interrelated forms of gender inequality do not stop when the household-based form of private patriarchy diminishes. Rather, we see new forms. The degree of patriarchy may change as well, but that is analytically separate from the issue of the form, even if, contingently, in Western history, there have been some changes in both simultaneously.

REFERENCES

AFSHAR, HALEH (1989), 'Women and Reproduction in Iran', in Nira Yuval-Davis and Floya Anthias (eds.), *Woman–Nation–State* (London: Macmillan).

AGARWAL, BINA (ed.) (1988), *Structures of Patriarchy: The State, the Community and the Household* (London: Zed Press).

ALCOFF, LINDA (1988), 'Cultural Feminism versus Post-Structuralism: The Identity Crisis in Feminist Theory', *Signs* (spring) 13/3: 405–36.

BARRETT, MICHÈLE (1990), *Women's Oppression Today*, 2nd edn. (London: Verso).

—— and Phillips, Anne (eds.) (1992), *Destabilizing Theory: Contemporary Feminist Debates* (Cambridge: Polity Press).

BOSERUP, ESTER (1970), *Women's Role in Economic Development* (London: Allen and Unwin).

BROWNMILLER, SUSAN (1976), *Against Our Will: Men, Women, and Rape* (Harmondsworth: Penguin).

BRYDON, LYNNE and CHANT, SYLVIA (1989), *Women in the Third World: Gender Issues in Rural and Urban Areas* (Aldershot: Edward Elgar).

CARBY, HAZEL (1982), 'White Woman Listen! Black Feminism and the Boundaries of Sisterhood', in Centre for Contemporary Cultural Studies, *The Empire Strikes Back* (London: Hutchinson).

DALY, MARY (1978), *Gyn/Ecology* (London: Women's Press).

EINHORN, BARBARA (1993), 'Democratization and Women's Movements in East

Central Europe: Concepts of Women's Rights', in V. M. Moghadam (ed.), *Democratic Reform and the Position of Women in Transitional Economies* (Oxford: Clarendon Press).

EISENSTEIN, ZILLAH (ed.) (1979), *Capitalist Patriarchy and the Case for Socialist Feminism* (New York: Monthly Review Press).

ELSON, DIANE and PEARSON, RUTH (1981), 'Nimble Fingers Make Cheap Workers: An Analysis of Women's Employment in Third World Export Manufacturing', *Feminist Review,* 7: 87–107.

FADERMAN, LILIAN (1981), *Surpassing the Love of Men: Romantic Friendship and Love Between Women from the Renaissance to the Present Day* (London: Junction Books).

FALUDI, SUSAN (1992), *Blacklash: The Undeclared War Against Women* (New York: Crown Publishers).

FIRESTONE, SHULAMITH (1974), *The Dialectic of Sex* (New York: Morrow).

FRANK, ANDRE GUNDER (1967), *Capitalism and Underdevelopment in Latin America* (New York: Monthly Review Press).

HARTMANN, HEIDI (1979), 'Capitalism, Patriarchy and Job Segregation by Sex', in Z. Eisenstein (ed.), *Capitalist Patriarchy* (New York: Monthly Review Press).

HOOKS, BELL (1984), *Feminist Theory: From Margin to Center* (Boston: South End Press).

JAYAWARDENA, KUMARI (1986), *Feminism and Nationalism in the Third World* (London: Zed Press).

JEFFREYS, SHEILA (1985), *The Spinster and Her Enemies: Feminism and Sexuality, 1880–1930* (London: Pandora).

KELLY, JOAN (1984), *Women, History and Theory* (Chicago: University of Chicago Press).

KOONZ, CLAUDIA (1987), *Mothers in the Fatherland* (London: Methuen).

LASLETT, PETER (1977), *Family Life and Illicit Love in Earlier Generations* (Cambridge: Cambridge University Press).

LEACOCK, ELEANOR and SAFA, HELEN (eds.) (1986), *Women's Work: Development and the Division of Labour by Gender* (South Hadley: Bergin and Garvey).

LERNER, GERDA (1986), *The Creation of Patriarchy* (New York: Oxford University Press).

MCFARLAND, ALAN (1978), *The Origins of English Individualism* (Oxford: Blackwell).

MACKINNON, CATHERINE (1989), *Towards a Feminist Theory of the State* (Cambridge, Mass.: Harvard University Press).

MANN, MICHAEL (1986), 'A Crisis in Stratification Theory? Persons, Households/Families/Lineages, Genders, Classes and Nations', in Rosemary Crompton and Michael Mann (eds.), *Gender and Stratification* (Cambridge: Polity Press).

MARK-LAWSON, JANE and WITZ, ANNE (1990), 'Familial Control or Patriarchal Domination? The Case of the Family System of Labour in Nineteenth Century Coal Mining', in Helen Corr and Lynn Jamieson (eds.), *Politics of Everyday Life: Continuity and Change in Work and the Family* (London: Macmillan).

MIDDLETON, CHRIS (1981), 'Peasants, Patriarchy and the Feudal Mode of Production in England', *Sociological Review,* 29/1: 105–54.

MIES, MARIA (1986), *Patriarchy and Accumulation on a World Scale: Women in the International Division of Labour* (London: Zed Books).

MILLETT, KATE (1977), *Sexual Politics* (London: Virago).

MITCHELL, JULIET (1975), *Psychoanalysis and Feminism* (Harmondsworth: Penguin).
MITTER, SWASTI (1986), *Common Fate, Common Bond: Women in the Global Economy* (London: Pluto Press).
MOGHADAM, VALENTINE (1992), 'Patriarchy and the Politics of Gender in Modernizing Societies: Iran, Pakistan and Afghanistan', *International Sociology*, 7/1 (March): 35–53.
OECD (1980), 'Women's Employment During the 1970s Recession', in A. H. Amsden (ed.), *The Economics of Women and World* (Harmondsworth: Penguin).
ROGERS, BARBARA (1980), *The Domestication of Women: Discrimination in Developing Societies* (London: Tavistock).
ROWBOTHAM, SHEILA (1981), 'The Trouble with "Patriarchy"', in Feminist Anthology Collective (ed.), *No Turning Back* (London: Women's Press).
SEGAL, LYNNE (1987), *Is the Future Female? Troubled Thoughts on Contemporary Feminism* (London: Virago).
SEN, AMARTYA (1984), *Resources, Value and Development* (Oxford: Blackwell).
—— (1987), *On Ethics and Economics* (Oxford: Blackwell).
—— (1987), *The Standard of Living* (Cambridge: Cambridge University Press).
STANDING, GUY (1989), 'Global Feminization through Flexible Labour', *World Development*, 17/7: 1077–95.
THOMAS, JIM (1992), *The Informal Economy* (London: Macmillan).
WALBY, SYLVIA (1988), 'Gender Politics and Social Theory', *Sociology*, 22/2 (May): 215–32.
—— (1990), *Theorizing Patriarchy* (Oxford: Blackwell).
—— (1992), 'Post-Modernism: Theorizing Social Complexity', in Michèle Barrett and Anne Phillips (eds.), *Destabilizing Theory: Contemporary Feminist Debates* (Cambridge: Polity Press).
WALLERSTEIN, IMMANUEL (1974), *The Origins of the Modern Wold System* (New York: Cambridge University Press).
WEBER, MAX (1947), *The Theory of Economic and Social Organization* (New York: Free Press).
YUVAL-DAVIS, NIRA and ANTHIAS, FLOYA (eds.) (1989), *Woman–Nation–State* (London: Macmillan).

From Agrarian Patriarchy to Patriarchal Capitalism: Gendered Capitalist Industrialization in Korea

John Lie

In this paper, I present a framework for analysing the role of women in the transition from agrarian patriarchy to patriarchal capitalism in peripheral nation states, and then illustrate it with a case study of Korea. In brief, I argue that peripheral industrialization entails 'gender' as a distinct axis of oppression. Whereas gender was embedded in other power relations and structures in agrarian patriarchy, gender emerges as a distinct locus of oppression in the course of peripheral industrialization—patriarchal capitalism. In agrarian patriarchy, there exists little possibility of women's political organization or gender consciousness. In patriarchal capitalism, industrialization contributes to the dissolution of agrarian patriarchal households and to a gendered division of labour in the economy and within the household. Paradoxically, the same dynamic creates the conditions for gender emancipation, providing both social and epistemological bases for gender-based politics and consciousness.

AGRARIAN PATRIARCHY AND THE SUBSUMPTION OF GENDER

As Mann (1986*a*: 31) observes: 'gender relations remained broadly constant, in the general form of *patriarchy*, throughout much of recorded history until the eighteenth and nineteenth centuries in Europe, when rapid changes began to occur' (see also Mann, 1986*b*: 41–4). The category of 'agrarian patriarchy' denotes male dominance in the social life of agrarian people.[1]

After 1948, Korea refers to the Republic of, or South, Korea. I wish to thank the organizer of the WIDER conference, Valentine M. Moghadam, for her kind invitation. Thanks also to Nancy Abelmann and Leslie Salzinger, as well as other participants of the WIDER conference, for their helpful suggestions.

[1] The situation was different in pre-agrarian societies. Mann (1986*a*: 34) writes: 'But from what we can guess about these gatherer-scavengers and gatherer-hunters, their social structure was extremely loose, *ad hoc*, and variable. They did not stably institutionalize power relations; they did not know classes, states, or even elites; even their distinctions between gender and age-sets . . . may not indicate permanent power differentials.' In a study otherwise sceptical of generalizations about women's status, Whyte (1978: 172) concludes: 'In the more complex cultures, women tend to have less domestic authority, less independent solidarity with other women, more unequal sexual restrictions, and perhaps receive more ritualized fear from men and have fewer property rights, than is the case in the simpler cultures.'

Agrarian patriarchy comprises macro-structural distinctions and contradictions between landlords and peasants, and micro-structural domination of the patriarch over his household. At neither level is gender socially significant; other social divisions and categories render gender oppression largely invisible and ineffective as a source of identity and mobilization. In other words, gender is embedded and subsumed in the fabric of social life.

In élite households, the patriarch rules over the household—the domination is exercised not only over women (wives and daughters), but over generation (children), and status (servants). The distinction can be expressed as 'autonomous' patriarchs versus 'dependent' non-patriarchs, including women, children, and non-élite men. Patriarchs dominate in relations between households and prevent non-patriarchs (including women) from participating in the public sphere (a concourse of household heads). In this context, élite women's status is mediated by and conjoined in patriarchal rule.[2] Gender is embedded and enmeshed in other social relations and structures. Although women are barred from public life and ideologically denigrated, their structural position prevents their organization as gendered subjects. The patriarchal domination of the public sphere circumscribes women's relations and associations outside of, while age gradations and status distinctions bar women's solidarity within, the household. It is of course true that there exists vast inequality between élite men and élite women, but the potential gender struggle does not become the major social dynamic of agrarian patriarchy.

In peasant households, the material conditions of agricultural production, which remains near the subsistence level, force both women and men to work. As with élite women, peasant women endure considerable oppression, working harder and longer than men in general (Chayanov, 1986: 180). Women's obvious and necessary contribution to material sustenance, however, prevents patriarchal ideology from fully penetrating peasant life. The patriarchal ideology is strongest in the public sphere, where élite control penetrates, and among those who emulate agrarian élites. Indeed, it is often in the cross-status difference in women's position that agrarian élites find the proof of their moral superiority and a justification for their rule. Unlike élite women, peasant women have more freedom in forming women's networks and thus creating a distinct sphere. However, their collective mobilization does not occur as gendered subjects, but rather as members of the household or the village community. The gender

I understand post-gatherer-hunter societies and 'the more complex cultures' to denote agrarian societies. See also Lerner (1986: 212–20) and Chafetz (1984: 113–16).

[2] On the concept of 'mediation', see Wright (1989: 62–3). Ironically, Goldthorpe's (1983) defence of ignoring women in the analysis of stratification is justified in agrarian patriarchy. It is of course possible to note the (vast) inequality between élite women and men, but that is somewhat beside the point in understanding the fundamental social dynamics of the time.

category is not historically dynamic since the basis of collective mobilization tends to rest on household rivalries or intercommunal conflicts.

To summarize, gender is subsumed in agrarian patriarchy. Gender-based organizing or consciousness is virtually absent; proto-feminist tracts or women's movements are far and few between in agrarian patriarchy. Polemically put, gender is *not* a useful category of analysis in understanding the historical dynamic of agrarian societies (cf. Scott, 1988). To highlight women as a distinct social category and to create knowledge about them is valid politically to reclaim the past from the vantage point of the present. However, although it is possible and important to make women 'visible' and analyse their contributions, we should not overlook the reasons for their lack of organized resistance or the paucity of proto-feminist ideology.

PATRIARCHAL CAPITALISM: GENDER DISEMBEDDED

The fundamental underlying dynamic of industrialization—capital accumulation—seems undeniable, if not as a systemic necessity, certainly as an empirical generalization. Capitalist industrialization entails relentless pursuit of cheap labour.

The pursuit of cheap labour assumes one of two major forms. Externally, colonial and neo-colonial relations constitute institutions and relations of surplus extraction. For example, core corporations establish operations abroad and employ workers from the periphery, or they rely on migrant workers. The external labour force, paralleling the world-systemic differentiation between core and periphery, becomes 'racialized': against the 'white' workers from the core emerge the 'racial' workers from the periphery (Wallerstein, 1991: 79–80). In addition to the creation of a racialized labour force, there are internally generated differentiation and hierarchization of the domestic labour force. These divisions usually exploit—in effect, invent—social divisions based on ethnicity, language, region, religion, and gender, and create pools of 'cheap' labour (Gordon *et al.*, 1982: ch. 5).

Peripheral industrialization entails enormous obstacles (for the case of South Korea, see Lie, 1992). By peripheral industrialization, I refer to the process of post-colonial industrialization exemplified in the 1980s by South Korea and Taiwan. Core industrializing countries in Europe and North America have already established formal or informal control over the periphery. In addition to dismantling the bonds of dependency, late industrializers cannot exploit external sources. External surplus extraction is impossible in the early, and crucial, stages of peripheral industrialization. Hence, peripheral industrialization demands greater domestic surplus extraction. The search for cheap labour becomes the pursuit of extra-cheap labour; in other words, there is a need for intensified hierarchization of the labour force.

In peripheral industrialization, agrarian patriarchy is transformed into industrial capitalism via intensified gender oppression: hence, patriarchal capitalism. There are several reasons for the gendered character of peripheral industrialization. The legacy of agrarian patriarchy renders non-patriarchs, including not just women, but children and men of lower status groups, ideologically fit for exploitation. However, as I will argue below, male workers' resistance and organization, along with the import of Western patriarchal ideologies and practices, contribute to female subordination in the workplace.

In addition, capitalist industrialization and associated social changes like urbanization contribute to household differentiation. As production becomes severed from the household, the line between work and family life separates. New household strategies utilize available labour for survival and social mobility. Thus, women—and especially daughters—become expendable for exploitation in the urban economy.[3]

These conditions underlie 'cheap' female labour. Although the use of female labour is often explained or justified in terms of their docility, skill, etc. (e.g. Elson and Pearson, 1984), gender differentiation and oppression is fundamentally a relational construct. It is not intrinsic and essential qualities of women, socialized as they may be, that make their labour cheap (cf. Bettio, 1988: 216). Rather, as an inferior group, they become relationally constructed as 'cheaper' than the normal male labour. It is a product—an invention—of the newly differentiated gender roles that pits the norm (male work) against other deviations, such as female (cf. Humphrey, 1985). Certainly, the legacy of agrarian patriarchal ideology plays an important role in the construction of 'cheap' female labour (cf. Bettio, 1988: 127). However, it is mediated by the construction of maleness, which is created both by capitalists and workers. On the one hand, management attempts to institute patriarchal control (in the agrarian tradition of the patriarch controlling not just women and children but other men as well). On the other hand, male workers struggle for autonomy and patriarchal status under the new, gender-segregated nuclear households. Male workers strive to achieve autonomy and in so doing differentiate themselves from dependents, such as women (cf. Roediger, 1991: 55–6, 69–71). Thus, the struggle for male work is often defined in terms of family wage (Baron, 1991), while women's work becomes devalued as

[3] As Accampo (1989: 211) writes of nineteenth-century France: 'In the industrial period, the tasks in both these categories [men and women] became more distinctively gender segregated and the lines between work and family life hardened.' On household strategies, see Lamphere (1987: 29–31). To the extent that they are bound by patriarchal households, they face new gender segregation in the worklace while still under agrarian patriarchal control (cf. Salaff, 1981).

superfluous, or 'working for lipstick' (Joekes, 1985; Joekes, 1987: 86). Hence, working-class men actively participate in destroying one form of patriarchal rule while erecting another, which denigrates female work and workers. In this process, the state contributes to the establishment of the new patriarchal ideology. The state's impact ranges from its labour laws to welfare policies. For instance, state policy does not allow for individual entitlement even as old patriarchal structures are breaking down, thereby negatively affecting women (cf. Elson, 1991: 4–7). In addition, core countries and corporations export Western patriarchal ideas and practices to the Third World.[4] In other words, Western patriarchal practices contribute to gender differentiation and exploitation in the periphery (cf. Amadiume, 1987: pt. 2). For example, gender-segregated wage policies and managerial strategies are used (e.g. Humphrey, 1985: 73–87), while the ideology of docile female labour is both assumed and propagated (cf. Lutz, 1988).

In addition, the economy becomes increasingly gendered—in effect, the new capitalist economy is 'male'. First, household work becomes the exclusive province of women. The process of 'housewife-zation' renders domestic duties as women's work as agrarian patriarchal households transform into nuclear families (Mies, 1986: ch. 4). Second, many of these women (housewives) work disproportionately in the informal sector, which is also defined as not 'real' work (Sen and Grown, 1987: 36–7). Third, women become purveyors of gendered labour, such as sexual work. The penetration of the core occurs in a variety of forms, ranging from military base to tourism, which also accelerates the greater gender exploitation to satisfy the male desires from within and without (Enloe, 1989). Finally, the capitalist economy destroys traditional economic organizations, such as women's trading networks (Hill, 1986: 140–5). In short, men work while women do not, at least not in the 'real' economy.

There are distinctive paths to industrialization. For example, proto-industrialization, relying on household production, results in relatively low inequality and undifferentiated gender roles, and hence, in the relative insignificance of patriarchal ideology (Medick, 1976). However, this and other alternatives are circumscribed by external and internal obstacles facing late industrializers. Just as peripheral industrialization cannot assume 'racial' or 'colonial' forms as in early industrialization, it cannot simply exploit serf or slave labour. The existence of slave or serf labour indicates the absence of other structural factors necessary for industrialization, such as land reform.

In summary, gender becomes a central axis of labour differentiation in peripheral industrialization—hence, patriarchal capitalism. Loosened from their moorings in agrarian patriarchal households, women engage in

[4] Indeed, the culture of capitalism—the reliance on abstract science and technology and the exploitation of nature—is of course a quintessential Western construct, which entails sexism (cf. Shiva, 1988).

devalued, 'female' labour in the new gender-segregated household and economy. Therein lies a major cause of women's lowered status and marginalization in the early stages of industrialization.

GENDER OPPRESSION AND RESISTANCE

Patriarchal capitalism creates the modern gender division of labour. Although it is in many ways oppressive, and often lowers the status of women, it also generates processes and ideologies that create the very conditions of gender-based consciousness, organization, and resistance. Thus, it is not simply a matter of quantitative evaluations and comparisons of women's conditions, but one of assessing the very potential for gender-based consciousness and organization. In this section, I explore these emancipatory dynamics by analysing two structural changes and two ideological sources of women's emancipation.

Patriarchal capitalism contributes to two structural changes which facilitate women's liberation. First, the dissolution of agrarian patriarchal households liberates non-patriarchs, including women, from the patriarch's rule. The 'rise of the egalitarian family'—the transformation from agrarian patriarchal (extended) households to modern nuclear families—occurs initially among élite households in industrialized societies and spreads with continuing industrialization (cf. Trumbach, 1978). The process is intimately intertwined with the destruction of agrarian patriarchy's economic and political base of power. Simultaneously, the public sphere is transformed from a concourse of patriarchs into one of property owners and citizens, in which non-patriarchs increasingly participate. The weakening of kinship ties dissolves the key institutional basis of women's oppression. Although the new gender division of labour creates the condition for 'housewife' and the associated cult of domesticity, it also enables women's gradual entrance into the public sphere as 'mothers', in the form of voluntary organizations for the care of society (Berg, 1978; Rendall, 1985). Indeed, middle-class women play an especially critical role in articulating the new family ideology and the new role for women (e.g. Coontz, 1988: 187–94). To be sure, their vision as the 'moral' guardians of society vitiates their role in liberating women of lower classes, different ethnicities, or other societies. Yet, middle-class women organize themselves by asserting their new gender-based ideologies (Ware, 1992).

The emergence of paid work also contributes to emancipation as women earn wages and become liberated from agrarian patriarchal households (e.g. Joekes, 1987: 10). Women enter their 'devalued' job role in part as liberation from the grip of agrarian patriarchy. Wage labour serves as an alternative to their oppression in agrarian patriarchy, which increasingly represents the 'traditional' against the modern wage-labour system. Indeed, the traditional sector becomes synonymous with continuing patriarchal rule, as agriculture and petty craft remain under the grip of agrarian patriarchal households. Capitalist industrialization, in contrast, destroys agrarian patriarchy. For working women, paid labour and changing household power dynamics represent a potential for freedom, however circumscribed it is in fact. Women workers may send the bulk of their earnings back to contribute to the sustenance of their household, but there is little doubt that, over time, their earnings translate into power and rising status within their households.

Paid work can also lead to organization among working-class women. Although both multinationals and host governments attempt to stifle women workers' organizations, their oppressed status *qua* women workers propels them into resistance. Here, again, the liberation from patriarchal control is critical in creating the possibility of mobilization. When the justification of their lower pay (in spite of roughly equal work) is their gender, it is not surprising that women should begin to resist gender segregation.

Gender-based ideology has two major sources: universalistic ideology and reaction against oppression.

First, the spread of universalistic ideology of emancipation, especially Enlightenment ideology, is a potent force of women's liberation. Early women's emancipatory ideology is associated also with its social basis: middle-class women (Evans, 1977: 29–32). The abstract character of the call for women's emancipation becomes concrete as the ideal touted by a universalistic ideology of emancipation comes in conflict with the patriarchal reality. For example, the contradiction between liberalism's universalist pretention and the continuing patriarchal rule is a source of feminist ideology (cf. Fauré, 1991). As Nehru (1961: 521) wrote while in British prison: 'The spirit of the age is in favour of equality, though practice denies it everywhere.' Equality in theory and inequality in practice generate tensions in ideologies and movements of emancipation. Hence, there is high propensity for women engaged in other emancipatory political movements and ideologies to become pioneers of women's liberation movements. For example, sexism within leftist movements, and their limitations on the 'woman question', are the proximate source of contemporary feminist theories and organizations (e.g. Evans, 1979). In general, the ideological justification for status privileges, once deprived of its mythical foundations, becomes difficult to sustain (Wallerstein, 1988: 6).

In peripheral areas, the 'import' of emancipatory, universalistic ideology is mediated by Westernizing élites. Hence, feminism spreads in late industrializing countries among upper-class women and men first, often by those who studied abroad or became exposed to Western 'missionizing' individuals. In this case, the reaction against traditional patriarchy is couched in terms of 'superior', 'universalistic' Western ideas. Especially for women of middle and upper classes, the Western influence becomes crucial. The public sphere under colonial influence becomes 'modern' or Westernized, with more 'advanced' ideas and practices about the status of women. In other words, the progressive stand on women's emancipation emerges as yet another way in which core countries can affirm their cultural superiority over the colonials and ex-colonials. Women in the periphery, then, begin to assert their independence *vis-à-vis* the tradition and lower classes of their society. The espousal of feminism at times becomes a mode of culturally differentiating the Westernizing élite from the tradition-bound lower classes.

A common ideological struggle in the periphery is nationalism articulated against Western imperialism. Women often join in the struggle against colonial oppression (cf. Jaywardena, 1986). As an emancipatory force, Third World nationalism often develops in tandem with feminist ideology, often affected by the very universalism touted by their colonial masters.

Second, gender-based oppression generates the conditions for gender-based emancipatory ideology. In so far as women are exploited *qua* women, there arise as reaction pro-woman ideologies and movements against traditional patriarchal ideology. The gender-based segregation comes into conflict with the individualistic and universalistic ideology; the sense of fairness transforms docile women workers, now loose from traditional control, and ripe for resistance.

Thus, the potential for gender-based resistance arises from the contradictions deriving from the structural changes in the household and the economy. There are two distinct ideological sources corresponding to different social bases: the universalistic ideology of the upper and middle classes, and the reaction against oppression experienced by working-class women.

THE CASE OF KOREA

To illustrate my analytical framework, I present the case of Korea. In the twentieth century, Korea transformed from an agrarian to an industrial society via colonialism. As a successful case of peripheral industrialization, Korea is an important case study.

Yi Dynasty Korea as agrarian patriarchy

Yi, or Chosôn Dynasty Korea, which lasted from the late fourteenth to early twentieth century, was a classic instance of agrarian patriarchy.[5] It was a quasi-caste system dominated by landlords (*yangban*), who maintained their privilege through the lineage system; patrilineality, patrilocality,

[5] Women's status was higher in the preceding Koryo Period, when matrilocality reigned and women had some 'rights', including property ownership (Kim, 1976: chs. 4, 8).

and primogeniture reigned. Although considerable differentiation existed within each group (Ch'oe, 1983: ch. 6), I will focus on *yangban* and peasant households.

In the patriarchal household of landed oligarchs, the status of *yangban* women was extremely low. As filial daughter, obedient wife, and wise mother, women's prescribed roles were inextricably intertwined with maintaining and reproducing the lineage system. Neo-Confucianism justified the subservience and inferiority of women, who were systematically excluded from political and economic life. For instance, women were not allowed to own property or appear in public without a veil; they were legally not responsible for their own actions (and hence could not stand trial). As Bird (1986: ii, 50) observed of late nineteenth-century Korea: 'Absolute seclusion [of women] is the inflexible rule among the upper classes.' In *yangban* households, men and women lived separately in outer and inner chambers, respectively, with different closets and bathrooms. Their social intercourse was largely proscribed (see Chang, 1983; Chung, 1986; Deuchler, 1977).

Being excluded from the public sphere and bound as a subservient member of the patriarchal household, *yangban* women's lives were extremely circumscribed.[6] An awareness of oppression can only be articulated socially; consciousness raising is wellnigh impossible for isolated individuals socialized into the ways of the *status quo*. Compounded by widespread illiteracy, *yangban* women failed to articulate proto-feminist ideology or to create women's organizations. Their relations with other women of their rank, for example, were limited; they could not build 'bonds' that are instrumental in producing proto-feminist consciousness and organization (cf. Cott, 1977: 197–206). Clear and deep social divisions—age gradations and status distinctions—separated women within the patriarchal household. Devoid of women's networks and informal associations, they became aligned with the major fault line of the larger society: *yangban* control over the vast majority of peasants. No doubt, personal resistance existed, but we have no records of women's organizations or proto-feminist writings from Yi Dynasty Korea.

Persistent poverty characterized peasant life in Yi Dynasty Korea (Palais, 1975: 67). Unlike the rigid hierarchy of *yangban* life, broadly egalitarian, communal practices existed in peasant life (Ko, 1986). The neo-Confucian patriarchal ideology penetrated peasantry slowly, albeit steadily, throughout the Yi Dynasty period (Deuchler, 1980). The agrarian patriarchal ideology manifested itself most strongly in the 'public' realm: for example,

[6] Ironically, three types of women were able to exercise limited freedom in aristocratic life. *Kisaeng*, or female entertainers organized by the state, constituted a minority who gained some knowledge of literature and the arts. Shamans and female doctors also belonged to the few educated women of Yi Dynasty Korea. However, they all belonged to the lowest strata (Kim, 1976: ch. 12).

the increasingly Confucianized family rituals. While the Confucian lineage system was hierarchical and patriarchal, the village social structure was broadly egalitarian. As Brandt (1971: 126) noted in his ethnography of a 'traditional' village: 'Male superiority is asserted in proportion to the formality of the situation'. Given the necessity of female labour in farm households, however, the ideological devaluation could not fully penetrate peasant life. One telling source of evidence derives from contemporary ethnographies of Korean farm life in which, in spite of the ideological profession of male superiority, male–female relations were relatively egalitarian.[7] This is not to deny that men dominated or that, because peasant women lived in less patriarchally oppressive households, their lives were in any way 'better' than those of *yangban* women (Bird, 1986: ii, 148; cf. Sorensen, 1988: 133–41). Furthermore, peasant women could not mobilize themselves *qua* women. Their social relations were deeply enmeshed in their household and community. Hence, to the extent that they became mobilized, they did so to resist local élites or political authorities (for a contemporary example, see Abelmann, 1990: ch. 8). None the less, unlike *yangban* women, peasant women created a distinct women's sphere in contradistinction to the male sphere pervaded by Confucianism (e.g. Brandt, 1971: 157–8; Janelli and Janelli, 1982: 24–5). One example is the persistence of shamanistic rituals, which were almost exclusively 'female' (Janelli and Janelli, 1982: 165–6; Kendall, 1985: 26–7, 167–70).

The absence of women's organization and consciousness characterizes agrarian patriarchy (cf. Mann, 1986*a*: 217). In spite of isolation and deprivation, élite women shared their relative privilege with *yangban* men, not their relative deprivation as women. On the other hand, peasant households were only partially infiltrated by dominant patriarchal ideology. Indeed, the differential subjugation of women was a major criterion of status distinction. The mastery of Confucian texts and rituals—embodying the Korean agrarian patriarchal ideology—became a cultural criterion to separate the élite from the masses. In both groups, however, the gender category was subsumed by other, more salient categories. In this sense, gender was rendered invisible and ineffectual. Having no basis for organization or consciousness, the social dynamic of agrarian patriarchy rested on other forms of social division and oppression.

By the late nineteenth century, Korea was encroached upon by the West (and Japan). In addition to the external threat, the state faced intra-élite

[7] For example, Sorensen (1988: 69) writes: 'The traditional élite pattern was for women not to participate in agricultural activities . . . but the women of Sangongni do much agricultural work.' Note the contrast between the following passages. '[In the yangban neighbourhood] women remain mostly inside their own homes' (Brandt, 1971: 46). '[In the non-yangban neighbourhood] women join in some of the discussions, talking back to men' (Brandt, 1971: 58). As Brandt (1971: 126) notes: 'It seems to me that the behavioral expression of this ideology of male dominance is even stronger among the traditional élite of provincial towns and in Seoul.' See also Osgood (1951: 47, 332).

conflicts and peasant uprisings. Eventually, the traditional order, and with it agrarian patriarchy, collapsed.

The super-exploitation of female workers in Korean development

Korea's industrialization began under the Japanese rule (1905–45) (Eckert, 1991: 253–9).[8] However, it was during Park's rule (1961–79) that Korea industrialized rapidly as the state pursued rapid GNP growth (Lie, 1992). Korea's export-oriented industrialization exploited its chief comparative advantage against the world: low-wage labour force.

In the process of rapid industrialization, the countryside yielded a plethora of cheap labor; indeed, Korea's rural exodus in the 1960s and 1970s averaged about 3 per cent annually (Lie, 1991*c*). To undercut global price competition, the state suppressed autonomous unions and exercised corporatist control over workers (Choi, 1989). There was no legal, autonomous union until the 1980s.[9] The state co-opted union leaders, while proscribing strikes through a variety of measures. In addition, institutions and practices upholding labour rights were all but absent in Korea. For example, there was no minimum wage law until 1988 (Lie, 1991*a*). Finally, even the *de jure* protection did not operate *de facto* because the authoritarian Yushin Constitution from 1972 overrode the extant protection and legislation.

Thus, there was an open, state-sanctified exploitation of Korean workers. The massive concentration of capital in large conglomerates (*chaebôl*) created immense power asymmetry between capital and labour. *Chaebôl* firms sought to institutionalize patriarchal control over workers in their 'family' firm. (To be sure, large conglomerates were family owned.) Capitalists were to be patriarchs over their 'family'—workers.

In spite of paternalist rhetoric, Koreans worked the longest hours in the world in 1986 and suffered one of the highest industrial accident rates in the world. Wages were low in comparison to other developing Asian economies, or to Mexico or Brazil in 1986. Perhaps the most telling is the differential between the average wage received by workers and the estimated subsistence wage. For example, the Korea Development Institute (KDI;

[8] Industrialization transformed some rural women into urban workers. In 1938, 30 per cent of industrial workers were women (the figure for the USA in 1930 was 13 per cent) (Grajdanzev, 1944: 184; Yi, 1989). Korean male workers earned one-half, while Korean female earned one-fourth, of Japanese male workers (Hanguk Minjungsa Yônguhoe, 1986: 151–61). In addition, women were exploited in a variety of ways, including being prostitutes for Japanese soldiers (Lie, 1991*b*).

[9] The rate of unionization was extremely low. For example, the level of unionization as percentage of the total employed workforce in the mid-1980s was 7.0 per cent in Korea, compared to 16.4 per cent in Singapore, 14.5 per cent in Hong Kong, and 20.9 per cent in Taiwan (Deyo, 1989: 70–3).

a government think-tank) estimated in 1980 that a minimum monthly income for a family of five was 270,000 won (about US$335). In fact, 31 per cent of all workers received less than 70,000 won; 56 per cent received less than 100,000 won; and 86 per cent received less than 200,000 won. In 1986, the Federation of Korean Trade Unions (FKTU) estimated that a family of four required a minimum of 524,113 won a month; the average wage was 339,474 won. In short, wages were low by international comparison and inadequate for many workers to acquire the basic necessities of life (see Lie, 1991*a*).

The super-exploitation of female workers occurred in the context of the exploitation of all workers. As I suggested above, peripheral industrialization necessitated an extreme hierarchization of the labour force. Female Korean workers played a crucial role in promoting export-oriented industrialization.

Throughout the 1960s and 1970s, female workers constituted about 30 per cent of the labour force (Ogle, 1990: 20). During this period, female migration to Seoul outpaced male migration by about 15 per cent (Hong, 1984: 192–3). However, the crucial factor is that 'In major export industries such as textiles, garments, electronics and food processing young women made up over 90 per cent of total production workers in 1980' (Cho, 1985*b*: 81). In Masan Free Export Zone, for example, young women made up over 90 per cent of the workforce (Cho, 1985*b*: 83). Thus, the crucial industries that fuelled export-oriented industrialization in South Korea relied predominantly on female workers.

The ideology and practice of male dominance was crucial in employing and dominating female workers. Male supervisors were used to control female workers (Ogle, 1990: 20). When female workers organized, male workers were mobilized to prevent worker unity and organization. For example, when a female worker was elected as the leader of a local union: 'Male workers, supported by management, combined with a few local thugs, beat and humiliated [female workers] in order to force a decertification of their union' (Ogle, 1990: 61).

Female workers' conditions were dire. In the official sector, they worked longer than men but received less than half of what they earned. In the 1984 Korea Development Institute report, 40 per cent of women workers earned less than 100,000 won a month. Of the 301,000 workers who earned less than 100,000 won a month in 1986, 261,000 were women (Lie, 1991*a*: 506). In 1985, 13.2 per cent of male workers earned less than the minimum cost of living for a single person, while the comparable figure was 63.9 per cent for women (Bello and Rosenfeld, 1990: 26). Many sweatshops employed women at lower wages. Women in textile factories worked over 12-hour work days, with virtually no vacation. They were cramped into small spaces without ventilation or adequate lighting; their health conditions deteriorated (Ko, 1988). They were goaded to work amidst deafening machine noises and the watchful gazes of taskmasters

(Spencer, 1988). For instance, Korean female textile workers made the following appeal in 1977:

> Our life in the factory is really miserable. Ours is a confined, stifling existence on the job—prohibited from talking to the workers next to us, poorly fed, not allowed to even go to toilet when necessary. The company side oppresses us by intervening in our personal lives . . . We are endlessly plagued by lung tuberculosis, athlete's foot, and various stomach diseases. Women workers have yellow, swollen faces from inadequate sunlight. We are also tormented by temperatures of 40 (centigrade) and by dust. . . . We are struggling to free ourselves from these miserable conditions which are too many to enumerate (*Asian Women's Liberation Newsletter*, 1983: 233–4).

In addition, many female workers suffered sexual harassment and other violence (Ogle, 1990: 20). Many of them were obliged to send their meagre earnings back to their rural homes. In a 1980 study, female textile workers on average saved nearly 50 per cent of their earnings (Oh, 1983: 195).

None the less, textile factories and related manufacturing industries presented the official, and in many ways, better opportunities for young women. Indeed, the simultaneous liberation from the condition of agrarian poverty and patriarchy and the relative privilege enjoyed *vis-à-vis* other women account at least in part for their willing incorporation into the capitalist world economy.

Many women worked in the informal sector, most prominently as housekeepers for middle- and upper-class households. From the 1960s to 1980s, one of the major sources of female employment was as domestic workers, many of them working as live-in help. These jobs were not registered in official government surveys, while their wages and working conditions were worse than the grinding factory jobs (Sin, 1989: 138–9; see also Cho, 1988). Women also worked in myriad manual and menial jobs, such as construction and peddling goods like cigarettes and candy bars. In 1989, there were 3 million female temporary workers, while nearly 2 million women, nearly 20 per cent of the workforce, worked in daily contract jobs in 1990 (Park, 1992: 16).

Three of the most important foreign exchange earners for Korea in the 1960s were wigs, textiles, and US military bases. Wigs literally came off women's bodies; textiles were produced by their sweat. The sex industry played a major role in foreign exchange accumulation. US soldiers in military bases created demands for venal entertainment. In a spectacle enacted wherever US bases exist, local 'entrepreneurs' organized sex-related entertainment for the American boys (Enloe, 1989: ch. 4). Another major market for the sex industry were Japanese businessmen. The 'sex tours' became a conspicuous presence in the major cities across Korea, where *kisaeng* (the Korean equivalent of the Japanese *geisha*) entertained Japanese men by acting as escorts and sexual partners. Perhaps the most shocking aspect of the sex industry was the government support. The precondition for being an official, i.e. government-approved, *kisaeng* was a licence issued by the government. In 1973, the Minister of Education publicly praised patriotic prostitutes (*kisaeng*), causing an uproar among the socially conscious public. Yet the government-approved *kisaeng* constituted the privileged section of prostitutes. Beneath the 'official' sector was the 'unofficial' one organized by pimps. These women did not require licences, but their working conditions were significantly worse than the 'official' prostitutes. In the mid-1970s, prostitutes numbered 200,000 (Lie, 1991*b*).[10]

Thus, labour exploitation, especially female super-exploitation, inside and outside factories was extremely crucial in promoting export through cheap labour. The exploitation of women was instrumental in accumulating crucial foreign exchange earnings critical for export-oriented industrialization. The gendered nature of capitalist industrialization in South Korea should be clear from the significance of female workers' contribution and exploitation.

Women's movements in Korea

In Korea, the first stirring of women's emancipation occurred in the context of Western encroachment in the late nineteenth century, primarily among Western-influenced élites. Enlightened *yangban* men received Western, 'progressive' ideas on women mediated through Japan.[11] In addition, Christian missionaries introduced women's education as well as spiritual equality between men and women. Influenced by Western ideology and Christianity, the first Korean women's organization, *Ch'anyanghoe*, was formed in 1989, dedicated to the causes of educating women and nationalism.

Substantial changes in women's conditions occurred in the Japanese Colonial Period. However, women's movements were led by élite women

[10] As Bryceson (1985: 151) writes of another context: 'The working-class woman prostitute represents the epitome of "freedom" under capitalism. She is "free" to sell her labour power and her sexuality, but in reality she is forced to do either or both to secure her subsistence.' Sexual exploitation went beyond straightforward prostitution. Some women were 'exported' as 'mail-order' brides or as prostitutes. The 'export' extended to babies (*Korea Times*, 1 Nov. 1989). The government also actively encouraged the export of male bodies. The most important was the boom in Middle East construction following the first oil shock of 1973. Tens of thousands of Korean workers worked as indentured labourers in Middle Eastern countries, repatriating their wages to Korea as construction companies generated tremendous profit. In 1978, for example, there were 122,000 South Korean workers abroad (Kurian, 1987: 1099). Another major 'export' was soldiers, who were dispatched to fight as mercenaries in the Vietnam war (Kurian, 1987: 1102).

[11] It should also be noted that the major indigenous movement against Western encroachment, the Tonghak rebellion, included calls for women's equality (Sin, 1987: 161–2).

and men and focused on nationalism. The adoption of 'Westernized' Japanese law provided some rights and privileges for Korean women. For instance, the colonial government (*Sôtokufu*) mandated primary schooling for girls. Many women entered the political sphere for the first time, either as participants in independence movements or in pro-Japanese organizations (Pak, 1989). Christian women were especially active (Kim, 1986; see also Chông, 1971). Also, working women struggled against their oppressed conditions as colonized workers (e.g. Kim, 1982). None the less, all these movements were limited, but they underscore my point regarding the sources of gender-based movements and ideologies. Furthermore, none of the movements enjoyed much autonomy from men and were focused on issues not directly related to women (Kim, 1986: 99). Early women's movements in Korea were almost inevitably articulated in conjunction with nationalism.

After 1945, most women active in the public sphere or women's rights movements came from élite, *yangban* backgrounds, especially those influenced by Western—notably Christian—ideologies. For example, the most prominent woman in the early stages of South Korean politics was Louise Yim, the leader of the Women's Democratic Party, who was educated in the United States (Yim, 1951). Perhaps the leading advocate of women's rights in contemporary South Korea was T. Y. Lee, a devoted Christian (Strawn, 1988).

About seventy women's groups were organized between the 1950s and 1970s. However, the vast majority of them were concerned with revising family law or dedicated to primarily middle-class issues, such as consumption (Ch'oe, 1989).

South Korean women's movements became more active in the 1970s, after the initial stages of rapid industrialization. A growing number of urban, middle-class women began to participate in the public sphere, roughly replicating the Western experience, albeit in a compressed time frame. First, they became active in a number of voluntary organizations. Second, they participated in women-related issues, such as movements against male violence. Third, they focused on a variety of legal issues, most prominently the revision of the family law (Josei Heiyûkai, 1986: 211–13). In the 1980s, predominantly middle-class women's groups participated in pro-democratic and other political movements (cf. Matsui, 1987; Palley, 1990: 1138).

Working women also struggled against their oppressive conditions in the 1970s. The intensification of labour movements in the late 1970s was spearheaded by women in textile factories. Some of the largest capital–labour confrontations involved 'docile' female workers. 'Women workers, unlike their male counterparts, often responded to the harshness of the enforcement system by direct resistance. Most of the disputes registered in the [1970s] were registered by women and the few cases of work stoppages were all by women' (Ogle, 1990: 84). The beginning of women's union activities can be traced to the early 1970s, especially through organizational activities by Christian groups (Hattori, 1987: 120–3; Josei Heiyûkai, 1986: 214–16). In spite of government repression, then, women workers resisted. For example, the physical assault and ideological effort of the government attempted to cast even day-care facilities as 'communist' (Rôdô Jôhô Henshû Iinkai, 1989: 120). However, by the 1980s, many working women's organizations began to demand changes in state child-care policies (Korean Women Workers Association, 1991). Particularly critical in women's mobilization were their separation from agrarian patriarchal households and their new experience as 'gendered' subjects. As Cho (1985*a*: 213) writes: 'young women workers in South Korea can be "autonomous" as "workers" and "free"'.

Ironically, the agrarian patriarchal ideology was more effective in curbing male workers' movements (as they struggled for a new patriarchal and sexist ideology). In contrast, 'docile' female workers were in fact much more militant. Indeed, 'the distinguishing feature of South Korea's labor movement' in the 1970s was that it was 'led by young women workers' (Cho, 1985*b*: 83). Sexist labour practices, then, contributed to the mobilization of gender-based labour movements.

In summary, patriarchal capitalism unleashed gender-based movements and ideologies in South Korea. They were, however, class divided. Middle-class women, influenced by Western ideology and Christianity, organized themselves on middle-class issues like consumption and the revision of family law. Working-class women labouring under the gender hierarchy became an active force as they organized to resist gender (and class) oppression.

CONCLUSION

In this paper, I proposed a framework for analysing the role of gender in peripheral industrialization. Although women are oppressed in agrarian patriarchy, they do not identify or mobilize themselves as gendered subjects. In peripheral industrialization, gender emerges as a crucial axis of oppression. Peripheral industrialization is *gendered*; patriarchal capitalism entails gender differentiation and exploitation. However, it also creates the condition for women's emancipatory ideologies and movements. The articulation of gender-based movements and ideologies, however, can be differentiated across class.

In this paper, I sought to stress gender and patriarchy as historically shifting categories. Rather than engaging in quantitative comparisons of gender inequality or oppression, I emphasized the qualitatively distinct nature of gender oppression in the transition from agrarian patriarchy to patriarchal capitalism. My intention is *not* to argue against empirical findings or to enter into debates about women's status in development.[12] Rather, my point is theoretical: I focus on a tendency to treat 'gender' as trans-historical. By assuming the universal usefulness of gender as a category of analysis, scholars apply it to assess the relative oppression or liberation of women across historical periods and cultures. In so doing, they neglect the historical character of 'gender' and miss critical social and epistemological shifts. In other words, rather than arguing about whether women's status is better or worse in one society or another, it is crucial to historicize not only the changing nature of male dominance and female oppression, but also to understand the ways in which gender is embedded or disembedded within fundamental social relations and structures. It is only through this process that we can assess the historical possibilities of gender emancipation. The imposition of 'gender' as a universally useful category misses some of the central dynamics of female oppression and emancipation.

REFERENCES

ABELMANN, NANCY (1990), *The Practice and Politics of History: A South Korean Tenant Farmers Movement* (Unpublished dissertation, Department of Anthropology, University of California at Berkeley).

ACCAMPO, ELINOR (1989), *Industrialization, Family Life, and Class Relations: Saint Chamond, 1815–1914* (Berkeley: University of California Press).

AMADIUME, IFI (1987), *Male Daughters, Female Husbands: Gender and Sex in an African Society* (London: Zed).

Asian Women's Liberation Newsletter (1983), 'Outcries of the Poor Workers: An Appeal from South Korea', in M. Davies (ed.), *Third World Second Sex* (London: Zed).

BARON, AVA (1991), 'An "Other" Side of Gender Antagonism at Work: Men, Boys, and the Remasculinization of Printers' Work, 1830–1920', in A. Baron

[12] In the 1960s, the received view in development studies suggested that women's status will gradually improve with 'modernization'. Modernizing forces—industrialization, urbanization, and so on—were to unshackle women from their premodern fetters (e.g. Inkeles and Smith, 1975). This optimistic formula—modernization liberates women—has come under suspicion; as Jacquette (1982: 271) summarizes: 'Feminists see urbanization, mobility, and the conversion to the cash economy not as unalloyed benefits, but as processes that cut women off from their traditional economic and social roles and thrust them into the modern sector where they are discriminated against and exploited.' By the late 1980s, the 'female marginalization thesis'—usually traced to Boserup's (1970) work—became perhaps the dominant view of women in development (Saffioti, 1978: 298; Fuentes and Ehrenreich, 1983; Ward, 1984: 147–9; cf. Tinker, 1990). In brief, the incorporation of women into the capitalist economy has further oppressed women; they are exploited in the workplace, while burdened by patriarchal rule and domestic duties at home (Fernández-Kelly, 1983; Mies, 1986). In spite of critiques of the female marginalization thesis (Scott, 1986), many scholars working in the field of women and development have compellingly delineated the deleterious consequences of industrialization for women (see in general Moghadam, 1992).

(ed.), *Word Engendered: Toward a New History of American Labor* (Ithaca: Cornell University Press), 47–69.

BELLO, WALDEN and ROSENFELD, STEPHANIE (1990), *Dragons in Distress: Asia's Miracle Economies in Crisis* (San Francisco: Institute for Food and Development Policy).

BERG, BARBARA J. (1978), *The Remembered Gate: Origins of American Feminism: The Woman and the City, 1800–1860* (Oxford: Oxford University Press).

BETTIO, FRANCESCA (1988), *The Sexual Division of Labour: The Italian Case* (Oxford: Clarendon Press).

BIRD, ISABELLA L. (1986), *Korea and Her Neighbours*, 1st pub. 1898 (Tokyo: Tuttle).

BOSERUP, ESTER (1970), *Women's Role in Economic Development* (New York: St Martin's Press).

BRANDT, VINCENT S. R. (1971), *A Korean Village: Between Farm and Sea* (Cambridge: Harvard University Press).

BRYCESON, DEBORAH FAHY (1985), 'Women's Proletarianization and the Family Wage in Tanzania', in H. Afshar (ed.), *Women, Work, and Ideology in the Third World* (London: Tavistock), 128–52.

CHAFETZ, JANET SALTZMAN (1984), *Sex and Advantage: A Comparative, Macro-Structural Theory of Sex Stratification* (Totowa, NJ: Rowman & Allanheld).

CHANG, YUNSHIK (1983), 'Women in a Confucian Society: The Case of Chosun Dynasty Korea', in E. Yu and E. H. Phillips (eds.), *Traditional Thoughts and Practices in Korea* (Los Angeles: Center for Korean-American and Korean Studies, California State University, Los Angeles), 67–96.

CHAYANOV, A. V. (1986) [1966], *The Theory of Peasant Economy*, eds. D. Thorner, B. Kerblay, and R. E. F. Smith (Madison: University of Wisconsin Press).

CHO, MI HYE (1988), 'Tosi pinmin yôsông ûi silt'ae wa ûisik', *Yôsông*, 3: 171–84.

CHO, SOON KYOUNG (1985*a*), 'The Labor Process and Capital Mobility: The Limits of the New International Division of Labor', *Politics and Society*, 14: 185–222.

—— (1985*b*), 'The Dilemmas of Export-Led Industrialization: South Korea and the World Economy', *Berkeley Journal of Sociology*, 30: 65–94.

CH'OE, CHAE SUK (1983), *Hanguk kajok chedosa yôngu* (Seoul: Ilchisa).

CH'OE, YANG JA (1989), 'Kankoku josei undôshi', in Yi Sun Ae (ed.), *Bundan kokufuku to Kankoku josei kaihô undô* (Tokyo: Ochanomizu Shobô).

CHOI, JANG JIP (1989), *Labor and the Authoritarian State: Labor Unions in South Korean Manufacturing Industries, 1961–1980* (Seoul: Korea University Press).

CHÔNG, YO SOP (1971), *Hanguk yôsông undong-sa* (Seoul: Ilchogak).

CHUNG, YO-SUP (1986), 'Women's Social Status in the Yi Dynasty', in Research Center for Asian Women, Sookmyung Women's University (eds.), *Women of the Yi Dynasty* (Seoul: Research Center for Asian Women, Sookmyung Women's University), 139–71.

COONTZ, STEPHANIE (1988), *The Social Origins of Private Life: A History of American Families, 1600–1900* (London: Verso).

COTT, NANCY F. (1977), *The Bonds of Womanhood: 'Woman's Sphere' in New England, 1780–1835* (New Haven: Yale University Press).

DEUCHLER, MARTINA (1977), 'The Tradition: Women during the Yi Dynasty', in S. Mattielli (ed.), *Virtues in Conflict: Tradition and the Korean Women Today* (Seoul: Royal Asiatic Society, Korea Branch), 1–47.

DEUCHLER, MARTINA (1980), 'Neo-Confucianism: The Impulse for Social Action in Early Yi Korea', *Journal of Korean Studies*, 2: 71–112.

DEYO, FREDERIC C. (1989), *Beneath the Miracle: Labor Subordination in the New Asian Industrialism* (Berkeley: University of California Press).

ECKERT, CARTER (1991), *Offspring of Empire: The Koch'ang Kims and the Colonial Origins of Korean Capitalism, 1876–1945* (Seattle: University of Washington Press).

ELSON, DIANE (1991) 'Male Bias in the Development Process: An Overview', in D. Elson (ed.), *Male Bias in the Development Process* (Manchester: Manchester University Press), 1–28.

—— and RUTH PEARSON (1984), 'The Subordination of Women and the Internationalisation of Factory Production', in K. Young (ed.), *Of Marriage and the Market: Women's Subordination Internationally and Its Lessons*, 2nd edn. (London: RKP), 18–40.

ENLOE, CYNTHIA (1989), *Bananas, Beaches and Bases* (Berkeley: University of California Press).

EVANS, RICHARD J. (1977), *The Feminists: Women's Emancipation Movements in Europe, America and Australasia 1840–1920* (London: Croom Helm).

EVANS, SARA (1979), *Personal Politics: The Roots of Women's Liberation in the Civil Rights Movement and the New Left* (New York: Knopf).

FAURÉ, CHRISTINE (1991) [1985], *Democracy without Women: Feminism and the Rise of Liberal Individualism in France*, tr. Claudia Borbman and John Berks (Bloomington: Indiana University Press).

FERNÁNDEZ-KELLY, MARÍA PATRICIA (1983), *For We Are Sold: I and My People: Women and Industry in Mexico's Frontier* (Albany, NY: SUNY Press).

FUENTES, ANNETTE and EHRENREICH, BARBARA (1983), *Women in the Global Factory* (New York: Institute for New Communications).

GOLDTHORPE, JOHN (1983), 'Women and Class Analysis: In Defense of the Conventional View', *Sociology*, 17: 468–88.

GORDON, DAVID M., EDWARDS, RICHARD and REICH, MICHAEL (1982), *Segmented Work, Divided Workers: The Historical Transformation of Labor in the United States* (Cambridge: Cambridge University Press).

GRAJDANZEV, ANDREW (1944), *Modern Korea* (New York: Institute of Pacific Relations).

HANGUK MINJUNGSA YÔNGUHOE (1986), *Hanguk minjungsa*, vol. 2 (Seoul: P'ulpit).

HATTORI, TAMIO (ed.) (1987), *Kankoku no kôgyôka: hatten no kôzu* (Tokyo: Ajia Keizai Kenkyûsho).

HILL, POLLY (1986), *Development Economics on Trial: The Anthropological Case for a Prosecution* (Cambridge: Cambridge University Press).

HUMPHREY, JOHN (1985), 'Gender, Pay, and Skill: Manual Workers in Brazilian Industry', in H. Afshar (ed.), *Women, Work, and Ideology in the Third World* (London: Tavistock), 214–31.

INKELES, ALEX and SMITH, DAVID (1975), *Becoming Modern* (Cambridge: Harvard University Press).

JACQUETTE, JANE S. (1982), 'Women and Modernization Theory: A Decade of Feminist Criticism', *World Politics*, 34: 267–84.

JANELLI, ROGER L. and JANELLI, DAWNHEE YIM (1982), *Ancestor Worship and Korean Society* (Stanford: Stanford University Press).

JAYWARDENA, KUMARI (1986), *Feminism and Nationalism in the Third World* (London: Zed).

JOEKES, SUSAN (1985), 'Working for Lipstick? Male and Female Labour in the Clothing Industry in Morocco', in H. Afshar (ed.), *Women, Work, and Ideology in the Third World* (London: Tavistock), 183–213.

—— (1987), *Women in the World Economy: An INSTRAW Study* (New York: Oxford University Press).

JOSEI HEIYÛKAI (1986) [1984], 'Kankoku josei undô no saikentô', in H. Wada and H. Kajimura (eds.), *Kankoku no minshû undô* (Tokyo: Keisô Shobô), 187–220.

KENDALL, LAUREL (1985), *Shamans, Housewives, and Other Restless Spirits: Women in Korean Ritual Life* (Honolulu: University of Hawaii Press).

KIM, CH'AN CHÔNG (1982), *Chôsenjin jokô no uta* (Tokyo: Iwanami Shoten).

KIM, YUNG-CHUNG (ed.) (1976), *Women of Korea: A History from Ancient Times to 1945* (Seoul: Ewha Womans University Press).

—— (1986), 'Women's Movement in Modern Korea', in S. Chung (ed.), *Challenges for Woman: Woman's Studies in Korea* (Seoul: Ewha Woman's University), 75–102.

KO, KYÔNG SIM (1988), 'Hanguk yôsông nodongja ûi kôngang munje', *Yôsông*, 3: 50–68.

KO, SÛNG-JE (1986), 'The Cooperative Practice of the Korean Village Community', in National Academy of Sciences (ed.), *Introduction to Korean Studies* (Seoul: National Academy of Sciences), 697–727.

Korean Women Workers Association (1991), 'Korean Women Demand Childcare Facilities', *Asian Women Workers Newsletter*, 10/2: 9–10.

KURIAN, G. T. (ed.) (1987), *Encyclopedia of the Third World*, 3rd edn. (New York: Facts on File).

LAMPHERE, LOUISE (1987), *From Working Daughters to Working Mothers: Immigrant Women in a New England Industrial Community* (Ithaca: Cornell University Press).

LERNER, GERDA (1986), *The Creation of Patriarchy* (New York: Oxford University Press).

LIE, JOHN (1991*a*), 'The Prospect for Economic Democracy in South Korea', *Economic and Industrial Democracy*, 12: 501–13.

—— (1991*b*), 'From Kisaeng to Maech'un: The Transformation of Sexual Work in Twentieth-Century Korea'. Paper presented at the American Sociological Association Annual Meeting, Cincinnati, Oh.

—— (1991*c*), 'The State, Industrialization and Agricultural Sufficiency: The Case of South Korea', *Development Policy Review*, 9: 37–51.

—— (1992), 'The Political Economy of South Korean Development', *International Sociology*, 7: 285–300.

LUTZ, NANCY MELISSA (1988), 'Images of Docility: Asian Women and the World-Economy', in J. Smith, J. Collins, T. K. Hopkins, and A. Muhammad (eds.), *Racism, Sexism, and the World-System* (New York: Greenwood Press), 57–73.

MANN, MICHAEL (1986*a*), *The Sources of Social Power, Vol. 1: A History of Power from the Beginning to AD 1760* (Cambridge: Cambridge University Press).

—— (1986*b*), 'A Crisis in Stratification Theory? Persons, Households/Families/Lineages, Genders, Classes and Nations', in R. Crompton and M. Mann (eds.), *Gender and Stratification* (Cambridge: Polity), 40–56.

MATSUI, YAYORI (1987), *Onnatachi no Ajia* (Tokyo: Iwanami Shoten).
MEDICK, HANS (1976), 'The Proto-Industrial Family Economy: The Structural Function of Household and Family during the Transition from Peasant Society to Industrial Capitalism', *Social History*, 3: 291–315.
MIES, MARIA (1986), *Patriarchy and Accumulation on a World Scale: Women in the International Division of Labour* (London: Zed).
MOGHADAM, VALENTINE M. (1992), 'Development and Women's Emancipation: Is There a Connection?', *Development and Change*, 23/3 (July): 215–56.
NEHRU, JAWAHARLAL (1961), *The Discovery of India* (Delhi: Asia Publishing House).
OGLE, GEORGE E. (1990), *South Korea: Dissent within the Economic Miracle* (London: Zed).
OH, SUN JOO (1983), 'The Living Conditions of Female Workers in Korea', *Korea Observer*, 14: 185–200.
OSGOOD, CORNELIUS (1951), *The Koreans and Their Culture* (New York: The Ronald Press).
PAK, YÔNG OK (1989), *Hanguk yôsông tongnip undong* (Seoul: Tongnip Kinyômkwan).
PALAIS, JAMES B. (1975), *Politics and Policy in Traditional Korea* (Cambridge: Harvard University Press).
PALLEY, MARIAN LIEF (1990), 'Women's Status in South Korea: Tradition and Change', *Asian Survey*, 30: 1136–53.
PARK, ANNA Y. M. (1992), 'South Korea: Mass Retrenchment vs Labour Shortage', *Asian Women Workers Newsletter*, 11/2: 14–16.
RENDALL, JANE (1985), *The Origins of Modern Feminism: Women in Britain, France and the United States, 1780–1860* (Chicago: Lyceum).
RÔDÔ JÔHÔ HENSHÛ IINKAI (1989), 'Nijû no yokuatuka no josei rôdôsha', in Rôdô Jôhô Henshû Iinkai (ed.), *Nodonja* (Tokyo: Kyôikushiryô Shuppankai), 115–20.
ROEDIGER, DAVID R. (1991), *The Wages of Whiteness: Race and the Making of the American Working Class* (London: Verso).
SAFFIOTI, HELEIETH I. B. (1978), *Women in Class Society*, tr. Michael Vale (New York: Monthly Review Press).
SALAFF, JANET (1981), *Working Daughters of Hong Kong: Filial Piety or Power in the Family?* (Cambridge: Cambridge University Press).
SCOTT, ALISON MACEWEN (1986), '"Women and Industrialisation": Examining the "Female Marginalisation" Thesis', *Journal of Development Studies*, 22: 649–80.
SCOTT, JOAN WALLACH (1988) [1986], 'Gender: A Useful Category of Social Analysis', in J. W. Scott (ed.), *Gender and the Politics of History* (New York: Columbia University Press), 28–50.
SEN, GITA and GROWN, CAREN (1987), *Development, Crises, and Alternative Visions: Third World Women's Perspectives* (New York: Monthly Review Press).
SHIVA, VANDANA (1988), *Staying Alive: Women, Ecology and Development* (London: Zed).
SIN, IN YÔNG (1989), Josei undô to josei rôdôsha', in Yi Sun Ae (ed.), *Bundan kokufuku to Kankoku josei kaihô undô* (Tokyo: Ochanomizu Shobô), 129–46.
SIN, YONG HA (1987), *Hanguk kundae sahoe sasangsa yôngu* (Seoul: Ilchisa).
SORENSEN, CLARK W. (1988), *Over the Mountains Are Mountains: Korean Peasant Households and Their Adaptations to Rapid Industrialization* (Seattle: University of Washington Press).

SPENCER, ROBERT (1988), *Yogong* (Seoul: Royal Asiatic Society, Korea Branch).

STRAWN, SONIA REID (1988), *Where There Is No Path: Lee Tai-Young, Her Story* (Seoul: Korean Legal Aid Center for Family Relations).

TINKER, IRENE (1990), 'The Making of a Field: Advocates, Practitioners, and Scholars', in Irene Tinker (ed.), *Persistent Inequalities: Women and World Development* (Oxford: Oxford University Press), 27–53.

TRUMBACH, RANDOLPH (1978), *The Rise of the Egalitarian Family: Aristocratic Kinship and Domestic Relations in Eighteenth-Century England* (New York: Academic Press).

WALLERSTEIN, IMMANUEL (1988), 'The Ideological Tensions of Capitalism: Universalism versus Racism and Sexism', in J. Smith, J. Collins, T. K. Hopkins, and A. Muhammad (eds.), *Racism, Sexism, and the World-System* (New York: Greenwood Press), 3–9.

—— (1991) [1987], 'The Construction of Peoplehood: Racism, Nationalism, Ethnicity', in Etienne Balibar and I. Wallerstein (eds.), *Race, Nation, Class: Ambiguous Identities* (London: Verso), 71–85.

WARD, KATHRYN B. (1984), *Women in the World-System: Its Impacts on Status and Fertility* (New York: Praeger).

WARE, VRON (1992), *Beyond the Pale: White Women, Racism and History* (London: Verso).

WHYTE, MARTIN KING (1978), *The Status of Women in Preindustrial Societies* (Princeton: Princeton University Press).

WRIGHT, ERIK OLIN (1989), 'Women in the Class Structure', *Politics and Society*, 17: 35–66.

YI, HYO CHAE (1989), 'Ilcheha ûi Hanguk yôsông nodong sanghwang kwa nodong undong', in Hyo Chae Yi (ed.), *Hanguk ûi yôsông undong* (Seoul: Chong'usa), 73–126.

YIM, LOUISE (1951), *My Forty Year Fight for Korea* (New York: A. A. Wyn).

Patriarchy and Private Property in Nicaragua, 1860–1920

Elizabeth Dore

ANALYSING WOMEN'S OPPRESSION

The dominant trend in feminist studies in the late 1980s and early 1990s was to abandon theories of patriarchy and to conclude that it is impossible to develop a theory of women's oppression. This flight from patriarchy was part of an academic wave that rejected the validity of all previously influential theories. Feminist critics of patriarchy discarded the concept for a variety of reasons: in the end many were left questioning the value of theory itself. In this introduction I examine the case against patriarchy theory and suggest methodological approaches to developing a theory about the systematic nature of men's oppression of women. Within this methodological framework, in succeeding sections I analyse changing forms of patriarchy in rural Nicaragua during the social revolution that accompanied the expansion of coffee production from 1860 to 1920. The conclusion explores the relationship between patriarchy and development.

Patriarchy is defined by the social relations of the systematic oppression of women by men.[1] Soon after patriarchy was popularized as an explanation of women's oppression, it fell into disrepute for failing to fulfil its analytical expectations.[2] Patriarchy theory was criticized on three grounds: first, for being ahistorical and not encompassing class and cultural diversity; second, for its reliance on dualism; and third, for its failure to specify the essence of women's subordination.[3] Feminists initiated the critique of patriarchy in an effort to develop a theory of women's oppression. But as that debate was overcome by the generalized rejection of existing orthodoxies patriarchy theory was discredited and pushed aside.

Theory is a body of general principles offered to explain phenomena. All analyses and descriptions are embedded in theory, though often not explicitly. Without a theory of patriarchy what we are offered, whether

[1] My definition of patriarchy is consistent with Sylvia Walby's. See her essay in this volume.

[2] For a literature review of the patriarchy debates see Sylvia Walby, *Theorizing Patriarchy* (Oxford: Blackwell, 1990).

[3] For a critique of patriarchy see Lourdes Benería and Marta Roldán, *The Crossroads of Class and Gender: Industrial Homework, Subcontracting and Household Dynamics in Mexico City* (Chicago: University of Chicago Press, 1987), 8–11. For an analytical review of literature critical of patriarchy see Ben Fine, *Women's Employment and the Capitalist Family* (London: Routledge, 1992), ch. 1.

acknowledged or not, is another theory: one that denies the systemic nature of women's oppression. Those who argue that it is impossible to develop theory about the general phenomenon of patriarchy must conclude that women's oppression is neither structural nor systematic. Recently some feminist writers have embraced this view. Self-consciously postmodern authors tended to be more overt in their rejection of the structural and systematic nature of women's oppression.[4] Their focus on gender hierarchies, rather than women's oppression, was a reflection of their analysis that the oppression of women is not systemic. For these authors, the central analytical task is to understand how gender difference is constructed rather than why and how men's oppression of women is sustained and reproduced. Although the difference in these two positions may appear subtle; it is key. The first approach explores difference; the second explores oppression. The *sine qua non* of feminism is that men's oppression of women characterizes most societies. Nevertheless, some feminist academics argue that it is erroneous to generalize about the asymmetric and exploitative nature of gender relations.[5] One consequence of rejecting theories of patriarchy, and concentrating on the social construction of gender, is that the political objective of women's emancipation is diffused, or lost entirely.

The critique that patriarchy theory is ahistorical and unable to account for class and cultural diversity reflects a misunderstanding of what theory is. Authors who reject patriarchy on these grounds assume that theory must explain as well as describe social reality. Patriarchy is an abstraction about the *systematic* oppression of women by men, a generalization from the complexities which obscure the systematic nature of that oppression. Its existence does not originate in the realm of ideas, but in social relations.[6] Patriarchy is an abstraction just as class is an abstraction, but a different abstraction. Class is 'ahistorical' in the sense that it has meaning,

[4] For a variety of theoretical perspectives, many postmodern, see Michèle Barrett and Anne Phillips (eds.), *Destabilizing Theory: Contemporary Feminist Debates* (Cambridge: Polity Press, 1992).

[5] Lynne Phillips stresses cultural relativism and argues that researchers in the US and Europe should refrain from imposing their views of women's oppression on Latin American rural women who may not think of themselves as oppressed. See 'Rural Women in Latin America: Directions for Future Research', *Latin American Research Review*, 25/3 (1990), 89–107. The postmodern approach to feminist studies has popularized examination of 'gender parallelism'. That there is only sketchy information about societies purported to be characterized by gender parallelism has detracted little from the credibility of this concept. For example, in *Moon, Sun, and Witches: Gender Ideologies and Class in Inca and Colonial Peru* (Princeton: Princeton University Press, 1987) Irene Silverblatt argues that pre-Inca society in Peru was characterized by gender parallelism. Because the evidence she presents is insufficient to sustain her argument, her presentation, while interesting, has more in common with myth-making than with historical analysis.

[6] For analysis of the difference between ideal and real abstractions see Susan Himmelweit and Simon Mohun, 'Real Abstractions and Anomalous Assumptions', in Ian Steedman *et al.* (eds.), *The Value Controversy* (London: Verso, 1981), 224–65.

but not existence, in the abstract. Class relations, defined by the appropriation of surplus labour, are sustained and transformed within a particular society. Only by analysing that society can we unravel the complexities of specific class relations. Similarly with patriarchy. Locating patriarchy at an abstract level does not imply that it is ahistorical. The social relations of men's oppression of women are sustained and transformed within specific societies. Only by analysing patriarchy as a facet of historically particular class and race relations can we analyse the forms of its existence. If this approach is correct, it is erroneous to reject the possibility of developing a theory of patriarchy on the grounds that the concept is inherently ahistorical. That argument fails to recognize distinctions between the levels of abstractions that characterize social relations.[7]

To analyse the ways in which class relations were differentiated by sex, and how patriarchy varied with class, writers developed theories which systematically related patriarchal relations to class relations. Known as dual systems theories, these explained the interaction of two separate yet interdependent systems of social relations. For example, they analysed the relationship between a mode of production and a sex-gender system, as in the articulation of capitalism and patriarchy.[8] Criticism of these theories focused on the problems of dualism. Critics argued that it was wrong to analyse patriarchy and capitalism, for example, as two systems with separate dynamics. This gave an autonomy to patriarchy that was misplaced.[9] In this view patriarchy and class are two facets of one system of social relations. This is a strong critique.

Another serious problem with dual-systems theories, one which has not been analysed before, is that patriarchal relations are viewed as class relations; the essence of patriarchy being the appropriation by men of women's labour. I suggest that conflating patriarchy and class has confused rather than clarified our understanding of both.[10] Because patriarchy is a different abstraction than class, it is more appropriate to think of one system of social relations which is inscribed by class and gender.

The most compelling criticism of patriarchy theory is that it has failed to specify the definitional element of women's oppression. This is not for lack of trying. Sophisticated theories which locate the essence of women's

[7] Fine offers another, I think compatible, analysis of the validity of patriarchy as an abstract concept. *Women's Employment and the Capitalist Family*, 27–8.

[8] Heidi Hartmann, 'The Unhappy Marriage of Marxism and Feminism: Towards a More Progressive Union', in Lydia Sargent (ed.), *Women and Revolution: A Discussion of the Unhappy Marriage of Marxism and Feminism* (Boston: South End Press, 1981), 1–41; and Zilla Eisenstein, 'Developing a Theory of Capitalist Patriarchy and Socialist Feminism', in Z. Eisenstein (ed.), *Capitalist Patriarchy and the Case for Socialist Feminism* (New York: Monthly Review Press, 1979), 5–40.

[9] Iris Young, 'Beyond the Unhappy Marriage: A Critique of the Dual Systems Theory', in Sargent (ed.), *Women and Revolution*, 43–69.

[10] An example of this is Walby's formulation that patriarchy is a mode of production in which housewives form one class and husbands another. See *Theorizing Patriarchy*, 7–13.

oppression in anatomy, sexuality, men's appropriation of women's labour, and male supremacist ideology abound.[11] Each has been shown to be unsatisfactory in explaining the general causes of women's oppression.[12] For this reason, a consensus emerged among academic feminists that it is not possible to do more than systematically describe and analyse the myriad forms that women's oppression assumes in different societies.

This resolution is unsatisfactory as well. We should be sceptical about the impossibility of developing a theory of the oppression of women by men on two grounds. First, because that conclusion mirrors the current academic fashion, and fashion is suspicious. Second, it is unlikely that it is not possible to systematically explain a phenomena that is found in virtually all human societies.

A strong current in the social sciences in the early 1990s is the idea that people make their own history to a large extent just as they please, with relatively few constraints transmitted from the past.[13] This forms the basis for denying the importance, even existence, of a material basis of social relations. Often this is what authors mean by their emphasis on historical contingency. Complementing the free play accorded to people's actions is the view that social relations are transparent. If what you see is what there is, there is no need for theoretical inquiry to reveal underlying structures and processes. Paradoxically, many academic feminists have accepted the validity of these principles, even though they clash violently with the history of women's experiences. Feminist studies has given a stamp of legitimacy to the reigning intellectual orthodoxy. Revitalization of debates on the theory of patriarchy is needed to advance feminist theory and practice.

THE GENESIS OF NICARAGUAN SOCIAL HISTORY

In addition to the difficulties of theory, the problem of analysing the changing forms of patriarchy in Nicaragua is that little is known about the history of women—and of men. Nicaraguan social history is in its infancy. The Somozas viewed history as so subversive that they eschewed even adulatory epics. With the Sandinista Revolution the country's official history was written as a kaleidoscope of US imperialism—bits and pieces of

[11] See S. Firestone, *The Dialectic of Sex* (New York: Morrow, 1970) for a theory based in women's reproductive monopoly. For a theory rooted in sexuality see Catharine MacKinnon, *Feminism Unmodified: Discourses on Life and Law* (Cambridge, Mass.: Harvard University Press, 1987). For appropriation of labour see Hartmann, 'The Unhappy Marriage of Marxism and Feminism'.

[12] For a clear and systematic critique of these positions see Walby, *Theorizing Patriarchy*.

[13] This, of course, turns upside-down Marx's approach to history: '[People] make their own history, but they do not make it just as they please; they do not make it under circumstances chosen by themselves, but under circumstances directly encountered, given and transmitted from the past.' *The Eighteenth Brumaire of Louis Bonaparte* (Moscow: Progress Publishers, 1972), 10.

canal routes, Washington-orchestrated coups, Marine occupations, Wall Street domination, Sandino's resistance and, crowning it all, the forty-three-year puppet-rule of the Somoza family dynasty. All these are critical elements of the country's past, but on their own they mystify almost as much as they clarify about the Nicaraguan people's history of struggles. Because of the absence of a tradition of writing history, analysis of social relations prior to the Sandinista Revolution is involved less with challenging national myths than with uncovering information to begin the task of analysing the past.[14]

Throughout Central America the expansion of coffee production in the second half of the nineteenth century revolutionized society. Class and patriarchal relations were profoundly altered in the course of the fifty years between 1860 and 1920. In rural Nicaragua, the rise of coffee production set in motion social changes more radical, perhaps, than any since the Spanish conquest. This paper focuses on the ways in which the social revolution associated with the privatization of land and the codification of coerced labour systems affected patriarchy. The protagonists of this history are the rural women and men, primarily peasants, in the municipality of Diriomo, one of Nicaragua's first and foremost coffee regions.

Diriomo, ten miles from the city of Granada, included the town centre and twelve rural hamlets scattered in the countryside around the town. Notwithstanding its geographical proximity to Granada, one of Nicaragua's leading commercial and cultural centres, Diriomo was a backwater at the time of the coffee boom, and so it remains. In the colonial period the Spanish crown granted Diriomo the status of indigenous community. Rural male inhabitants of the township selected officials who spoke in the name of the indigenous community until the early twentieth century. Nevertheless, what it meant that Diriomo was a *Comunidad Indígena* in the 1860s was far from straightforward. It did not imply the perpetuation of pre-Hispanic or even colonial social institutions. What 'indigenous' signified, along with the social relations of the indigenous community, transformed radically over the centuries since the Spanish conquest.[15]

[14] Recent books on Nicaraguan history include E. Bradford Burns, *Patriarch and Folk: The Emergence of Nicaragua, 1798–1858* (Cambridge, Mass.: Harvard University Press, 1991); Jeffrey L. Gould, *To Lead as Equals: Rural Protest and Political Consciousness in Chinandega, Nicaragua, 1912–1979* (Chapel Hill: University of North Carolina Press, 1990); Charles R. Hale, *Resistance and Contradiction: Miskitu Indians and the Nicaraguan State, 1894–1987* (Stanford, Calif.: Stanford University Press, 1994); Elizabeth Dore, 'La Producción Cafetalera Nicaragüense, 1860–1960: Transformaciones Estructurales', in Héctor Pérez Brignoli and Mario Samper (eds.), *Tierra, café y sociedad* (San José, Costa Rica: FLACSO, 1994), 377–436; Alberto Lanuza, Juan Vázquez, Amaru Barahona, and Amalia Chamorro, *Economía y sociedad en la construcción del estado en Nicaragua* (San José, Costa Rica: Instituto Centroamericano de Administración Pública, 1983); Walter Knut, *The Regime of Anastasio Somoza, 1936–1956* (Chapel Hill: University of North Carolina Press, 1993); Jaime Wheelock Róman, *Imperialismo y Dictadura: Crisis de una formación social* (Mexico City: Siglo XXI, 1975).

[15] For interesting analyses of the transformation of the meaning of 'Indian' and of indigenous communities in Central America see Carol A. Smith (ed.), *Indians and the State in Rural*

With growing recognition in the second half of the nineteenth century that great wealth could be made in coffee cultivation, a portion of Diriomo's common lands increasingly were sought after, especially land on the slopes of the Mombacho Volcano. Previously residents of the area had considered those tracts of common land marginal for agriculture and of little value. Their volcanic soils and steep gradients were not well suited to the cultivation of corn, beans, plantains, cotton, cacao, sugar, tobacco, or any other important crop. These same qualities proved ideal for coffee, however. Residents of Diriomo—the Indians and the mixed-race mestizo élite—discovered, unfortunately for most of them, that their township occupied some of the most coveted land in Nicaragua.

PATRIARCHY BEFORE PRIVATE PROPERTY

It is commonly held that men's oppression of women is a product of colonialism and capitalism. Engels argued that before capitalism, men's and women's spheres of labour were separate but equal. With capitalism men's sphere—production—became more important, and women's sphere—reproduction—less. As a result men increasingly dominated women.[16] A variant of this view is popular among anthropologists, many of whom argue that patriarchy is an aspect of 'Western culture' that was imposed upon pre-colonial societies characterized by gender equality.[17] Neither of these interpretations withstands historical examination. Nicaraguan society before the coffee boom was pre-capitalist. Yet both indigenous and mestizo culture were definitively patriarchal. Women in indigenous communities were subordinated to men, as were women in mestizo society, although not in the same ways. This challenges the anthropological stereotype of Indian gender egalitarianism. It is crucial to stress, however, that this analysis has nothing to do with pre-colonial societies. What gender relations might have been in pre-conquest Nicaragua has little or nothing to do with this history. Indigenous communities in nineteenth-century Central America were as much a product of Hispanic colonialism as was the mestizo society which overtly associated itself with European culture.

Guatemala, 1540–1988 (Austin: University of Texas Press, 1990), especially the chapter by David McCreery, 'State Power, Indigenous Communities and Land in Nineteenth Century Guatemala, 1820–1920'.

[16] Frederick Engels, *The Origin of the Family, Private Property and the State* (New York: International Publishers, 1972).

[17] Etienne and Leacock state, '[I]t is critical to clarify the fact that egalitarian relations between women and men are not an imported Western value and that, instead, the reverse is true. Egalitarian relations or at least mutually respectful relations were a living reality in much of the world in precolonial times, which was far from the case in Western culture.' Mona Etienne and Eleanor Leacock (eds.), *Women and Colonization: Anthropological Perspectives* (New York: Praeger, 1980), pp. v–vi.

Nicaragua's official history, in so far as there is one, paints a picture of a country of mestizos of mixed Spanish and Indian descent who identified with a popular form of Hispanic culture. The few histories that treat the indigenous people at all claim that through a process of acculturation the indigenous population in the Pacific region all but ceased to exist in the eighteenth century.[18] Historical research reveals the Euro-centrism of this interpretation. In addition to Monimbó and Sutiava, long considered the only cases of indigenous survival in western Nicaragua, many indigenous communities existed in the early twentieth century. Diriomo was one of these. This has major implications for understanding class and patriarchal relations in Nicaragua.

Beginning in the 1870s the cultivation of coffee for export radically altered the landscape and social fabric of rural Granada. Before that social upheaval, class distinctions in Diriomo were based less on ownership of land than on political power, wealth, and ethnic culture. Private property of natural resources was the exception rather than the norm in the municipality. As numerous court cases in later years attest, even when people claimed private property in land, hardly ever did they possess legal documents or titles to support their claims. Access to land was based, more than anything else, on continual cultivation or usufruct 'from time immemorial'. The very idea of private property in land defied the imagination of most of the inhabitants of Diriomo. The vast majority of the population of the municipality was considered Indian by both the town's mestizo population and by Indians themselves. In documents written by town officials, 'Indian' was used in two ways: ideologically, synonymous with poor and rustic; and more concretely, indicating association with Diriomo's indigenous community. Before the coffee boom the difference between Indian and mestizo was rooted as much in culture and community as in wealth. Although wealthy in comparison with Indians, mestizo families in Diriomo by necessity lived modestly in the town centre. Local officials complained that because of their humble lifestyle oligarchs from Granada did not condescend to acknowledge the distinction between Indian and mestizo: to the city's merchants and landowners all Diriomeños were Indians. For the town's mestizo élite this was the ultimate insult, for they prided themselves on their European culture and disdained anything indigenous.

Cloaked by some superficial similarities that accompany relative poverty were important differences in the social relations of the two communities in Diriomo. Among these, different forms of patriarchy stand out. Prior to the onslaught of coffee, Indians' access to most means of production were organized by and through the indigenous community. The community's

[18] Germán Romero Vargas, *Las estructuras sociales de Nicaragua en el siglo XVIII* (Managua: Editorial Vanguardia, 1988), 343–77.

all-male hierarchy assigned lands for cultivation to male heads of household, and male members of the community had rights to graze animals, hunt, gather wood, and draw water on the common lands. Male descent governed the distribution of plots for cultivation. In the absence of male heirs, a members' lands reverted to the community to be reassigned. Adhering to custom, women's access to collective resources was mediated exclusively through the men of the community: fathers, husbands, partners, sons, and brothers. If and when practice varied from custom, it left no traces.[19]

Men's monopoly over political power mirrored their control over material resources in so far as institutionalized politics within the community was a male arena. Religious brotherhoods, or *cofradías*, which controlled community resources such as cattle herds and land, formed another locus of power in the community. These were exclusively male institutions. Women too were organized into religious sisterhoods. But where brotherhoods had responsibility for productive resources, the sisterhoods' purview was religious devotion. Yet even in that realm men dominated. The prestigious positions responsible for maintaining churches and shrines and organizing religious festivals were held by men. The interconnected civil and religious hierarchies of the indigenous community of Diriomo were both restricted male domains.

Documents from Diriomo, as well as from other indigenous communities in the region, attest to an Indian tradition of collective decision-making. In a well-documented case from nearby Nindirí, legal records describe how men of the community for several years debated selling their communal lands.[20] As only men appear in these sources, it suggests that such collectivity excluded women. This may or may not be true. Women's absence from the legal records implies, however, that what role they played was informal rather than formal, at least as seen through the eyes of the male mestizo who transcribed the testimonies of the men of Nindirí. Available historical evidence indicates that essential to patriarchy in the indigenous communities of western Nicaragua was women's formal separation from control over material resources and from political power.[21]

Women's marginalization from politics was not unique to indigenous society. Throughout Nicaragua mestizo women's official exclusion from institutionalized politics was central to the social relations of patriarchy. In Diriomo derivative from this was the practice, as opposed to the law, of male access to land within mestizo society. State intervention in the

[19] My analysis of the Comunidad Indígena de Diriomo in the middle nineteenth century is drawn from documents in the Archivo Municipal de Diriomo (AMD).

[20] 'Deliberaciónes: Comunidad Indígena de Nindirí, 18 febrero, 1878', Archivo Municipal de Diriomo (AMD), Ramo de Agricultura, 1878.

[21] Elizabeth Dore, 'Patriarchy Before Private Property: Gender Oppression in Rural Nicaragua, 1830–1875', ms.

regulation of women's sexuality was a third critical element of mestizo patriarchal relations. Formal political power in Diriomo was invested in the forty or fifty men who formed the municipal government, the *Junta Municipal*. By virtue of their sex and wealth they were granted national citizenship and administrative control over the town. In accordance with Nicaraguan Constitutions of the first half of the nineteenth century, males over the age of twenty who owned 200 pesos worth of property or had a profession were citizens. All other Nicaraguans—all women, of course—were merely inhabitants of the country, barred from participating in institutionalized politics.[22]

Unlike Indian society, where the political exclusion of women mirrored their formal separation from access to land, mestizo women were permitted to own land. In keeping with Hispanic legal tradition, Nicaraguan law stipulated that women could own, inherit, and dispose of all forms of property. However, in Diriomo this was of little significance because private property in land was uncommon prior to the coffee boom. Most of the meagre wealth of the town's élite was embodied in carts, draft animals, tools, mills, clothing, jewellery, furniture, and their modest houses. Only a few members of the élite claimed property in land: among these were several women.[23] Private farms were small; the largest comprised about thirty manzanas (fifty acres) on the valley floor surrounding the town. As a rule mestizo citizens cultivated small plots and grazed animals on the town's common lands. At one time these were legally distinct from the common lands of the indigenous community. However, by the late nineteenth century frequently the two were confused in practice.

That private property in land was neither customary nor common in the township had a different significance for the women than for the men of mestizo society. Men's political rights gave them access to land. Women's political exclusion denied them what was permitted in law. Despite the law, and notwithstanding the existence of women landowners, the citizens of Diriomo perpetuated the norm of male monopoly over material resources. The municipal council allocated land only to men for use, analogous to the practice of the Indian community. In this manner custom and ideology denied direct access to land to all but a few women in the town. Where private property in land was rare the legal possibility of women's ownership of property did little to challenge the social relations of patriarchy. In practice, mestizo women's access to land was mediated through men, similar to the practice of the Indian community. When fathers, brothers, or husbands were alive women often were excluded from possession of property. Even when women owned land, patriarchal relations were the norm. In general women's wealth was procured through men, as sole heirs

[22] E. Bradford Burns, *Patriarch and Folk*, 80.

[23] AMD, Juzgado Municipal Constitucional, 'Demanda verbal entre el Sr. Víctor Ayala, Luciano Torres y la Sra. Vicenta Gómez por la compra de una huerta', 22 Oct. 1866.

and widows. Also, it was customary for women to defer to men in the administration of their property.

Agriculture in the township was predominantly for household consumption. Diriomo's mestizo élite wanted to produce sugar, tobacco, fruits, and cereals for sale in Granada, but their aspirations were thwarted because the citizens had no effective means of systematically appropriating the Indians' labour. With access to ample land on which they practised shifting slash and burn cultivation, the indigenous population did not form a regular labour force for the local élite. Sharecropping and debt peonage existed, although both were uncommon. Occasionally an Indian or mestizo in need of cash or food would enter into such an agreement with a citizen. However, such relationships deviated from a norm of household-centred production in both Indian and mestizo society.[24]

A major distinction between Indian and citizen was that as the latter exercised local political power, they attempted to wield their corporate authority to appropriate Indian labour. But this was limited by Indians' ample access to the means of production and citizens' meagre command over the forces of coercion. So from independence until the spread of coffee production the major systematic labour drafts within Diriomo appear to have been to construct the Church and the town hall, to maintain the paths and cart-tracks in and around the municipality, and to do whatever was needed to venerate the numerous saints whose intercessions were seen as necessary to the well-being of the community. Mestizo citizens attempted to embed these drafts in an ideology of the common good, and seemed overall to have been successful. Although labour drafts occasionally were resisted, I found little evidence to suggest that the rural poor perceived these demands on their labour as particularly onerous.[25]

The military draft was different. Independence unleashed a wave of civil strife in Nicaragua which raged with little interruption until the coffee boom.[26] Oligarchs from Granada fought their counterparts in Léon for control over the feeble nation state. This drew the entire Granada region into the wars. To avoid the recruiters from both sides who swept the countryside, forcing men into military service, men hid in the hills and fled to the agricultural frontier. This left the women at home to work the fields and sustain the household. In other contexts wars and military drafts

[24] While mestizo and Indian formed the two dominant strata in the region, the class structure was not as binary as this picture might suggest. The mestizo lower orders included artisans, cart drivers, and labourers who qualified neither for citizenship nor for membership in the indigenous community. Likewise, the population of the Indian community was stratified by wealth, prestige, power, and, of course, by gender. But key to the structure of local society was that all adult men had rights and access to land and household production was the prevailing economic form.

[25] Burns argues that the popular rebellions of 1845–50 were sparked by Indian resistance to the state's role in promoting privatization of land. *Patriarch and Folk*, 145–59.

[26] For analysis of these civil wars see Dore, 'La Producción Cafetalera Nicaragüense', 384–94.

altered the form of patriarchal relations: and they must have done so in the towns and villages surrounding Granada. Unfortunately, numerous references to the flight of men is accompanied by virtual silence about the plight of women.

One associates marriage with Hispanic-Catholic societies. But marriage was the norm only for the mestizo élite. Parish records, paternity suits, and all sorts of civil and criminal litigation indicate that legal matrimony among mestizos and Indians alike was the exception rather than the rule. Among Diriomo's élite, marriage was an aspect of European culture which was central to their social identity. Stressing the importance of marriage, they linked their customs and lifestyle with the élite culture of Granada, to which they aspired, though for the two groups marriage had very different associations. For the oligarchs of Granada marriage was important in securing, centralizing, and inheriting wealth, also in maintaining the fiction of their European lineage. For Diriomo's citizens, who had neither the substantial property nor the social pretensions of the merchants and landowners of Granada, marriage was one means of differentiating themselves from the masses. In addition, it served to consolidate the town's citizens into a local political, and later economic, élite. As such, there was social and familial pressure on women of this class to marry, and within their ranks.

Motherhood, wifehood, and honour were the prevailing criteria by which these women were judged by their neighbours. Court proceedings in Diriomo provide insights into gender norms. However, as the legal arena was exclusively male, in examining these cases we are forced to view events and morals through a male prism. In keeping with custom, women of the upper classes almost never directly participated in court proceedings. Their testimony was presented by a man: her husband, son, or lawyer. The judge, the two witnesses present at all proceedings, and the scribe all were male. In other words, in the judicial system women's views were filtered through men. Even exceptional women who owned property were represented in court by men. On the rare occasions when an élite woman participated directly in legal proceedings, she did so with the express permission of her husband, standing by her side.[27]

In that overtly gendered context women contested their honour—their sexual purity and fidelity. The vast majority of court cases involving women were about honour—a major obsession of élite women and men in Nicaragua in the middle nineteenth century. Legal cases brought, indirectly, by women who claimed to be victims of defamation are revealing of custom and deviance in women's roles within mestizo society. These cases, usually involving one woman who accused another of sexual promiscuity, were

[27] AMD, Juzgado Municipal Constitucional, Libro de Conciliaciones, 1843. 'En el pueblo de Diriomo, 14 marzo de 1843, ante mi el alcalde municipal compareció la Señora Juana Isabel López con previa licencia de su marido . . .'

serious. In some, a woman's husband sued on her behalf; in many, lawyers were hired to restore a woman's honour. In all cases numerous witnesses testified about the reputations of both the accused and the accuser.[28] In one case, which dragged on for three years and involved appeals to a higher court in Granada, the woman accused of calumny was convicted of criminal slander for besmirching the honour of a 'good wife and mother'. Sent to jail for eighteen months, she was last heard from serving out her sentence in a Granada prison.

These cases demonstrate that sexuality was not a private affair.[29] The state was a male monopoly which played an active role in adjudicating the sexual behaviour of women. Presiding over women's sexuality on an everyday level, the state sustained the power not only of individual men over individual women, but of the patriarchal order. Clearly, sexual purity was a critical element of female identity in the upper echelons of the town's social order. Why female honour was so important to the mestizo élite in that culturally isolated town probably has less to do with the particularities of political and social relations in Diriomo, than with material and ideological role of patriarchy more generally in nineteenth-century Central America.

For centuries 'honour' was exalted by the dominant classes in the Hispanic world as a female virtue. *Marianismo*, or the cult of women's purity, had its origin in Spanish obsession with racial purity and religious orthodoxy.[30] When Spain battled against the Moors, expelled the Jews, and fought throughout Europe to defend Catholicism, racial and ideological purity were prized. In this context women's honour was associated with maintaining the purity of the 'race'. In Spanish America marianismo played a similar role in perpetuating racial and cultural separatism. Linked to the racism of marianismo, élite women were supposed to embody and transmit European values.

In Latin America the cult of female honour was not a relic from the past. Gender roles were constituted, modified, sustained, and transmitted within specific social struggles. In different times and places marianismo was constituted in different ways, consciously and unconsciously manipulated—propagated or repressed—for different reasons. In nineteenth-century Central America, women's sexual purity was a central definitional element of the élite by which they distinguished themselves from the region's indigenous people. In particular, marianismo was key to the oligarchs' myth that they were racially distinct from the masses of Indians. For these

[28] AMD, Juzgado Municipal Constitucional, 'Demanda verbal motivada por Juana Carballo y Olaya Vásquez por defamación de delito', 14 Nov. 1865.

[29] In general the private–public distinction often made in analyses of patriarchy is problematical. Family relations, the household, sexuality, etc. are shaped by the 'public' system of social relations, by the state, etc.

[30] 'Marianismo' means literally the cult of Mary.

reasons, female honour was an important ideological element of class and ethnic hierarchies for élite women as well as for men in Diriomo.

Historical records, especially parish registers and court cases, from mid-century Diriomo indicate that sexual relations and family structures among the Indian and mestizo peasantry did not conform to the Catholic-Hispanic prototype exulted in marianismo. Marriage, monogamy, and pre-nuptial virginity were the ideals, and possibly the norms, of women of the mestizo élite. For peasants, evidence suggests that mothers most often were unmarried; and that women's sexual liaisons, as well as residence patterns, tended to be monogamous and serial. Since women's access to land was mediated by their relations with men, women tended to establish households with male partners, but these households shifted over time.[31] Contemporary newspapers and pamphlets were replete with condemnations by male politicians and writers of the sexual promiscuity of the rural poor. These self-styled patriarchs failed to include in their polemics any mention that sexual promiscuity was the norm for men of their class, and considered an essential element of their male identity.[32]

The cult of female honour and purity affected the lives of Diriomo's women in various ways, differentiated by class and ethnicity. For the wives and daughters of the town's citizens marianismo meant that they accepted as inevitable their fathers' and husbands' numerous extra-marital sexual liaisons. For the women of the lower classes and of the Indian caste, the cult of sexual honour and purity provided little protection from abduction and rape. Diriomo's court transcripts record many cases where a parent accused a man of abducting and raping her or his daughter.[33] Often these accusations were brought against one of the town's leading citizens. In most instances no documents survive other than the initial accusation. Possibly the cases were abandoned or resolved out of court. Or the records were destroyed. Despite these incomplete records, it is clear that sexual violence against women, especially women of the lower classes, was commonplace.

Paternity and child-support cases were adjudicated with regularity by the town's mayor. In most of these, mestizo women of the lower classes claimed financial support for their 'illegitimate' children, often from leading citizens of the town. These women overcame the social stigmas which were associated publicly with single motherhood. These cases follow a pattern. Women declared they were impoverished, with insufficient resources to feed themselves and their children. The accused man did not

[31] Evidence for this is drawn from a number of court cases from Diriomo where after the death of a parent children from various unions claim rights of inheritance. Usually the sums contested are small in quantity.

[32] For analysis of patriarchal discourse see Burns, *Patriarch and Folk*, 66–109.

[33] AMD, Juzgado Municipal Constitucional, Libro de Terminaciones Verbales, 'Gertrudis Banegas exponga que el Sr. Tómas Vasconcelos has perpetrados los delitos de rapto y estrupo . . .', 11 June, 1869.

contest paternity but agreed to support the children only if the mother relinquished all claims to the children, who would then live with the father.[34]

These cases are particularly revealing of the feminization of poverty in nineteenth-century rural Nicaragua. They highlight the plight of women in a rural society where resources were allocated to men; where peasant women's access to land was mediated exclusively through their relationships with males. Also, they shed light on class differences in family relations and household composition. Frequently, illegitimate children of members of the male élite lived in their father's household, occupying a status somewhere between kin and trusted servant. This pattern underscores the gap between the cult of motherhood and the reality of poverty of peasant women. Élite culture extolled the special bonds of motherhood and the natural role for women as mothers. However, the social distribution of resources prevented some—probably many—women from fulfilling that role. Dedication to that ideal of motherhood may have been consistent with the life experiences of the town's élite women. For poor women of Diriomo it was not. For them, motherhood often meant selling or giving away their children.

Child-support claims were fraught with tensions, both emotional and material, which reveal dynamics of patriarchy. In Diriomo labour was scarce: children were valued for their capacity to work. Contests over children, in particular men's desire to have custody of the children they supported, were struggles over resources. The importance of children as economic resources was a factor in the historical and material construction of marianismo and machismo in rural Nicaragua. Women were esteemed for the number of strong, healthy children they produced. Most women bore from eight to twelve children; although many died in infancy, and mothers in childbirth. This explains, in part, why women's fecundity was socially revered. Central to 'classic' machismo in Nicaragua, then and now, was a man's 'fecundity', or his paternity of many children. These cases suggest a material side to men's desire to sire scores of children, and

[34] AMD, Juzgado Municipal Constitucional, Libro de Terminaciones Verbales, 'La Señora Josefana Bermudez contra Sr. Eufreciano Alvarez', 30 Apr. 1866. AMD, Ramo Judicial, Sección Jueces Locales, Francisca López Cano contra Sr. Dionesio Marquez, 26 Nov. 1865. The most illustrious child-support case of the period was brought by Luisa Vallecillo against Andrés Marcía, one of the most prominent citizens of Diriomo and later to become mayor. Able to secure the services of a lawyer to prosecute her case, Vallecillo was probably from the strata of ladino artisans in the town. The case was bounced back and forth between judges in Diriomo and Granada, clearly a hot potato which neither wanted to decide for fear of antagonizing the powerful Marcía. Litigation in the case lasted eighteen months. Finally Marcía was ordered to pay Vallecillo five pesos fuertes per month until the children reached the age of 25. AMD, Juzgado Municipal Constitucional, Libro de Terminaciones Verbales, 'Luisa Vallecillo contra Andrés Marcia por alimentos', 22 Feb. 1873. The case was closed 21 March 1874. In August 1874, six months after the final sentence, Vallecillo asked the judge in Diriomo to embargo Marcía's property since he had not paid her any child support.

to gain custody. Although this argument reeks of functionalism, if it has some validity it suggests that in addition to men's desire to demonstrate their sexual prowess, an aspect of the cult of male virility may have been the quest for control over children as a source of labour.

In rural Nicaragua, before class and exchange relations were deeply monetized and commercialized, women's class status was less definitive, as well as less secure than that of men. For women of the indigenous community as well as for poor peasant women, access to material resources, most particularly to land, was mediated exclusively through relationships to men. Only a tiny fraction of élite women had direct access to resources, and control of these often was delegated to males. While class, caste, and gender hierarchies divided women in Diriomo, one thread united them. Access to common land was guaranteed to all adult men regardless of class or ethnicity; no women enjoyed this right, again regardless of class or caste. This reinforced women's dependence on men, and ensured that their social and economic status remained more precarious than men's. Class is conditioned by access to the means of production. Therefore, my analysis suggests that the women of Diriomo did not share automatically the same class position as their male counterparts. This is not to argue that women formed a separate 'female' class; rather that social relations in rural Nicaragua before the commercialization of the economy and society were characterized by the interaction of class and patriarchy.

PATRIARCHY AND PRIVATE PROPERTY

According to Engels' interpretation of the origins of gender inequality, privatization of property along with the rise of capitalism marked a watershed in the subordination of women. With private property men's labour was publicly recognized and valued, women's hidden and devalued. Many anthropologists support this view, although rarely within a Marxist framework. The coffee boom in Central America was associated with rapid privatization of lands which had been communal.[35] Therefore, analysis of the social revolution that accompanied the expansion of coffee production in Nicaragua provides a strong case to test this theoretical hypothesis. Contrary to Engels' theory, in the process of privatization of land in rural Granada a significant minority of women became small proprietors. This altered the form of their sudordination to men, and reduced the degree of their gender oppression. Such evidence from Nicaragua indicates that

[35] The coffee revolution was not associated with the rise of capitalism. On the contrary, it systematized non-capitalist social relations of production. See Elizabeth Dore, 'Coffee, Land and Class Relations in Nicaragua: 1870–1920', presented at the Annual Meeting of the American Historical Association, Dec. 1991, Chicago, Ill. My analysis is similar to David McCreery's in *Rural Guatemala, 1760–1940* (Stanford: Stanford University Press, 1994).

Engels' analysis is not universally valid. My argument underlines the need to reappraise his theory by examining the relationship between private property and patriarchy in specific historical contexts.

In the 1860s, when Nicaragua's political and economic élite became aware of the potential profitability of coffee cultivation, the municipal council of Diriomo received an occasional legal writ which initiated the process of privatization of land.[36] Most of these were filed by wealthy residents of Granada impressed with the success of coffee cultivation in other countries of Central America. Their attention was drawn to the common lands of nearby Diriomo because of their potential for coffee production. There were few precedents to guide the procedure, and each case was handled by the town council in an *ad hoc* manner. Private property in land was more common in other parts of the country. However, in Diriomo the process of privatization was postponed by the town's economic isolation and its indigenous tradition. At the beginning, even citizens who soon grasped the lucrative possibilities of privatization, expressed their belief that private land went against the principles of natural law.[37] Hundreds of lengthy legal disputes originated in the process of appropriation of land. These show that in Diriomo there was little agreement even about the meaning of private property in land before the 1870s.

In the 1870s there was an avalanche of claims to landed property in Diriomo. After a bewildering assortment of affidavits, testimony, and payments, the Junta usually awarded title to possession.[38] The year 1874 marked a watershed in Diriomo. The press of claims, and of self-interest, led the town council to institutionalize the process of privatizing land. In drawing up its annual budget, the council regularized procedures for registering claims to land.[39] It decreed that anyone who had not cultivated their allotment within the common lands for the preceding five years would lose their rights to those plots. In addition, the decree was a turning point in the erosion of the indigenous community for it made no distinction between the common lands of the town and those of the community. The town council assumed the power to legally recognize private claims to all of the common lands. Although the decree stipulated that each applicant could claim a maximum of ten manzanas, this was applied selectively.[40] Leading citizens of the town and from Granada were granted hundreds of manzanas of land suitable for coffee cultivation.

In theory any resident of Diriomo could register a claim to private property within the common lands. In practice this process was tightly

[36] AMD, Libros de Actas Municipales, 1864, 1866, 1868.

[37] AMD, Libro de Actas Municipales, 13 Oct. 1875, fos. 7–14.

[38] At first this was a vague claim which, by emphasizing possession and not private property, failed to clearly distinguish it from the earlier tradition of usufruct rights to common lands.

[39] AMD, Libro de Actas Municipales, 'Plan de Arbitrios' (25 Aug. 1874), fos. 11–20^{v}.

[40] Manzana is the traditional measure of land in Nicaragua. 1 manzana = 1.72 acres = 0.7 hectares.

controlled by and for the town's citizens. The town council, exercising the corporate and class power of the local élite, used the institutions of municipal government to carefully control the process of privatization. In the course of the next fifteen years Diriomo's citizens and Granada's oligarchs expropriated those common lands which promised a lucrative future in coffee production.

In the initial stages of privatization of the common lands the Indians and poor mestizos of Diriomo largely were unaware of the dramatic transformation that was altering the legal and social framework of the world around them. The fields they and their ancestors had cultivated for generations, and thought of as inseparable from their community, were expropriated often without their knowledge. Only when fences were erected and coffee trees planted did they discover that the town council had expropriated their ancestral lands. Many peasant men, learning of impending privatization, tried to stop the process. In the 1870s and 1880s hundreds of men threatened with expropriation appealed to the municipal council. Some won their cases. But most men with subsistence plots and plantain groves on choice coffee land failed to preserve their rights to the land. Most were too poor to hire a legal representative to pursue their case. And being illiterate, they encountered difficulties in negotiating the maze of bureaucratic steps involved in registering and contesting claims to land. Some subsistence agriculturalists, intimidated by the meagre wealth and petty power of the citizens of Diriomo, were expropriated silently. Others refused to accept their fate in silence. Litigation by those who fought against expropriation occupied the town council for two decades.[41] Peasants argued that their lands were not abandoned, as the citizens claimed, but were used and cultivated according to their prevailing custom of shifting slash and burn agriculture.

The process of privatization of land was neither linear nor rapid. It was fraught with conflicts between the expropriators and the peasantry, and it generated struggles within the élite, as well as within the peasantry. By 1900 most of the area that straddled the shifting border between Diriomo and Granada was private property, even if the bureaucratic steps whereby titles were legalized still were incomplete.

Élite mestizo women largely were excluded from this first wave of privatization of land. The process was political more than it was economic. As women were barred from participating in formal politics, they had few opportunities for acquiring land. A few women who claimed prior title to land, or whose husbands or fathers died in the midst of the lengthy procedure of acquiring title, secured property in their names.[42]

[41] For details of these struggles see Dore, 'Coffee, Land and Class Relations in Nicaragua'.

[42] AMD, Juzgado Municipal Constitucional, 'La Señora Timotea Amador demanda a Julian del mismo apellido por un terreno', 10 Oct. 1874. In this case Amador claims title to lands which her deceased father had claimed. AMD, Corporación Municipal, Asunto

Women at the other end of the social spectrum remain hidden from history. Documents which record men resisting privatization and enclosures through litigation and occupation of land say nothing about the struggles of peasant women. Minutes of the heady meetings of the town council record conflicts surrounding the claims and counter-claims to land. In these, except for the Virgin Mary and the Virgin of Candelaria (the town's patron), women are absent. It would seem that the council limited its concern with women to the two Virgins, to whom it prayed at every session. However, we should not presume from these records that women played no role in these struggles over land. Silence about women reflects the patriarchal attitudes of the town fathers: it indicates little about women's activities. Peasant women were members of households, and part of a community that lost land. More likely than not they actively opposed that expropriation.

This stage in the privatization did not mark the dispossession of the peasantry. The vast majority of male heads of household in the township retained access to subsistence plots for cultivation of staples. In good years a household's parcel of land provided enough for the family to eat, fodder for the animals, and seeds for cultivation. If fortunate, a family might sell a small quantity of corn, beans, or plantains in Granada. However, drought, plagues, flooding, or misfortunes such as sickness and death, meant the family ate less or went into debt. Nevertheless, peasant production for subsistence remained the norm in Diriomo.

As a consequence of privatization peasants' agricultural practice changed radically. Before the rise of coffee and the privatization of land, agriculture based on slash-and-burn techniques predominated in Diriomo. That agricultural system was predicated on common rights to land. Every few years households moved their cultivation plots to new locations, allowing fields to lie fallow and regrowth to restore the soils' fertility. Enclosures and privatization spatially fixed peasant agriculture in one location. The possibility for most peasant households to allow fields to lie fallow was significantly reduced, if not eliminated. In addition, because of increasing pressure on land, areas not suitable for agriculture, because of the steepness of the grade or the quality of the soils, were planted—and rapidly eroded. This accelerated depletion of the soils, decline in agricultural productivity, and the ecological degradation of a large area. These changes in agricultural practice and in the ecology of the region undoubtedly were associated with changes in household composition and the sexual division of labour.

Tierras Ejidales, 'Josefa Rodriguez demanda tierras de Santiago Rodriguez', 1895. Rodriguez claims title to lands which her deceased husband had received. Burns cites a case where Sra. Jerónima Morales claimed land in the common lands of the Laguna de Apoyo in May 1878. *Nicaragua, Indice de los documentos que comprende la sección de tierras y que existen en depósito en el Archivo Nacional*, vol. 1 (Managua: Tipografía Nacional, 1900), cited by Burns in *Patriarch and Folk*, 134.

Another major change associated with the spread of coffee production for export was the commercialization and monetization of the economy. Nicaragua had no regular currency in the 1870s. Towards the end of the century money more frequently served as a means of payment for labour and for products. Throughout this period elimination of common lands, privatization of property in land, ecological degradation, and increasing monetization of the economy were aspects of a social revolution in class and patriarchal relations.

Around the turn of the century, from the 1890 to 1915, the process of privatization of land took on a different character. Realizing that custom and law governing rights to land had shifted fundamentally, small agriculturalists—women and men, mestizo and Indian—registered claims to the subsistence plots they cultivated and, in the case of men, considered their own. Usually these plots were small; often no more than three manzanas. New laws hastened and consolidated the major change in land tenure. In the first decade of the twentieth century the municipal council required all claimants to land to secure title or forfeit their land. Common property rights no longer were legal.

This second phase of privatization consolidated Diriomo's poor and medium peasantry. Surprisingly, the process incorporated women. Land records indicate that approximately 15 per cent of titles to small plots were in women's names. Given women's former exclusion from rights to common land, and their continued disenfranchisement, this incidence of women's land ownership is high. The important question, and one not easily answered, is what enabled women to engage in the political process of privatization? Part of the answer lies in entrenchment of the legal process of privatization. The new laws which governed access to land eroded custom and practice. Traditional male rights to common lands were abolished, replaced by laws of property, which, in the Hispanic legal tradition, were gender neutral.

How some peasant women overcame patriarchal relations which governed land requires explanation of a range of social relations. A significant factor was the absence of the norm of marriage among peasant women. In a peasant society, for women who had serial relationships with men it was very important to own land, if at all possible. Also, the dissolution of the indigenous community, with its allocation of land to men, was associated with a decline in the power of custom in male control over land. Finally, the number of peasant women who became small holders raises the question whether women were as marginalized and powerless in the previous period as the silent records might suggest.

While the causes of these changes are not clear, their effects were more obvious. Most of the peasant women who acquired title to parcels of land were single. No longer constrained by relationships with males to have access to land, most of these women became head of a household which engaged in subsistence production. These households included males—brothers, sons, and itinerant lovers. The difference was that they were constructed around female rather than male control over material resources. These were strong women, litigating against men who challenged their title to land, and against male neighbours who encroached on their parcels. This hardly conforms to the dominant stereotype, historical and contemporary, of the submissive, downtrodden peasant women of Nicaragua.

Nevertheless, turn-of-the-century Diriomo remained a patriarchal domain. These women were viewed, and viewed themselves, as vulnerable. Court transcripts record their laments that as single mothers and heads of household, with no husband to protect them and their children, they deserved special consideration. Such discourses appeared frequently. They indicate the strength of patriarchal ideology, and also how 'liberated' women used that ideology to their benefit.

The township remained a citadel of machismo despite the expansion of women's participation in property ownership. A few women in control of land did little to reduce the systematic oppression of women by men. Women continued to be excluded from politics. In addition, language and ideology denied women any role other than domestic. In official and popular discourse a woman's trade or profession was listed invariably as 'domestic' (*oficios domesticos*), even when the woman was an important landowner who administered her own estate. Similarly, in legal documents and everyday use all unmarried women were 'girls' (*niñas*), regardless of age or social position. Eighty-year-old Blanca Morales, matriarch of the town, was Niña Blanquita because she did not marry.

In all, about fifty years elapsed before the transformation of property relations was more or less completed in Diriomo in the 1920s. The privatization of land in Diriomo involved almost no buying and selling. Virtually all land that changed hands did so as the direct result of the actions of the municipal council. The process was, in the first instance, political and social more than narrowly economic. It was a contest over the meaning and practice of private property. An important aspect of this contest was a struggle over the patriarchal norms that governed access to land.

COERCED LABOUR: EXPLOITATION OF GENDER DIFFERENCES

In altering custom and law governing access to land, the spread of coffee transformed social relations of production in the township. Prevailing subsistence household production clashed with planters' needs for a steady labour force throughout the year, but particularly during the harvest which, in the Granada region, lasted two months from December to February. In the 1870s owners of large coffee estates offered cash advances to entice peasants into contracting their labour throughout the harvest season. At first these agreements were private; enforced by custom, by the political authority of the planter, and if necessary, by his or her personal armed guards. By the 1880s planters' need for labourers was so great that this informal system proved inadequate. Gradually the state created and imposed a labour draft which obligated men in the coffee regions to work for the planters during the harvest season.[43] Over time the system became more draconian in law as well as in practice, reflecting expansion in planters' demand for workers and peasants' increased resistance to the labour draft. The state created tiers of confusing and often contradictory institutions in its attempt to ensure that the system worked. These included passbooks carried by the rural poor, agricultural judges responsible for rounding up, registering, and controlling the reluctant labourers, a rural police that captured and returned fugitives, prison terms, road gangs, and military service for evaders, and possibly most effective of all, a nation-wide telegraph system which tied together the coercive apparatus of every city and town.

The complex nature of the legislation, competition among planters for workers, and peasant resistance created great variety in how the system worked in different regions. However, in almost all its forms, coercion was key to these social relations. Although many peasants were impoverished through the process of privatization of land, at the turn of the century this alone was insufficient to forge a stable labour force for the coffee planters.

The 1901 law which codified the forced labour system stipulated that all men and women who had neither 500 pesos in 'capital' nor a profession were required to register with the local authorities and work for a planter (a *patrón*).[44] Despite the letter of the law, only males were required to comply with the decree. Nevertheless, in practice the productive unit was often the family, real or fictive, rather than an individual male labourer. As remuneration was according to piece work, it suited the planters, as well as the peasants, for an entire family to pick coffee.

The normal labour contract was an agreement between men. Often the planter provided a cash advance to a male head of household, with the stipulation that he, his wife, and children would pick coffee. The debt would be cancelled according to an established piece rate, and might require the family to work the harvests for several years to repay the loan. This labour relation perpetuated the convention of a male-headed family unit. Also, it established the principle of a man's authority to contract the labour of family members and to collect their pay—or amortize their debt. Another form of agreement, again between planter and male head of

[43] For analysis of the origins, transformations, and resistance to this forced labour draft see Dore, 'Coffee, Land and Class Relations in Nicaragua'.

[44] *Diario Oficial, La Gaceta*: Managua (Oct. 1901) vol. VI, no. 1480.

household, specified the precise tasks and remuneration of men, women, and children. Such contracts are particularly illuminating about the extreme exploitation of women and girls. In one typical contract, of two years' duration, the husband earned 14 pesos per month, the son 8 pesos, the wife and daughter each 2 pesos. Female members of the family were required to work a longer working day than the males, even though their pay was a fraction of what the males earned.[45]

Although women were not forced to work, labour contracts record numerous examples of women who indebted their labour and that of their children in return for a cash advance. These were single peasant women, some of whom owned small parcels of land. The terms of these contracts are similar to those signed by men. However, they differ markedly in two areas: the cash advanced and the rate of pay. Both are significantly lower than in contracts between men. Planters systematically took advantage of women's oppression and possibly of their extreme poverty, to impose particularly onerous terms on an already onerous relationship of indebtedness.

Similarly, women and children often were brutally exploited in domestic service in the planters' homes. Payment of one-half or one peso per month was the norm, in contrast to men's pay of 15 pesos per month for agricultural work. In addition, legal transcripts indicate the frequency of complaints involving sexual abuse, oppressive working conditions, and fraud on the part of the patrón. The mayor, serving as judge, would lament the distressing conditions common in domestic labour. Nevertheless, he reminded plaintives that they had agreed to contracts which could not be dissolved.

Flight, the most frequent form of resistance to oppressive labour conditions, was more difficult for women than for men. There are examples of entire family units abandoning a coffee estate, attempting to leave behind their debt. However, the most frequent and successful fugitives were single men. It was more difficult for a family, than for a single man, to flee and evade pursuit by the rural police. With this in mind, planters indicated their preference for contracting entire families. Most difficult of all was for a woman with her children to abandon the confines of a coffee plantation. Among the hundreds of cases of fugitive workers I found no record of flight of a single woman with her children.

A pattern of systematic discrimination of females in payment for labour is evident. This raises the question why women and girls were paid less than males for the same or longer hours of work. A male conspiracy, uniting planters and peasants, to perpetuate men's oppression of women is an unsatisfactory explanation. It is doubtful that poor men forced to labour for coffee planters would collude, consciously or unconsciously, to

[45] AMD, Libro de Matricula, 1903, Libreta 343, 'Entre Don Feliz Castillo y Francisco Tardencilla Dávila'.

keep women's pay low, since this depressed the family wage.[46] Part of the explanation is that it was advantageous for the planter class to perpetuate the myth of female weakness and inferiority, then use this as justification to exploit women and girls more ruthlessly than men. The pay differential between women and men in the early years of coffee production had major repercussions for the future of women's rural employment in Nicaragua. Coffee was one of the first economic activities in which men and women systematically worked for wages. As such, it established a precedent for paying women substantially less than men.

ON PATRIARCHY AND DEVELOPMENT

The control over land that women achieved in the process of privatization eroded in the succeeding decades. The proportion of smallholders who were women declined in Diriomo in the 1930s and 1940s. This is suggestive of the problems of viewing changes in patriarchy in a linear mold. Changes in the forms and degree of patriarchy are aspects of diverse relations at different levels of society.[47] Arguments about the inevitability of the decline of patriarchy as societies develop fail to consider the multiple ways in which patriarchal relations are sustained and reformed in every society.

The impact of capitalist development on the subordination of women by men became the object of debate more than a century ago. As the controversy re-emerged in the last twenty years it resumed its characteristically binary form. Although terrains and patterns of discourse shifted, the terms of debate remained: does capitalism alleviate or exacerbate the oppression of women? Protagonists divided into two camps—each the mirror image of the other. One side held that capitalist development accentuated women's subordination. Constructing an idealized past where sexual divisions of labour were neither asymmetrical nor exploitative, romanticists proposed that we should not presume that sexual differentiation in some cloudy historical era translated into women's oppression. They argued that as capitalism increasingly divorced private and public spheres women's labour was denigrated and subordinated to men's. Separate became unequal. The opposition also adhered to a romantic and schematic view. They argued that capitalism renders women's oppression obsolete by progressively eliminating the material basis of women's subordination.

[46] Ben Fine reviews the debate about women's differential pay under capitalism in *Women's Employment and the Capitalist Family*, ch. 3. Carmen Diana Deere analyses women's differential pay in a rural setting in *Household and Class Relations: Peasants and Landlords in Northern Peru* (Berkeley: University of California Press, 1990), 265–91.

[47] For analysis of the relationship between the forms and degree of patriarchy see Walby's chapter in the present volume.

The debate was fruitful in so far as it explored theoretical issues involving the nexus between domestic labour, modes of production, and women's oppression. Also, it generated abundant empirical studies of the impact of socio-economic change on women's status.[48]

This study of the changing forms and degree of patriarchy in a period of major social upheaval in rural Nicaragua challenges the linearity of both interpretations. Rather than discovering progressive evolution or regressive devolution in women's oppression, this historical analysis underscores the ephemerality of improvements in women's status, and disjunctures between changing material conditions and alterations in gender hierarchies. While these conclusions might not appear striking, they go against the grain of most approaches to history and theory. For most historians either accept an implicit teleology or reject the possibility of developing theory. This chapter endeavours to contribute to the development of patriarchy theory by exploring the tendencies and counteracting tendencies in patriarchal relations in rural Nicaragua. Above all, my research highlights the importance of combining analyses of class and gender. I hope it puts another nail in the coffin of gender-neutral class analysis by demonstrating that analysis of class transformations in an epoch of intensified commercialization in Nicaragua is incomplete if separated from analysis of transformations in patriarchal relations.

[48] Recent studies of patriarchy in Latin America include Carmen Diana Deere, *Household and Class Relations: Peasants and Landlords in Northern Peru* (Berkeley and London: University of California Press, 1990); Verena Stolcke, *Coffee Planters, Workers and Wives: Class Conflict and Gender Relations on São Paulo Plantations, 1850–1980* (London: Macmillan Press, 1988); Fiona Wilson, 'Women and Agricultural Change in Latin America: Some Concepts Guiding Research', *World Development*, 13/9 (1985); Diane Elson (ed.), *Male Bias in the Development Process* (Manchester: Manchester University Press, 1991); Elizabeth Jelin (ed.), *Family, Household and Gender Relations in Latin America* (London: Kegan Paul International, 1991); and Benería and Roldán, *The Crossroads of Class and Gender*.

Gender and Status Inequalities in Yemen: Honour, Economics, and Politics

Sheila Carapico

INTRODUCTION

Studies of women in Arab countries fit into two other wider inquiries. Within the anthropology of the Middle East, as Abu Lughod shows in her review, 'harem theory' is one of the three 'theoretical metonyms', the other two being segmentation theory and Islam. Because ethnographic debates on segmentation among tribes and orientalist studies of Islam are largely male dominated, and Western stereotypes of Arab women are so sexist, studies of women initially strove merely to show elements of power and individualism within the 'harem' and have only more recently moved on to analyse the ideologies of patriarchy and sexual modesty, the epistemological issues involved in 'knowing the Other', and the relationship between studies of women and studies of men (Abu-Lughod, 1990).

Arab women are also included under the broader rubric of women-in-development (WID), where general questions concern the impact of modernization on women's lives and the specific questions asked about the Middle East have often been whether Islamic or Arab culture is inimical to women's liberation. In this literature, as Moghadam shows, more recent research considers how male-dominated patriarchal structures in the public and private spheres of tribal societies and 'neo-patriarchal' states restrict female access to the public domain. She deals with the impact of wealth, status, power, and public policy on gender relations. It is also important in this context to examine changes in personal status, political rights, education and health, and employment (Moghadam, 1990, 1992).

The aim of this national case study, a synthetic summary of the work and evidence on women in a tribal, Muslim, Arabian, rapidly changing society, is to contribute to the intersection of the Middle Eastern and women-in-development literatures by situating women first within tribal and Islamic settings and then in the context of rapid changes in political and economic circumstances during the past thirty years. It therefore considers feminine roles in the different historical social strata before examining how new services brought by modernization, class formation associated with the penetration of capitalism, and political struggles between right and left all affect women's positions in modernizing Arab societies.

What I hope to show is that the relationship between modernization and women's status is not a straightforward one, even in an apparently patriarchal Arab context.

TRIBES, ÉLITES, AND SERVICE PEOPLE

A mountainous, semi-arid farming region on the south-west Arabian peninsula, historic Yemen was partitioned in the nineteenth century when the British colonized the area around and later east of the important natural harbour at Aden, while the north remained in the Ottoman sphere of influence until World War I and independent under a Zaydi imam afterwards. Within North Yemen, there are three major geo-cultural regions: the northern highlands, a semi-arid zone characterized by grain production and sheep and goat herding; the southern uplands, washed twice annually by Indian Ocean monsoons, greener and supporting a peasant population; and the Tihama, the Red Sea coastal plain, with tropical agriculture in the mountain-fed *wadis* and near-desert conditions in between. In the South, colonial capitalism and post-revolutionary socialism affected Aden city and the nearby Lahej agricultural region most directly, whereas the irrigated Wadi Hadramawt and the more tribal eastern mountains remained quite isolated. The northern highlands are predominantly Zaydi (Shi'a) whereas the rest of Yemen is mostly Shafa'i (Sunni).

The ethnographic literature, most of which (with the exception of Bujra) comes from the north in the late 1970s and early 1980s, describes a tripartite status hierarchy consisting of the tribes (*qaba'il*), the élite or religious aristocracy (*sa'ada*), and the 'deficient' or 'service' groups at the bottom of the social ladder. The three groups' status and roles were interdependent. While the tribespeople engaged in grain farming and/or herding, and the educated élite practised the legal, administrative, and educational professions, the lower-status groups performed personal and market services on a contractual or, more recently, a commercial basis. Like ascribed status categories in most cultures, membership in each group was based on descent or at least a myth of common ancestry, maintained through endogamous marriage patterns (Bujra, 1971; Caton, 1990; Dresch, 1977).

'Tribe' has two distinct connotations. In political histories, 'the tribes' are the great Hashid and Bakil confederations of the northern plateau, who maintained through a combination of honour and force a 'tribal peace' that protected unarmed people including religious élites, service people, and women. Tribalism in this sense embodies a set of folk codes of behaviour (*'urf* or *'ard*) and a form of political organization under the leadership of quasi-elected *shaykhs*. In the second connotation 'tribesman' (*qabili*) or 'tribeswoman' (*qabiliyya*) means tribal, as distinct from non-tribal, status. Beyond Hashid and Bakil territory, 'tribes' are less of a political force, farmers are often called 'peasant' (*ra'iyya*) as opposed to *qabili*, tribal codes are relaxed, and the term *shaykh* connotes exploitation more than election. However, tribespeople are distinguished from both higher- and lower-status groups, as 'independent' cereal farmers and/or herders.

Independent cereal and dairy production was not pure subsistence, for tribal households relied on others to provide the goods and services their 'honour' prevented them from undertaking, including growing vegetables, especially local onions and horse-radishes; and the activities of barbers, builders, cosmeticians, healers, criers, musicians, artisans, builders, traders, innkeepers, and, particularly, street-sweepers and bath-cleaners. Dishonoured by these tasks, tribal communities or families contracted with market people or ritual specialists, exchanging grain, butter, and meat for services. Service professionals, referred to collectively as *muzayyin*, as 'deficient' (*nuqqas*), or as 'market people' (*ahl al-suq*), traditionally entered contractual agreements to provide certain goods and services in exchange for grain and protection from a tribe, or subsistence from an élite community. Group-to-group contractual arrangements were preferred by both farmers and Muslim and Jewish service people for their reliability and dignity.

The élite non-tribal religious aristocracy consisted of the descendants of the Prophet, the *Sa'ada* and/or *Ashraf* (singular *sayyid or sharif*); and the judges (singular *qadi*) whose status came not from birth (for by blood they were tribesmen) but from education which, as in Europe, tended to be passed on within families. Honour attached to piety, scholarship, and mediation of disputes rather than, as among tribesmen, to acts of valour and violence (Caton, 1986). These two groups tended to concentrate in a dozen or more historic towns, where a combination of fees for legal services, rent-taking, religious endowment, and royal largess gave them a standard of living somewhat, but not dramatically, better than that of either rural tribesfolk or the service people in their midst. Under tribal practice, *sayyid* communities, like the market domain, were *hijrah* or 'protected' from warfare.

At the very bottom of the social hierarchy were the *Akhdam* (servants), employed in urban and market areas as street-weepers and bath-cleaners for the municipalities or *awqaf*, where taxes or endowments paid their wages, or on large estates in the Tihama and some parts of the southern uplands as migrant harvest workers, a step below the permanent share-croppers. Often seen lodged in temporary housing on the edge of towns, markets, and estates, the *Akhdam* are very nearly a distinct ethnic group, who evidently have African as well as Arab heritage, dress distinctively, and rarely interact socially with other Yemenis. Although when camped they appeared to be propertyless, a careful study in 1977 of Luhayyah district in the near-desert northern Tihama showed that families abandoned their land in drought years to seek employment as migrant farm workers, urban sanitation workers, or unskilled labourers in Saudi Arabia (Steffen *et al.*, 1978).

The distinctions among these groups were status inequalities rather than class divisions because independent farmers and tradespeople owned their own means of production—land, livestock, and the tools of their trades—and engaged in contractual exchange with other groups. Moreover, it was not the religious élite but a distinct tribute-collecting class-in-the-making that expropriated wealth through a sharecropping system not corresponding directly to status (Tutwiler, 1987). Unlike inter-household sharecropping in the semi-arid zones, on some irrigated estates in the southern uplands, the Tihama, and the Hadramawt, sharecroppers paid up to three-quarters of their crop to landlord-*shaykhs* or urban masters. Among the largest landowners in the early twentieth century were the imam's family and some other prominent *sayyid* families, but also northern *shaykhs* who conquered verdant valleys and traders who took land as collateral against loans. Independent farmers then became sharecroppers and gradually lost their tribal identity along with their independence. Class and status overlapped most closely for the *Akhdam*; otherwise, the class relation between owners and sharecroppers should not be confused with the status distinctions in the ethnographic literature.

Nor did low status prevent some coffee merchants, importers, and businessmen who moved to British Aden from amassing economic and political fortunes (Messick, 1978). The imams also selected some bright sons of low-status families for higher education or military posts precisely because, unlike either tribal military leaders or other descendants of the prophet, they could presumably broker no claim to political power. Thus although the monarchy derived its ideology and legitimacy from the religious aristocracy, status did not coincide exactly with wealth and power. When the son of a blacksmith, in his capacity as captain of the palace guard, seized the reins of state in September 1962, the *sa'ada* lost influence, but merchants and officers were posed to come to the fore.

THE ROLES OF WOMEN

Gender, the second major source of inequality in Yemeni society, has been the subject of more journalistic and impressionistic writing than serious scholarship. The major published studies of Yemeni women remain Myntti's general overview and Dorsky's study of Amran, while the bulk of the analysis of extended fieldwork by Najwa Adra, Christine Ansell, Mary Herbert, Martha Mundy, and Delores Walters remains unpublished.

Evidence suggests a great deal of regional and situational variation, within which, ironically from a contemporary liberal feminist political perspective, the greatest honour is attached to feminine seclusion and the greatest shame to market activity. This section begins with the role of women farmers and sharecroppers, and then considers *sayyid*, service, and *Akhdam* women.

The predominant farm system consisted of three interdependent elements: the fields, the livestock, and the kitchen. The fields supplied cereal and tinder to the kitchen and fodder for the livestock, who, in turn, returned fertilizer and traction to the fields as well as milk and sometimes meat to the kitchen. This was a use-value-maximizing system with virtually no waste, since grasses and stalks were culled for feed and fuel, leftovers fattened livestock, and even droppings were used as fuel or to replenish the soil. The farm system produced a nutritious, high-fibre diet of grain, beans, dairy products like buttermilk and clarified butter, sometimes eggs or meat, and herbs and seasonal fruits. Water had to be collected daily, often from natural streams.

Within the tribal household, men performed the mainly seasonal tasks associated with the land and women did nearly everything else. Men maintained the terraces contouring the rugged highlands, or irrigation systems in the Tihama, rebuilding walls, ploughing, levelling fields, and turning the soil under after harvest, using drought stock. Women's responsibilities for dairy stock and the kitchen entailed a long list of daily chores, including cutting fodder and collecting fuel, feeding and milking, preparing a fire, grinding grain, making bread or porridge, collecting water, and, of course, serving meals and raising children (Dorsky, 1986; Myntti, 1979; Carapico and Tutwiler, 1981).

Women's work was not 'housework'; it was the basis of production and subsistence, with high value added. Measured in terms of hours, it was way more than half the work, depending on the ratio of land to livestock. Within share-cropping and nearly landless families women's economic power was greater relative to males because the value of their livestock exceeded that of the land; on marginal and even medium-sized holdings, planting decisions were often predicated on the importance of sorghum and alfalfa as fodder. In the most destitute farm families that sharecropped even their livestock, women usually contracted independently. In all farm families women managed all the products (grain, milk) as well as most of the inputs (fodder, fuel, water), which required daily handling, while men were condemned to seasonal unemployment during fallow and growing seasons. Whereas entirely female households could survive, it was culturally inconceivable and physically untenable for men to live 'alone' until markets began to supply bread, milk, and water.

Most tribeswomen inherited a bit of land, about half as much (under Islamic laws) as their brothers, but all land in the household was managed as a unit by the men (Mundy, 1979). The preferred marriage patterns kept both people and property within the extended family, or tribal fraction. The ideal household consisted of two or more adult males, one of whom could be off-farm, and three or four women. Polygamy occurred, but the extended household of male kin was preferred. When women married, they looked after their mothers and sisters-in-law, with whom they would spend their lives dividing day-to-day chores. A brideprice composed of gold, livestock, or other goods was paid to the bride and her father. If a man divorced his wife, he regained part of the brideprice but lost her labour, her land, her livestock, and the alliance of her male kin. It happened, but was not taken lightly. The other women in the household and the necessity of her labour minimized wife abuse.

Under tribal law, women were not at all equal to men. They did have tribal status and membership, but they were also treated as 'protected' people. Therefore, they would not bear arms, and should never be attacked; if they were harmed, the blood-money compensation might be as much as eleven times that of a man's. No tribeswoman should set foot in a marketplace, engage directly in trade, or betray her sexual honour. Tribeswomen were thus the object of a chauvinistic code of chivalry that denied direct participation in the military–political sphere or in the market.

Women from *shaykhly, qadi*, and administrative families exercised a certain power as intermediaries and as consummators of political alliances. Except under very dire circumstances when a distraught widow burst into a *shaykh*'s *diwan*, women approached political leaders through their menfolk or the *shaykh*'s womenfolk. Women in political families often married into potentially allied tribes, where they enjoyed membership in their fathers' as well as protection by their husband's tribe. Depending on her temperament, relationship with her family, and the specific circumstances, such a marriage could be an entré into influential behind-the-scenes politics or into social and psychological exile.

Although the daughters and wives of tribal chiefs shared with *sayyid* women the potential for political marriages, there was a clear difference between the 'ladies' of the upper crust and tribeswomen. For the women of the religious aristocracy exemplified the seclusion and modesty of Muslim wives, mothers, and daughters. The privileged 'ladies' of the 'best families' were also the most 'protected' group in society: from work, from public view and interaction with strangers, and from violence. Daughters of *sayyid* families, who always married other *sa'ada*, veiled heavily after the fashion of Ottoman Turks who partly conquered Yemen in the seventeenth and again in the nineteenth century. In centres of administration and learning in the highlands, post-pubescent females lived a cloistered existence, venturing from their homes only to visit other women, cloaked from head to foot in yards of fabric, while in élite Tihama towns a labyrinth of passages allowed them to visit without entering the street. The veil symbolized not just honour but freedom from the drudgery and physical exertion of the fields. Unlike rural tribeswomen familiar with all the men in their own communities, the ladies of the well-born and learned families refrained from contact with males beyond their immediate families, and were therefore far more likely to marry utter strangers. Their extreme modesty were marks of privilege, mimicked by women of *qadi* families that could afford it.

The veiled ladies enjoyed a further privilege open to no other women: schooling. Within *sayyid* and *qadi* families literate women trained their brightest daughters and nieces to read the Quran, practice calligraphy, or, sometimes, in herbology or other arts. For the apt pupils in the best urban families tutors might be brought. Such learning conferred tremendous prestige because it was so rare.

In other ways the women of all but the royal family shared certain things in common. Although *sayyid* families were more likely to have a public fountain, often endowed through a pious foundation (*waqf*), near their homes, they still had to haul water. Although they might take in poor relatives, orphans, or women of 'service' strata to lighten the load, unlike the ladies of Europe they did not rely on servants to prepare meals, keep house, or raise children. Their neighbours were frequently of different status. And like women throughout Yemen they tended cows and goats for milk and breeding, typically feeding them with alfalfa and other crops from nearby *waqf* gardens. And it must be noted that the men and women sharecroppers on the *waqf* gardens chequering *sayyid* communities were not infrequently themselves *sayyids* whose association with the pious foundation or a mosque conferred prestige on tasks otherwise performed by the untitled lower strata. Other *sayyidat* earned money, grain, or goods by reading or performing at feminine celebrations, healing, tutoring, and so forth.

Finally, the untitled *muzayyin* and *Akhdam* women were the least constrained and least privileged: having neither land nor status, they had only their labour to barter or sell and (as the others saw it) no particular honour to protect. Yet within their families low-status women wielded more economic power than their ladylike or even tribal sisters. Although a complete ethnography of the trades has not been done, apparently there are a number of trades where women and men each have special skills (pottery), some where they do similar tasks (straw weaving, sewing), some where each gender serves its own (barbering, cosmetics, entertaining), and some performed only by men (carpentry, metal work, fishing) whose wives tended livestock or vegetable gardens. For the wholly shameless it was even possible to enter the market, unveiled, to hawk wares, serve in a restaurant, or tend to traveller's needs at a hostel. Even these market women looked down on the *Akhdam* street sweepers.

Polygamy rates seem to have been highest among the most and the least privileged families. Among the political élites, men took second and third wives to cement political alliances and head households in more than one location. At the other end of the spectrum, peddlers, itinerant traders, caravaneers, and other travelling men found a wife in each of several destinations, leaving each to fend for herself much of the time, raising livestock, selling crafts or services, or ingratiating themselves to more affluent families. The latter—landless wives of shiftless men—enjoyed little honour or wealth, but (so) they enjoyed more freedom of physical mobility, economic independence, and personal access to *shaykhs* and judges than any other women.

The ways in which status distinctions were constituted, reflected, reinforced, or, more recently, modified in the course of daily interaction and crisis resolution have been a major theme in the ethnographies of Yemeni men. Social inequalities among men are enacted almost daily in the seating arrangements at a *qat* session, where the most prestigious seats are in the far corner of the *diwan* or *mafraj*, opposite the windows, and the least desirable places are near the door (Dresch, 1985). Forms of greeting and rhetorical style also mark the status of both the speaker and the person being addressed (Caton, 1986).

Within the female domain, the cues to status seem far more subtle, since social interactions coalesced around physical rather than status proximity. In traditional neighbourhoods and villages, a feminine social network revolved around water sources and afternoon social gatherings. At the water-hole or fountain, fights might break out in dry periods but no one could pull rank. In more urban neighbourhoods where market, élite, and tribal households often shared common spaces and facilities, women attending wedding and post-natal parties filled the *mafraj* two and three deep, on a first come, first served basis, quite oblivious to status ranking, and convention required either equal greetings to each individual or a single collective blessing. While everyone knew who could and could not marry whom, in women's gatherings only the visiting, special-occasion professionals, like ritual Quran readers, by definition *sayyidat*, and *muzzayina* entertainers, stood out. Even wealthy, powerful women married to *shaykhs*, governors, or princes took pains not to show off. Within the group, women ignored status distinctions, and felt it rude to speak of them. One's personal honour depended on personal traits like generosity, piety, wit, and motherhood.

THE IMPACT OF CHANGE ON STATUS

The Yemen Arab Republic (YAR) was a separate state from 1962, when the imamate fell, until 1990, when North and South Yemen unified. During that period, a political, economic, and social transformation unleashed by the civil war (1962–70) destroyed not only the imamate but also the political basis of aristocratic preferences and privileges. The oil bonanza in the neighbouring Arab Gulf opened up wage and entrepreneurial opportunities for over a million Yemeni sojourners whose remittances, peaking at over a billion dollars a year, flooded a formerly 'closed' economy of fewer than ten million residents with hard currency and imported commodities. Within a generation class had substantially replaced status as the principal denominator of social inequality. In the late 1980s, deflation in the price of oil reduced the YAR's foreign currency transfers, sending the economy into recession. In the meantime, however, Sana'a had negotiated a political agreement for unification with the heretofore Marxist post-colonial regime of the People's Democratic Republic of Yemen (PDRY), noted, among other things, for its progressive family and gender policies. Soon on the heels of unification came another major shock from the 1991 Gulf War, which precipitated an influx of returned migrants and sharply reduced international assistance. These rapid, major changes affected men and women differently, and among women the effects of rapid modernization and political developments depended on both prior status and subsequent class position.

In the North Yemeni bourgeois society, with its commercial economy and bureaucratic state, status inequalities continued to differentiate men but they lost their material and occupational underpinnings. With political upheavals and the advent of modern urban education old élites lost their monopoly over learning and their domination of the expanding apparatus of the state. Traders as a group and certain importers and money-changers in particular flourished, and were indeed able to transform new wealth into prestige and power. Sellers of certainly traditionally valuable and now widely available commodities like meat and *qat* now prospered while some artisan categories like potters and weavers lost most of their trade to cheap uniform imports. The latter joined the thousands of smallholders and some tenant sharecroppers in the growing exodus to the Gulf where some established small businesses but the majority worked for wages. Migrant remittances entered Yemen via money-changers who transmitted them to families for expenditure on consumption. This economic 'demand' pulled markets, roads, electricity, and pumped water into the countryside. Soon, the market for wage labour spread into the Yemeni towns and eventually the villages.

With the availability of imported white flour, tinned milk and food, and, more unevenly, gas, electricity, and piped water, the economic basis of household grain and livestock production on dry land began to collapse. Those who could dig or drill wells to irrigate their land for *qat* or commercial food crops did so, and the *qat* farmers made a small fortune (Weir, 1985). Others gradually concluded that the old grain and livestock regime was more trouble than it was worth, and the men moved further into the wage economy. By the late 1980s, when the bonanza ended, most families were almost entirely dependent on the market.

Women's access to the fruits of North Yemeni modernization projects was uneven, for water, electricity, roads, education, and health-care services distribution was affected by factors ranging from technology and terrain to politics and foreign aid. The extension of these services affected, and reflected, urban–rural as well as class and gender differences. Overall, only a small, privileged proportion of women enjoyed enough access to education, health services, and transport to really transform their lives, to support and express themselves individually in the new public spheres of market and state.

The single most significant change for women came from piped water. In the two decades after the end of the civil war in 1970, the Yemen Arab Republic, with international assistance, delivered water to much of the population: 29 per cent of households, mostly in cities and towns, had piped water by 1981, and the proportion of households reached may well have doubled in the next decade with the completion of an additional 1,223 water projects (CPO, 1988: 65, 111). Women who now had water piped to the house or at least the neighbourhood were freed of one of the most time-consuming and strenuous of their traditional tasks, the carrying of water. This was a most welcome relief especially to rural highland women, many of whom spent hours walking several kilometres a day to provide their families with a couple of buckets full of water. However, it should also be noted that the water collection spot previously gave women a gathering place outside the home, and that going for water afforded a particular sort of physical mobility and, indeed, exercise, so that household or neighbourhood taps removed their main excuse for leaving the home even as it relieved them of an arduous task.

The second service gradually reaching most households was electricity, extended gradually from the cities, along the main roads, into the countryside, reaching 64 per cent of households by 1981 and nearly tripling in generating capacity by the end of the decade (CPO, 1988: 65, 112–13). Electric lights and televisions bought with migrants' remittances now lit most homes. This made a difference in the rhythm of daily life once tied to sunrise and sunset and in the nature of leisure time once filled only with social conversation. Women liberated from the task of hauling water, and in many cases from livestock rearing, now settled in the afternoon or evening in front of the TV to watch Yemeni, Arab, and Western programmes. Television mesmerized, reducing the incentive to attend women's parties, and to talk when one did visit. It introduced a partial, rarified glimpse of lifestyles and technologies never imagined a decade earlier, from Caireen middle class sitcoms to improbable scenarios with talking, flying, anthropomorphic animations or real men in space flight. This exposure raised certain expectations but also created confusion and even revulsion about the world outside. Electrification also introduced basic appliances like washing machines, blenders, and refrigerators, whose utilization were less labour saving than housework modifying. There is little evidence of time saved fetching water or chopping vegetables being put towards 'economic' purposes (Myntti, 1979).

Female access to other services was more limited. Roads brought appliances, building materials, and consumer goods, but relatively few women travelled, and then only heavily veiled. Indeed the arrival of vehicular traffic brought strangers whose presence made most girls and women more reluctant to venture from home and more likely to veil. Although in medical emergencies women might ride to a clinic or hospital, few travelled by car to clinics or schools on a routine basis.

Although schools and clinics were built throughout North Yemen in the 1970s and 1980s, female access to education and medical care, especially beyond the main cities, was limited and spotty. Some aggregate statistics illustrate this point. By 1985, female literacy rates in the YAR were estimated at 3 per cent, compared with 27 per cent for males, and 25 per cent for females in South Yemen. Between 1986 and 1988, 40 per cent of primary school-aged girls were enrolled (compared with 141 per cent for boys, indicating large numbers of older male students). At the secondary level, the proportion of the female age group dropped to six per cent (Moghadam, 1992: table 13), reflecting parents' reluctance to send pubescent daughters to school, due to the acute shortage of women teachers, to fathers' refusal to have their daughters more educated than themselves, to mothers' desire to have them help at home, and to the widespread perception that advanced education for girls is 'wasted'. City girls were going to school at twice the rate of their country cousins. During 1986–7, girls constituted one-fifth of those in grades one to six, including 42 per cent in Sana'a and probably the other cities, but a commensurately lower proportion elsewhere. At the preparatory and secondary levels females were only 11 per cent of pupils, and 19–20 per cent in Sana'a city alone (CPO, 1987: 157–62). There was a comparable urban bias in female education in the PDRY, where two-thirds of Adeni girls but around one-third elsewhere attended primary school, and at the secondary level 43 per cent of teenage females in Aden were students, but in other governorates the figures mirrored the YAR's (Al-Noban, 1984: 121). The ratio of female to male enrollment in all of Yemen in the mid-1980s was 24 at the primary level, 22 at the secondary level, and 40 for higher education (Khalidi and Tucker, n.d., p. 5).

The rate of college entry of female graduates of YAR secondary schools being equal to men's, women represented 12 per cent of Yemeni student body at Sana'a University, and of various faculties as follows: medicine, 56 per cent; arts, 31 per cent; science, 24 per cent; education, 21 per cent; commerce and economics, 9 per cent; engineering, 7 per cent; law, 2 per cent; agriculture, 2 per cent. At the Taiz faculty of education, 31 per cent of the Yemeni students were women (CPO, 1987: 177). Fourteen per cent of YAR graduate students, and a quarter of trainees at teachers' institutes were women (CPO, 1987: 169). In comparison, women were in the absolute numerical majority at Aden University of South Yemen, where they represented 72 per cent of students in the college of education and half of medical students (Lackner, 1985: 114).

Indicators of health care, like school attendance, put North Yemeni females behind women in almost all other Middle Eastern countries. In 1981–5 the contraceptive prevalence rate of 1 per cent was the lowest in the Middle East, and the fertility rate of 8.5 per cent was the highest. A World Fertility Survey in the early eighties reported that only a quarter of Yemeni women were aware of family planning methods, again far lower than elsewhere even within the Arab World, and less than 5 per cent were reportedly willing to use contraceptives, perhaps because child mortality under age one remained an alarming 162 per thousand, and 237 under the age of five (Moghadam, 1992, table 12). Acceptance of contraception (and/or the results of surveys) varied regionally, however, as a 1977 survey in Sana'a found that 21 per cent of women had used contraceptives and 37 said they might in the future, whereas the Family Planning Association reported that 13 per cent were using contraceptives and in another, rural, survey, Myntti found that 9 per cent of ever-married women practised family planning (Myntti, 1985: 50). In 1985, according to World Health Organization estimates, 12 per cent of births were attended by a recognized professional attendant, and maternal mortality could not even be estimated (World Bank, 1989: 226).

One profound difficulty with first-generation access to either education or medical care, despite the fact that access was theoretically free and universal, was the acute shortage of female teachers, nurses, and doctors. Indeed, during the 1970s and 1980s most teaching and health practitioner positions were filled by Egyptian, Sudanese, or Palestinian professionals, predominantly male. Only 13 per cent of primary teachers, 5 per cent of preparatory teachers, and 4 per cent of secondary teachers in 1981–2 were Yemeni (CPO, 1983: 220). By 1986, half of all physicians, one-third of qualified nurses, one-quarter of midwives, but 98 per cent of assistant nurses were Yemeni (CPO, 1987: 230–9). The likelihood of exposure to a foreign man exacerbated cultural inhibitions against Yemeni women's secondary school attendance and, particularly, physician care, thereby restricting access to schools and clinics to a predominantly urban, educated, wealthy segment of female society.

During this process, women were becoming housewives, professionals, workers, or farmers. First the housewives. Freed of the back-breaking daily drudgery of hauling water and firewood, hundreds of thousands of women discovered leisure for the first time. During the 1970s, as their husbands' and sons' jobs or businesses afforded more and more purchases, women gradually abandoned field chores and then, a bit more reluctantly, cows and goats. These changes afforded them a kind of pampered luxury unimagined by their mothers, and an opportunity to imitate the *sayyid* ladies of a bygone era by veiling and going into seclusion. With urbanization, as more families moved to larger cities, villages became towns, and streets became filled with strangers, everybody but the *Akhdam* and the Western-educated adopted the formerly aristocratic full black *sharshif*. Yet women exchanged symbolic prestige and freedom from hard physical labour for a considerable loss of economic autonomy. As men's earnings from the cash economy replaced an interdependent production unit, women's work became tedious housework with marginalized economic value: cooking, cleaning, laundry. Their only productive activity is now child-bearing. Since they are now dependent on their husbands' disposition as never before, those in nuclear households in new suburban neighbourhoods removed from old feminine networks, particularly, are subject to unprecedented physical and emotional abuse.

Some combination of education, personal drive, family wealth, and parental support has propelled about two thousand female members of the Yemeni bourgeoisie into careers in broadcasting, education, medicine, public service, and other fields. Not more than a handful run their own businesses. College educated in Sana'a, Aden, or abroad, they dress stylishly but modestly. Although of course there may be conflicts within marriages, their families are prepared to cope with the potential breach of 'honour' associated with open professionalism: wealthy merchants, *muzayyin* officers, educated *sayyid* and *qadi* families, and modernizing republican *shaykhs*. And they earn prestige on their own in the public sphere. Even so, career women must juggle multiple family and professional responsibilities (El Duais, 1991).

The new female urban wage earners, numbering perhaps in the tens of thousands, include civil servants, unskilled industrial workers, and maids, probably in that order. Clerks and secretaries are literate and thus privileged relative to manual workers. Urban factory and household workers, among them Vietnamese- and African-Yemenis ('half-breeds') as well as some *muzayyin*, tribal, and even *sayyid* women, divorced, widowed, or married working mothers or unmarried daughters, typically aspire to be housewives. Often working women must keep their daughters out of school to help out at home or with piece work. They are at the bottom of every pay scale, and suffer from loss of prestige, but cannot afford not to work. Their veils are not a mark of luxury but a way of retaining anonymity and dignity on public transportation and among strange men in offices, factories, and shops.

Other women though not formally employed earn a living in the informal sector, displaying their own bread, eggs, baskets, or needlework in the market, or selling clothing and other items at women's parties. Certain weekly markets including Suq at-Talh near the Saudi border, Suq Bayt al-Faqih and others in the Tihama, and Taiz markets frequented by Jabal Sabr women are notable for their women traders, but these are the exception rather than the rule. Elsewhere food, retail, and craft operations are managed by couples or families, or, more exceptionally, by women through their children and younger brothers. Male service workers, servants, petty traders, and sharecroppers also engage their wives and daughters for tasks that can be done in relative privacy.

In the farm sector, women remain active mainly within the use-oriented system of cereal and dairy production, for virtually all market and cash cropping activities, including *qat*, are designated as men's work. Although women and girls are sometimes hired as day-labour to harvest cotton, tomatoes, or other annual crops, at a wage about two-thirds of that of unskilled men, and although there is evidence that a growing proportion of sharecropping is done by females, and some fresh kitchen products like butter, eggs, and yoghurt had excellent market value, the introduction of mechanical irrigation, tractors, chemical fertilizers, and production-for-the-market put more and more capital and responsibility in the hands of men. In other words, on functioning integrated farms feeding cattle, goats, sheep, and chickens from the fields women play a role at least as vital as before massive male migration. But increasingly commercial-scale egg, meat, and dairy production and mono-cropping farm enterprises owned by male merchants and politicians replace domestic production.

There are now very clear class differences between a small number of families with property or rents that guarantee a high level of consumption and hired help from drivers, door-keepers, and maids, and larger, increasing numbers of households whose earnings fluctuate seasonally, monthly, or even daily to the point of uncertainty about basics like food and housing. Depending on life-cycle, personal, and family circumstances, bourgeois women, with access to all services and rights, may be professionals or housewives, and those without guaranteed income and probably illiterate may be poor housewives or working women. Unlike in the old days, in urban areas the two groups do not socialize, for their lifestyles are too different.

Although there is much less field evidence, it would seem that some of the same processes had occurred in South Yemen almost a generation earlier, when services in and around Aden created a lifestyle very different from distant Wadi Hadramawt and Mahrah mountain, and the entrepôt economy created class differences sharp enough to spark a revolution. Although politically repressive in some other ways, the Aden regime purported to treat men and women equally. The PDRY not only recognized women as full citizens in the constitution, but also made an effort to equalize access to education, employment, and the professions (Molyneux, 1985). Although this theoretical goal was never achieved, female participation in government and the professions compared favourably not only to other Arab states but to many Western systems as well. Like many socialist policies of the PDRY, however, the impact of progressive gender policies was felt mainly by the 42 per cent of the population living in Aden. As in the North, poor rural women fell behind just by staying where they were.

Politics was relevant to North Yemeni women's participation in modern services and employment in a complex way. YAR law was relatively liberal in terms of post-natal and family-leave-with-pay policies, women's suffrage, and property rights. Women's suffrage was theoretical because elections were in any case rare and female participation as either voters or candidates was low; but within the Arabian peninsula, Yemeni women had more political rights than most. Although seclusion was preferred in practice, women were not prohibited by law from participating in public life as in neighbouring countries.

Yet family and gender policies were very much at issue. Feminine modesty, education, and rights were politicized partly by the YAR's relationship with its two immediate neighbours, Saudi Arabia and the People's Republic, with drastically opposed gender policies. These positions were represented politically by the opposition Islamic and National 'fronts', respectively, since parties were outlawed. During the period between the early 1970s and the late 1980s, when Saudi influence was at its zenith and cold-war tensions flared between the YAR and the PDRY, the two neighbours offered very conflicting models for gender roles. While the YAR rejected some reactionary Saudi restrictions on the rights, appearance, and activities of women, the Kingdom's wealth gave it tremendous influence in policy areas including education. Bankrolling salaries for non-Yemeni Arab teachers, Riyadh recruited religious conservatives who supported its preference for gender segregation and women's seclusion. Religious partisans established a large base among faculty and students at Sana'a University where, in several ugly incidents, bare-headed Arab or Yemeni women were humiliated or even pelted with stones. The Islamic front also had a following of genuinely pious men and women attracted by their religious message, were capable of making temporary regional alliances with Hashid and Bakil, and could sometimes count on the support of Aden *émigrés* and anti-communist merchants.

By contrast, the progressive gender policies of South Yemen were admired by opponents of royalist influences in the YAR, by some Shafa'i communities with familial, tribal, and political ties to Aden and the Hadramawt, by whole southern uplands and Tihama districts full of sharecroppers wanting social and particularly land reform, and by some secular lawyers, journalists, professors, and students. Here the political conundrum was particularly complex, for the radical, unificationist National Democratic Front, which won popular backing in a number of southern uplands districts around Ibb and Taiz, was defeated militarily in the early 1980s, and seemingly discredited politically by the terrible, destructive intra-party blood-bath in Aden in January 1986. During 1986 some ten thousand of the PDRY's intellectual, political, and economic élite moved to the North. In Taiz and Sana'a, the Adeni women, wearing the *abayya*, a loose cloak which, though acceptably Islamic was none the less considerably less restrictive than the Northern *sharshif*, were socially visible, shopping in urban markets, applying for jobs, visiting with their husbands' friends. While some conservatives murmured that their behaviour was disgraceful, a lot of people found an increasingly acceptable model of the modern Muslim woman.

The historical confluence of Yemeni unity and the Gulf War transformed the political landscape within which gender relations were constructed. Unity heralded new political liberty for Yemenis, northern and southern, men and women—the new constitution defined citizenship in gender-neutral terms and guaranteed freedom of the press, of assembly, of expression, of political organization and participation, from arbitrary arrest, and from 'discrimination . . . due to sex, colour, racial origin, language, occupation, social status, or religious beliefs' (Article 27, p. 9). Yet within months of this historic juncture in Yemeni history came the Gulf War, in which the new republic, trying to remain neutral, was perceived as tilting towards Iraq, and was consequently punished by Saudi Arabia with a cancellation of its substantial foreign assistance budget and expulsion of three quarters of a million Yemenis living in the Kingdom.

The gender effects of these events were far-reaching. First, the aid cut-off meant that foreign educators, health practitioners, and other professionals working in the North would no longer be paid in hard currency. They left in droves, opening up thousands of positions to be filled by Adeni teachers, nurses, and clerks, including many more women than had ever been employed in North Yemen. As part of the anti-Saudi sentiment in the immediate aftermath of the expulsions, at least a few women were thrust to the political forefront, for instance addressing crowds of tens of thousands who gathered in public squares to protest the war. Gender and family statements were also at issue in the constitutional referendum of May 1991, when a coalition of Hashid and Islamic leaders unsuccessfully called for a boycott of the constitutional referendum unless *Sharia* were made the sole basis of law.

Yet the post-war economic crisis also created widespread unemployment and inflation as the nascent republic struggled to cope with resettlement and soaring budgetary deficits even as it forged a brand new political order. With domestic politics on the verge of chaos and Saudi money now funding rightist, tribal-separatist, and religious factions at unprecedented levels, politics became increasingly polarized. Appeals to family and religious values resonate among returned migrants and other disenfranchized groups. In this context, the role of women, laden with cultural, religious, economic, and political implications, is of tremendous ideological and symbolic importance, and has become a front-line political issue.

CONCLUSION

In this chapter, I have tried to demonstrate that one cannot easily generalize about the role of Yemeni women, either by bemoaning oppression or by apologizing for 'chivalry'. Traditional roles varied according to family status, and women's status in the home and in society is nowadays affected by class. One irony that emerges from studying gender relations in Yemen is that the relative autonomy, participation, and self-reliance valued by Western feminists attaches to economic necessity and low prestige in the South Arabian context, where (non-professional) working women tend to envy housewives. Conversely, greater leisure for housewives is accompanied by a reduced economic role and eroding sense of feminine solidarity. Only at a high level of comfort and education do women begin to consider 'careers'. The larger point I have tried to make is that while cultural artefacts like the veil loom large in the eyes of foreigners, within a cultural setting economic and material conditions on the one hand and national and international political circumstances on the other mould gender relations in ways that have direct impact on women's lives. *Sayyid*, tribal, and partisan interpretations of 'family values' exist and are emphasized politically in time of economic or political crisis. I would argue that it is not Islamic, Arab, or tribal culture *per se* but rather their relationship to the political economy within which they operate that restricts or liberates women. In the same way that Pearson, in this volume, argues that industrialization does not have a uniform impact on women, likewise, I maintain that 'modernization' does not have a unilinear, universal, or automatic impact on gender relations. Women's roles and rights depend rather on more specific features of status, class, and the politics and economics of development.

REFERENCES

ABU LUGHOD, LILA (1990), 'Anthropology's Orient: The Boundaries of Theory on the Arab World', in Hisham Sharabi (ed.), *Theory, Politics, and the Arab World: Critical Responses* (New York: Routledge).

AL-NOBAN, SAEED ABDUL KHAIR (1984), 'Education for Nation-Building: The Experience of the People's Democratic Republic of Yemen', in B. R. Pridham (ed.), *Contemporary Yemen: Politics and Historical Background* (London: Croom Helm).

BUJRA, ABDALLA S. (1971), *The Politics of Stratification: A Study of Political Change in a South Arabian Town* (Oxford: Oxford University Press).

CARAPICO, SHEILA and TUTWILER, RICHARD (1981), *Yemeni Agriculture and Economic Change: Case Studies of Two Highland Regions*, Development Series Number 1 (Milwaukee: American Institute for Yemeni Studies).

CATON, STEVEN C. (1986), 'Salam Tahiya: Greetings from the Highlands of Yemen', *American Ethnologist*, 13/2: 290–308.

—— (1990), 'Anthropological Theories of Tribe and State Formation in the Middle East: Ideology and the Semiotics of Power', in P. Khoury and J. Kostiner (eds.), *Tribes and State Formation in the Middle East* (Berkeley: University of California Press).

Central Planning Organization (CPO) (1983), *Statistical Year Book 1982* (Sana'a: Prime Minister's Office).

—— (1988), *Statistical Year Book 1987* (Sana'a: Prime Minister's Office).

DORSKY, SUSAN (1986), *Women of 'Amran: A Middle Eastern Ethnographic Study* (Salt Lake City: University of Utah Press).

DRESCH, PAUL (1977), 'Imams and Tribes: The Writing and Acting of History in Upper Yemen', in P. Khoury and J. Kostiner (eds.), *Tribes and State Formation* (Berkeley: University of California Press).

EL DUAIS, NAGAT N. (1991), 'Yemeni Women in Public Life', *Yemen Times*, 10 April, p. 9.

GERHOLM, TOMAS (1977), *Market, Mosque, and Mufraj* (Stockholm: University of Stockholm).

KHALIDI, RAMLA and TUCKER, JUDITH (n.d.), *Women's Rights in the Arab World* (Washington, DC: Special Middle East Research and Information Project (MERIP) publication).

LACKNER, HELEN (1985), *P.D.R. Yemen: Outpost of Socialist Development in Arabia* (London: Ithaca Press).

MESSICK, BRINKLEY (1978), 'Transactions in Ibb: Society and Economy in a Yemeni Highlands Town', unpublished Ph.D. thesis, Princeton University, Princeton, NJ.

MOGHADAM, VALENTINE M. (1992), *Development and Patriarchy: The Middle East and North Africa in Economic and Demographic Transition*, WIDER Working Paper No. 99 (Helsinki: UNU/WIDER).

—— (1993), *Modernizing Women: Gender and Social Change in the Middle East* (Boulder, Colo.: Lynne Rienner Publishers).

MOLYNEUX, MAXINE (1985), 'Legal Reform and Socialist Revolution in Democratic Yemen: Women and the Family', *International Journal of the Sociology of Law*, 13: 147–72.

MUNDY, MARTHA (1979), 'Women's Inheritance of Land in Highland Yemen', *Arabian Studies*, 5: 161–87.

MYNTTI, CYNTHIA (1979), *Women and Development in Yemen Arab Republic* (Eschborn: GTZ).

—— (1985), 'Women, Work, Population, and Development in the Yemen Arab Republic', in J. Abu Nasr, N. Khoury, and H. Azzam (eds.), *Women, Employment, and Development in the Arab World* (The Hague: Mouton/ILO).

STEFFEN, H., *et al.* (1978), *Yemen Arab Republic Final Report of the Airphoto Interpretations Project of the Swiss Technical Co-operation Service, Berne* (Zürich: April, for the CPO, San'a, II).

TUTWILER, RICHARD (1987), 'Tribe, Tribute, and Trade: Social Class Formation in Highland Yemen', unpublished Ph.D. thesis, State University of New York at Binghamton, New York.

WEIR, SHELAGH (1985), *Qat in Yemen; Consumption of Social Change* (London: British Museum Publications).

World Bank (1989), *World Development Report 1989* (Washington: Oxford University Press).

Yemen Times (1991), 'Yemeni Career Women Carry a Double Burden: at Home and at Work', Interview with Amat Al-Aleem Sousuwah, Assistant Deputy Minister of Information, 10 April, p. 12.

Development, Patriarchy, and Politics: Indian Women in the Political Process, 1947–1992

Leela Kasturi

INTRODUCTION

In India, as elsewhere, women's development has to be related to national development. This is no mean task, as the problems of women are not uniform. There are marked differences by rural and urban residences, occupational and gender role diversities across caste, class, and community. Further, there are five separate systems of personal law for the five major religious communities—Hindu, Muslim, Christian, Parsee and Jew—apart from innumerable and diverse customary laws that continue to be practised by smaller ethnic or regional groups or tribes. Finally, state policies affect various categories of women differentially, while gender-blind development plans evade the major issue of women's economic and political participation as equal partners, decision-makers, and agents of national development (*National Perspective Plan*, 1988).

In this chapter, I propose to give an overview of various aspects of women's status by relating it to succeeding waves of the women's movement with the help of three seminal documents which span a period of over fifty years (1940–92) and perhaps four generations of women. Set in three historical periods—pre-independence, post-independence, and post-1975, the documents roughly chart women's progress and/or regression over time, and articulate the hopes and demands of women. The first of these is the *Report of the Sub-Committee on 'Woman's Role in Planned Economy'* (1947); the second is the *Report of the Committee on the Status of Women in India* (Government of India, 1974), and the third is the *National Perspective Plan for Women, A Perspective from the Women's Movement* (1988).

The content of the three reports reflects the way the women's movement or women leaders tried to articulate the issues and analyse contemporary conditions in relation to women. They could see that change was not uniform and that in all spheres women were unequal. The documents prove that Indian women were not willing to be passive spectators or victims of the process of transformation but intended to be active participants in directions of their own choice. Challenging the patriarchal social order was a central goal. The shifts in emphasis and priorities demonstrated through these three documents indicate the evolution of a political understanding of the process of development and a recognition that the development process has actually strengthened patriarchal structures in India.

Before examining the documents, a discussion of the unevenness of Indian development is in order.

Uneven socio-economic development

India, as one writer put it, is 'a congeries of micro-regions' (M. N. Srinivas, 1978). There is considerable variation among regions, classes, religions, and ethnic and caste groups. (See Table 1 for an illustration of the social and religious heterogeneity of contemporary India.) Family structure and kinship patterns, social and economic milieux, culture, and social practices vary widely within the country. The rural–urban divide has also to be taken into account as a consistent factor. This great diversity was complicated further by the changes wrought by colonial rule. Traditional and modern values have been perennially in conflict since then and many ambiguities have resulted. The absence of social, cultural and economic homogeneity makes it difficult to generalize about Indian women in the crucible of change and images of Indian women are paradoxical and contradictory. For instance, in one context, a subordinate status can coexist with advanced education. In another, a free status coexists with illiteracy and low caste. But an impression has gained ground that Indian women are developing fast in various spheres. The fact is that the vast mass of Indian women has still to be emancipated. Complex socio-economic processes implicit in development—such as modernization. urbanization, industrialization, commercialization, technological change in the methods of production, and the spread of education—have had a differential impact on Indian women in terms of the diversities indicated above. How far has such socio-economic development helped women's development? Has change been wholesome and egalitarian? This is a question that has been exercising activists and researchers since the publication of *Towards Equality, the Report of the Committee on the Status of Women in India* (CSWI) in 1974.

An investigation on the position of Indian women cannot be done outside the social framework (Government of India, 1974). Indian society is a traditional and hierarchical social structure based on caste, community, and class. It has fostered numerous inequalities which affect both men and women. Caste/class/social group configurations occur with such regularity that the implications of these connections cannot be easily brushed aside. Certain patterns—social as well as economic—correlate positively with class and caste, distinguishing members of one class or caste from others.[1]

[1] Caste and class are, historically, closely interlinked, acquiring special significance in the nineteenth century consequent upon the development of 'stunted capitalism' specific to colonial India. See Bipan Chandra (1979).

Despite recent socio-economic changes which have tended to blur such caste/class identifications, class status can still be often identified with caste status; this is especially true at the lower levels of the caste hierarchy in the rural areas. For instance, members of the Scheduled Castes and Scheduled Tribes[2] are among the poorest sections in rural areas accounting as before for a substantial percentage of agricultural wage workers. On the other hand, several 'middle' castes have been pushed or moved upwards (and play the role of 'vested interests') as a result of changes brought about by land reform, the 'green revolution', or political success. It is also quite common for members of upper castes to have suffered downward mobility as a result of the same or other changes and lost class dominance.

It is interesting to note that some regions/sub-regions of India are clearly better developed than some others. These differences are evident in terms of health, literacy, education, sex ratios, fertility and mortality patterns, employment, social and economic development, the incidence of poverty, economic disparities, and political participation. Four sets of factors are relevant to an analysis of regional differences: (*a*) pre-existing levels of development; (*b*) agro-ecological endowment in terms of climate, soils, natural resources, topography, farming systems, crop choices, traditional economic practices, and so forth; (*c*) development strategies and priorities pursued by individual states as well as the central government; and (*d*) socio-cultural norms and practices and religious beliefs. While regional imbalances in development may be directly traced to a greater or lesser extent to the first three sets of factors, the last-named is particularly crucial in determining the relative strength of the ideology of gender not only among the population in a given region but in government policies and programmes at state level as well. Gender bias in the community and in state policies have had negative consequences for women and, indirectly, as studies have shown, for the level of development in individual regions or states. Judged by the measures of economic development and the high or low incidence of poverty, the better-developed states include the north-western states of Punjab and Haryana. The poorest less-developed states are headed by the states of Bihar, Orissa, Uttar Pradesh, and Madhya Pradesh.

The processes of development have been fraught with contradictions;

[2] Under Articles 341 and 342 of the Indian Constitution, certain castes and tribes, specified by public notification, have been deemed to be Scheduled Castes and Scheduled Tribes. These categories were and still are among the poorest and most backward sections of Indian society. Considered unclean, hence untouchable, and outside the pale of the caste system, the Scheduled Castes were subjected to various types of discrimination ranging from physical avoidance to exclusion from temples. The tribes of India are diverse, spread out, and isolated, their customs and culture different from those of the mainstream. Hindered in their development by socio-economic and cultural factors, these categories receive protection under provisions of the Constitution and special laws which safeguard their civil rights and representation in various spheres, such as education, employment, and elected bodies.

Table 1 Castes and religions of contemporary India[b]

States and Union Territories	Religion (%)—1981							Scheduled caste (%)			Scheduled tribe (%)		
	Hindu	Moslim	Christian	Sikh	Buddhist	Jain	Other	1961	1971	1981	1961	1971	1981
All India	82.6	11.4	2.4	2.0	0.7	0.5	0.4	14.7	14.6	15.7	6.9	6.9	7.8
Andhra Pradesh	88.8	8.5	2.7	neg	neg	neg	neg	13.8	13.3	14.8	3.7	3.8	5.9
Assam	n.a.	n.a.	n.a.	n.a.	n.a.	n.a.	n.a.	6.2	6.1	—[a]	17.4	12.8	—
Bihar	83.0	14.1	1.1	0.1	neg	neg	1.7	14.1	14.1	14.5	9.0	8.7	8.3
Gujarat	89.5	8.5	0.4	0.1	neg	1.4	0.1	6.6	6.8	7.1	13.3	14.0	14.2
Haryana	89.4	4.0	0.1	6.2	neg	0.3	neg	—	18.9	19.0	—	—	—
Himachal Pradesh	95.8	1.6	0.1	1.2	1.2	neg	0.1	27.4	22.2	24.6	8.0	4.1	4.6
Jammu & Kashmir	32.2	64.2	0.2	2.2	1.2	neg	neg	8.0	8.3	8.3	—	—	—
Karnataka	85.9	11.1	2.1	neg	0.1	0.8	neg	13.2	13.1	15.0	0.8	0.8	4.9
Kerala	58.2	21.2	20.6	neg	neg	neg	neg	8.5	8.3	10.0	1.3	1.3	1.0
Madhya Pradesh	93.0	4.8	0.7	0.3	0.1	0.8	0.3	13.1	13.1	14.1	20.6	20.1	23.0
Maharashtra	81.4	9.2	1.3	0.2	6.3	1.5	0.1	5.6	6.0	7.1	6.1	5.9	9.2
Manipur	60.0	7.0	29.7	0.1	neg	0.1	3.1	1.7	1.5	1.2	31.9	31.2	27.3
Meghalaya	18.0	3.1	52.6	0.1	0.2	0.1	25.9	18.1	0.4	0.4	—	80.5	80.6
Nagaland	14.4	1.5	80.2	0.1	0.1	0.1	3.6	—	—	—	93.1	88.6	84.0

Orissa	95.4	1.6	1.8	0.1	neg	neg	1.1	15.7	15.1	14.6	24.1	23.1	22.4
Punjab	36.9	1.0	1.1	60.7	neg	0.2	0.1	20.4	24.7	26.8	0.1	—	—
Rajasthan	89.3	7.3	0.1	1.5	neg	1.8	neg	16.7	15.8	17.0	11.5	12.1	12.2
Sikkim	67.3	1.0	2.2	0.1	28.7	neg	0.7	—	—	5.7	—	—	23.3
Tamil Nadu	88.9	5.2	5.8	neg	neg	0.1	neg	18.0	17.8	18.3	0.7	0.8	1.1
Tripura	89.3	6.8	1.2	neg	2.7	neg	neg	10.5	12.4	15.1	31.5	28.9	28.4
Uttar Pradesh	83.3	15.9	0.2	0.4	0.1	0.1	neg	20.9	21.0	21.1	—	0.2	0.2
West Bengal	77.0	21.5	0.6	0.1	0.3	0.1	0.4	19.7	19.7	21.9	5.9	5.7	5.6
Union Territories													
A & N Islands	64.5	8.6	25.6	0.5	0.1	neg	0.7	—	—	—	22.2	15.7	11.8
Arunachal Pradesh	29.2	0.8	4.3	0.2	13.7	neg	51.8	—	0.1	0.5	88.6	79.0	69.8
Dhandigarh	75.3	2.0	1.0	21.1	0.1	0.4	0.1	—	11.3	0.4	—	—	—
Dadra and Nagar Haveli	95.6	1.9	1.9	neg	0.2	0.3	0.1	1.7	1.8	1.9	88.4	86.9	78.8
Delhi	83.6	7.8	1.0	6.3	0.1	1.2	neg	12.8	15.6	18.0	—	—	—
Goa, Daman & Diu	65.9	4.5	29.3	0.1	neg	0.1	0.1	—	1.9	2.1	—	0.9	1.0
Lakshadweep	4.5	94.8	0.7	—	—	—	neg	—	—	—	97.0	92.9	93.8
Mizoram	7.1	0.5	83.8	0.1	8.2	neg	0.3	—	—	0.3	—	94.3	93.5
Pondicherry	85.6	6.1	8.3	neg	neg	0.1	neg	15.4	15.5	15.9	—	—	—

[a] In 1981, the Census was not conducted in Assam. [b] Based on state and union territory division in 1981.
Source: Census of India, 1981.

benefits have accrued alongside inequalities, and beneficiaries have often been the haves rather than the have-nots, defeating in some settings the aims of development. The effects of development have thus been variable not only by region but by class within regions, and within classes, by gender. Class- and gender-specific consequences (of development) for women are visible at both ends of the spectrum. Middle- and upper-class women are the obvious beneficiaries whereas proletarian women have been the worst affected. To take only one dimension: work—while educated middle-class women have been increasingly entering the modern sector of employment as professionals, encouraged by an expanding structure of opportunities, illiterate, poor rural women lost their traditional economic opportunities and with it the traditional status conferred on them by economic participation. The material situation of the latter has been further worsened by the entire gamut of discrimination resulting in lower wages, unequal access to technology, information, credit, training, resources, and the double burden of work, and so forth. State policies have aggravated poor women's marginalization and exploitation in the economic sphere. The majority (94 per cent) of the female workforce is dependent on the informal sector.[3]

Tables 2–5 and Figure 1 present descriptive data on infant mortality, child school enrollment, literacy, age-specific economic activity (including child labour), and the sex ratio by region. Although there are variations across regions—and of course within regions, variations by caste and class—one striking constant is the impressive results attained by Kerala. On all counts, the state of Kerala does better than any of the other regions. For example, Figure 1, on rates of infant mortality throughout India, shows that Kerala has the lowest rate; at 27 per 1,000 live births, this figure is considerably below the national average. Similarly, Kerala boasts the highest primary school enrollments (see Table 2), and the highest literacy rates (see Table 3). Child labour, which is extensive in India, is lowest in Kerala. As can be seen in Table 4, labour-force participation rates for girls aged 10–14 range from highs of 59 per cent in Dadra and Nagar Haveli and 35–6 per cent in Rajasthan and Andhra Pradesh to lows of about 2 per cent in Kerala, Assam, Manipur, Punjab, Tripura, and Andaman. Likewise, India suffers from an adverse sex ratio, a result of high rates of maternal mortality and preferential treatment of boy babies, the latter leading to higher than normal mortality of baby girls. Once again, Kerala departs from this pattern, and is the only state with a sex ratio favourable to women (see Table 5).

[3] See National Commission on Self-employed Women and Women in the Informal Sector, *Shram Shakti* (1988) for a detailed account of the working lives of women in the poorest groups. For an excellent documentation of the implications of development for Indian women (for the period 1947–74), refer to Government of India (1974). For the post-1975 period, see among other studies, Desai and Krishnaraj (1987), and Desai and Patel (1985).

Table 2 Proportion of six-year-old children attending school: 1981

State	Male	Female	All
Rural:			
Uttar Pradesh	20.70	10.05	15.67
Bihar	22.98	11.85	17.53
Maharashtra	41.24	31.12	36.25
West Bangal*	26.97	21.08	24.06
Andhra Pradesh*	37.25	25.40	31.47
Madhya Pradesh*	25.67	12.83	19.34
Tamil Nadu	58.61	49.72	54.31
Karnataka	32.18	23.33	27.83
Rajasthan*	23.94	07.92	16.34
Gujarat	33.35	23.98	28.80
Orissa*	42.23	29.62	35.99
Kerala	72.84	72.55	72.69
India	31.29	21.19	26.39
Urban:			
Uttar Pradesh	39.53	33.85	36.77
Bihar	49.67	41.15	45.56
Maharashtra	61.70	57.73	59.76
West Bangal*	52.12	47.47	49.88
Andhra Pradesh*	60.82	53.52	57.22
Madhya Pradesh*	51.56	44.49	48.07
Tamil Nadu	69.99	67.01	68.54
Karnataka	52.51	48.33	50.46
Rajasthan*	46.87	37.12	42.13
Gujarat	51.51	46.63	49.16
Orissa*	56.93	49.68	53.36
Kerala	80.64	79.71	80.19
India	55.02	49.65	52.40

* educationally backward states.
Source: Census of India, 1981.

A variety of interlinked historical, ideological, economic, and cultural factors underlie these differences. In general, the northern states are noted for lower female work participation rates, greater discrimination against females, lower female survival rates, higher incidence of dowry, violence against women, and thus a lower status of women. Among the southern states which provide a dramatic contrast, human resource development is best in Kerala, the development of women being central to the difference. This state compares well with developed countries in many respects and stands out among the states of India for this reason.

Kerala has the highest population density of any state (655 per square

Table 3 Number of literates in 1991 and literacy rates for 1991 by sex

India/State/Union Territory	Literate population aged 7 years and above			Percentage of literates to estimated population aged 7 and above		
	Persons	Males	Females	Persons	Males	Females
India	361,713,246	230,150,363	131,562,883	52.11	63.06	39.42
States						
Andhra Pradesh	24,840,456	15,675,060	9,165,396	45.11	56.24	33.71
Arunachal Pradesh	282,147	190,691	91,456	41.22	51.10	29.37
Assam	9,631,529	5,862,115	3,769,414	53.42	62.34	43.70
Bihar	26,854,389	19,176,364	7,678,025	38.54	52.63	23.10
Goa	782,002	440,396	341,606	76.96	85.48	68.20
Gujarat	21,265,395	13,070,534	8,194,861	60.91	72.54	48.50
Haryana	7,431,708	4,872,757	2,558,951	55.33	67.85	40.94
Himachal Pradesh	2,724,609	1,602,266	1,122,343	63.54	74.57	52.46
Jammu & Kashmir	n/a	n/a	n/a	n/a	n/a	n/a
Karnataka	21,074,117	12,868,146	8,205,971	55.98	67.25	44.30
Kerala	22,657,985	11,508,235	11,149,750	90.59	94.45	86.93
Madhya Pradesh	23,491,956	16,101,046	7,390,910	43.45	57.43	28.39
Maharashtra	42,800,914	26,193,454	16,607,460	63.05	74.84	50.51
Manipur	894,923	542,213	352,710	60.96	72.98	48.64

Meghalaya	689,419	377,281	312,138	48.26	51.57	44.78
Mizoram	462,246	250,962	211,284	81.23	84.06	78.09
Nagaland	621,048	360,526	260,522	61.30	66.09	55.72
Orissa	12,911,905	8,392,320	4,519,585	48.55	62.37	34.40
Punjab	9,952,965	5,897,599	4,055,366	57.14	63.68	49.72
Rajasthan	13,618,272	10,143,275	3,474,997	38.81	55.07	20.84
Sikkim	186,779	115,502	71,277	56.53	64.34	47.23
Tamil Nadu	30,383,416	18,066,226	12,317,190	63.72	74.88	52.29
Tripura	1,368,567	821,403	547,164	60.39	70.08	50.01
Uttar Pradesh	46,871,095	33,268,503	13,602,592	41.71	55.35	26.02
West Bengal	32,719,340	20,053,418	12,665,922	57.72	67.42	47.15
Union Territories						
Andaman and Nicobar Islands	170,349	102,839	67,510	73.74	79.68	66.22
Chandigarh	426,009	252,922	173,087	78.73	82.67	73.61
Dadra & Nagar Haveli	45,073	30,582	14,491	39.45	52.07	26.18
Daman & Diu	61,497	35,968	25,529	73.58	85.67	61.38
Delhi	5,949,528	3,570,973	2,378,555	76.09	82.63	68.01
Lakshadweep	33,562	19,046	14,516	79.23	87.06	70.88
Pondichery	509,746	287,441	222,305	74.91	83.91	65.79

Note: n/a stands for not available. The 1991 Census has not yet been conducted in Jammu and Kashmir. The figures are as per projections prepared by the Standing Committee of Experts on population projections October 1989.

Table 4 Age-specific work participation rates according to usual (principal) status—NSSO—38th round (1983); by milieu, sex, and age group

State Union Territory	Rural				Urban			
	Males		Females		Males		Females	
	5–9	10–14	5–9	10–14	5–9	10–14	5–9	10–14
Andhra Pradesh	5.66	42.45	3.43	36.16	2.07	18.22	0.83	8.90
Assam	0.30	7.97	0.25	2.54	0.12	3.63	0.80	7.46
Bihar	1.79	14.29	1.55	8.93	1.25	9.48	0.32	4.86
Gujarat	1.19	16.35	1.02	16.74	0.15	6.61	0.25	2.23
Haryana	0.44	11.39	0.40	9.59	0.33	10.25	—	4.47
Himachal Pradesh	0.67	9.58	2.13	17.11	—	5.10	—	—
Jammu and Kashmir	1.10	13.58	1.45	7.56	0.57	10.38	0.50	4.20
Karnataka	4.24	35.41	3.37	27.64	0.98	11.29	0.73	9.05
Kerala	—	3.35	0.08	2.25	0.25	3.06	—	0.64
Madhya Pradesh	2.36	28.17	1.34	25.95	0.04	7.21	0.27	4.27
Maharashtra	2.22	22.30	2.12	25.31	0.24	6.17	—	2.01

Manipur	0.24	1.85	0.32	2.28	—	—	0.71	0.65
Meghalaya	1.27	25.24	0.75	16.89	0.59	8.68	—	2.01
Orissa	1.71	25.95	1.39	20.04	0.44	10.05	0.71	5.49
Punjab	2.80	26.84	0.33	2.42	0.60	8.13	—	2.49
Rajasthan	3.33	24.91	7.21	34.45	0.31	7.76	1.95	9.30
Sikkim	—	3.06	—	5.39	—	14.54	2.51	15.17
Tamil Nadu	2.30	26.17	2.40	27.17	0.64	13.08	0.86	8.91
Tripura	0.30	11.64	0.60	1.75	—	3.62	1.44	1.29
Uttar Pradesh	0.80	17.27	0.98	8.81	0.25	11.34	0.49	3.44
West Bengal	0.97	16.25	0.19	4.14	0.26	6.31	0.11	8.31
Andaman and Nicobar Islands	—	7.26	0.25	2.47	—	8.57	—	—
Dadra and Nagar Haveli	8.22	36.67	1.36	59.23	—	—	—	—
Delhi	—	2.13	—	—	0.46	4.28	0.20	1.27
Goa, Daman & Diu	—	2.13	—	—	0.46	4.28	0.20	1.27
Mizoram	—	6.17	—	4.59	—	1.09	—	0.73
Pondicherry	—	16.56	2.74	20.10	—	10.05	—	6.96
India	1.97	21.28	1.78	16.97	0.54	9.31	0.50	5.41

Source: Government of India, Sarvekshana XI (4), issue no. 35; April 1988. Dept. of Statistics, Ministry of Planning, pp. 25–8.

Table 5 Distribution of population and sex ratio

India/State/Union Territory	Population 1991			Sex ratio	
	Persons	Males	Females	1981	1991
India	843,930,861	437,597,929	406,332,932	934	929
States					
Andhra Pradesh	66,304,854	33,623,738	32,681,116	975	972
Arunachal Pradesh	858,392	461,242	397,150	862	861
Assam	22,294,562	11,579,693	10,714,869	910	925
Bihar	86,338,853	45,147,280	41,191,573	946	912
Goa	1,168,622	593,563	575,059	975	969
Gujarat	41,174,060	21,272,388	19,901,672	942	936
Haryana	16,317,715	8,705,379	7,612,336	870	874
Himachal Pradesh	5,111,079	2,560,894	2,550,185	973	996
Jammu and Kashmir	7,718,700	4,014,100	3,704,600	892	923
Karnataka	44,817,398	22,861,409	21,955,989	963	960
Kerala	29,011,237	14,218,167	14,793,070	1,032	1,040
Madhya Pradesh	66,135,862	34,232,048	31,903,814	941	932
Maharashtra	78,706,719	40,652,056	38,054,663	937	936
Manipur	1,826,714	931,511	895,203	971	961

Meghalaya	1,760,626	904,308	856,318	954	947
Mizoram	686,217	356,672	329,545	919	924
Nagaland	1,215,573	643,273	572,300	863	890
Orissa	31,512,070	15,979,904	15,532,166	981	972
Punjab	20,190,795	10,695,136	9,495,659	879	888
Rajasthan	43,880,640	22,935,895	20,944,745	919	913
Sikkim	403,612	214,723	188,889	835	880
Tamil Nadu	55,638,318	28,217,947	27,420,371	977	972
Tripura	2,744,827	1,410,545	1,334,282	946	946
Uttar Pradesh	138,760,417	73,745,994	65,014,423	885	882
West Bengal	67,982,732	35,461,898	32,520,834	911	917
Union Territories					
Andaman and Nicobar Islands	277,989	152,737	125,252	760	
Chandigarh	640,725	357,411	283,314	769	
Dadra and Nagar Haveli	138,542	70,927	67,615	974	
Daman and Diu	101,439	51,452	49,987	1,062	
Delhi	9,370,475	5,120,733	4,249,742	808	
Lakshadweep	51,681	26,582	25,099	975	
Pondicherry	789,416	398,324	391,092	985	

Note: The figures are as per projections prepared by the Standing Committee of Experts on population projections, October 1989.

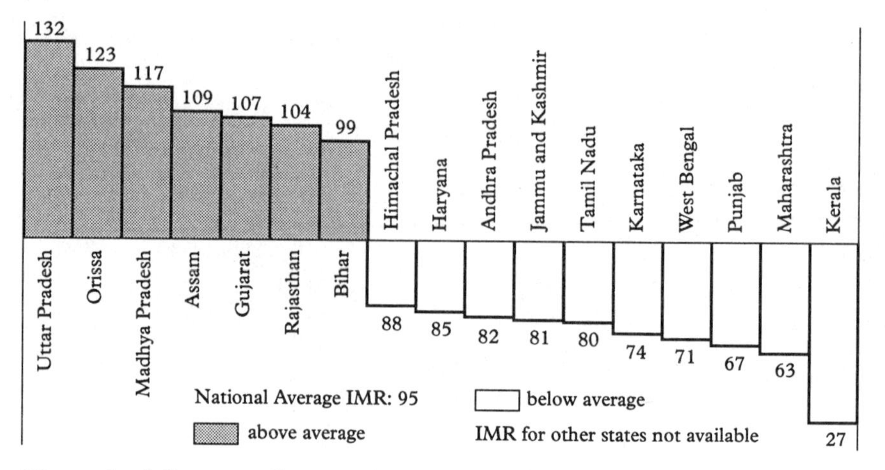

Figure 1 Infant mortality rates by region

Source: Graph based on figures cited in *The Hunger Project/Planning Commission* (1990), mimeo (Madras: M. S. Swaminathan Research Foundation).

kilometre) and despite limited economic development, has the lowest crude death rate.[4] It has lower birth rates, higher levels of contraceptive use, lower infant mortality rates and higher estimates of life expectancy at birth than many other states (Jayasree, 1989: 114–28; Nayar, 1986), and the highest literacy rates in India. The rural areas are less rigidly demarcated from the urban (in fact, the percentage of urban population is lower than the all-India average) in terms of amenities such as water, electricity and roadways,[5] elementary education, and primary health care. Medical and health facilities,[6] particularly in the rural areas, are extensively available as well as utilized. This is reflected in the decline of births, deaths, and morbidity, a pattern that was clear from the beginning of this century (Nag, 1983).

Kerala has a long history of progressive government. Since the early nineteenth century, the royal families of the erstwhile States of Travancore and Cochin (now part of Kerala) paid great attention to the promotion of literacy and education, and public health, a tradition which has been

[4] Since the beginning of this century, the death rate in Kerala has been falling, the decline in the 1970s being particularly sharp. In 1978 it was 7.0% as against 14.2% for India as a whole. Since the 1940s Kerala has had the lowest recorded crude death rate or CDR (annual number of deaths per thousand population), but this does not take into account the age distribution of the population. Differentials in CDR among the States of India reflect more or less differential mortality in all age groups since there is not much difference in their age distribution. For more details, see Nag (1983).

[5] In Kerala, there are more roads in relation to its area than in other states. It is the only state where all villages are connected to all-weather roads (UNFPA, 1992; Nag, 1983).

[6] Kerala has the highest rate of hospital beds to the population (UNFPA, 1992) and Primary Health Centres are widely spread out to serve the rural population throughout Kerala (Nag, 1983).

Table 6 Labour-force participation rates by age: 1987–8

	Age group (in years)					
	5–14	15–29	30–44	45–59	60 +	Total
Urban						
Male	7.4	79.7	98.7	95.7	64.7	61.4
Female	6.3	36.9	47.6	42.2	16.3	29.2
Rural						
Male	4.2	69.7	98.7	93.1	46.6	59.6
Female	2.4	17.2	23.9	22.4	9.3	14.6

Source: National Sample Survey Organization (43rd round), 1987/8.

continued after independence and is reflected in higher public spending in these two areas in Kerala than in other states of India. Female education was promoted from the early nineteenth century onwards through indigenous as well as modern institutions, a policy that has contributed to the existence in Kerala today of the largest number of women teachers, nurses, health workers, legislators, and professionals (Jayasree, 1989: 155). Literacy has clearly contributed to the higher utilization of maternal and child health services with consequences of demographic significance (Nag, 1983). Literacy and education have shown, in general, a direct relationship with political and social awareness. Kerala has the largest circulation of vernacular newspapers in India, assured through a chain of over 5,000 libraries (Jayasree, 1989: 154). An extensive and sustained pace of social change has thus depended on state intervention as well as the power of functional literacy and education.

Widespread poverty and economic mismanagement in India have prevented the expansion of waged and salaried employment for both men and women, but the situation is especially acute for women. There is a marked gender disparity in labour-force participation rates for both rural and urban areas. In 1988, whereas nearly 60 per cent of urban men were economically active, the corresponding figure for women was 14.6 per cent (see Table 6). Notwithstanding the advantages that have accrued to a segment of middle-class women, Indian feminists have been very critical of the development process for its marginalization of women and for the exploitative conditions suffered by labour, including child and female labour.

Patriarchy

Women's status is affected by relations in the family, class status, and the ideology of the social group to which they belong. It is inherited through historical institutions and culture. The social relations of gender as well as class relations are part of a historical inheritance. Among the ideologies underlying our inheritance is that of patriarchy. This is a term in which inequality and hierarchy are implicit and is a concept and institution which is discussed in sociological and feminist literature in a variety of ways, as Sylvia Walby shows in her chapter in this volume. Literally 'power of the father' and indicating male supremacy, it is understood variously as 'a symbolic male principle' governing social and gender relations, an institutional structure of male domination, or an ideology based on the power of men. Zillah Eisenstein (1979) suggests that patriarchy provides the sexual hierarchical ordering of society for political control. It is a feature of a large number of societies predating capitalism; a separate phenomenon and independent dynamic observed in connection with social relations between men and women as well as the organization and control of production (Rowbotham, 1981). Thus it is a useful analytical tool with which to investigate both class and gender relations.

Operating in some or all of these senses, patriarchy as an ideology is deeply embedded in several societies, cultures, and institutions as well as in the minds of men and women. From experience and a variety of studies we are able to conclude that women over whom such power and authority is exercised are socialized suitably to 'fit in'. Prejudices coloured by patriarchy are inherent in many traditions. Where tradition rules, institutions, cultures, social mechanisms, norms, and practices tend to become resistant to change and hinder women's development.

Despite being ruled by such traditions, Indian history offers innumerable examples of protests against such submission and domination. Protest, struggle, and the urge for equality are as old as constricting structures such as caste, hierarchy, patriarchy and inequality of power, wealth and knowledge. Subaltern groups have always tried to be upwardly mobile.[7] This too is part of the Indian heritage. Although research on women's role in such protests is only of recent origin, it is known that women were not only involved in protests in large numbers but were leaders as well. They challenged existing patriarchal structures and systems, becoming poets, saints, rebels, and drop-outs.

'Patriarchy' is pervasive in India but varies in degree depending on region, community, class, caste, and religious or social group. Therefore, in this regard it would not be possible to generalize. Researchers are aware that within the broader universe of Indian women, women must be studied in specific contexts, whatever the historical period.

Broadly speaking, three classes of women emerge: the economically secure at one end of the spectrum, and at the other, women below the

[7] The term 'subaltern' implies the general attribute of subordination in south Asian society whether this is expressed in terms of class, caste, age, gender, and office or any other way. See Guha (1982).

subsistence or poverty level (which is relative), and in between, women who shift continuously between subsistence (that is, minimum economic security) and starvation (Government of India, 1974: 5). The latter two classes of women are more likely to be of a lower caste than others. There may be a cultural divorce between the élites and the masses but women as a category are objects of patriarchal control. Therefore, it may be safe to assume that male strength, authority, and power contribute to the oppression of women of all three classes. Such values are visible in all the indicators of women's status: health, education, political status, economic participation, law and its implementation. Women face these values in their day-to-day life in all areas of living, for such attitudes are widely held mainly by men, whether they are leaders, members of families, or others, in agencies of the state. In sum, Indian women live within patriarchal frameworks.

Politics

There are several definitions of politics, but common to all is the view that it is inevitable in any society. In plural societies, where interests are diverse, tensions are likely to be greater. Theorists have long held that politics is about representation, policy, position and power, with government as the arena of politics. Political activity is any activity which aims at bringing government to bear in a particular direction to secure particular results (Miller, 1962: 14–16, 254–87). The definition of politics has, however, in the recent past widened considerably from merely denoting the area of formal government in its widest sense, including all processes directly or indirectly associated with it and in which in a democracy every citizen has a share (Nettl, 1967: 29–30).

The concept of politics in terms of spheres, objectives, and activities has evolved much further than this. Political theorists have accepted now that movements, protests, and struggles are legitimate expressions of political behaviour and 'argue for theories that use availability of resources and opportunity structures to explain why, when and how people protest and make claims' (West and Blumberg, 1990: 5). The political sphere thus includes the 'spheres in social relations where power relations are generated, institutionalized and used to encourage, control or move people's behaviour, attitudes, beliefs in a specified direction—to control and regulate the distribution of resources'. It should be noted that this broader definition of the political sphere and political action was drawn up by a group of women scholars and activists who participated in a UNESCO seminar on the 'Participation of Women in Political Life' held at Lisbon in 1983. Two years later, this definition was endorsed by a non-aligned Ministerial Level Conference on 'Role of Women in Development' (New Delhi, 1985). Political issues now include every kind of issue, including those of everyday life, of survival itself. Collective actions of ordinary people on such issues symbolize the challenge that the powerless throw to the powerful. Cross-culturally and across classes women have participated in open confrontations and collective actions which are now accepted both definitionally and on the ground as established ways of doing political business.

The shape and direction of development, its priorities, allocation of resources, and targets are determined in the political sphere and by political processes. More narrowly, it is the government which decides these; but more broadly speaking political processes are initiated by disagreement with state policy in the wider society as a result of which state policy is ultimately either modified, cancelled, or replaced. Political struggle is not only for power but for change. Development planning is thus a political process where objectives, resource allocation, and implementing strategies call for a firm ideological perspective, and opportunities for the participation of the people from planning to implementation (*National Perspective Plan for Women*, 1988).

In modern India, the political participation of women took place at several levels. Not so well documented are women's struggles in rural areas on survival issues, where anti-imperialism was often mixed with anti-landlord feeling. Better documented are women's entry into the struggle for freedom and the activities of women's organizations working for women's uplift and development. The quality and extent of women's role in the national movement drew praise and admiration from the nationalist leaders. The work of educated élite women leaders of the first women's movement was equally important, although it did not involve itself deeply with the mass of rural women or reflect on issues relevant to them. Participating in both the national and women's movements élite women campaigned for legislative action in the areas of education, political rights, marriage, and property. To their credit it must be said that they highlighted the socio-economic phenomena which hampered the progress of Indian women while occupying themselves with welfare activities. Some of them never gave up campaigning for equal rights as opposed to women's uplift.

Women's search for equality was given an impetus by the historic decision of the Indian National Congress at its Karachi session in 1931 to adopt a Resolution on Fundamental Rights by which the nationalist leadership committed itself to the principle of equality for all citizens irrespective of caste, creed, or sex. Gandhi was emphatic that the reconstruction and development of the Indian nation would not be possible without the full participation of women as equal partners.

India's Constitution which came into force in 1950 incorporated this Resolution twenty-five years before the World Conference in Mexico, and twenty-nine years before the UN General Assembly's Declaration on the Elimination of All Forms of Discrimination against Women in 1979.

Five significant features of the new political system were:

1. universal adult franchise;
2. legal equality of all citizens;
3. certain fundamental right and freedoms such as freedom of speech, protection of life and personal liberty;
4. prohibition of discrimination on grounds of sex, caste, or creed;
5. special protective measures for sections of the population traditionally marginalized in Indian history.

The last named provision was designed to assist 'weaker sections of society' to transcend their traditional inequality through a system of reservations and special supports in education, employment, and political representation. The women's movement rejected the proposal for similar support for women and demanded complete equality. However, Article 15 (3) empowers the state to 'introduce special measures for the protection of women and children irrespective of its obligation not to discriminate on grounds of sex'. Thus the Constitution provided positive as well as negative rights (Basu, 1955).

The values embodied in the Constitution are present in the Directive Principles of State Policy, the Preamble, and its various provisions, all of which reflect the high ideals of a liberal democratic polity. They function as a guide to social transformation and embody the objectives of a social, economic, and political revolution. Further, they seek to confer upon Indian women an equal position and status in society. Finally, the Constitution assigns primacy to law as an instrument of directed social change. It demands of the government continuous vigilance and responsiveness to the relationship between law and social transformation in contemporary India (Government of India, 1974).

The government undertook the massive task of nation building and planned to eliminate poverty and the several forms of social inequality and to raise the standards of living of the masses. This was how we embarked on national development taking into account the wide disparities between different sections of people including women.

REPORT OF THE SUB-COMMITTEE ON 'WOMAN'S ROLE IN PLANNED ECONOMY'

One of the important documents which has turned out to be a little-noted landmark in the evolution of the perspectives of the Indian women's movement is the *Report of the Sub-Committee on 'Woman's Role in Planned Economy'*. The Sub-Committee was appointed in 1939, many years before independence. As Chairman of the National Planning Committee (NPC), Jawaharlal Nehru appointed several sub-committees—as many as twenty-nine—to report on various aspects of 'national life and work' and to make recommendations in accordance with a predetermined plan. One of these dealt with the place of women in the planned economy of a free India. This report was reviewed by the National Planning Committee and some resolutions were passed on the basis of the Sub-Committee's recommendations (Report of the Sub-Committee, 1947: 225–31).

The terms of reference of the Sub-Committee were comprehensive. The Sub-Committee was to consider the social, economic, and legal status of Indian women and, in particular, was to concern itself with family life and organization and women's employment in the house; marriage and succession, and the laws governing these; the conditions of employment of women in various sectors; social customs and institutions which hindered women's development, and appropriate types and methods of education which would enable women to play their due roles in the household, professions, and national services (1947: 27).

Woman, according to the Sub-Committee, 'still labours under disabilities which must be removed before she can take her proper share in the social life of the community. She has special problems and duties which require adjustment in the social scheme.' Even more than man, 'she is a guardian and trustee of future generations . . . it is essential that woman should have her proper place in the scheme of things, and that she should be considered as an individual and . . . have the same rights as man. If freedom and equality are the bases of human development, woman must share in them . . . It follows, therefore, as a natural corollary that woman should be recognized as an equal unit in the social order with man, and that she should gain the same political rights, civic and legal status, social equality, and economic independence' (1947: 28–9). But a lot remained to be achieved in terms of freedom. This would mean an entire reorganization of life. 'Woman cannot be free until the means and training for economic liberty have been assured to her, and until the functions which nature and society impose on her are organized in such a way that while fulfilling them woman still retains the right to mould her social and economic life in any way she chooses' (1947: 30).

The work of the Sub-Committee was hampered by scarcity or unevenness of information. Questionnaires, quite stunningly comprehensive, were issued widely and the replies and reports analysed. These form the basis of the text of the Report. The Sub-Committee could not 'build a structure of any firmness on the foundations supplied to [it] in the shape of data' (1947: 32), but laid down the main principles on which a structure could be built. The Report may therefore be regarded as a framework of principles—a sort of work plan. The Sub-Committee stressed the importance of social and economic planning in an era of change. Special care would be required in the period of transition when moving from existing conditions to a future based on recommendations which at first glance might appear to be drastic.

The Sub-Committee did not seek to belittle traditions 'which have in the past, contributed to the happiness and progress of the individual . . . We do not wish to turn woman into a cheap imitation of man or to render her useless for the great tasks of motherhood and nation-building. But in demanding equal status and equal opportunity, we desire to achieve for woman the possibility of development under favourable circumstances of education and opportunity, and while so doing, urge upon the State its responsibility towards women in this respect' (1947: 32–3).

The Sub-Committee fully endorsed the 1931 Fundamental Rights Resolution of the Congress. In the light of this resolution, one of the first demands made by the Sub-Committee was adult franchise. Woman had not been granted the right to vote as an individual but had been given only a limited right to vote as a wife. Additional qualifications were education and ownership of property (1947: 37). No impediments should be placed in the way of women holding public office or employment, which might in effect prevent women from taking their full and equal share in civic duties and obligations. They should be eligible in the same way as men and on the same conditions in all branches of public service. The right to work, free from social prejudice, was not articulated but implied in demands for equality of access to the public services. Women were debarred from several Class I services under the Act of 1935.[8] For example, in the Post and Telegraphs Department women were employed only as 'telephone girls' (1947: 50–1).

Another important right demanded was that every India-born national should be regarded as an Indian citizen and that every Indian woman should have the right to choose her own nationality in the event of marrying a non-national (1947: 43).

Among the rights discussed under 'civic rights' are women's right to an identical moral standard as men, the right to health, leisure, and recreation. For the first time, the drudgery of the housewife was openly acknowledged. The demands for health, leisure, and recreation for women emphasize two things: the hard work a woman puts in as mother, wife, and home-maker, and the right of a woman to recover her energies and to have something left over for herself as an individual. The concept that housewives are also working women is clear throughout the Report. There should be cessation of all work during the day at a fixed hour so that the housewife is released from duties in the kitchen. This may not be a practical possibility but the suggestion implies the need to allow the housewife some time for herself, and thereby to establish her identity as an individual. Co-operative services could relieve her burden by providing meals

[8] This term refers to the group of government services at the top of the hierarchy of services. Class I services are characterized by greater power, prestige, remuneration, and scale of benefits. Recruitment is made through open competitive examinations to draw young people of merit and ability into the bureaucracy to become decision-makers in due course.

and doing the laundry. Local bodies should provide opportunities for recreation. The need for crèches is repeatedly articulated. They should be available to all women. There is an emphasis throughout on local bodies for action, as the need is greatest at that level (1947: 38–43).

Thus the Report of the Sub-Committee established that all women work regardless of class, and the meaning of work was extended to include housework. In homes where men and women work, they should not only share expenses but domestic responsibilities as well. Men of every class should learn housework and 'domestic science'. The Sub-Committee was far in advance of the times when it stated that housework receives no recognition from state or society as having an economic value and that it should not be considered in any way inferior to other types of work done outside the home. Woman's function as home-maker and her labour are indirect contributions to family income. However, her economic dependence on man has reduced her to the position of a slave. This social degradation has brought into contempt the work of the woman in the home. Unless the homeworker/maker is considered as much a productive worker as the one who is engaged in work outside, it will be difficult to raise the dignity of labour in the home (1947: 104–5).

The Report discussed the lives and inequalities of working-class women at length in a chapter on Economic Rights. The problems of the mass of women were distinguished from those of middle-class women for whom employment for wages carried a certain stigma. There were very few educated women in employment; if they were employed it was while waiting for marriage and motherhood, which were their ultimate goals. Wage earning was abandoned after marriage despite grave financial circumstances, social attitudes being what they were (1947: 51–2).

On the other hand, the majority of Indian women were 'instruments of labour' who had to seek work to feed their families. One third of all workers were women. They worked on land, in cottages and factories, in retail trade and family units, and as indentured and forced labour, for meagre returns. In addition, they had to shoulder a double burden: child care and domestic tasks awaited them after working outside. Working-class women's problems were too numerous:

1. They had difficulty reconciling economic activity with their domestic roles.

2. At work they faced endless problems—gender bias ruled their work lives in every sector. Wage differentials existed obviously because of the low status given to women's place in the economic life of the nation. As illiterate, unskilled unorganized abundant labour, women were paid low wages. What worsened the situation was the theory (*a*) that women's labour is not equal to men's; (*b*) that woman is a supplementary worker with no dependents and is supported by the family. Women's work is not

recognized, said the Report, as separate and essential, particularly in agriculture, family production, and even in the management of the household.

3. Further, women were victimized by both employers and the state's 'protective actions'. Women were thrown out of work in the interests of rationalization. Certain occupations and industries were banned to them; special legislation to protect them, such as maternity benefit acts, resulted in employers' refusal to employ women, especially married women. Trade Unionists colluded with management against women workers in the interests of male workers. The government itself was guilty in this respect by not selecting married women in its various departments (1947: 52–5).

While demanding equal wages for equal work the Sub-Committee was clear that this right should be enforced without endangering employment opportunities for women. The right to work would be meaningless without equal opportunities. Further, training facilities, security, and protection from exploitation through control and regulation of general conditions of work (wages, working hours, membership in trade union), child care, medical and health care, would have to be provided.

Women's right to work was affected not only by low work opportunities but by social attitudes in all classes. Baldly put, gender bias, assumptions of woman's place in society, and failure to assess woman's economic value resulted in a range of effects. Middle-class women could not enter all spheres of economic activity. Retail trade, and the theatre, for instance, were considered off limits regardless of the necessity to work and earn a livelihood. Working-class women suffered the prejudices of employers particularly if married, and the non-recognition of the value of their work denied them fair and equal wages.

It was quite clear to the Sub-Committee that

1. women of all classes have to work out of economic necessity;
2. social attitudes at all levels (the state, employers, family members) operate against women of different classes in different ways;
3. women's labour is not valued at all or sufficiently, inside or outside the home;
4. as a consequence, the work women do is not socially valued and therefore neither recognized nor remunerated;
5. working women have great difficulty in balancing work outside with housework;
6. there is a dire need for state action to help women in all these respects in order to further gender equality and bring justice to women.

The issue of women's economic dependence exercised the Sub-Committee throughout their analysis of women's economic rights. Economic independence has to be seen as very distinct from equal access to employment, which still remains the current slogan in much of the WID literature.

Women are dependent on men for all the reasons stated above. Disparity in wages, unpaid labour performed by women as housewives, in family production, and in manual work as helpers and team-mates, absence of any right for women to the collective income of the family, the belief that marital status cancels out the right to receive equal wages, lack of control over their earnings reinforce women's economic dependence and subordinate status.

One of the objectives of a planned economy is that women must be made economically independent. To achieve this end, one of the important recommendations made by the Sub-Committee was that women should be made co-sharers in the collective income of the family (1947: 61). The economic value of women's work at home and in family production must be recognized. As this is difficult to measure in terms of wages, women should have absolute control over some part of the family income, have a share in the husband's property which he cannot will away, and the husband should contribute to any appropriate state social insurance scheme on his wife's behalf (1947: 105).

Equal wages should be given to women; equal work opportunities must increase; child care should be provided, and it should be possible for married women to earn an independent income, without facing social prejudice and familial control. Economic independence rests on a woman's absolute control over the money she earns. Unfortunately, even educated women in the middle class regard their salary as part of the family income (1947: 62–3).

Women's prospects for economic independence would be improved if they could claim equal rights to property as well. Property rights of women varied under different personal laws; such rights are not absolutely denied but are limited. Under Muslim and Parsee laws women have better rights than under Hindu law: inequality flows from the diversity of laws and the differences in custom and practice in different sections of the same community. This has resulted in the lowering of women's status in the eyes of law and society. Equality exists only under the Indian Succession Act.

As early as in 1939 the Sub-Committee was once again most far-seeing. It said: 'no national plan can entertain such communal diversities which result in inequalities among men and women governed by the same state . . . We therefore recommend that a common civil code for the whole country based on the fundamental principle of equality between man and man and between man and woman be evolved incorporating the best points of the personal laws' (1947: 118).

In the opinion of the Sub-Committee a common civil code should be evolved in India on the pattern of a common criminal code. It should cover inheritance and succession, divorce and marriage. The recommendations of the Committee were aimed at giving Hindu women—wives and daughters—a larger share than granted by traditional laws. Daughters should be entitled to the same rights pertaining to maintenance, education, marriage, succession or inheritance, and the acquisition of property as sons. This recommendation was a seminal departure from tradition. Vigorous propaganda should be carried on to educate Muslim women of their existing rights, and glaring defects in other laws should be remedied (1947: 216–18).

Another really admirable concept introduced by the Sub-Committee was that of matrimonial property, although not defined as such. The Sub-Committee stated: 'The income or acquisition from any sources whatever, made or acquired during coverture will be owned by the husband and wife jointly.' On the death of a spouse 'half of the property jointly acquired with the help of the income during coverture should devolve on the surviving husband or wife and their children'. The division of the joint property in the event of divorce should be left to the discretion of the court (1947: 125).

These recommendations and the ideas relating to women's share in the collective income of the family together comprise the concept of matrimonial property which was alien until then, not to be found in tradition.

The Sub-Committee even considered the rights of children and made several modern pronouncements. The child is an individual who has rights and needs help and protection from the state (1947: 43–4). Child labour particularly in the unorganized sector was recognized as an evil and described by the Sub-Committee. Among its recommendations were compulsory universal education up to the age of fourteen and a legal prohibition of such labour (1947: 81–3, 149).

Legislative action

The importance of legislative action by the state was undeniable. Only law could guarantee and ensure essential measures for women's equality and development. It was quite clear that social, political, and economic rights of women needed to be written into state-sponsored legislation backed by state power. The role of the state was clear in several situations.

1. The state must uphold the rights of children. Child labour should be prohibited by law. Children, especially girls, are liable to various kinds of exploitation and require special protection. Parents and guardians bind children to lifelong commitments through child marriage, dedication to temples, sale into prostitution, etc. Children should be given a choice on reaching the age of maturity to repudiate such commitments and pledges (1947: 44).

2. *The need for crèches was reiterated throughout the Report:* Whole-time creches should be provided where *all* mothers needing leisure, rest, tension-free convalescence, or child-care arrangements during working hours could

leave their young children. This Sub-Committee realized the needs of mothers other than those working outside the home. Crèches are normally associated only with the latter. This is an extraordinary acknowledgement of all women's need to be free of child care for reasons of personal development and the recovery of their health. The State must provide for the maintenance of crèches and nursery schools under a system of social insurance, suggested the Sub-Committee (1947: 42–3).

3. To ensure the economic rights of women and the provision of support services to enable women to work for a living out of financial necessity, the state must legislate on several issues including crèches, equal wages for equal work, prohibition of dangerous work in terms of health and safety (night work need not be totally abolished except for pregnant/nursing mothers and girls under eighteen), medical care, better working conditions (reasonable working hours, leave, sickness insurance, maternity benefits, welfare, union membership), and training for the work she is required to do, whether it is factory work, agriculture, or home-based production.

The issue of reservation occurs even in relation to women's employment. Should any occupation be either legally prohibited or set apart for women to protect their social and economic rights? The Sub-Committee believed that it would be undesirable to advocate reservation. It may be noted here that the Sub-Committee was against reservation in principle even in the electoral process. It endorsed the views of three women's organizations who raised a hue and cry against such reservations on the ground that women could contest on equal terms with men. This belief was justified when women were elected from general constituencies (1947: 37). 'Women's demand is for equal rights and opportunities: the question of preferential treatment cannot arise' (1947: 50).

The Sub-Committee did not overlook the fact that social legislation has its dark side, that good intentions could backfire, that the letter could defeat the spirit of the law. The equal right to work and the right to equal opportunity underlay various measures which have had the effect of decreasing women's employment. Employers would rather not employ women than go to the trouble and expense of providing them benefits or of clashing with the state over this issue (state legislation had been mostly preoccupied with maternity benefits for women workers in the 1930s). Therefore, women were dismissed or discriminated against in employment, and marriage automatically disqualified women. Social legislation for the benefit of women would not act against women's interests in the long run if such legislation thoughtfully went hand in hand with measures to ensure absorption into other new sectors of employment. For instance, no occupation should be prohibited unless an alternative scheme of employment is provided *by law* for those thrown out of work as a result of such prohibition (1947: 54).

Summary and assessment

The Report of the Sub-Committee may be summed up as the first attempt to assess the status of Indian women and to define the parameters of their development. Although the analysis was not that of a group of professional sociologists or economists, as committed intelligent women they based their conclusions on their knowledge of society and the data they received. Some aspects of women's lives were emphasized and some not, but most of the issues were outlined. We see that they were not against tradition or in favour of modernization, but they were certainly in favour of women's development as individuals.

They attempted a class analysis and divided women into the middle class and the mass of poor women who had to work outside their homes for wages. However, they did not belittle the work of the middle-class woman—the housewife. They knew more about women in industry than women on land and less about the landless. But they could clearly see that all of them were economically dependent and badly off despite their hard labour and toiling lives. Economic independence for women, they averred, should be one of the objectives of a planned economy. They also realized the importance of legal rights in the pursuit of women's equality and asked for a uniform civil code which even now finds few supporters among men. They recommended that working women's conditions should vastly improve, demanded crèches for the benefit of both mothers and children, and emphasized the rights of children in many contexts, from child labour and child marriage to protection from immoral purposes, and education. Social attitudes cannot be abolished by law and the Sub-Committee could only pray for a change in such attitudes. For the rest, they relied on law to bring about change. By emphasizing the crucial role of legislative action, the Sub-Committee was laying the responsibility for bringing about a social order based on gender equality squarely on the government, the sole law-making and law-enforcing authority. Progressive for its time, this document disappeared in the years after independence, was forgotten, misplaced, and overlooked.

Members of the Sub-Committee were eminent or distinguished women active in public life during the nationalist period. They were freedom fighters from different political parties, legislators, social workers, office-bearers in women's organizations, or otherwise working in fields connected with the rights of women or the poor, bound together by the common cause of national freedom. They pooled their ideas and talents when working together on the Sub-Committee to articulate and describe the rights, hopes, and new roles of all classes of Indian women in a free India. The Report, however, went into cold storage along with the Final Reports of the other Sub-Committees of the NPC. As documents, they were valuable and were published immediately after independence, but have been out of sight and out of print ever since. It is hoped that the Report of the Sub-Committee discussed here will soon be reprinted as an important document relevant to the history of Indian women.

REPORT OF THE COMMITTEE ON THE STATUS OF WOMEN IN INDIA

The political response to the issue of equality was contained in the breaking down of formal barriers to women's access to legal, political, educational, and economic institutions. It was hoped that this step would bring about an increase in women's participatory roles. However, the guarantees of the Constitution and protective and just laws passed in favour of women failed to eliminate structures of subordination deeply rooted in all our social institutions. Legal equality was not followed by change either for the poor or for women as a category.

Legislation can only reflect desirable social values and provide the framework for change. Translation of equal rights into reality is the task of other agencies of government. Implementation of the law is as important as the law itself (Government of India, 1974: 103). Change also requires a transformation in the value structure. There was a great deal of ambivalence towards the idea of equality, as is clear from the discussions and debates on women's rights in the 1930s, 1940s, and 1950s (Everett, 1979; Government of India, 1974: 103). In addition, women face numerous constraints that restrict their social, economic, and political roles.

The distance between the intention of the framers of the Constitution and the reality was measured by the Committee on the Status of Women in India appointed for evaluating the status of Indian women. This it did, conditioned by the ideals of the Sub-Committee of 1939. The Committee stated that equality of women is necessary not merely on the grounds of social justice but as a basic condition for the social, economic, and political development of the nation (Government of India, 1974: 8). Both the Committees thus echoed the importance of women as a national resource.

The terms of reference of the Committee clearly indicated three major dimensions of the enquiry:

(*a*) to assess the impact of the constitutional, legal, and administrative provisions on the social status of women, their education, and employment, particularly in the rural sector during the period since independence;
(*b*) to examine the status of women in the changing social pattern; and
(*c*) to suggest remedial and other measures in the fields of law, education, employment, population policy, etc., 'which would enable women to play their full and proper role in building up the nation'.

The framework for the study was provided on the one hand by constitutional provisions that have a bearing on the status of women, and on the other, by the clear objective specified in the last term of reference (1974: 1).

The Committee's task was a formidable one as it involved a wide perspective including all aspects affecting the life of women in diverse contexts. Uneven rates of development between regions, communities, and sections of the population and contradictory trends made generalizations difficult and analysis by quantitative methods baffling. There was a basic paucity of data which the Committee tried to overcome by studying all types of existing documentary sources, preparing special studies covering numerous aspects of the lives of various categories of women, organizing tours, interviews and discussions with knowledgeable men and women working in various fields. The Committee studied gender roles and status, social, economic, and cultural institutions, and the structure of rights and opportunities provided by the state (1974: 7). The Committee's report was published in 1974. This is the second document which I wish to use to give an overview of the impact of development and the activities of nation building on the women of India between 1947 and 1975.

The Committee's findings highlighted the fact that the development process instead of helping to promote equality, had itself accentuated inequality. Planned development, education, legal reform, and political rights had been seen as the main instruments of social transformation. But the Committee found that these various indices faithfully reflected the stratification of society, systematic discrimination against women leaving them with narrow life options and choices, and distributional inequities. While tradition, custom, caste, and class were assuredly among the prime constraints holding back large sections of the general population from realizing equal rights and economic freedom, the Committee did not believe that these alone constituted obstacles to equality. The Committee laid stress on the structural aspects of both the old and modern systems as providing a base for discriminatory and marginalizing attitudes and factors.

The class dimension of inequality in the wake of development was noted by the Committee. It reported that 'while opportunities had widened immensely at certain levels of society and enabled women to forge ahead in areas which had been completely closed to them in earlier years, for the other levels of society, this was not the case' (1974: 5). The population of the middle and upper classes had better access to the benefits of development.

The gender dimension underlying every type of inequality was next fully exposed by the Committee. Imbalances were seen in every sector; at work and within the family women were affected by the unequal distribution of roles, resources, rewards, and authority. The Committee identified certain trends in society which had resisted time, the British intervention, and twenty-eight years of independence. Though women do not constitute a

Table 7 Sex ratio—India: 1901–91

Census year	Sex ratio
1901	972
1911	964
1921	955
1931	950
1941	945
1951	946
1961	941
1971	930
1981	934
1991	929*

* provisional.
Source: Census of India, 1991. Series 1, India. Paper 1 of 1991. Provisional Population Totals. Office of the Registrar General, Ministry of Home Affairs, New Delhi.

minority numerically, they were acquiring the features of one by experiencing inequality of class, status, and political power (1974: 301).

The lower status of women was visible in the adverse sex ratio which reflected son preference, lower life expectancy, early marriage for girls, high female mortality and morbidity rates, unequal access to health care, and inadequate nutritional intake. (See Table 7 for an illustration of the adverse sex ratio.)

Literacy is crucial to women's development but the vast majority of Indian women were illiterate—this is a great barrier to an improvement in their position in employment, health, exercise of legal and constitutional rights, equal opportunity in education, and attaining equality of status (Government of India, 1974: 204). Female literacy did not increase at a rapid rate after independence either in absolute numbers or in relation to the growth of literacy among men (1974: 265). There were also disparities among different regions and sections (low literacy among Scheduled Castes and Tribes, and Muslims, but high literacy among Christians) and between urban and rural areas. (See Table 8 for general literacy rates 1951–91.)

Similarly, school enrolment rates showed wide differences between the sexes, poverty, and rural residence working against the girl child. There was an improvement in enrolment at various levels of higher education but the disparity between male and female rates was striking in all disciplines. Biases in curricula continued to reflect social attitudes to women's roles and place (1974: 234–82).

The Committee was greatly exercised over disparities and regional/local imbalances in literacy and educational levels, noting with care that local

Table 8 Literacy rate—India: 1951–91

Year	Persons	Males	Females
1951	18.33	27.16	8.86
1961	28.31	40.40	15.34
1971	34.45	45.95	21.97
1981	43.56 (41.42)	56.37 (53.45)	29.75 (28.46)
1991	52.11	63.86	39.42

Note: Literacy rates for 1951, 1961, and 1971 relate to population aged five years and above. The rates for the years 1981 and 1991 relate to the population aged seven years and above. The literacy rates for the population aged five years and above in 1981 have been shown in brackets.
Source: Census of India, 1991. Series 1, India. Paper 1 of 1991. Provisional Population Totals. Office of the Registrar Genera, Ministry of Home Affairs, New Delhi.

conditions varied, needing particular solutions. No set solutions could be universally applicable. There must be universalization of elementary education and attention must be paid to the retention of girls in schools; gender biases must be removed from curricula. Equality is a major value which can be taught through the educational process to counteract socialization, rather indoctrination, into sex roles. As it stands today, reflected the Committee, the system strengthens the traditional prejudices of inequality and has not even attempted to undertake this responsibility. In this respect, the educational system must make a planned and sustained effort (1974: 282).

A review of the legal position of women convinced the Committee that there was widespread violation of laws which laid down the government's social policy. This was due to the persistence of tradition and custom. Further, every personal law was seen to reinforce women's subordination and inequality. The Committee considered the issues of bigamy/polygamy, age at marriage, dowry, divorce, adoption, guardianship, maintenance, inheritance, and recommended parity of rights and the enactment of a secular law applicable to all women to remove existing discrimination against women under different personal laws.

The main theme running through the Chapter on law is that there should be a unified law as primary rights continue to be vested in men. Even when fundamental changes were made by the Hindu Succession Act (1956), legislators compromised and retained in some respects the inferior position of women (1974: 135). But the Committee found the Hindu Adoption and Maintenance Act (1956) an improvement on the previous law in some ways, for instance, by allowing single women to adopt a son or a daughter (1974: 125).

The Committee followed the Sub-Committee (1939) in upholding the economic value of a woman's contribution to the family economy and her right to matrimonial property on the basis of her work, be it inside or outside the house. Mothering, child care, and housework are activities without economic remuneration, but these keep women dependent. Why should ownership of property be determined on the basis of financial contribution alone? (1974: 140–1) This line of thinking is in consonance with a current world-wide trend. It may be reiterated here that the Sub-Committee had thought of it decades ago.

The Committee also recommended that Indian women's right to Indian nationality should be unaffected by marriage to a foreigner; that the age at marriage for girls be raised to eighteen, and that adultery cease to be a criminal offence, an implication of the latter being that the wife ceases to be regarded as the husband's property. Another important recommendation made was that the right to initiate proceedings for bigamy can also be made by anyone other than the aggrieved party—a forerunner in principle of the right to initiate public-interest litigation accepted in the post-1975 period.

In the political sphere too there was no equality for women. Throughout India, except as voters, women's participation as contestants, elected representatives, members of the government, and so on, was negligible. Regional and sectional patterns in political participation manifested themselves with familiar correlations. Two of the chief reasons for women's poor performance in this sphere were laid at the door of both political parties and a moribund women's movement.

After independence, Indian women had not been unified by political, economic, and social issues on a national scale as they had been in the struggle for freedom. The women's movement petered out after the passage of the Hindu Code Bill in 1956. Nor did political parties seek out women as a constituency or encourage them within their own ranks. Thus women were neither mobilized by political parties and organizations nor by women's organizations and women leaders. Meagre attention was given to women's issues as a result, and the plight of rural women remained neglected, lacking spokeswomen (1974: 294–300).

The question of reservation, however, cropped up again and was debated by the groups of women the Committee met; some wanted reservation as a transitional supportive measure but the Committee rejected it. However, at the local level the Committee recommended the establishment of village-level statutory women's councils to ensure greater participation by women in the political process (1974: 302–5).

The Committee came into its own in its examination of the economic roles of women. It was mainly concerned with the majority who have to work out of necessity. The majority of women were found in the unorganized sector in a variety of occupations too numerous to enumerate and where working conditions were appalling and inhumane. A considerable number of women therefore had no equal rights in the economic process, they had unequal access to employment opportunities, knowledge and skills, and did not therefore have an adequate means of livelihood nor anything like equal pay. In family production and home-based activities they had little or no return and recognition. Policies and processes of economic development had clearly marginalized women in the primary sector. A higher degree of concentration of capital, exploitative relations of production, modernization in agriculture, export-oriented production, and technological change had pushed women into the unorganized sector, led to the feminization of certain production processes, increased female migration and female-headed households. Discriminatory attitudes not only by private employers but also by the state (such as the assumption that women are supplementary earners); lack of successful unionization among women workers; and a lack of alternatives compounded the problem, increasing women's economic dependence on the family.

The Committee called for a well-defined state policy to provide equality of opportunity in employment for women. Special attention to women's disabilities and needs has to be given, and the policy implemented carefully. The Committee recommended that maternity benefits be extended beyond the organized sector, crèches be provided, and wages equalized by law. Integrated development of training and employment, provision for re-entry, steps to organize labour unions in agriculture and other sectors were needed, as well as formation of women's wings in all trade unions to look after the problems of women workers and to improve women's participation in trade-union activities (1974: 148–233).

Summary and assessment

Although the Sub-Committee's outline of a proposal for the realization of women's equality was not retained as a guide, the women's question remained on the economic and political agenda until 1956. Some legislative changes pertaining to labour laws and personal laws were made, but they were piecemeal and incomplete. Gradually, the social perceptions of the political leadership, including women in political parties, moved away from the hopes, norms, and ideals set out before women in the nationalist period. There was also no investigation during this period of the role women were playing in development until the Committee was set up.

The CSWI was a product of the earlier women's movement and influenced by the message of the Sub-Committee. Using the Constitution as a point of reference, it undertook a critical analysis of trends since independence. Its findings in various spheres were that development had not been guided by the Constitution and that inequality was rampant in society in terms of class as well as gender.

The condition of the mass of women had worsened, except for that of a fraction of women in the middle and upper class in terms of higher education and white-collar employment in a few professions. This is not to suggest that economically secure women were free from gender oppression or that they were politically effective. The blame for the predicament of the mass of women was equally distributed among the following: educational institutions which played a role in perpetuating gender role socialization and prejudices leading to inequality, the indifference of political parties to the women's question, the absence of the pressure that could have been provided by a women's movement, and trends in society that ran contrary to the earlier political commitment to equality.

The state itself did not take up the task of creating a new social order. Issues relating to women did not enjoy a high priority for a government besieged by problems of poverty, a slowing growth rate and political factionalism. The women's question as such and the commitment to eliminate gender disparities disappeared from the political agenda between 1956 and 1975. Existing laws were not enforced by the state nor were they comprehensive or complete. For instance, maternity benefits were granted only to a limited number of women workers in plantations and mines, although 95 per cent of women workers are in other sectors. The legislation on equal remuneration was delayed until 1975. Furthermore, the persistent debate within economic development has been centred not so much around equity as productivity. The argument was that a large section of the human labour force, i.e. women, were left out of the strategies for development. Women were seen as an economic issue but not in terms of equality even within that issue.

These varied failures strengthened 'the structures' of patriarchy and increased inequality and exploitation of women. The Committee suggested several important measures in every sphere for the reduction of such inequality. Its emphasis throughout has been on greater legislative support; implementation of laws; greater decentralization with an emphasis on action at the local level, whether it was non-formal education, human resource development, or child care; and the inclusion of women in political parties, women's *panchayats*, committees, commissions and so on, that is, in all decision-making bodies.

1975—1988—1992: DEBATES ON THE DRAFT *NATIONAL PERSPECTIVE PLAN FOR WOMEN*

The publication of the Report of the CSWI was an event that took place in a period of political ferment. The political emergency imposed in 1975 by Indira Gandhi (and which ended in 1977) coincided with several democratic people's movements, labour strikes, and a mood of questioning. Agrarian and student unrest, protests against food shortages, inflation, unemployment, deforestation, public corruption, and so on had been on the increase since the 1960s, culminating in the Total Revolution Movement initiated by the late Jaya Prakash Narayan in 1974.[9] All these protests had attracted substantial participation by women. Once they were mobilized, they also raised women-specific issues like alcoholism and atrocities against women which gave rise to the growth of women's groups even before the declaration of the UN Decade for Women. The Emergency suppressed this discontent for two years, but from 1977 onwards women's protests gathered momentum along with the general upsurge of popular movements.

The CSWI's report by itself had produced only token gestures by the government, though the report created extraordinary interest in the media, because of its unexpected findings. Between 1975 and March 1977 the government created a Cell on Women's Employment within the Ministry of Labour. A Women's Welfare and Development Bureau within the Ministry of Social Welfare formulated a National Plan for Action for Women (which had no legal status as it was not incorporated within the activities of the Planning Commission) and constituted a National Committee under the chairmanship of the Prime Minister with undefined powers, to ensure a fair deal for women. Though an Empowered Committee drawn from various ministries had examined the fifty-nine recommendations of the CSWI and decided on follow-up action, none of this was initiated during the period of emergency.

From 1977 to 1980, however, the successor Janata Government (after the General Elections of 1977 in which Mrs Gandhi was defeated) initiated various policy reviews. Some of them included a search for new or alternative strategies to undo the damage done to the large majority of women through the government's neglect in the past. Even these new strategies, however, concrete as they were, did not ultimately find favour with the ruling government or its Planning Commission. Three Working Groups were set up by the government: on village-level organizations for rural

[9] Jaya Prakash Narayan, popularly known as J.P., was an illustrious freedom fighter who occupied the position of an elder statesman in Indian politics. A Gandhian and a socialist, he did not aspire to public office but exerted himself outside the realm of party and power politics, speaking out for greater popular participation and the protection of democratic principles in a state that was becoming increasingly centralized. The term 'Total Revolution' is Marxist in origin, is ingrained in Gandhi's political thought, and has taken a place in Indian political discourse. The concept connoted for J.P. a vision of systemic change and a new social and economic order to be achieved by non-violent mass action. In the early 1970s, the Indian state faced a crisis and popular discontent challenged the legitimacy of the prevailing system. In 1974, young people in Gujarat and Bihar turned to J.P. for leadership. The movement he led was treated as a law and order problem and ended with his imprisonment and the imposition of a political emergency in 1975 by the Prime Minister, Indira Gandhi. When released in late 1975, J.P. was a very sick man and died four yours later in 1979. Suggested readings on his life and thought are: Bimal Prasad (1992), Selbourne (1985), Ostergaard (1985).

women, in the Ministry of Rural Development; on employment, in the Planning Commission; and on adult education for women, in the Ministry of Education.

Another general election in 1980 brought Indira Gandhi back to power. In the same year, seven national women's organizations presented a Memorandum to the government (*Indian Women in the Eighties: Development Imperatives*) which resulted in the Planning Commission's decision to include for the first time a chapter on Women and Development in the Sixth Five-Year Plan and some of the recommendations made in the Memorandum. Most of the recommendations drew on the analysis and the approaches of the three official Working Groups mentioned above, and carried political weight with the backing of the larger national women's organizations. It is from this point that intervention by the women's movement became intense and effective and a dialogue was opened up between the government and the women's movement. However, by September 1980, a new approach to the Sixth Five-Year Plan produced by the Indira Gandhi government did not reflect the exercises undertaken by the official Working Groups between 1977 and 1980, or the contents of the Memorandum.

In 1985, another national consultation was convened by the same groups of organizations to review the developments in the Women's Decade. Some of the recommendations of this conference formed a basis for discussions on new policies during the Seventh Plan period. Some were reflected in the strategies recommended by the Ministerial-level Conference of Non-aligned and Other Developing Nations hosted by the government of India in 1985.

In the post-1975 period women's organizations conscientized the wider society, worked with all classes of women, combining developmental activities with mobilization for socio-economic rights, put a limited but successful pressure on the state for legislative action to curb exploitation of women in matters relating to marriage, rape, and workers' rights. They raised many questions specific to women and challenged patriarchal values in all spheres and structures through agitational tactics, propaganda, and lobbying. Many problems of women are class-related. Therefore, while separateness as a gender-based movement was regarded as essential to unify women vertically and horizontally, collaboration with other socio-economic and political movements was also seen as necessary. The women's movement joined civil rights movements, struggles in rural areas, people's and workers' movements. It challenged state policies on population, women's employment, environment, training and organization of women workers, planning for rural development, agriculture, education, and so on, and protested against atrocities against women, distorted portrayal of women in the media, and so forth. As a consequence of all these activities, the movement grew increasingly political. Its concerns have shifted to such basic issues as the state of the polity, the state of the economy, the criminalization and communalization of politics, communalism *per se*, violence and the rise of fundamentalism.

Two events, the furore over the Shah Bano case and the self-immolation or *sati* of a young widow in Rajasthan, brought the issues of fundamentalism and revivalism into the open.

The Shah Bano case

The Shah Bano case threw up many issues: the rights of religious minorities, the rights of women, the role of the judiciary, and so on. Before briefly commenting on the case it would be useful to explain that Muslim Personal Law provides for *mahr*, a payment by the groom (or his family) to the bride (or her family) whose amount is stipulated in the marriage contract. Its intent is to represent an insurance against divorce or widowhood; thus divorced women do not have any right of maintenance beyond a limited period (*iddat*). However, Section 125 of the Criminal Procedure Code of India acting as a preventive against destitution and vagrancy, permits wives, including ex-wives, to seek a summary maintenance order from a court. This maintenance provision is subject to a ceiling of 500 rupees per month, depending on the economic capacity of the husband or ex-husband. The Criminal Procedure Code, being a secular law, applies to all citizens, and many Muslim women have been able to obtain this remedy through the courts. In 1985 in the case of Shah Bano, the Supreme Court, while upholding the order given by the High Court for maintenance under Section 125, commented that it was time for the government to consider drawing up a uniform civil code as directed by the Constitution (Article 44).

The opinion of the Supreme Court was interpreted by Muslim fundamentalists as an attack on minority rights and Islamic personal law. Since the political situation was already tense over the issue of the construction of a temple on a site where a mosque was located in Ayodhya, the legendary birth place of the Hindu epic hero, Rama, in pursuit of its policy of appeasing Muslim opinion, the government of Rajiv Gandhi enacted the Muslim Women's (Protection of Rights on Divorce) Bill in 1986, which deprived Muslim women of their right to maintenance under the relevant section of the secular Criminal Procedure Code. The women's movement and all progressive opinion condemned this measure as an invasion of women's constitutional rights. Several writs challenging its validity filed by various women's organizations are still pending with the Supreme Court. Other suits by young Muslim women challenging their personal law were also filed.

The sati *at Deorala*

Hard on the heels of the Muslim Women's Bill, an act of *sati* occurred in Deorala in 1987. Hindu revivalism legitimized this heinous act by the deification and worship of the young woman, Roop Kanwar, and the formation of a Dharma Raksha Samiti (Organization to Protect Religion). The government passed a Commission of *Sati* (Prevention) Act 1987 which, while penalizing the glorification of *sati*, treats the act as suicide, placing the onus of responsibility on the victim. The half-hearted, loopholed, and hurried legislation in response to protests against the outrage was not followed up by firm implementation of the law.

In both cases women's issues became communalized and the government was seen in a poor light. Caught between political expediency, appeasement of fundamentalists, and minority rights, the main issue was totally blurred and lost.

In 1987, the government announced the appointment of a National Commission to study the problems of self-employed women and women in the informal sector. Its report was published in 1988. In 1989 the recommendation for a National Commission on Women made by the CSWI in 1974 and which had not been acted upon, was finally considered. A Bill on the National Commission was introduced, then passed in 1990, and in 1992 the members of this Commission were eventually appointed. One can assume that these were attempts to pacify the women's lobby which had been badly upset by the enactment of the Muslim Women's Act and the Bill on *sati*.

The National Perspective Plan for Women (NPP) was an exercise internal to the government in which women's organizations had not been at all involved. The first that the women's organizations heard of it was when they were confronted with the announcement that the NPP would be placed before Parliament for endorsement as a policy. No one knew what the plan contained. The fragments of information which trickled out in the press were sufficient to disturb the women's organizations which then issued a public statement that there should be a national debate on the Plan before it was adopted as a policy. When no response was received from the government, seven national women's organizations convened a public debate in which thirty-nine organizations from all India participated. Their comments and reactions to the NPP were basically a critique along with many constructive alternative suggestions. These were collected under the title: *The National Perspective Plan for Women, 1988–2000: A Perspective from the Women's Movement*. This is the third text I propose to discuss here.

The NPP reviews women's condition in nine areas: rural development and agriculture, employment and training, education, health and family welfare, legislation, media and communication, supportive services, political participation and decision-making, and voluntary action. It incorporates many of the recommendations of the CSWI which have not yet been implemented. It stresses enforcement of laws, new legal safeguards, and support mechanisms for women in all spheres.

The government's awareness that women need better protection from the state and more legislative action is expressed in every chapter. Women have been viewed as a human resource and as producers making major contributions to family and national income. The Plan speaks of a national labour policy, education for development, a uniform civil code, and echoes various suggestions made by the CSWI and the women's movement in regard to family law and women workers. It even mentions measures to ensure protection from destitution, domestic violence, and non-implementation of the law. However, nowhere in the Plan is the role of government mentioned nor how much of women's situation is the *consequence of the government's own policies*. The NPP does not take note of the major issues which women face overall.

The women's movement's critique of the NPP is contained in the text I have referred to. It appreciated the government's admission of its failure on various fronts but felt that there are great gaps between the government's analysis of problems and recommendations made for needed measures. The issues of resource allocation, their distribution between infrastructural development and participatory human development, and the question of accountability have been evaded. The social and political constraints, and the adverse impact of mainstream development policies are inadequately articulated in the Plan. (For example, Table 9, on per capita income and poverty across India, shows that despite a decline in the percentage of the population living below the poverty line in almost all states and territories, the percentages are still high, and of course the absolute figures are even higher.)

The Plan does not take into account the wide disparities between different sections of women, and does not clearly call for the active participation of the people in the development process from planning and resource allocation to implementation. The expressed need to bring women into the mainstream of development ignores the reality that women's marginalization is the *result* of such development. Several deficiencies of the NPP were pointed out by the women's movement. The NPP indicates a *departure from* the existing 'convergence' approach in development assistance programmes. Strategies were evolved during the last two Five-Year Plans to achieve women's economic independence through additional employment opportunities, and 'social strength' through organization and support services. There is little evidence of this in the NPP. The proposal to distribute responsibility for monitoring and/or implementing state policies on women at various levels appears to be contradicted by centralizing strategies also mentioned in the NPP. The women's movement stresses *the need for greater decentralization of the planning process*. In the case

Table 9 Basic economic indicators

States/Union Territories	Per capita income (in Rs)	Percentage population below poverty line	
	1981	1977–8	1984–5
All India	1,559	48.13	36.90
States			
Andhra Pradesh	1,313	42.18	35.80
Assam	1,221	51.10	37.99
Bihar	927	57.49	47.87
Gujarat	1,828	39.04	22.92
Haryana	2,331	24.84	17.02
Himachal Pradesh	1,521	27.23	19.10
Jammu & Kashmir	1,496	34.06	23.43
Karnataka	1,314	48.34	33.48
Kerala	1,379	46.95	24.74
Madhya Pradesh	1,131	57.73	46.23
Maharashtra	2,261	47.71	33.83
Manipur	1,052	29.71	22.67
Meghalaya	1,135	48.03	37.33
Nagaland	—	—	n/a
Orissa	1,101	66.40	41.47
Punjab	2,771	15.13	13.20
Rajasthan	1,238	33.76	33.87
Sikkim	—	—	n/a
Tamil Nadu	1,197	52.12	36.99
Tripura	1,206	59.73	47.39
Uttar Pradesh	1,280	59.09	42.88
West Bengal	1,553	52.54	48.01
Union Territories			
Andaman and Nicobar Islands	—	21.69	15.85
Arunachal Pradesh	—	—	—
Chandigarh	—	—	—
Dadra Nagar Haveli	—	—	—
Delhi	2,872	—	—
Goa, Daman & Diu	2,794	—	—
Lakshadweep	—	—	—
Mizoram	—	—	—
Pondicherry	2,930	—	—

Note: Based on state and union territory divisions in 1981.
Source: Compiled from Census of India, 1981.

of women's development, the situational diversity calls for greater flexibility than centralized, streamlined programmes can provide.

Instead of having a Commissioner in the Department of Women and Child Development to prevent atrocities against women (and children), it would be far better to bring legal redress within reach of all women through informal courts, legal literacy, and by making legal procedures quick and inexpensive. Penalties need to be enforced on those who do not apply the law. This would revitalize the principle of accountability and spread awareness of women's rights.

The NPP acknowledges the need to increase women's participation and representation in the political process and recommends 30 per cent reservation in legislatures, administrative bodies, and positions of power as a 'transitional' measure. It also suggests the method of co-option for filling such reserved seats in all elective bodies. This, in the opinion of the women's movement, would be a subversion of the Constitution and all democratic norms.[10] The CSWI had recommended the promotion of genuine representative women's bodies at the lowest level of the representative structures for wider participation, articulation of women's concerns, and the emergence of genuine leadership. Co-option would be a dangerous threat to the future of democracy.

Strategies and policies of the government continue to subvert employment opportunities. There is ample evidence that the government has contributed to the expansion of the unorganized sector. The participatory right of poor working women in trade unions and struggles to articulate their problems were sought to be denied by certain recent measures of the government (e.g. Hospitals and Other Institutions Bill 1988, which attempted to deny the basic rights of workers under labour laws; withdrawal of the Minimum Wages Notification for garment workers in Gujarat and incentives provided to employers in the Export Promotion Zones). Several recommendations of various working groups, and of women's organizations, and various laws continue to be unimplemented.

[10] Whereas a nomination is an act of an authority which has the power to do so, co-option is a collective decision of a democratically constituted committee, board, commission, or official group whereby groups or interests which have not succeeded in getting representation (through the democratic process implied above) are given representation. Although the two processes of selection are different, their objective is often the same. The number or percentage of seats 'reserved' for co-option may vary, depending on the size of the body, its purpose, and the population it represents and serves. In India, the alternative of co-option is provided as a device whereby representatives from the weaker sections of society, such as women, Scheduled Castes, and Scheduled Tribes, who may fail to be elected, may be given a voice and a place in representative institutions, particularly at the local level. However, in practice, this method is often misused or manipulated in such a way that co-option smacks of arbitrariness and high-handedness. Through co-option, individuals or groups often maintain dominance and control over elected assemblies. Where this is a standard practice, democratic norms are, obviously, subverted. Reservation is a form of affirmative action for weaker groups and is utilized generally *during* the electoral process, whereas co-option is resorted to *after* elections to redress any imbalance that may have resulted.

The NPP, in short, appears to believe that by creating a few top-heavy structures and co-opting women into decision-making bodies, an immense, complex problem involving women's subordination, inequality in power and resources, and active opposition from powerful and organized forces, can be solved.

The women's organizations representing the women's movement demanded the ratification by the government of the United Nations Convention on the Elimination of All Forms of Discrimination against Women, as also adoption of Article 2 of the Convention as part of our Constitution. The women's movement also demanded the recognition of the right to work as a fundamental right.

The other demand of the women's movement was for the establishment of statutory autonomous Commissions on Women at the Centre and the States as recommended by the CSWI. The shape and powers of these commissions were outlined so that they could function as watchdog bodies with rights to question, suggest, and censure. Further, 30 per cent reservation for women in local government institutions and planning groups should be assured with special emphasis on representation of women from the Scheduled Castes and Scheduled Tribes. These seats are to be filled by election, not co-option. Other critical demands were: allocation of resources for women's development within sectors; free compulsory elementary education; widespread child care; land reform, new laws, implementation of all laws; cessation of all anti-labour and anti-democratic measures of the state; more accountability, sensitization of educators and members of government at all levels to women's issues; association of women's organizations in the enforcement of laws for the protection of women and at different levels of planning.

As the NPP was formulated without discussion and debate, the women's movement termed it an undemocratic exercise. The women's movement's critique of the NPP was a critique of the government—unlike the CSWI's Report, which was an investigative analysis that divided the blame. To this extent the critique is a political document and proof of the increasingly political nature of the women's movement.

CONCLUSION

An analysis of these three documents shows that Indian women have been associated to a greater degree with political processes in the wider society and less with the formal political system and with government. In the twentieth century they broke the mould of the traditional woman by joining the national movement in their thousands. Simultaneously, the first wave of the women's movement fought for access to equal rights including political and civic rights for women as individual and social beings. Equality was the dream of the women's Sub-Committee of the NPC. The Constitution guaranteed equal rights but in practice women did not experience equality. As the second report—that of the CSWI—has shown, women have not been able to get into mainstream or formal politics, into decision-making or representative structures on account of the constraints of poverty, illiteracy, ill health, traditional attitudes in society, inequality in class, status, and power.

Secondly, over time the political leadership grew away from the promises made to women in the nationalist era. Thirdly, the entire social system and state structure followed a particular path of growth in the course of which the whole question of gender equality was jettisoned. The pattern of development, especially economic development and changing social institutions, did not eliminate the stranglehold of patriarchy. Instead, the structures of patriarchy including the state, the community, and the household, have been strengthened through the processes of development.

Macro- and micro-level studies in India have pointed out that although socio-economic development depends to a certain extent on the quality of natural as well as human resources, the root causes of poverty are often man-made. These include economic policies, political factors, and socio-cultural norms. Interacting with one another they not only reinforce poverty but inequality. In addition, the so-called beneficiaries of development have to contend with ever-increasing violence in society caused by divisions based on class, community, ethnic, and religious separatism. All these trends have affected women far more adversely than men. Gender bias in pernicious forms, unfortunately encouraged by the state in various ways, has weakened the social and economic position of women. Specifically, male bias in development thinking, planning, and implementation has affected women's position in the family, the community, and society. Women perform the lion's share of the work on a national scale but are unequal in terms of benefits, entitlements, and allocation of resources. The question therefore seems to be not whether women should be integrated into development and existing structures but whether structures and strategies should be changed in order to benefit women.

Institutions based on religious and social traditions are opposed to woman's equality, dignity, and status. Women's rights have been increasingly subjected to social and religious oppression to such an extent that they are unable to avail of the minimum protection given to them under existing secular civil and criminal laws. Clear examples are the revival of *sati*, 'witch hunting' in rural areas, the resistance to the prohibition of dowry and a divorced woman's right to maintenance. Crimes against women such as rape, dowry murder, female foeticide, and child prostitution are widespread, affecting all classes. The increase in brutality and force are related to consumerism, religious revivalism, and the hardening of feudal, sexist, and patriarchal values in society. In the media—the cinema and TV mainly—women are portrayed either as powerless commodities or parasitical consumers. Projecting such stereotypes reinforces the influence of patriarchal values, dangerous when directed towards a vast illiterate audience. These perverse trends have been creating a wide dispersal of anti-women values. Most women thus live in a state of threat and reprisal, coercion and fear.

It is the duty of the state 'to ensure that its citizens' rights and dignity are not violated by its own laws or by other citizens. No state should benefit from the violation, abuse or neglect by its own agents or by others, of the rights of its citizens. But in reality, all states violate citizens' rights because of their failure to create real and reliable equity and equality for the female sex' (Ashworth, 1986). The Indian state is not gender neutral, whatever its protestations. Society and state are influenced by patriarchal values, and atrocities against women are being used as instruments of political action. The basic objective underlying the demand for statutory autonomous commissions on women is the restoration of the rule of law breached also by the government. Law is the only powerful instrument to support women's status, and must be strengthened, and the Constitution must be upheld. In placing this emphasis, the women's movement of today has not veered from the perspective of the women's Sub-Committee and the CSWI. At the same time, the women's movement recognizes that women's political participation is central to the struggle against patriarchy and for women's emancipation.

I would like to end with what Gandhi said about women's role in society. He had great faith in the women of India: in their forbearance, capacity for sacrifice, dedication to the family, and steadfastness. Gandhi went even further than the 1931 Congress Declaration on Fundamental Rights in viewing political and legal equality for women as only the beginning:

> Women must have votes and an equal legal status. But the problem does not end there. It only commences at the point where women begin to affect the political deliberations of the nation.[11]

REFERENCES

AGARWAL, BINA (1988), *Structures of Patriarchy* (New Delhi: Kali for Women).

All India Women's Conference (n.d.), *Indian Women in the Eighties: Development Imperatives* (New Delhi: AIWC).

ASHWORTH, GEORGINA (1986), *Of Violence and Violation, Women and Human Rights* (London: Change).

[11] M. K. Gandhi in *Young India*, 17 Oct. 1929.

BASU, DURGA DAS (1955), *Commentary on the Constitution of India*. 2 vols. (Calcutta: S. C. Sarkar and Sons Ltd.).

BÉTEILLE, ANDRÉ (1965), *Caste, Class and Power* (Berkeley and Los Angeles: University of California Press).

BIMAL PRASAD (1992), *Jayaprakash Narayan* (New Delhi: Vikas).

BIPAN CHANDRA (1979), *Nationalism and Colonialism in Modern India* (New Delhi: Orient Longman).

DESAI, NEERA and PATEL, VIBHUTI (1985), *Indian Women: Change and Challenge in the International Decade 1975–1985* (Bombay: Popular Prakashan).

—— and KRISHNARAJ, MAITHREYI (1987), *Women and Society in India* (Delhi: Ajanta).

DUMONT, LOUIS (1966), *Homo Hierarchicus: Essai sur le système des castes* (Paris: Gallimard).

EISENSTEIN, ZILLAH R. (1979), 'Developing a Theory of Capitalist Patriarchy and Socialist Feminism', and 'Some notes on the Relations of Capitalist Patriarchy', in Eisenstein (ed.), *Capitalist Patriarchy and the Case for Socialist Feminism* (New York and London: Monthly Review Press), 5–55.

EVERETT, J. M. (1979), *Women and Social Change* (New Delhi: Heritage Publishers).

Government of India (1974), *Towards Equality, Report of the Committee on the Status of Women in India* (New Delhi: Department of Social Welfare, Ministry of Education and Social Welfare).

—— (1987), *A Social and Economic Atlas of India* (Delhi: Oxford University Press).

—— (1988), *National Perspective Plan for Women 1988–2000 AD* (New Delhi: Department of Women and Child Development, Ministry of Human Resource Development).

GUHA, RANAJIT (ed.) (1982), 'Introduction', in *Subaltern Studies: Writings on South Asian History and Society*, vol. 1 (New Delhi: Oxford University Press).

JAYASREE, R. (1989), *Religion, Social Change and Fertility Behaviour. A Study of Kerala* (New Delhi: Concept Publishing Co.).

JOSHI, PUSHPA (compiled by) (1988), *Gandhi on Women* (Ahmedabad: Navajivan; New Delhi: CWDS).

MANDELBAUM, DAVID G. (1979/1984), *Society in India*, vols 1 and 2 (Bombay: Popular Prakashan).

MASANI, M. R. (1975), *Is J.P. the Answer?* (New Delhi: Macmillan).

MILLER, J. D. B. (1962), *The Nature of Politics* (London: Gerald Duckworth & Co. Ltd.).

NAG, MONI (1983), 'Impact of Social and Economic Development on Mortality', *Economic and Political Weekly*, 18/19, 20, 21 (May): 877–900.

National Commission on Self-employed Women and Women in the Informal Sector (1988), *Shram Shakti*, a report.

National Perspective Plan for Women, 1988–2000: A Perspective from the Women's Movement. Report of a Debate, 22–3 Aug. 1988, New Delhi.

NAYAR, P. K. B. (1986), 'Factors in Fertility Decline in Kerala', in K. Mahadevan *et al.* (eds.), *Fertility and Mortality: Theory, Methodology and Empirical Issues* (New Delhi: Sage).

NETTL, J. P. (1967), *Political Mobilization: A Sociological Analysis of Methods and Concepts* (London: Faber and Faber Ltd.).

New Delhi Document on Women in Development: Report of the Ministerial Level Conference of Non-Aligned and Other Developing Nations, Apr. 1985.

OSTERGAARD, GEOFFREY (1985), *Non-Violent Revolution in India* (New Delhi: Gandhi Peace Foundation).

Report of the Sub-Committee on *Woman's Role in Planned Economy* (1947): National Planning Committee Series (Bombay: Vora and Co.).

ROWBOTHAM, SHEILA (1981), 'The Trouble with Patriarchy', in R. Samuel (ed.), *People's History and Socialist Theory* (London: Routledge and Kegan Paul).

SHARMA, KUMUD (1989), *Shared Aspirations: Fragmented Realities*, Occasional Paper no. 12 (New Delhi: CWDS).

SELBOURNE, DAVID (ed.) (1985), *In Theory and in Practice: Essays on the Politics of Jayaprakash Narayan* (Delhi: Oxford University Press).

SRINIVAS, M. N. (1972), *Social Change in Modern India* (New Delhi: Orient Longman).

—— (1978), *The Changing Position of Indian Women* (New Delhi: Oxford University Press).

UNESCO (1983), *Report of the Meeting of Experts on the Participation of Women in Political Life and the Means for Increasing this Participation* (13–16 Dec.) (Lisbon: UNESCO).

UNFPA (1992), *The State of World Population* (New York: Oxford University Press).

WEST, GUIDA and BLUMBERG, RHODA (eds.) (1990), *Women and Social Protest* (New York, Oxford: Oxford University Press).

World Bank (1991), *Gender and Poverty in India: A World Bank Country Study* (Washington, DC: World Bank).

Young India, 17 Oct. 1929.

Gender, Patriarchy, and Development in Africa: The Zimbabwean Case

Jane L. Parpart

INTRODUCTION

The relationship between women's access to the benefits of development, the existence of patriarchal structures and ideology, and the emancipation or subordination of women is particularly difficult to assess in Africa. Dramatic economic decline combined with endemic civil wars and widespread autocratic rule muddies the picture, as does the variety of social, political, and economic circumstances in the continent's many countries. Continent-wide generalizations are clearly impossible, but the analysis of one country may shed some light on the relationship between economic development, patriarchy, and women's position in society.

To that end, this chapter will examine these issues in post-independence Zimbabwe. Drawing on the various theoretical approaches for analysing the development of women, particularly the insights of both postmodernist feminism and the gender and development perspective, the chapter examines the economic changes in Zimbabwe since independence in 1980, their impact on women's employment and educational opportunities, and the degree to which patriarchal structures and ideas have continued (or failed) to restrict women's opportunities in economic and political spheres. Case studies of inheritance disputes, collected by the Zimbabwean research team of the Women and Law in Southern Africa Research Project (WLSA),[1] will be used as a prism to examine the possibility that some women have managed to use the benefits of economic development to challenge patriarchal authority and control.

[1] The Women and Law in Southern African Research Project (WLSA) has been carrying out a six-country comparative research project into women's experiences concerning maintenance and inheritance law in southern Africa. The project emphasizes women's experiences of the law rather than simply the laws themselves or women's knowledge about those laws. I am very grateful to WLSA for giving me access to its data and for educating me about women and the law in southern Africa. I am particularly grateful to Alice Armstrong, the former director, to all the country research teams, and especially to the Zimbabwean research team which provided the crucial data for this paper. All members of the Zimbabwean team provided invaluable advice and data for which I am most grateful, but above all I want to thank Julie Stewart, who spent many hours explaining the intricacies of Zimbabwean customary law. This paper could not have been written without her.

THEORETICAL APPROACHES

Before considering the Zimbabwean case, it is important to clarify the concepts being used to discuss the issues at hand. The literature on women's status in the Third World has been dominated by the Women in Development (WID) approach to the study of women. Steeped in the liberal tradition, this perspective generally accepts Western gender stereotypes as given. While calling for greater equity between women and men, particularly in regard to education, employment, and other material benefits, WID advocates for the most part accept the notion that women are fundamentally responsible for reproductive labour. As a result, their policies and prescriptions have sought to increase women's access to social benefits such as education, employment, property, and credit, without challenging basic gender stereotypes. The double and triple day, in which women struggle under the burden of both reproductive and productive labour, is thus simply seen as an inevitable part of women's lives. Women's development consequently becomes largely logistical—that is, how can women obtain greater access to male-dominated benefits—rather than something requiring the reassessment of societal assumptions about the responsibilities, rights, and relations between men and women (Boserup, 1970; Parpart, 1993; Rathgeber, 1990; Afshar, 1991).

In the 1970s, critiques of both mainstream development and liberal feminist assumptions began to emerge. Some Latin American economists and social scientists, most notably Andre Gunder Frank and Raul Prebisch blamed Third World underdevelopment on the machinations of capitalist leaders in the industrialized North and their allies (or collaborators) in the South (Frank, 1976; Prebisch, 1980).[2] They called for self-reliant development, free from the self-interested 'assistance' of capitalist élites and their indigeneous henchmen. In the same period, radical feminists began openly questioning the possibility that women's lives could be improved within patriarchal structures of power, and they too called for delinking from male-dominated institutions (O'Brien, 1981; Daly, 1978). These two perspectives inspired a new approach to the development of women, one that focused on small-scale, women-only projects designed to circumvent male domination, both from the North and the South. This approach, known as Women and Development (WAD), influenced the policy and

[2] I use the word Third World with trepidation, recognizing that it has little explanatory value other than as a short-hand description for three regions of the world: Africa, Asia, and Latin America. While these regions share some common economic problems, they can no longer be seen as a homogeneous, less-developed part of the world. Many differences exist as well. I use the terms South and North to indicate my belief that global economic rivalries and status are no longer defined on an East–West axis, but rather that they are more defined around the less-industrialized economies in the South and the more-industrialized economies in both the North and the South (particularly in Asia). I use the term 'the West' to refer specifically to Europe and North America.

programmes of many non-governmental organizations (NGOs) and became a staple of NGO activities. Some mainstream development agencies supported this approach through their NGO programs as well (Parpart, 1989; Rathgeber, 1990).

WID policy-makers responded to these critiques by modifying mainstream development policy for women. Concern with equality between women and men fell by the wayside as planners emphasized basic human needs, particularly for health, education, and training. WID specialists argued that this approach would increase women's effectiveness and efficiency at work, thus assisting both economic development and women's lives. Reduced fertility would be a side benefit. Planners also called for more credit, greater access to land, legal reform, and for more female involvement in development planning.[3] As a USAID report on women in development put it, 'a focus on the economic participation of women in development is essential' (USAID, 1982: 1). The possibility that fundamental change might be required, particularly attitudinal change, was rarely discussed (Kandiyoti, 1990; Mueller, 1987; Moser, 1989).

In the 1980s, some scholars and activists from both the North and the South began to argue for a new approach to women's development. Drawing on the dependency literature with its concern about widespread poverty and international capitalism, as well as radical feminist ideas about global patriarchy, a socialist-feminist position gradually emerged in various parts of the world. Feminists in the South began looking for their own answers to women's developmental problems. The 1985 Nairobi Conference, celebrating the end of the UN Decade for Women (1975–85), encouraged contacts and better understanding between feminists worldwide. It provided a springboard for South–South linkages among women, including the creation of an international organization, Development Alternatives with Women for a New Era (DAWN), which grew out of discussions among Third World feminists before the conference. DAWN has continued to organize and deliberate about development issues of concern to women in the South. The group has published a book which emphasizes the importance of listening to and learning from women's diverse experiences and knowledge, and to maintaining a commitment to long-range strategies dedicated to breaking down the structures of inequality between genders, classes, and nations. It's political goals thus maintain a belief in modernization, but with greater sensitivity to cultural differences and Third World agendas (Sen and Grown, 1987).

The Nairobi conference also facilitated dialogue between some feminists in the South and the North, particularly those working within the socialist-feminist framework. Links between these groups had been growing rather

[3] Mainstream development planners rarely acknowledged their debt to dependency theorists, but the intellectual roots of this more populist move are easy to discern.

tentatively in North America, and rather more surely in Europe (most notably at Sussex University and The Institute of Social Sciences (ISS) in The Hague), but they received a boost at Nairobi. DAWN members had been influenced by the writings of socialist-feminists (Beneria and Sen, 1981) and the deliberations of the Sussex workshops on the subordination of women (Young *et al.*, 1981). This perspective, with its commitment to understanding class, race, and gender inequalities in a global context, provided an intellectual meeting point for some like-minded feminists from around the world. The resulting dialogue, increasingly known as Gender and Development (GAD), rejects the liberal and radical emphasis on women, and focuses on gender instead, particularly the social construction of gender roles and relations. 'Gender is seen as the process by which individuals who are born into biological categories of male or female become the social categories of men and women through the acquisition of locally-defined attributes of masculinity and femininity' (Kabeer, 1991: 11). The possibility of transforming gender roles is thus established. This approach also emphasizes the importance of examining the gender division of labour in specific societies, particularly the more invisible aspects of women's work, their spatial arrangements, and the relation between these labour patterns and other aspects of gender inequality. It looks at the issue of power as it relates to gender and at strategies for empowering women and challenging the structures and ideas maintaining gender hierarchies (Kabeer, 1991).

While this approach has had considerable influence on academic development discourse, its willingness to consider fundamental social transformation does not sit well with the large donor agencies who prefer government-to-government aid, with its assumed respect for the sovereign rights of member states. Although some government agencies (most notably the Scandinavians, Dutch, and Canadians) and some non-governmental organizations have adopted a more gender-oriented approach to women's development, adding gender analysis training to established WID training programs, this approach is rarely integrated into development planning (Moser, 1989). However, as Rathgeber points out, sometimes gender-sensitive approaches are partially incorporated into WID policies, but without changing the official discourse (Rathgeber, 1994).[4] Moreover, while GAD proponents rarely reject/question modernist assumptions, the GAD perspective provides the possible (discursive) space to do so.

[4] The GAD approach offers development planners a way to differentiate between practical (i.e. specific, daily) gender needs and strategic (or long-term, empowerment) needs for women. This approach is making some inroads into mainstream development thinking, at least at the level of rhetoric. The CIDA/WID policy, passed in 1992, acknowledges gender equity's fundamental nature and the need to see gender equity as a societal, economic, and political matter. (CIDA, 1992; interview with Sherry Greaves, CIDA, WID Unit, Ottawa, 28 Feb. 1992.)

Most development practitioners have seen no reason to alter their comfortable belief in modernization. However, new thinking is questioning the validity of this assumption. Drawing on the postmodern critique of the modern and the crucial relationship between power and language (Foucault, 1976), some scholars are questioning the underlying assumptions of development with its uncritical identification with Westernization/modernization (Escobar, 1984–5; Ferguson, 1990). This critique of the modern, concern with difference, and focus on the power of language has influenced the thinking of some feminists concerned with women's development in the Third World (Parpart, 1993; Marchand and Parpart, 1994). It has led to new questions, particularly a critique of development specialists' representation of the Third World as the vulnerable 'other', and an awareness that these representations have often undermined indigenous women's knowledge and self-confidence. It overestimates the knowledge of Western 'experts' and devalues developmental solutions coming out of the South. This approach argues for a more careful attention to language and to the specific contexts and locales in which peoples lives are played out. It rejects analysis that draws primarily on macro-economic data and broad generalizations, and urges scholars to investigate the interstices of daily life, the small exchanges between women and men, which reveal changes in gender relations that cannot be seen at the macro-level (Marchand and Parpart, 1995; Crush, 1995).

In this spirit, the Zimbabwe case discussed below will adopt a multi-pronged approach to its analysis of the relationship between women, economic development, and patriarchy in post-independence Zimbabwe. While drawing on broad economic and political indicators, the chapter will also examine the struggles of seven widows to protect their interests and obtain control over marital property. These cases offer insights into the discursive construction of gender ideology and gender relations which are difficult to obtain from macro-economic data alone.

THE ZIMBABWEAN CASE: GENDER AND ECONOMIC DEVELOPMENT

When independence was finally won in 1980, the new Zimbabwean government publicly recognized African women's crucial role in the liberation struggle. It called for new laws and programmes to ensure that women reaped the benefits of independence. To that end, several major pieces of legislation were enacted to protect women's interests. Most importantly, in 1982 the Legal Age of Majority Act (LAMA) granted all Zimbabweans, both male and female, full majority at the age of eighteen. This legislation gave women full jural rights, something they had not had in either colonial or pre-colonial Zimbabwe. The 1985 Matrimonial Causes Act made civil marriages dissoluble on no-fault grounds and the maternity leave regulations guaranteed that women could take up to ninety days maternity leave without losing their job. The Sex Disqualification Removal Act (1985) declared that women with the requisite qualications could not be barred from holding the same offices and positions as men (Jacobs and Howard, 1987; Kazembe and Mol, 1985).

The government officially supported welfare programmes for women (both donor driven and government sponsored) and set up a Ministry for Community Development and Women's Affairs (MCDWA) to protect women's interests. The ministry called for the removal of discriminatory laws and labour practices, the mobilization of women in development projects, literacy campaigns, and an end to discriminatory practices such as *lobola*.[5] In line with its official commitment to socialism, government leaders acknowledged the importance of providing incentives to draw women into waged employment (Jacobs and Howard, 1987; MacKenzie, 1986; MCDWA, 1985).

However, this rhetoric and the legal and government structures set in place to help Zimbabwean women have not achieved as much as one would have hoped. Only a small minority hold government positions. In 1986, only two government ministers (or 6.25 per cent) were women. No women held provincial governorships. Women were 8 per cent of the deputy ministers, 9 per cent of the MPs, and 1.82 per cent of local councillors. These figures hardly represent women's 52 per cent of the population. In 1985, the Politburo (the ruling party's top decision-making body) had only one woman out of fifteen members (MacKenzie, 1986; MCDWA, 1985). Furthermore, only three to four per cent of the employees in public administration were women (Spence, 1986).

Moreover, if one looks at economic performance and individual access to education, employment, property, and other benefits, men have clearly gained more from independence than women, particularly in the rural areas. For example, males continue to benefit disproportionately from education. Literacy levels for women continue to lag behind men. In 1970, 75 women for every 100 men could read. By 1990, the figure had only risen to 82. Schooling for Africans expanded dramatically after independence. While girls benefitted at the lower levels, where by 1988 girls and boys had equal access to education, the gender gap continues to widen as one moves up the educational heirarchy. In 1988–9, 85 girls for every 100 boys attended secondary school; the ratio fell to 36 in tertiary institutions. At the graduate level, the figures are even lower. Moreover, women in higher education are predominantly in the humanities and social

[5] *Lobola*, otherwise known as bridewealth, is a payment made at marriage which guarantees the husband's right to the progeny of that marriage. It is not a purchase of the bride. Among matrilineal peoples rights to the children remain in the mother's line, although a bride's service payment may occur.

sciences, where job opportunities and pay are lowest (UNDP, 1993: 151–3; Batezat and Mwalo, 1989: 28–9).

Historically, men have dominated waged employment in Zimbabwe, and this trend has continued. In 1981, African women held 1.9 per cent of the jobs in production, 2.5 per cent in agriculture, animal husbandry, and foresty, 7.2 per cent in service, 8.5 per cent in clerical and related employment, and 16.6 per cent of professional and technical jobs. Women with skills were concentrated in the clerical and service occupations, such as medical assistants, nurses, midwives, teachers, social workers, typists, and telephonists. More than any other group, African women worked in the lowest paid, least secure sectors of waged employment (Jacobs and Howard, 1987). Since independence, women have increasingly entered the waged labour force. In 1990, 35 per cent of the waged labour force were women. However, these women still cluster in the least skilled, worst paid and most insecure jobs. Moreover, women in industry report considerable sexual harassment, lack of promotion, limited training opportunities, and little support from administration. And since only 41 per cent of the population have waged jobs, many people, particularly women, are left struggling to survive in the informal sector, which has become increasingly competitive and unremunerative in the current economic crisis (UNDP, 1993: 169; Made and Lagerstrom, 1985).

At independence, most African women worked in the rural areas as unwaged family workers on small holdings or in the communal areas. They received little reward for their work. Men generally controlled the sale of produce and thus the little money that came into the household. This situation has changed little for many rural women. They continue to do much of the work, receive little training, and control very little land. In 1986, for example, only 14 out of 1,400 extension agricultural workers were women, thus making it difficult for women farmers to receive training (Spence, 1986; Batezat and Mwalo, 1989; MCDWA, 1985).

Men continue to have easier access to property and credit than women. In the resettlement schemes set up to provide land to liberation fighters, individual land grants were awarded to heads of households, i.e. men. Married women thus could not own land, and in case of a divorce, the female settler lost rights to stay on the land in her estranged husband's name. Thus only widows and single women could obtain land, and even they had trouble acquiring land because officials were sceptical about their potential productivity. Women found it easier to gain access to land in co-operatives, but this membership generally brought increased workloads with limited control or rewards (Jacobs, 1989: 169–78). Because women rarely own land, and if they do, usually obtain marginal land with little chance for capital accumulation, they are poor credit risks, and thus have more difficulty obtaining loans than men. Special projects to offer women credit have generally focused on entrepreneurs rather than farmers (Spence, 1986).

These inequalities are not easily explained. Laws and institutions designed to improve women's status have had to contend with deeply entrenched patriarchal beliefs. While no one can be sure how much these beliefs are the residue of pre-colonial patriarchy, which was very powerful, most scholars agree that patriarchal attitudes grew in strength during the colonial period (Schmidt, 1992). It is clear, however, that patriarchal assumptions, with their preference for female subordination, abound in Zimbabwe and have undermined the progressive legislation mentioned above. Indeed, Joan May and Joyce Kazembe have concluded that 'the intention of the legislature was a symbolic goal setting only. It was the result of ideological and social pressures, and probably demonstrated that there were conflicts and contradictions among the legislature itself' (1985: 21–2). Moreover, poor women, especially in the rural areas, often have little knowledge of the law nor do they have an opportunity to use the law, as most decisions regarding their lives are made at the household and community level where customary law dominates. And since customary law is for the most part defined and controlled by men, it can often be manipulated to protect male interests (Maboreke, 1987; Shenje, 1992; Stewart, 1992).[6]

Patriarchal assumptions have inhibited women's ability to achieve in male dominated sectors of the economy and the government. Public statements glorifying women's roles as mothers and wives have encouraged women to stay home and raise children rather than enter the workforce or seek more training. The current economic crisis has reinforced the notion that women should stay home and let men (i.e. the breadwinners) have well-paying waged jobs (Batezat and Mwalo, 1989: 26–7). In the cities, 'clean-up' campaigns, which have attacked unescorted women in public places, have blamed economic problems on these 'prostitutes', making it difficult for women to take up employment that requires travel and in-hibiting collective action and organizational activities, particularly when meetings must be held at night (Ranchod-Nilsson, 1992; Jacobs, 1989: 166–8; Seidman, 1984).

While it is difficult to quantify the impact of such attitudes and behaviour, evidence suggests that patriarchal ideology, particularly concerning the sexual division of labour, has affected many women's ability to take up the opportunities available in the post-independence period. It has also, no doubt, contributed to the chronic underfunding meted out to the Women's Bureau (which received just over one per cent of the national budget in 1983), and to widespread disinterest in the fact that laws ostensibly designed to help women have been poorly enforced and institutions that hamper women's opportunities have rarely been challenged. (Seidman, 1984: 431; May and Kazembe, 1985; Batezat and Mwalo, 1989).

[6] Julie Stewart, a Zimbabwean lawyer and expert on inheritance law, is increasingly convinced that women can manipulate customary law as well if they know how to do it. She believes customary law may have more potential for women's rights than the creation of new statutory laws which would probably be ignored for the most part.

However, while men have benefited from economic and political development more than women, it is important to recognize that some African women have reaped the benefits of economic development which have emerged since independence. In 1988 a study reported that 21 per cent of the University of Zimbabwe's academic posts were held by women. While far from representative, this figure compares favourably with similar statistics in North America. Admittedly, women academics are largely in the middle and lower academic ranks and continue to be concentrated in the humanities. However, African women academics are an increasingly forceful group on campus (Dorsey *et al.*, 1989). The current economic crisis has forced middle-class families to adopt a dual-income strategy to maintain their living standards. Women with education and capital are entering employment in increasing numbers and many have professional jobs in government or the private sector. Indeed, African women working in professional, technical, and related jobs rose from 59 per cent of the female labour force in 1981 to 79 per cent in 1985 (Batezat and Mwalo, 1989: 33).

Thus some women have profited dramatically from economic developments during the independence period. Other women's lives have improved, if only marginally. The question at issue is whether women have been able to use these economic advances to challenge patriarchal beliefs and authority in post-colonial Zimbabwe. The above statistics offer some insights at the macro-level, but tell us little about struggles between women and men over property. Inheritance cases provide an opportunity to examine specific struggles over property. These cases are particularly interesting because they offer a glimpse into the way women have sought to protect their interests within often deeply patriarchal family and community structures.

WOMEN AND INHERITANCE IN ZIMBABWE

The following cases were collected by the Zimbabwe research team of the Women and Law in Southern Africa Research Project, a six country research project which has been investigating issues around women and inheritance in six southern African countries.[7] This is raw data, collected in the field during 1992. The informants are both Shona and Ndebele speakers,[8] rich and poor, urban and rural. The data offer some insights into the way a number of widows have struggled to acquire and control property after the death of their spouse. Their ability (or inability) to manage

[7] This data was collected during 1992 and is currently being analysed and written up.

[8] The Shona people predominate in Zimbabwe. They were the original inhabitants. In the 1800s, the Ndebele moved into southern Zimbabwe, fleeing from disturbances in their home country of Natal.

the inheritance process reveals a good deal about women's capacity to control their lives and protect their interests, and consequently is particularly appropriate for analysing the relationship between women's access to the benefits of economic development and their ability to challenge patriarchal attitudes and practices. The cases are summarized below.

Case 1: Mrs A., lives in a high-density (crowded) suburb of Bulawayo in Southern Zimbabwe

Mrs A.'s husband died in 1980. She had been married by customary law, with *lobola* (bridewealth). The marriage was monogamous, with no children. Both were Ndebele. Neither had much formal education. He worked as a hotel cook. They owned a three-roomed house and the husband transferred the house to her name while he was still alive. He had no will.

The husband died suddenly at work of suspected food poisoning. The relative accepted the death as being of natural causes.[9] The employers catered for the funeral. The widow received a small pension and four months rent. There was no insurance. Clothing and effects of the deceased were distributed in accordance with customary practices about a year after death and there was no conflict over this. The widow kept the radio and some clothes, which she sold. The relatives took the car and cupboards. The widow accepted this distribution since she had no children and could not drive the car.

There was no question of her entering into a lineage (levirate) marriage; she was too old.[10] She followed accepted mourning practices—the relatives bought her the traditional black dress. After the standard year of mourning, the relatives bought her some new clothes to symbolize the end of mourning. She tried to earn some money by making trading trips to Botswana, but poor health and age put a stop to that. Now she survives on assistance from the Department of Social Welfare and her relatives. She had no views on what could be done to improve things.

Case 2: Mrs B., rural Matabeleland (southern Zimbabwe)

Mrs B. was married under customary law. Both were Ndebele. She has three children of her own and numerous step-children, since her husband had four other wives (they had all left before he died). She completed standard six education. Her husband was a wealthy chief and already married when they met. She never worked. He worked as a buthcher in

[9] African religions have often ascribed death to intervention by a deceased's enemies, whether alive or dead. Accusations of witchcraft around the death of a person are still fairly common, particularly if there is any question of the cause of death or a suspicion that someone wanted the death to occur.

[10] Leviratic marriage (*nhaka*) involves the 'inheritance' of a widow by one of her husband's brothers. It was a long-held tradition designed to provide a male protector for the widow and her children, and as a means to keep the children under the control of their father's family. It still occurs, though less often, but only with the widow's consent.

Bulawayo before taking up the chieftainship. They lived in the rural areas and had lots of cattle. She was resourceful and bought household goods for the home.

She had a harmonious relationship with her spouse and in-laws, but the co-wives were quarrelsome and difficult to live with. There had been no pre- or post-death protection measures. The husband died in a scooter accident. The in-laws did not raise allegations of witchcraft against her concerning the husband's death. At the end of mourning, the property was distributed among all the children by the next of kin. No conflict ocurred. The property was taken from her and given to the deceased's other children. The widow believed the next of kin thought they were being fair by giving the property to all the children, including those of wives who had left the husband, but she didn't agree. 'After all,' she said, 'I worked for that property.' She took no action against the relatives, however, not knowing what she could do. She is still aggrieved at how the property, especially the household effects, was distributed.

She has had health difficulties since her husband's death, but has been coping financially since she has no dependents. She had no proposals for changing the inheritance system to offer the research team. The chieftainship has gone to her husband's eldest son by another wife.

Case 3: Mrs C., poor housing in a low-density suburb of Bulawayo

She is about 25 years old, and had been married under custom, although without *lobola*. She has four children and no step-children. Her husband was Shona, she is Ndebele. The husband had a grade seven education and she has grade five. The husband worked as a security guard. They were married for about ten years. Relations with husband and in-laws were good. No pre- or post-death measures had been taken to protect the wife.

The husband complained of a headache and died in hospital the next day. The relatives were angry and blamed her for the death. There was no property worth talking about. She has the sofas and the wardrobe, but the in-laws took the bicycle and said they would come for the sofas. The relatives forcibly took the children. The wife seemingly had no resource person to help her. She has taken no apparent action to protect her interests. Her relatives told her to let the in-laws be. She didn't know her rights. She was surprised when the research team told her that despite being unmarried (technically), the custody and guardianship of the children lay with her and she could assert these rights.

She was not asked to go through mourning. The in-laws have been difficult to deal with. They are not happy with the explanation of the death of their son and have been asking the children how he died. They have even taken the death certificate and won't let the widow have access to it. The widow is worried about the children because the sister-in-law who took them back to Mashonaland does not work and does not have the resources to adequately look after them.

The deceased had no pension or insurance and the widow is destitute. She has virtually no formal education and is unlikely to find employment. She doesn't seem to have much moral support from her family—perhaps because she isn't regarded by them as properly married. She had no ideas for change.

Case 4: Mrs D., lives in Highfield, a high-density suburb of Harare

The widow was living with her husband in Highfield when he died. The Highfield municipality housing scheme superintendent, in accordance with municipal policy, transferred the lease agreement into her name, so she could continue living there. The rent is paid by having lodgers. Seventeen people live in the house, including a sister, two brothers, their children, and the lodgers.

There was no other property to speak of at the husband's death. All his savings had been put into building a home in Mount Darwin. His clothes were distributed by a nephew of the deceased, in accordance with custom. Two uncles were present at the funeral, but played no role in it. Neither of them work so could not be of much financial assistance at the funeral.

The mother lives on handouts from her children. They find it increasingly difficult to provide her with money as their families are expanding and needy. Each family in the house cooks separately and they take turns giving her food. On occasion the widow complains that she is not being looked after adequately, but the sons dismiss these as the remarks of someone who does not realize how tough things are for everyone. She also complains that the sons-in-law whom she supported during their unemployment have moved away now that they have jobs and have forgotten about her. They do not send money to help support her.

Case 5: Mrs E., lives in Greendale, a low-density suburb of Harare

Mrs E. married young and had four children. Her husband worked as a senior accountant for an industrial firm. She completed secondary school and has been involved in business. The husband died in 1990 in a car accident. The company was supportive, paid most of the funeral expences, and gave the widow some financial assistance while working out the pension monies.

While this was going on, the widow heard rumours that some people believed she 'caused' the death of her husband and that she didn't care about the children. This didn't bother her a bit because 'she knew that a lot of our African people always talk like that and anyway I loved my husband and could never have even dreamt of harming him'.

Her husband had a will and on his death the widow left the lawyers to handle all the insurance policies. Her in-laws went to the lawyers thinking they would be entitled to some of the deceased's property. The lawyers told them that their son had left a will which gave the Greendale home and a rural home, including the household effects, to his wife and their little boy. He left the car to the first-born child, a girl. The widow is closing down two shops from which she receives the proceeds. The widow did not know the contents of the will until after the husband's death.

When the company had worked out the pension monies, the husband's father and brothers went with the widow to discuss the payments. The company officials told the relatives that they only wanted to talk to the widow, who had to bring the children's birth certificates and a marriage certificate before she could get the money. The company recovered the cost of the wrecked car from the money, so it was much less than expected. The pension was paid to the widow (for life) and to the children (until 18 years).

Since the company and lawyers made it clear to the husband's relatives that all property would be given to the widow and children, they have become less interested in them. They rarely phone or visit. 'You see my brother-in-law had wanted the car. They thought that since I didn't have a driver's licence, I would either let go of the car completely or I would let them use the car, and have come and pick me up and take me where I want to go. At some stage they were even thinking that they could get the house. Anyway all their ambitions came to nothing. The lawyers, anticipating that the car might create a lot of problems for me from the brothers, decided to sell it and put the money in the children's accounts. It's up to the kids to do what they want with the money when they reach 18.'

According to the deceased's father, the widow chased a second wife (who was not formally married) away from her home and refused to let her have any benefits from the estate. The deceased's father was angry about this. He had wanted both wives to live in the Greendale house and for the first wife to be 'inherited' by one of his sons so there could be someone (i.e. a male relative) in the house who would oversee the care of the children and the spending of the estate. He complained that the widow arranged for the heir to be her small son. She did this by getting her sister-in-law to agree to be her nominal 'husband'. The father was furious, claiming that 'my daughter [the sister-in-law] in Glen View is a government into herself. No one can control her. She interfered with a lot of things and put her own rules and decisions, most of which I did not agree with. She interfered not only on the issue of *kugara nhaka*, but also regarding the property of the second wife and eventually giving marching orders to the second wife.' The father-in-law feels he should have been consulted about the use of the pension money and the sale of the car and he is increasingly dissatisfied with the way his son's property is being used.

Case 6: Mrs F., a low-density suburb of Bulawayo
The husband was a lecturer in the training sector with a government parastatal. The wife is a nurse. The husband died in a car crash. They married in 1963 and had three children.

The benefits and pension were straightened out in two weeks and were given to the widow. The insurances and other monies were handed over to the family lawyer who was executor of the estate. The husband left no will, and his brother arranged to have the eldest son appointed heir without consulting the widow. The widow convinced the son to cede his heirship to her, thus giving her control over the property in question. The widow told the researchers that 'I am quite opposed to the notion of heir because it is a bad law. If you work as a twosome, the remaining spouse must be the heir'.

Her relationship with her in-laws has remained very poor. Her brother-in-law asked for money only three weeks after the funeral and she refused. He has not taken that refusal well. The mother-in-law does not visit any more. The widow wore black for a year. She set a date for the ceremony ending the mourning. The mother-in-law and brother-in-laws tried to change it. The widow refused and the original date was celebrated. The brother-in-laws refused to come and went a year without talking to her. There was no question of *kugara nhaka*.

After a year, the two brother-in-laws arrived saying they had come for the clothes of the deceased. The widow was ready to call the police if they stole the clothes, but 'fortunately they just threw open all the suitcases and left without anything. They told my son to take anything he wanted and discard the rest through sale or donation.'

The sister-in-law was content with the arrangement. She agreed that the eldest son should be the heir and that the guardian of the children would be the mother. The brother-in-laws were unhappy with the way the son handed the estate over to his mother at the High Court, but they could do nothing about it. The son reported that he and the rest of the family are not on good terms with the uncles as they want to oversee and control everything. Despite much pressure from his uncles, the heir decided to give everything to his mother. He reported that 'I do not need help from him [the uncle], I've never gone there for it. Even if I face hardships I won't look back. I believe the widow must have everything. If I had taken over this home would have been upside-down by now.'

Case 7: Mrs G., Highfield, a high-density suburb of Harare
The widow was married in 1955 and had eight children (four died). Her husband worked as a cleaner in an office building. They had lived in a house in Highfield since 1961. Now the widow lives in the house with her youngest son, his wife and a baby, and one daughter. They started living in the house in 1961. The house was in both their names.

The funeral was held without problems. Some of the deceased's clothes were distributed to his relatives. The rest were given out three years later at the ceremony to mark the end of mourning. This usually takes place after a year, but because the deceased had no brothers, the widow had to rely on a cousin, who didn't seem to care whether the ceremony was completed or not. Finally, when that family began experiencing misfortunes, they decided to arrange for the ceremony in order to appease the spirit of their dead cousin.

There were no problems about the house. When the husband died, the superintendent's office asked the son to come to the office to discuss the matter. They asked him what he wanted done with the house. He said it should go to the widow. She signed some papers and the house was then in her name. The widow praised her son for this attitude as not all sons wanted their mother to own the home. He may have been influenced by custom, as the family came from Chipinge where wives and children generally inherit a man's property.

The widow also received a pension so has had no problems with money. She tried to make some extra money from crotcheting and travelled south to sell her goods, but now has stopped because she is tired. Her children take good care of her.

ANALYSIS

These cases raise a number of important issues. First, a woman's access to economic resources, particularly her own income, seems to be a crucial factor in her ability to influence the inheritance process. Mrs E. (case 5) and Mrs F. (case 6), were able to challenge relatives who wanted to control both the widow and the property left by the deceased. They both hired lawyers to protect them from over-zealous relatives. Mrs E., for example, quickly handed over insurance policies rather than let her husband's relatives have them. Mrs F. took the insurances and other monies to the family lawyer. Both women were employed and thus could afford expert advice. Thus, their education and position in the waged economy, as well as the position of their husbands, provided important resources in their struggle to maintain control over the family assets and to challenge patriarchal authority.

However, access to lawyers, money, and other sources of support do not tell the whole story. Both widows successfully resisted the plans of their in-laws and manipulated the system for their own ends. The brothers of Mrs F.'s husband met with the family lawyer and indicated that they wished the eldest son to become the heir, in the expectation that they could control the son. But the widow circumvented this by convincing the son to let her control the family property, although he would remain the heir. She helped him arrange the transfer of the family property to her. When the brother-in-laws showed up to take her husband's clothing, she threatened them with the police. Mrs E. sold one of her husband's shops against the wishes of his relatives and sold the car rather than let the brother get ahold of it. Both widows proved remarkably confident and resourceful in their struggles to obtain control over the marital property. It is striking that both widows are reasonably well educated and employed. They had resources to draw on, both economic and experiential, which played a crucial role in their willingness and ability to challenge the patriarchal assumptions of male family members, particularly the expectiation that property should be controlled and monitored by men. This confidence and poise, which is often seen in women with a high degree of economic autonomy, was a crucial factor in the widows' willingness to take on established authorities and to challenge the dominance of men (and their female allies), both in the family and in society at large.

At first glance, the widows in the urban areas with less education and fewer economic resources seem to have been more vulnerable to inheritance problems than their more privileged sisters. This is true to some degree. Mrs A. lost the car and cupboards to her husband's relatives. Mrs C.'s relatives took the children, the bicycle, and are threatening to take the sofa. She is destitute. Both Mrs D. and Mrs G. live on the margins economically, and share their Highfield homes with numerous relatives. However, it is important to note that all of these widows, with the exception of Mrs C., have maintained control over the matrimonial home. The husband of Mrs A. had transferred the house to his wife's name before his death. The two widows living in Highfield benefited from municipal regulations which obligated the municipality to transfer the title of the home to the widow. This regulation has been crucial for many widows' survival and prosperity. Women who control a home may have to share it, but they cannot be expelled. Significantly, Mrs C., the widow in the greatest difficulty, had no permanent home. Relatively poor urban widows also frequently received some help from their husbands' employers, particularly with the funeral and over pension monies. Thus many of the institutions and regulations associated with economic and political development have permitted even relatively unprivileged women to challenge the widespread belief that men should control their lives. Women do not have to be professionals or managers to use the modern economy for their own ends. These inheritance cases remind us that women who are marginal, but located in formal structures, may be able to draw on those institutions to protect their interests and to challenge received notions about women's rights and access to property.

Widows in the rural areas for the most part have had less access to these formal structures, and thus have been more reliant on customary practices. This can lead to unhappiness. Mrs B., for example, clearly disagreed with the way her husband's relatives distributed the marital property, although she admitted they were following local custom. Another widow, who lived in a communal area, fled the shop she had built up with her husband, after a family council meeting of her in-laws decided she no longer had rights to it. She believed this was unjust, but saw no way to fight it (WLSA, 1993: 15). The WLSA research team has discovered that the disposition of property in the rural areas is still largely determined by the deceased's male relatives. Family decisions are ostensibly based on 'custom', but the research has revealed just how fluid custom can be. While some families have upheld the traditional focus of customary inheritance law, with its commitment to the well-being and security of the widow and her children, others have bent the law to serve their own material interests. Customary law has proven a flexible medium, and it continues to be so. This can work against widows, as in the two cases above (WLSA, 1993).

However, the very flexibility of customary law offers possibilities for negotiation and contestation as well. The WLSA research team discovered many cases where widows refused to accept *nhaka* and managed to gain the use (if not control) of land and other property. Good relations with one's children and in-laws clearly helped, although no doubt personal charisma also made a difference. As one informant from a more prosperous rural area stated, 'I think that every family has its own laws here in Bikita. What happens when a man dies, with regards to his property, depends on the relationship that existed between the widow and her husband's parents. If the relationship was good, there is no reason for the widow to alienate herself from her husband's family. . . . If the relationship was bad, then the widow will most likely do everything without consulting her in-laws' (WLSA, 1993: 19–20).

In the matter of inheritance, even urban women were affected by the quality of their family relationships. Despite considerable material resources, the Greendale widow (Mrs E.) relied on a sympathetic sister-in-law in order to resist the pressures of her husband's male relatives. She also benefited from a sympathetic and supportive son. Thus, good relations with children (especially the heir) and in-laws generally affect a widow's ability to negotiate a favourable conclusion to inheritance issues. This is particularly true if the widow has few outside resources, as in the case of Mrs C. The custom of blaming a death on witchcraft is more apt to happen when relatives dislike the widow and are looking for a reason to mistreat her. Women in polygynous unions, such as Mrs B., can suffer from hostile co-wives and their children as well.

Urban widows are also affected by the flexibility of customary law. While widows with economic and personal resources can sometimes ignore tradition, such as Mrs E.'s dismissal of accusations about the cause of her husband's death, at other points, following 'tradition' or at least an acceptable version of 'tradition' may be more beneficial. Mrs E., for example, convinced her sister-in-law to be her nominal 'husband', thus precluding the possibility of marrying one of her husband's brothers. Mrs G. waited three years before taking off mourning clothes rather than break with custom. But at the same time, she felt no compunction about obtaining control over property left to her son. Thus it appears that custom is important in the urban areas, but the urban widows we have encountered freely adapted custom to their specific circumstances. In both the urban and rural areas, customary law thus offers a flexible instrument which can provide innovative and determined women a means for challenging the *status quo*.

CONCLUSION

This chapter has considered the relationship between economic development, women's status, and patriarchy in Zimbabwe since the declaration of independence in 1980. If one measures women's status by their access to education, employment, property, credit, and other material benefits, while some Zimbabwean women have managed to reap the benefits of economic and political development, most have not. At the macro-level, statistics reveal continued bias towards men and males in Zimbabwe. Men dominate the highest levels of government, education, and employment. Moreover, patriarchal values are still very much a force to be reckoned with. Male hostility to women's advancement and to progressive legislation aimed at assisting women explains the continued underfunding of the Women's Ministry, the attacks on 'prostitutes', and the refusal to acknowledge the full implications of the Age of Majority Act. Thus, macro-economic indicators paint a rather grim picture, one that suggests little improvement over patriarchal domination during the colonial era.

However, if one adopts a more localized, discursive approach to the question of women's emancipation, a different picture emerges. The widows we have encountered have not just capitulated to male domination. They have developed myriad, and often effective, ways of challenging male domination. As we have seen, widows with economic resources of their own have used these resources to protect their access to marital property. They have been remarkably successful in challenging patriarchal authority and maintaining control over their lives and property. This evidence supports Moghadam's conclusion that education and employment are crucial factors in women's emancipation (see the Introduction to the present volume). However, we have seen that even relatively poor, less educated women have managed to use the structures and regulations put in place since independence to their own end. Witness the Highfield widows and the widow in Bulawayo, all of whom obtained control over the marital home. Here again, we see the importance of property for women, but the data remind us that women need not be from the most advantaged groups to be able to benefit from the outcomes of economic and political development.

Moreover, even poor rural women are rarely completely defenceless. True, they must adapt more to local (often male) pressures, but even here, women with strong family support and forceful personalities have often managed to bend 'tradition' to their own ends. Men, after all, require female knowledge and co-operation for many activities, and while this co-operation is no doubt sometimes achieved through force, it often requires negotiation as well. The inheritance cases offer only a glimpse into this world of female–male negotiations and contestations, but even that glimpse reminds us that maintaining patriarchal authority and domination is not a simple matter.

This chapter thus points out the danger of excessive reliance on macro-data, and the importance of discovering the voices of specific women, of learning about the concrete, lived experiences of specific women. Only then can we begin to see through the smokescreen of figures and statistics that too often obscure more than they reveal. While the power of patriarchal authority and ideology should not be minimized, it is important to recognize women's power as well. If we argue that women can only challenge patriarchy after they have conquered male-dominated educational and occupational institutions, we are ignoring women's history. We are throwing away the knowledge and power women have used to challenge patriarchy. Women need new tools, they need to reap the benefits of economic and political development, but women also need to remember and recognize their long-held knowledge and power as well.

REFERENCES

Afshar, H. (ed.) (1991), *Women, Development and Survival in the Third World* (London: Longman).

Batezat, Elinor and Mwalo, Margaret (1989), *Women in Zimbabwe* (Harare: Southern Africa Political Economy Series (SAPES) Trust).

Beneria, L. and Sen, G. (1981), 'Accumulation, Reproduction and Women's Role in Economic Development: Boserup Revisited', *Signs*, 7/2: 279–98.

Boserup, E. (1970), *Woman's Role in Economic Development* (New York: St Martin's).

Canadian International Development Agency/WID Unit (1992), 'Women in Development: A Policy Statement' (Ottawa: CIDA, Feb.).

Crush, Jonathan (1995), *The Power of Development* (New York: Routledge).

Daly, Mary (1978), *Gyn/Ecology: the Metaethics of Radical Feminism* (Boston: Beacon Press).

Dorsey, Betty Jo, Gaidzanwa, Rudo and Mupawaenda, Anna (1989), *Factors*

Affecting Academic Careers for Women at the University of Zimbabwe (Harare: Ford Foundation).

ESCOBAR, ARTURO (1984–5), 'Discourse and Power in Development: Michel Foucault and the Relevance of his Work to the Third World', *Alternatives*, 10: 377–400.

FERGUSON, JAMES (1990), *The Anti-Politics Machine* (Cambridge: Cambridge University Press).

FOUCAULT, MICHEL (1976), *Rower/Knowledge* (New York: Pantheon Books).

FRANK, ANDRE GUNDER (1976), *Latin America: Underdevelopment or Revolution* (New York: Monthly Review Press).

GILLESPIE, KAMLESH (1989), 'The Key to Unlocking Sustainable Development', (Washington, DC: World Bank, mimeo).

JACOBS, SUSAN (1989), 'Zimbabwe: State, Class, and Gendered Models of Land Resettlement', in J. Parpart and K. Staudt (eds.), *Women and the State in Africa* (Boulder, Colo.: Lynne Rienner).

—— and HOWARD, TRACEY (1987), 'Women in Zimbabwe: Stated Policy and State Action', in H. Afshar (ed.), *Women, State and Ideology: Studies from Africa and Asia* (London: Macmillan).

KABEER, NAILA (1991), 'Rethinking Development from a Gender Perspective: Some Insights from the Decade'. Durban: Conference on Women and Gender in Southern Africa, University of Natal.

KANDIYOTI, DENIZ (1990), 'Women and Rural Development Policies: the Changing Agenda', *Development and Change*, 21/1: 5–22.

KAZEMBE, JOYCE and MOL, MARJON (1985), 'Traveller, There is no Path. Paths are Made by Walking'. (Harare: Centre for Applied Social Sciences, University of Zimbabwe, mimeo).

MABOREKE, MARY (1987), 'The Love of a Mother: Problems of Custody in Zimbabwe', in Alice Armstrong (ed.), (with W. Ncube), *Women and Law in Southern Africa* (Harare: Zimbabwe Publishing House).

MACKENZIE, CLAYTON (1986), 'Educating for Equality: Women's Rights in Zimbabwe' (mimeo).

MADE, PATRICIA and LAGERSTROM, BIRGITTA (1985), *Zimbabwean Women in Industry* (Harare: Zimbabwe Publishing House).

MARCHAND, MARIANNE and PARPART, JANE (eds.) (1995), *Feminism/Postmodernism/Development* (London: Routledge).

MAY, JOAN and KAZEMBE, JOYCE (1985), 'Beyond Legislation' (mimeo).

Ministry of Community Development and Women's Affairs (MCDWA), Zimbabwe (1985), *National Seminar on Women in Construction and Reconstruction in Post-Independent Zimbabwe* (Harare: MCDWA with UNESCO).

MOSER, CAROLINE (1989), 'Gender Planning in the Third World: Meeting Practical and Strategic Gender Needs', *World Development*, 17/11: 1799–1825.

MUELLER, ADELE (1987), 'Peasants and Professionals: the Production of Knowledge about Women in the Third World', paper presented at the Association for Women in Development, Washington, DC.

O'BRIEN, MARY (1981), *The Politics of Reproduction* (Boston: Routledge and Kegan Paul).

PARPART, JANE (1989), *Women and Development in Africa* (Lanham, Md.: University Press of America).

—— (1993), 'Who is the Other?: A Postmodern Feminist Critique of Women and Development Theory and Practice', *Development and Change*, 24/3: 439–64.

PREBISCH, RAUL (1980), 'The Dynamics of Peripheral Capitalism', in Louis Lefeber and Lisa L. North (eds.), *Democracy and Development in Latin America* (Toronto: Toronto University Press).

RANCHOD-NILSSON, SITA (1992), 'Women and Democratization in Southern Africa: The Legacy of Zimbabwe's Liberation War for Women's Politics After Independence', paper presented for the International Studies Association Mid-west Meeting (Nov.).

RATHGEBER, EVA (1990), 'WID, WAD, GAD: Trends in Research and Practice', *Journal of Developing Areas*, 24: 489–502.

Report of a Commonwealth Expert Group on Women and Structural Adjustment (1989), *Engendering Adjustment for the 1990s* (London: Commonwealth Secretariat).

SCHMIDT, ELIZABETH (1992), *Peasants, Traders, and Wives: Shona Women in the History of Zimbabwe, 1870–1939* (Portsmouth, NH: Heinemann).

SEIDMAN, GAY (1984), 'Women in Zimbabwe: Postindependence Struggles', *Feminist Studies*, 10/3: 419–40.

SEN, GITA and GROWN, CAREN (1987), *Development, Crises, and Alternative Visions* (New York: Monthly Review Press).

SHENJE, A. (1992), 'The Forgotten Victims? African Widows and their use of the Provisions of the Deceased Person's Family Maintenance Act', in Julie Stewart (ed.), *Working Papers on Inheritance in Zimbabwe*, Working Paper no. 5 (Harare: Women and Law in Southern Africa Research Project (WLSA)).

SPENCE, NANCY (1986), 'Women in Zimbabwe: Needs/Future Directions', compiled for the Zimbabwe Desk, CIDA (Ottawa: CIDA).

STEWART, JULIE (1992), 'Inheritance in Zimbabwe: The Quiet Revolution', in J. Stewart, *Working Papers on Inheritance in Zimbabwe*, Working Paper no. 5 (Harare: WLSA).

SYLVESTER, CHRISTINE (1991), '"Urban Women Cooperators", "Progress", and "African Feminism" in Zimbabwe', *Differences*, 3/1: 39–62.

United Nations Development Program (1993), *Human Development Report 1993* (New York: Oxford University Press).

United States Agency For International Development (USAID) (1982), 'Women in Development' (Washington, DC: AID Policy Paper).

WILTSHIRE, ROSINA (1988), 'Indigenisation Issues in Women and Development Studies in the Caribbean: Towards a Holistic Approach' (mimeo).

WLSA (1993), 'WLSA, Inheritance Project, Zimbabwe Data' (mimeo).

World Bank (1989), *Sub-Saharan Africa: From Crisis to Sustainable Growth* (Washington, DC: World Bank).

YOUNG, K., WALKOWITZ, C., and MCCALLOGH, R. (eds.) (1981), *Of Marriage and the Market* (Berkeley: University of California Press).

PART II

INDUSTRIALIZATION, THE STATE, AND FEMALE LABOUR

Industrialization and Women's Subordination: A Reappraisal

Ruth Pearson

The purpose of this chapter is twofold. First it addresses some of the issues which have been raised since the earlier analysis of women's work and industrialization in the third work initially published some fifteen years ago (See Elson and Pearson, 1980, 1981*a*, 1981*b*). Secondly it argues for an extension of the debate beyond the narrow focus on factory employment to consider the multiple experiences of women's work, the links between women's productive and reproductive work and the interplay between gender relations, the gendering of the workforce, and the changing patterns of global industrialization.

WOMEN WORKERS AND EXPORT MANUFACTURING

Since Diane Elson and I published a series of articles in the early 1980s analysing the increasing employment of women in the export manufacturing industries in various Third World countries—then a relatively new phenomenon—much more empirical research has been carried out. Much of our initial analysis was of necessity conceptual and analytical rather than based on empirical and case studies. We were concerned to understand why this kind of industrial process was so universally and heavily dependent on a female workforce, and we concerned to use this conjunctural phenomenon to begin to examine the interplay between gender and capital accumulation.

In the course of subsequent research and case-study material, we are now in a much stronger position to continue this examination, and to respond to criticisms from other writers who rightly point to the limited empirical base of our earlier analyses. Linda Lim (1990) charges that we presented a 'stereotypical' view of women workers 'which is remarkably homogenous and generally negative'. She writes (Lim, 1990: 111):

> The predominant stereotype is that First World multinational factories located in Third World export processing zones employ mostly young, single, female, rural-urban migrants, who are ruthlessly exploited in harsh factory environments where they suffer long hours, poor working conditions, insecure and unhealthy and unsafe jobs, and wages so low that they are not even sufficient to cover individual subsistence. This together with discriminatory practices by employers and *disruptive work patterns*, results in a high turnover rate, as women are 'exhausted' by their

employment, or are forced to resign when they marry or are laid off in frequent recessions. They face constant harassment by employers, supervisors, and even the government, especially if they attempt to unionize or take any labour action. The women are forced to work by poverty and exploited by their families, who claim a disproportionate share of their wages yet do not accord them more power or status within the family. They thus suffer a double oppression, that of imperialist/capitalist exploitation on the one hand and of gender subordination on the other—and benefit little from their employment. (Elson and Pearson, 1981*a* and 1981*b*)

According to Lim the conclusion that she (erroneously) finds in the cited works—that women benefit little from Third World factories—is flawed. She considers that this is an analysis which sees patriarchy and gender subordination as crucial underpinnings and inevitable consequences of all capitalism and refuses to recognize any benefits to women in the Third World from employment in export factories, insisting that such employment intensifies rather than alleviates their gender subordination.

Lim's presentation of our work is largely rhetorical, in order to set up a straw person against which she can hang her own principal point—namely that waged work under capitalism is by definition exploitative, but also, by definition, progressive for the worker, a view which echoes earlier debates about the progressive nature of capitalist exploitation expounded by Warren and the world-systems school of development. Waged work in export processing factories, she argues, confers varied benefits on the women employed. She continues (Lim, 1990: 112):

Although in most but not all cases, wages, working conditions and job security in the export factories are inferior to those in the developed countries, they are comparable if not superior to those found in women's (and even men's) jobs in most other sectors of these still poor underdeveloped local economies. The length of time that women work in these factories varies by country, individual and overtime, and is usually truncated by the mounting domestic responsibilities women face when they marry and have children, rather than by employer compulsion or market disruption. The women working in these large modern factories are better able to organize in unions than are women in most other sectors of the economy and forms of employment, and despite obstacles they have in many cases become more unionized than sections of the male labor force in their countries or than the female labor force in similar industries in the developed countries. They have also not hesitated to undertake sometimes militant labor actions, such as strikes and slowdowns, and in countries like the Philippines and South Korea, they have even been involved in wider political actions. Women textile workers are considered to be among the most militant in South Korea's labor unions.

Women export factory workers do not come from the poorest segments of society, who are usually found in the rural areas, but from families located in or near more prosperous urban areas, or those who had the resources to educate them more than the average male or female in their societies and/or to finance their migration to cities from rural locations. Although some women do work because they would otherwise be destitute, most do so in order to improve their own living standards and that of their families, even where families object to their working or have no pressing need for their income. They are motivated by social and cultural as well as economic factors, and they typically are accorded more respect and more say in their families and households because of their employment and contribution to family income, though this is insufficient to completely undermine the traditional sexual division of labor and its cultural constructs.

This is not to say that women export factory workers from the élite of the working class in Third World countries, though in some cases (e.g. Mexico) this may be close to the truth. *But they are unambiguously better off than they would have been without these jobs* [emphasis added].

Lim's concluding assertion is also inevitably an ahistorical generalization. But it does alert us to two separate points which are instructive. First, it *is* necessary to incorporate differences in the experiences and situations of women workers in different countries, in different sectors, and in different time periods. An earlier attempt to take account of such differences was made in Pearson (1986), where the differences in age, marital status, education and skills were reviewed. However, this analysis was focused only on trying to understand the different ways in which capital could obtain a productive female labour force in circumstances where women's reproductive characteristics and behaviour varied. Thus, in south-east Asia single women provided the labour force most unfettered by domestic responsibility; in northern Mexico it was childless women who were targeted in the initial expansion of maquiladora industries (Pearson, 1992), whilst in the Caribbean many women factory workers are older than those employed elsewhere, often at the end of their active reproducing years, rather than before they start.

But we also need to take into account the experiences of women workers as export factories have become a long-stay phenomenon in many countries. In many cases, women's employment experience extended beyond the short five-year interval predicted in the earlier analysis. Whether women are able to stay in the factory workforce and even to obtain higher skilled qualifications and employment depends on the tightness of the labour market, and the willingness of family and state to support women simultaneously being mothers and factory workers. Pongpaichit (1988) argues that in Singapore, this was an option for many women as the deepening of technological sophistication coincided with labour shortages in the early 1980s, and with the need to retain and train labour; but in South Korea, where labour markets for women workers were over-supplied, and family norms required women not only to directly care for their children but their parents and parents-in-law as well, most women are expelled from their factory jobs on marriage and motherhood, though many continue to carry out industrial work in the form of subcontracted and irregular home work (Kim, 1991; see also Lie, this volume). In Mexico, many women with maternal responsibilities also remained in the industrial workforce, though often displaced to the lower-paid and lower-status textile and garments sector, rather than the electronics sector, which retained its preference for young, childless women (Fernandez-Kelly, 1983; Pearson, 1991).

The burden of these lessons from empirical case studies should alert us to two issues. First and uncontroversially, the nature of employment opportunities in export processing does indeed vary, as Lim asserts, with the dynamics of industrial growth in a particular situation, and the characteristics of the labour market. These factors will affect the ways in which different sectors of the female population are targeted for incorporation into or expulsion from the industrial labour force. But having said that, it is important not to generalize from the very particular case of Singapore, where—as argued above—the combination of tight labour markets and skill-intensive industrial development gave (some) women a purchase on upgrading their level of employment and state-supported (if not supplied) services to enable them to combine motherhood and extended employment in the industrial sector. It may be relevant that much of Lim's analysis is based on empirical work undertaken in Singapore in the late 1970s and 1980s.

But secondly, such refinements to the original analysis are not especially revealing. All they tell us is which women, in which circumstances are the preferred labour force, and thus which women have opportunities for factory employment, and for how long. They do not get to the interesting question for feminist analysis of the interplay between capital accumulation and gender relations—the interesting question being what is the significance behind such employment trends. Can we equate employment in factories as being unequivocally in the interests of women workers, on the basis, as Lim argues, that these women earn an income, contribute to their own and their families' subsistence, and thus 'are accorded more respect and more say in their families and households' (Lim, 1990: 112)?

To address such a question we have to leave the phenomenon of the factory floor and re-enter the household. Pongpaichit's analysis implied that decisions about women's availability for factory employment are strongly constrained by quite pervasive requirements for women's reproductive labour. If the household requires women's wage income more than it requires their unwaged reproductive (or agricultural) labour, then it may well be the case that women will be available for factory employment, should there be a demand from such labour. But we cannot automatically assume that such employment is either unequivocally the woman's choice, or in her interests. As Wolf (1990) most cogently argues, a household strategy which actively encourages daughters in households to seek and retain factory employment is the result of a decision made *within* the household but not *by* the household:

[T]he household can neither decide nor think, since analytic constructs are not so empowered. Rather, certain people within the household make decisions. Since few household strategies operate in democratic fashion, household strategies necessarily embody relationships of power, domination and subordination if a strategy is formulated by the decision-maker(s) and successfully executed by those for whom decisions are made. (Wolf, 1990: 60)

Wolf compares the circumstances in which Javanese and Taiwanese women come to seek factory employment in situations of expanding demand for women workers. In her own field in Java in 1982, she found that women from the poorest rural households, those at an early and expanding stage of the family's life cycle—could not afford to forgo the daily labour or returns to the labour of one female productive member needed at home or on the farm. But many young women workers defied their parents' wishes, following their own preference for factory employment. 'Whilst younger daughters (aged 13 to 14) accepted parental disapproval of factory employment, older daughters usually disobeyed and rebelled. In not one case did a parent suggest to a daughter that she seek factory employment. Rather, most parents were on the defensive, responding and adapting to a daughter's decision' (Wolf, 1990: 51). Rather than seeking factory employment because of the need to contribute to the household income, 'many workers sought factory employment to gain some financial autonomy from their families', even though 'low wages forced workers to remain economically dependent upon their families'. In contradiction to many other empirical studies, Wolf found a high degree of income retention by women factory workers, in Java, rather than the more familiar (stereotypical) pattern of remittances or income pooling. 'Unlike their Taiwanese counterparts who turn over 50 to 80 per cent of factory wages to families, these Javanese factory daughters controlled their own income, remitting little if anything from their weekly wages to the family till, and often *asked* their parents for money' (Wolf, 1990: 52–3).

The contradictions demonstrated by the labour-market behaviour of these different groups of women coincides fully with our earlier analytical assertion that it is necessary 'to distinguish three tendencies in the relation between factory work and the subordination of women as a gender: a tendency to *intensify* the existing forms of gender subordination; a tendency to *decompose* existing forms of gender subordination and a tendency to *recompose* new forms of gender subordination' (Elson and Pearson, 1981*b*: 157).

The relative autonomy in terms of choice of employment, reflected also in relatively more choice of timing of marriage and selection of marriage partner reported by Wolf, can be seen as corresponding to a tendency to decompose existing forms of gender subordination; however, even in the same case study, tendencies for recomposition of gender subordination are also apparent. Wolf goes on to report that 'most [young women factory workers] participated in rotating savings associations through which they accumulated substantial sums of money. That money was used to buy their clothing, consumer goods for the household, and was made accessible to parents for lifecycle events (birth, death, circumcision, marriage, emergencies and debts)' (Wolf, 1990: 53). So although they achieved relative autonomy in employment and marriage choice, the capital they were able to save was at the call of, if not under the control of their families.

The study of Taiwanese women factory workers, reported by Wolf (and based on empirical research by Greenhalgh, Gates, and others) reflects the tendency to intensify existing forms of gender subordination. Wolf writes that in Taiwan:

> [W]ithout question, historically parents controlled a daughter's labour—the decision to work, where to work, and her wages. In the 1920s and 1930s in Taiwan and elsewhere parents controlled their daughter's labour and received her work directly. Fathers often signed labour contracts, turning their daughters into factory workers who were then treated as indentured servants. Margery Wolf found that parents still controlled the decision of where their daughter worked. Since daughters have been socialized to feel that they must pay back their debt to parents, it is not a question of whether to work, but when and where. While parents in the 1950s were hesitant to allow their daughter to leave home for factory work, eventually factory employment became automatic for young women. In contemporary Taiwan, parents are still involved in their daughter's work related decisions, and parental opinions are obeyed. Parents make the decision as to when their daughter will stop schooling and where and when she will start working. When an occupation is selected 'parents are insistent about having daughters abide by their decision' (Kung, 1983: 54). Parents exert authority over which factory she should work in if she is seeking employment or attempting to change factories. (Wolf, 1990: 55)

In the Taiwanese situation there is no question of daughters using factory employment to obtain (relative) autonomy from the household: 'Since a daughter's labour and returns to it are seen as economic resources which families control, parents do not demand money from daughters; there is an implicit contract and daughters fulfil their obligations by remitting 50–100 per cent of their wage' (Wolf, 1990: 56). According to Greenhalgh (cited in Wolf), employment in factories has increased the subordination of daughters within the family, as parents invested more in their daughter's education, thus increasing their daughter's obligations to them. In a different study on Taiwanese factory workers, Niehoff (1987) found that parents were reducing the schooling offered to their daughters, forcing them to start factory work at an earlier age, so that the daughters could spend a full ten years in work before marriage at the average age of 23, whilst there was no corresponding reduction in male schooling. Other researchers have argued that Taiwanese young women 'sell their youth to the company', having no choice but to work selflessly for years, in boring, low-paid, and monotonous jobs, contributing most of their wages to their family. Since parents are aware that marriage will end the economic contributions of daughters to the household budget, they have encouraged an earlier entry to the labour market, and a later age at marriage; in contrast, parents are giving sons considerable freedom to develop their own careers so that they secure their son's continuing allegiance to their natal household. In her contribution to this volume, Gallin stresses the role of the family system in organizing women's work and men's work.

These and other empirical studies do indeed confirm the competing tendencies we hypothesized in our original analysis; and do indeed indicate that the implications of factory employment for Third World women have to be sought within the household as well as in the significance and nature of women's experience of employment on the factory floor. Lim may well be correct in pointing to the economic returns of factory employment, the absence of desirable alternatives, and the contra-indicatory experience of women's organization and militancy over the last 25 years of factory employment in a changing and shifting global economy. Perhaps the questions have been posed too simplistically. Submission to the authority of factory management and the discipline of modern management techniques is not necessarily an alternative to more 'traditional' forms of subordination of women; in some situations it can be a new manifestation of the same pattern of subordination; in others the experience of working with other women in the context of formal organization of work offers the basis for more individual autonomy compared to household production. In any situation women workers will devise strategies to maximize the benefits of their situation—in terms of personal autonomy, resistance to certain aspects of industrial discipline, socialization and organization with other workers, taking advantage of educational and other opportunities available to factory workers. But whatever the response of the individual worker is to her work situation, the fact that her relationship with her (natal) household is still determined through gender relations, and that the organization of the production process, the system of remuneration and supervision, the style of management and of training are all organized on the basis of women's particular and subordinated gender position indicate that such employment is likely to mediate rather than dissolve the gender subordination of women factory workers.

INDUSTRIALIZATION AND WOMEN'S SUBORDINATION: TOWARDS A NON-ESSENTIALIST ANALYSIS

Yet in spite of attempts to deconstruct any simple association between women's status and industrial employment, much of the debate is still focused on a specific subset of women workers—those who are employed in factories—and corresponds to a particular view of industrialization which traces a particular trajectory of capitalist development and concentration in which the factory becomes the visible and central location of production and accumulation. Thus the debate on the relationship between gender relations and industrialization has become enclosed in a discussion about whether and which women should be employed in factories; leading, as we illustrate above, to a discussion about the implications of such employment for those employed, and by extension, for the general female population.

This approach owes much to the Marxist tradition, particularly the writings of Engels, which posited women's incorporation into the waged labour force as the key element in the undermining of women's oppression in the capitalist society. The link between waged work and women's liberation was echoed by the emphasis laid by former Socialist regimes in formal declarations of women's emancipation enshrined in political manifestos and national constitutions.[1] The influence of this analytical tradition continues to underlie debates about women's employment and industrialization—indeed, the morphology of much of the literature can be described by what I have termed elsewhere the three consensuses (Pearson 1992), which are theories about women's employment generalized from specific historical experiences of industrialization. The earlier consensus—that women were excluded from employment opportunities offered by industrialization—reflected the growth of import substituting industries in Latin America, particularly after the 1950s, and was grounded in an unproblematized view that the generation or not of jobs for women encapsulated the relationship between gender subordination and women's employment. The next consensus—that industrialization is grounded in the employment of women workers—is exemplified by the debate summarized in the previous section, which asserts that the economic opportunities offered by factory employment in export-oriented industrialization inevitably have a positive effect on dissolving women's oppression.

The most recent consensus—that of global feminization—again reflects a particular phase of industrialization, in this case *flexibility*. Instead of industrial efficiency being related specifically to economies of scale, smaller units of production equipped with programmable and flexible technology are found to be more cost-effective under certain conditions. Flexible production systems require flexible labour that can be deployed over a variety of production tasks, whereas the major feature of large-scale production is labour socialization. Rather than continually expanding the size of production units or firms in order to benefit from scale of economies, it can be more efficient to have a series of small firms linked together, or to divide enterprises into smaller autonomous units.

[1] The implications of this argument are elaborated in Pearson (1994).

A flexible labour system does not only require multiple skills, but also flexibility in terms of supply. The demand for such labour can be both immediate and temporary. It is employed only when directly needed in production—an extension of the Japanese 'just in time' principle: rather than hoarding stock (which has the labour element built in), the parts, components, and final goods are produced only when they are needed. This kind of labour force usually has no permanent status, no statutory protection against dismissal, is subject to short-time working or retrenchment, and cannot demand a wage above what is competitive in the market. This concept of the flexible workforce, in which the norms of previously 'inflexible' or male jobs are replaced with conditions historically associated with women's work (that is, irregular forms of employment) has been described by Standing (1989) as *global feminization.* By this he refers not only to the increase in women's share of industrial employment, but to the terms and conditions of work and employment, and the substitution of women in activities previously carried out by male workers under 'inflexible' conditions.

This is also a partial and problematic analytical framework. Firstly because industrialization cannot be reduced to a single trend. Whilst it is true that in some sectors and places the downsizing of industrial production in association with programmable machine tools and computerized production control to meet niche markets is the norm, in others, large-scale mass production, often labour-intensive, is still the basis of a chance to compete in an international market. Moreover new areas of employment, such as export of computer services, or of fruit and flowers, to first world markets have also produced a *feminized* labour force, which conforms to Standing's notions of global feminization, but which remains profoundly *gendered* in terms of composition of the labour force and of the construction of male and female jobs and skills within the labour process. Jobs within these new labour processes are still 'men's' or 'women's' jobs, requiring a modification of the technology of production to effect a change in the sexual composition of the labour force, as Sklair (1989) reports for Mexico, or the redesignation of jobs from male to female, and thus the change in employment conditions and rewards, in order to recruit women to previously male occupations (see Humphrey 1987).

One of the profound problems with the previous discussion is that the association of emancipatory trajectories for women being routed directly through industrial employment abstracts women, as bearers of gender relations, from their reproductive reality. It is clear from all accounts that export processing targets a particular cohort of women workers, specifically those who are not burdened by the responsibilities of motherhood or marriage. There is some acknowledgement that such women are a minority of working women, particularly in third world countries; but there is less recognition that the factory work experience of the women involved is likely to be a small part of their total life cycle and that reproductive responsibilities play a profound role not only in the extent to which women can retain industrial employment and wages but also the way in which gender is experienced even by those who have found the emancipation of industrial employment.

The contrast described by Pongpaichit (1988) between the experiences of the female workforce in Singapore and South Korea makes it clear that although women were incorporated into the rapidly expanding export-oriented industrial workforce in both countries, the potential impact of this employment differed because of the different ways in which reproductive tasks were organized in each country:

> Towards the early 1970s the extended family system went into a decline as the result of the mushrooming of public housing through the Housing Development Board which aimed at resettling families from kampongs that often housed large extended families, into modern flats designed for nuclear families. In this situation only women who could afford child care remained in the workforce. Here too, the household played an important role: kin members were prepared to look after the children of working mothers in return for some compensation, which was usually cheaper than private child-care services.
>
> In the second phase of industrialization, tight labour markets and higher wages compelled the government to shift its industrialization strategy from labour-intensive to capital- and skill-intensive enterprises. In order to achieve this the development of human resources was of utmost importance, and since Singapore had a small population, it could not afford to discriminate against women. Thus public policies to upgrade the educational levels and skills of all those who had not had the opportunity to do so in the previous phase, were open to both men and women. In this second phase more women entered professional occupations, and in industry, more were upgraded into supervisory positions. The need for female labour compelled the government to provide assistance in child care, and even encourage men to play a more active role in household work. (p. 157)

Pongpaichit concludes that by the early 1980s women in Singapore had become 'a permanent part of the industrial labour force, in every sphere of work from unskilled to skilled and professional'.

In contrast, the long-term consequences of industrialization on women and the household in South Korea is markedly different from Singapore. According to Pongpaichit (1988: 158), women workers 'still constitute what may be termed a "floating" or "peripheral" labour force'. The following passages (from Pongpaichit, 1988: 158–61) are instructive:

> Women's industrial working lives are still rather short, extending from their late teens up to the time they get married or have children. The reasons for this can be found both in the economic and the social spheres. In the economic context South Korea has a much larger population than Singapore (40 million as against

2.5 million), and thus in terms of the labour market it has a much larger supply of both male and female labour; the competition between males and females for industrial jobs is thus much keener overall. Further the source of supply of workers, females included, for factories in the early phases of industrialization was the large rural hinterland. Migrant women workers had to travel a long way from home and were thus deprived of their family support systems.

In South Korea, a woman's place is still seen to be very much in the home. A married woman is supposed to look after the household affairs of not only her immediate family but her husband's as well. Despite the emergence of the nuclear family, this custom is so prevalent that, even where a woman is living with her parents-in-law, she is not in a position to ask them to help with child care or other household chores, to enable her to continue working. This is in marked contrast to Singapore, where, as we have seen, the extended family is very supportive to the working woman.

Without family support, factory women are at a great disadvantage in the labour markets, as they find it difficult to remain in the labour force long enough to acquire tenure and skills. In most cases, therefore, they cannot return to industrial jobs until after their child-rearing responsibilities are over. In the urban slum of Seoul there is now a large number of poor married women in their late 30s and 40s who were factory workers in the labour-intensive industries of the 1960s. Most of them came from rural areas as migrants, and married and settled in the outskirts of Seoul.

Another striking difference between Singapore and South Korea is society's or government's view of women with regard to policies on human resource development. Whereas in Singapore women are not discriminated against in education and professional jobs because of the shortage of labour, in South Korea they do not seem to enter the government's development goals as part of the human resource factor in economic development at all. They are pushed into the labour market when required, as during the labour-intensive phase of industrialization, but must leave their jobs and return home when their families demand. While government policy in Singapore attempts to upgrade the educational level of both men and women who could not benefit from compulsory education in the early phase of industrialization there is no such policy in South Korea; all vocational school education and attempts to upgrade skills in the private sector have been concentrated on men.

The Korean government is only just beginning to talk about ways to encourage married women to continue working in those occupations where male labour is tight. Yet, neither government or employer is prepared to subsidize the cost of childcare. The general feeling is that this is the responsibility of NGOs [non-governmental organizations] or social welfare organizations, and family norms, as we have seen, provide little support for women.

This account, together with Lie's analysis of the patriarchal nature of capitalist development in South Korea in this volume, illustrates the dangers not just of generalizing about women and industrialization in third world countries, but also of dissolving notions of gender relations entirely into opportunities or exclusion from factory employment. Moreover a factory focused notion of industrialization also ignores the large percentage of the workforce of developing countries who work in the informal sector where, as Scott (1992) demonstrates, women are over represented.

INDUSTRIALIZATION BEYOND THE FACTORY: WOMEN'S WORK IN THE INFORMAL SECTOR

Pongpaichit's account assumes that women factory workers are excluded entirely from industrial work when they marry and have children. In recent years it has become apparent that large numbers of married women and young mothers, many of whom are ex-factory employees, are involved in a network of industrial subcontracting within their own homes.

A survey undertaken in a low-income area of Seoul, South Korea, found that at least 10 per cent of the economically active female population was engaged in some form of industrial home-working, involving production activities using materials delivered from large factories. The range of activities carried out included the sewing of sweaters, sheets, and suits, embroidery (by hand machine), and the stitching of hats, socks, scarves, leather luggage, jackets, boots, gloves, and jogging shoes. A substantial percentage of women carrying out home-based activities were involved in some kind of 'finishing' task, chiefly removing threads from factory-sewn garments or textiles. Women were also employed in food processing (chiefly garlic peeling and packaging), in sub-assembly of electronics and electrical goods, and in a variety of miscellaneous packaging and other activities (Kim, 1991).

The reasons for using homeworkers, who operate through a web of subcontractors, are various. Outworking allows the main supplier responsible for the export contract to minimize overheads, to adjust the size of the workforce to changes in demand, and to save on labour costs. The study estimated that main contractors saved between 20 and 40 per cent on wage costs, with additional savings through avoiding non-wage payments such as taxation, social insurance, and welfare payments, not to mention factory space, storage space, utilities, and materials.

The women interviewed complained of low earnings (only 57.3 per cent of the equivalent factory wage), overdue payment from subcontractors, living space being overrun by uncollected sweaters and other goods, and instability in the supply of materials or work (and therefore of earnings). But the reasons why they undertook the work are very clear: at least half of the women had children under the age of six and/or elderly or sick relatives for whom they were responsible. The majority of husbands in the households worked in manual occupations such as construction work, as mechanics or taxi or truck drivers, and earned only half of the average urban wage. Without the continued earnings of the women, the household would find it impossible to survive.

In many parts of the world subcontracting and outworking have long been part of production of manufactures for export as well as for domestic markets, as Moghadham observes for the Middle East in this volume. Moreover the very mobility of export industrialization has transformed factory-based employment in Hong Kong as factories have been relocated to the more profitable sites in the newly emerging Chinese economy, leaving women in Hong Kong either unemployed or facing work in sweatshops and outwork, which were more characteristic of their emerging economy in the 1950s than the image of the most successful industrializing economy of the 1990s. The ways in which gender relations within the sphere of work as well as within the family and household will be affected by this transition has yet to be understood.

CONCLUSIONS

Exploring the gendered nature of the workforce reveals the variety of forms of industrial organization; moreover, many of these forms are not alternatives to factory production, or remnants of pre-factory production, but are new and contemporary adaptations to prevailing conditions. The prevalence and variety of non-factory industrial work should warn us against linear models of industrialization in which 'superior', higher-productivity organization or production technology supersedes 'pre-industrial' forms. Non-factory production is a facet of the industrialization process rather than a feature of pre-industrial economic organization.

To understand fully the implications of industrialization for women, we would also need to examine the impact of women's earnings on intra-household decision-making, as Walby has noted in her chapter. In this book, Safa discusses intra-household decision-making in her case study, but we need research to analyse whether earning a wage empowers women within households, and increases their autonomy and ability to resist coercion or oppression. We would also need to examine in each case whether such employment in factories is 'women's choice', or whether such employment carries costs such as reduced access to education, restrictions in timing and choice of marriage partner, or alternatively, whether employment actually increases women's choices in these spheres, or—as is likely—the effect is contradictory, increasing choices in some areas and for some women, and restricting choices for others. Without such an examination we are not in a position to make categorical statements about whether women are better off or not as the result of such employment.

REFERENCES

ELSON, DIANE (1991), 'Male Bias in the Development Process: An Overview', in D. Elson (ed.), *Male Bias in the Development Process* (Manchester: Manchester University Press).

—— and PEARSON, RUTH (1980), 'The Latest Phase of the Internationalisation of Capital and its Implications of Women in the Third World', *IDS Discussion Paper* no. 150, University of Sussex.

——, —— (1981*a*), 'Nimble Fingers Make Cheap Workers', *Feminist Review*, 7.

——, —— (1981*b*), 'The Subordination of Women and the Internationalisation of Factory Production', in Kate Young *et al.* (eds.), *Of Marriage and the Market* (London: CSE Books; republished by Routeledge and Kegan Paul, 1984, repr. 1992).

FERNANDEZ-KELLY, P. (1983), *For We Are Sold, I and My People: Women and Industry in Mexico's Frontier* (Albany, NY: SUNY Press).

GREENHALGH, SUSAN (1985), 'Sexual Stratification: The Other Side of "Growth with Equity" in East Asia', *Population and Development Review*, 11/2: 265–314.

HUMPHREY, JOHN (1987), *Gender and Work in the Third World: Sexual Divisions in Brazilian Industry* (London: Tavistock).

KIM, S. (1991), 'Industrial Outworking in South Korea', paper presented at Workshop on Organising Women Industrial Workers, Institute of Social Studies, The Hague, Apr.

LIM, LINDA (1990), 'Women's Work in Export Factories: The Politics of a Cause', in Irene Tinker (ed.), *Persistent Inequalities: Women and World Development* (New York: Oxford University Press).

NIEHOFF, JUSTIN (1987), 'The Villagers as Industrialists: Ideologies of Household Factories in Rural Taiwan', *Modern China*, 13/2: 286–307.

PEARSON, RUTH (1986), 'Women Workers in the First and Third Worlds: The "Greening" of Women's Labour', in K. Purcell *et al.* (eds.), *The Changing Experience of Employment* (London: Macmillan). Repr. in Ray Pahl (ed.), *On Work: Historical, Comparative and Theoretical Approaches* (Oxford: Blackwell, 1988).

—— (1991), 'Male Bias and Women's Work in Mexico's Border Industries', in Diane Elson (ed.), *Male Bias in the Development Process* (Manchester: Manchester University Press).

—— (1992), 'Gender Issues in Industrialisation', in Tom Hewitt, Hazel Johnson, and Dave Wield (eds.), *Industrialisation and Development* (Oxford: Oxford University Press).

—— 'Gender Relations, Capitalism and Third World Industrialization', in L. Sklair (ed.), *Capitalism and Development* (London: Routledge).

PONGPAICHIT, P. (1988), 'Two Roads to the Factory: Industrialisation Strategies and Women's Employment in South East Asia', in Bina Agarwal (ed.), *Structures of Patriarchy: The State, the Community and the Household* (London: Zed Books).

SEN, AMARTYA K. (1990), 'Gender and Cooperative Conflicts', in Irene Tinker (ed.), *Persistent Inequalities: Women and World Development* (New York: Oxford University Press).

SCOTT, A. (1992), 'Informal Sector or Female Sector? Gender Bias in Urban Labour Market Models', in D. Elson (ed.) *Male Bias in the Development Process* (Manchester: Manchester University Press).

SKLAIR, LESLIE (1989), *Assembling for Development: The Maquila Industry in Mexico and the USA* (Boston and London: Unwin Hyman).

STANDING, GUY (1989), 'Global Feminisation Through Flexible Labour', *World Development*, 17/7 (July): 1077–96.

WOLF, DIANE L. (1990), 'Daughters, Decisions and Domination: An Empirical and Conceptual Critique of Household Strategies', *Development and Change*, 21: 43–74.

Gender Inequality and Women's Wage Labour: A Theoretical and Empirical Analysis

Helen I. Safa

Export-led industrialization has become the principal development strategy during the 1980s in several developing countries, particularly in the small, open economies of the Caribbean Basin. Many countries have been pushed into export-led industrialization to generate foreign exchange to meet their payments under the debt crisis, as well as to reduce growing unemployment. In the Latin American and Caribbean region particularly, export-led industrialization has been spurred on by the US government, which saw export manufacturing as a way of improving the stagnant economies of this region, and of promoting political stability, or 'security through development' (Deere *et al.*, 1990: 154). As part of its trade development policy to stimulate private-sector investment in the region, the US Agency for International Development (AID) provides funds for improvement or construction of export processing zones, training projects, and export market information (Joekes and Moayedi, 1987: 1–6). Several special tariff programmes, including the Caribbean Basin Initiative, were designed to reduce or abolish US duties on certain imports, though some programmes require imports to be assembled from US components. These AID and tariff programmes also aided US business, which faced with increasing competition for foreign imports, particularly from the newly industrializing countries in Asia, sought to cut labour costs by shifting the labour-intensive phase of production to cheaper wage areas abroad (Safa, 1981). The debt crisis further reduced wages in developing countries through currency devaluation. Though in the Caribbean Basin, export-led industrialization is largely confined to labour-intensive industries such as garments and electronics, it now includes such heavy industries as automobile assembly, much of which is relocating to the Mexican border.

The shift toward export manufacturing in the Caribbean Basin implies a profound restructuring of their economies away from traditional exports, such as sugar, coffee, or bauxite into a source of cheap labour for US light industry. Agricultural exports have been the primary development strategy in these small countries since colonial times, due to the lack of capital, technology, and a viable internal market hampered by small size and low purchasing power. However, starting in the 1960s, there was an increase in manufacturing, following the 'industrialization by invitation' strategy initiated by Puerto Rico a decade earlier. Export manufacturing accelerated in the 1980s due to the US government initiatives detailed earlier and economic conditions in these Caribbean countries, including the debt crisis and the greater need for foreign exchange; the decline in the price of agricultural commodities in international trade; and the cut in the US sugar quota, which was particularly devastating for the Dominican Republic. Export manufacturing lessens the need to develop an internal market required under import substitution; on the contrary, the external demand for export manufacturing requires the maximum reduction of production costs, principally wages, in order to compete effectively on the international level. In fact, the availability of cheap labour appears to be the prime motivation for investment in the region; this helps explain why most of the jobs generated through export manufacturing are for women, who previously represented a small percentage of the industrial labour force under import substitution. In this way, import substitution industrialization reinforced the demand for male workers, while the emphasis in export-led industrialization on a cheap, disciplined labour force gives preference to women workers.

Most workers in export-led industrialization are young, single women with no previous job experience, which increases their vulnerability. Employers are often US multinationals who can move freely from one country to another in search of cheaper and more docile labour. They are lured by governments anxious to attract this new form of investment and offering tax holidays, exemption from import duties, unrestricted profit repatriation, and special free-trade zones constructed at public expense to house these plants complete with water, electricity, and roads. The state also tries to guarantee a quiescent labour force by prohibiting unions or strikes in export-processing zones. This compact between the state and capital weakens resistance to subordination on the part of women workers in export processing, as we shall see in the case of the Dominican Republic.

Standing (1989) has documented the rising labour-force participation rates of women and the falling participation rates of men in several advanced industrial as well as developing countries in the 1980s. He argues that 'global feminization through flexible labor' results from the need in both developed and developing societies to cut labour costs through labour deregulation in order to meet growing international competition. Labour-market deregulation cheapens wages through explicitly abandoning formal labour regulations or simply weakening their implementation, as in informal agreements between the state and multinationals to prohibit unionization in export-processing zones. It is manifest in a global trend to a shift from full-time wage and salary workers with fixed wages and fringe benefits to unprotected casual or temporary workers employed in export processing, subcontracting, and homework in the informal sector, all of which favour female employment. The debt crisis also forced more women, especially married women, into the labour force through inflation, the fall in real wages and the rising cost of living, reinforced by the cut or privatization of public services formerly provided by the state. As a result, in many advanced industrial as well as developing countries, women are now taking more responsibility than ever for the economic support of their families, while the man's role as principal breadwinner is weakening.

This paper will explore the impact of global restructuring and increases in women's wage labour on gender subordination from both a theoretical and empirical perspective. However, I shall not confine my analysis to export-led industrialization, but examine the effect of wage labour generally on gender subordination in both advanced industrial and developing societies. A theoretical framework of the changing historical relationship between gender subordination and women's wage labour will be constructed based largely on studies conducted in advanced industrial societies. I shall then test the validity of this theoretical framework for a developing country by applying it to the Dominican Republic, in which the growth of export-led industrialization has contributed to substantial increases in female labour-force participation since 1960. Why have women become the preferred labour force in the labour-intensive phase of export-led industrialization? What has been the impact of increased labour-force participation on gender subordination and does it differ in advanced industrial and developing countries? Has wage labour merely added to their burdens or has it led to greater autonomy for women and raised their consciousness regarding gender subordination? These are some of the questions this paper will explore.

THEORIES OF GENDER SUBORDINATION AND WOMEN'S WAGE LABOUR

The world-wide increase in women's wage labour in export manufacturing has generated intense debate over its effects on women's status (Tiano, 1986; Lim, 1990). Champions of export-led industrialization stress its benefits in providing women with a new source of employment, while critics argue that export-led industrialization exploits women through low wages, poor working conditions, high turnover, occupational segregation, lack of possibilities of advancement, and harassment by employers and the state.

Much of this debate depends in part on differing theoretical perspectives. Theories regarding the effects of wage labour on women's status can be grouped in two broad categories, the modernization school and Marxist-feminist analysis. They differ dramatically in how they view the effects of capitalist development on women. Modernization theorists such as Rosen (1982) maintain that women are held back by the traditional ascriptive criteria found in pre-capitalist societies which denies them access to jobs and education on the basis of gender. Capitalist development and wage labour liberates women by replacing these prescriptions with universalistic criteria based on individual achievement and merit. Wage labour undermines patriarchal control by increasing women's financial independence and providing them with productive skills and modern attitudes. Thus, the modernization school believes that capitalism liberates women by integrating them into development and by promoting upward mobility through the development of human capital.

Marxist-feminists, however, see capitalism in alliance with patriarchy as a source of women's subordination. Rather than weakening inequality, capitalism builds upon pre-existing hierarchies based on gender, race, and class and utilizes these to create an exploitable labour force for the capitalist élite. Marxist feminists differ in the emphasis placed on either patriarchy or capitalism as a source of women's subordination, and on the relationship between them. Those emphasizing capitalism focus on class exploitation of labour by capital at the work place, while those emphasizing patriarchy emphasize male domination over women in the family as the primary source of women's subordination. Most Marxist feminists have abandoned a dualist approach and now conceptualize patriarchy as relatively autonomous yet coexisting with capitalism (Walby, 1986). Patriarchy pre-dates capitalism but is intensified through the growth of wage labour in which men are designated the principal wage earners and women are confined to the home as unpaid domestic labour. Women's domestic labour performs an important function for capitalism through the maintenance and reproduction of the labour force, but housework is increasingly devalued as only wage-earning activities in the public sphere confer status and prestige. Even when they are employed, women are at a distinct disadvantage in the labour market because of their dual productive/reproductive role. Thus, most women serve as a cheap labour reserve to supplement male labour and keep wages down.

However, like the modernists, Marxist feminists also see wage labour as potentially liberating for women. Following Engels, wage labour is seen as one way of breaking down patriarchy and women's isolation and dependence on men; it is expected to give women greater economic autonomy, to increase their authority in the household, and to develop their class consciousness as workers and their gender consciousness as women. The emphasis on consciousness differentiates the Marxist feminist from the modernist approach to wage labour; wage labour liberates women (and men) not through the development of human capital, but through making workers aware of their common exploitation and of the need to adopt collective strategies to combat capitalist exploitation. There are many obstacles to the formation of consciousness among women, however, including the segregation of women into poorly paid, unstable jobs (such as export manufacturing), their double burden of paid employment and domestic labour, and a gender ideology which continues to portray women as 'supplementary' workers even when they are fully employed (Hartmann, 1981).

In short, for Marxist feminists, women's dual productive/reproductive role weakens the liberating effects of wage labour on gender subordination. Women workers continue to function as a cheap labour reserve because they are still primarily defined in terms of their domestic role, and therefore not given the same legitimacy as men as workers. This has led feminist scholars like Barrett (1980: 211) to argue that the family is 'the central site of the oppression of women'. According to Barrett, gender ideology is formed principally within the family through a woman's dependence on a male wage and is reflected at other levels of society such as the work place and the polity.

I argue, however, that there are various levels of women's subordination, in the family, the work place, and the polity, and that these different levels need to be kept analytically separate. Like Hartmann (1981: 15) I define patriarchy as male control over female labour, which is maintained by excluding women from access to productive resources (including jobs and wages) and by restricting women's sexuality. Like Hartmann, I argue that this control exists not only in the family, but in the work place and in the polity as well. Gender hierarchies are reproduced in the work place, with male management, owners, and unions controlling women workers, and in the polity, where women continue to be under-represented. Both capital and the state, like individual men, are interested in control of women's labour and sexuality, in order to preserve their role as a cheap labour reserve while at the same time preserving their reproductive functions in child rearing and domestic labour. This can be seen in the preference of employers for young, single women and in the state enforced re-domestication of women workers in the USA after World War II. Thus, patriarchy is manifest not only in the family, but in the work place and the polity, which over time become equally important sources of gender subordination.

Changes in the form of patriarchal control

However, the relationship between patriarchy and capitalism shifts over time. In the early stages of capitalism, patriarchy resides primarily in individual male heads of household, who maintain control over women's labour and sexuality. The home is the primary locus of production and reproduction and is the primary agent of women's subordination. With the development of industrial capitalism and the growth in importance of the nation state, patriarchy shifts from being primarily in the private realm of the family to the public sphere of the work place and the state (Mann,

1986; Walby, 1990). The development of advanced capitalism also results in the increasing importance of women as wage earners, and challenges the status of men as principal breadwinners.

With the growth of industrial capitalism and a market economy, the control of the state and capital over women's labour grew at the expense of the individual male heads of household. Patriarchy shifted from private to public control over women's labour (Brown, 1987). As production moved outside the home into factories and offices, the household declined in economic and political importance. Many family functions such as education, health, and even child care were taken over by the state, and the household declined in size, while extended families and kin ties were weakened by increased residential and social mobility. This shift was marked by increasing tension between the state, capital, and individual men over women's labour, and reflected in increasing state intervention in the economy against capital (e.g. protective legislation, minimum wages) or against individual male heads of household (e.g. laws guaranteeing women's property rights or rights to divorce and child custody). Universal suffrage strengthened the state, which no longer represented merely the ruling class, and made women a more important political constituency. However, women's collective representation in political parties and labour unions has never been as strong as that of men, reflecting their diminished role in the public sphere. Despite women's increasing presence in the public sphere, both women and men continue to regard it as the domain of men. The notion of separate spheres for men and women maintains gender differences and defines women as family members whose work roles are secondary (Kessler-Harris, 1990).

Women were not passive victims of patriarchal control, but actively resisted in the home, work place, and polity. Many of the rights women won, such as suffrage and legal equality in family law, were due to women's pressure on the state and capital to replace their status as dependent minors with that of equal citizens. These pressures, in turn, were partly a result of women's increased labour-force participation, which raised their consciousness regarding their dependent status and their desire to acquire greater economic independence to bolster their demands for greater equality. Wage labour was not the only stimulus to greater gender consciousness; increased educational levels also made women more aware of their subordinate status, and more able to overcome it, while declining fertility rates freed them from some child-rearing responsibilities. All three factors interacted to produce women more able and willing to enter the public sphere. Women's rights were also the result of feminist movements led largely by middle-class and educated women, who openly championed women's right to vote, to hold property, and to control their own sexuality.

Clearly wage labour is not the sole source of consciousness among women, nor does paid employment have the same impact on women of different cultures, races, and classes, even within advanced capitalist societies. Bonds among women based on race, ethnicity, neighbourhood, and kinship also offer women collective forms of resistance to capitalist exploitation (Sacks, 1989). However, as long as the normative ideal was based on separate spheres, with women confined to the home and men dominating the public sphere, women lacked legitimacy to press demands that were not extensions of their domestic role. The notion of separate spheres was heavily dependent upon the man's role as principal breadwinner, which gave the man control over family income and family labour and insured woman's economic dependence. This myth of the male breadwinner persists, despite the increasing importance of women's wages in the household. The origins of this myth must be sought in the changing sexual division of labour accompanying the rise of industrial capitalism.

Changes in the sexual division of labour

The 'unproductive housewife' itself was a product of the rise of a market economy and industrial capitalism in the nineteenth century (Folbre, 1991). As production moved outside the home into the factory, women ceased to be seen as productive members of a household unit and became increasingly dependent on male wages earned outside the home. Women were relegated to the reproductive sphere of child rearing, enshrined in the 'cult of domesticity', despite the economic devaluation of housework. The state institutionalized the concept of the unproductive housewife in the census and through family law, while male unions strove for a family wage which would exclude women from the labour force and enable men to support their dependent wives and children (Hartmann, 1981). The family wage strengthened the control of the male head of household over his wife's labour by defining men as the principal wage earners. Single women worked, but their wages could not support a family and most left employment upon marriage. These changes were strongest in advanced industrial societies such as the United States and England, and even here the bourgeois ideal of the 'idle housewife' did not hold for black and immigrant women and some of the white working class, who could not survive without their wives' wages.

As increasing numbers of women, particularly married women, began to enter the labour force in advanced capitalist societies during and after World War II, the concept of housewife began to change to that of supplementary wage earner. Fewer than 15 per cent of all married women and 30 per cent of black women with wage-earning husbands were regularly employed by the 1930s (Kessler-Harris, 1990: 29). Women's labour-force participation in the US increased from 20 per cent in 1900 to 55 per cent in 1988, with much of the growth among married women and mothers (Sassen and Fernandez-Kelly, 1995). Wage differentials and occupational segregation reinforced the view that men were still the primary breadwinners and justified women's attachment to their families. In the USA state benefits such as social security or AFDC to women were directly linked to their maternal or parental status, and designed to substitute for the wage of the absent father, thereby extending the notion of female dependence from the male breadwinner to the state (Acker, 1988). Despite differential male access to training and education, by 1981 college enrolments were approximately equal for men and women, with greater numbers of women in non-traditional disciplines (Hartmann, 1987: 42–4). As a result, women entered white-collar and professional jobs, changing as well the class composition of the female labour force and adding to its importance and legitimacy.

The 'demise of domesticity' in the USA did not begin until the 1960s with ever-increasing numbers of married women in paid employment (Kessler-Harris and Sacks, 1987). The change from working daughters to working mothers (Lamphere, 1986) was important, because the employment of mothers directly challenged the traditional sexual division of labour in the family. Many married women had to work because of the increase in female heads of household, or because their husbands were unemployed or did not earn enough to support a family. Male blue-collar workers (as well as women in labour-intensive jobs such as the garment industry), suffered a sharp decline in employment and earnings as a result of industrial restructuring and the movement of production abroad. Middle-class women were motivated to work by an increase in consumerism and their desire for more personal economic security and autonomy, fuelled by the women's movement (Hartmann, 1987). Married women also remained employed rather than leaving at childbirth as previously. This enabled children to prolong their education and to qualify for expanding white-collar and professional jobs. As children no longer contributed to the household economy, there was increasing pressure on mothers to remain in the labour force, to supplement their husbands' wages or to support children on their own (Safa, 1983). The increasing employment of married women also contributed to decreasing fertility, as a woman's reproductive labour shifted from an emphasis on large families to a smaller number of educated children capable of entering an increasingly skilled labour force.

Gradually in the USA the concept of the family wage has been replaced with that of the two wage-earner family, as 65 per cent of mothers in dual parent families were in the workforce in 1990 (Alt-WID, 1992: 10). Most mothers no longer withdraw from the workforce to raise small children and instead see themselves as permanently employed. The possibility of earning their own, independent wage represents a basis for resisting gender and generational subordination within the family, giving women more autonomy and the ability to dissolve an unhappy marriage and head their own household. Divorce rates have increased, contributing to the rising percentage of female heads of households and reinforcing the importance of women's wages in the household. Employed women have become more active in unions and have begun to press for wider family-oriented benefits from the state and employers, such as paid maternity leave and child care, as well as the right to control their own bodies through family planning and abortions. While women pressed the state, unions, and employers to assume greater responsibility for the costs of reproduction, these institutions have been slow to respond because to assume all of these costs would negate the notion of women as cheaper labour. Although women's wages in the USA have improved relative to men's wages, women in 1988 still earned on average 66 cents for every dollar earned by men (ibid.). As both women and men become recognized as providers, a woman's wage is now increasingly seen as job-based rather than need-based as previously (Kessler-Harris, 1990).

The 1963 US law guaranteeing equal pay for equal work embodies this shift, for as long as women were seen as dependents or supplementary wage earners, their wages were based on need and not on the jobs they performed. Women were expected to be self-supporting or to contribute to the family income, but not to maintain a family as men did. Earlier need-based concepts of women's wages rested on the ideology of women's separate sphere, which idealized the domestic sphere at the same time that it restricted women's presence in the public sphere. Underlying the notion of separate spheres was a clear division between the public male world of work and the private female world of the home, which was being increasingly eroded with the increasing number of women in the labour force. Equal pay for equal work acknowledged this change and embodied a very different notion of gender roles based on individual rights rather than family responsibilities (Kessler-Harris, 1990). Though its effects were diluted by continued occupational segregation, it moved away from an identity based on gender differences to one based on gender equality.

In large part, women's struggle against gender subordination in advanced industrial societies has now shifted from the home to the work place and increasingly the polity. The increasing importance of women as wage earners has facilitated this transition. In part, a shift in focus has been made necessary by the attack during the past decade on the welfare state and social services in countries such as the USA and England. The growing crisis over the redistributive functions of government in advanced capitalist societies and the movement to reduce family planning services and to overturn the right to abortion can be seen as a way of reasserting private patriarchy, as the state withdraws from its responsibilities for social reproduction and shifts this back to the individual family. However, cuts in social services and transfer payments drive more women into the labour force, while the number of blue-collar and service jobs continues to shrink, so that female as well as male unemployment figures continue to grow.

Women who have become permanent members of the labour force can no longer retreat into the category of housewife in order to disguise their unemployment.

In sum, patriarchy underwent two major modifications in Western industrial societies with the development of industrial capitalism: primary control over women's labour shifted from individual male heads of households to capital and the state, as the household declined in economic and political importance; and the sexual division of labour in the family changed as women became increasingly important wage earners and economic providers. These changes were marked by an increase in the percentage of women employed, particularly married women, and in the importance of their contribution to the household economy. An ideological shift accompanied these structural changes. As women began to move into the workforce in greater numbers, the notion of women's separate sphere was gradually replaced by the notion of individual rights for men and women. Separate spheres is based on complementarity between men and women, on the assumption that each can excel in their own sphere, women in the home, and men in the public world of work and politics. It extols motherhood and sees women's public role as basically extensions of their domestic role. The decreasing importance of the family and of housework undermined their value for women. Women demanded a greater presence in the public sphere and began to claim individual rights based on equality with men and not simply on the basis of protecting women's separate domestic sphere. This marked a fundamental change in women's conceptualization of gender roles and gender subordination. With the massive incorporation of women into the labour force, gender subordination was no longer defined solely on the basis of male domination in the home, but on the limitations to gender equality in the work place and in the state. Women looked increasingly to the state to achieve greater equality, thus reinforcing the shift from private to public patriarchy.

Changing forms of patriarchy in Latin America and the Caribbean

Can this theoretical framework documenting historical changes in the relationship between women's wage labour and gender subordination in advanced industrial countries be applied as well to developing countries differing in historical and cultural formation, in racial and ethnic composition, and in levels of development? Has the ideological shift away from separate spheres into equal individual rights for men and women occurred as well in these Third World countries? Obviously, there are dangers here in assuming that developing countries will follow the same changes in gender roles described for the West. I shall not attempt to conduct a global analysis of the impact of wage labour on women, but confine my discussion to Latin America and the Caribbean. As Kandiyoti (1991) has shown, regional differences in the form of patriarchy can range from the relatively autonomous mother–child units found in sub-Saharan Africa to the belt of 'classic patriarchy' found in North Africa, the Muslim Middle East, and south and east Asia, based on the patrilocally extended household, which totally appropriates women's labour and progeny. Latin America lies between these extremes, combining a bilateral kinship system with control of women's sexuality and labour through an emphasis on family honour and female virginity, but as in other regions, patriarchal norms vary by country, class, and ethnicity as well as over time. The cultural differences in the form of patriarchy point up the importance of kinship and the patrilineal household in providing a base for patriarchy, but their importance is also declining with the development of industrial capitalism.

Historical analyses of women in Latin America indicate strong patriarchal control over women's labour in the colonial period, when most women were largely confined to the home. Under Hispanic colonial law, *patria potestad* or paternal authority gave a husband exclusive control over his children and most of his wife's legal transactions, property, earnings, and sexuality (Arrom, 1985: 65–70). The Catholic Church reinforced civil authority and male domination, through its moral insistence on female virginity and male superiority. Family honor was based on following the Spanish adage '*El hombre está hecho para la calle y la mujer para la casa*' (Men are made for the street and women for the home), which defined dual standards of sexuality and insured women's economic dependence on men. However, there were clear class and racial/ethnic differences between élite white or mestizo women and poor indigenous or black women, who assumed greater economic responsibility for the family and never established the same patterns of male dependency. For example, in Mexico City during the early nineteenth century, though women constituted almost one-third of the labour force, it was largely the poorest women who worked (rural migrants, Indian women), and the majority were single women who were employed as domestic servants (Arrom, 1985: 157–8). In all *castas* or racial groups, single women and widows worked more than married women, who were clearly expected to 'subsist on the earnings of their male head', as a petition by women tobacco factory workers noted (ibid.: 200).

As in the USA the development of industrial capitalism in Latin America helped to advance the notion of individual rights and to lessen the control of male heads of household over their wives and children. Legislation for women's rights was stronger in some Latin American countries with higher levels of development and a strong feminist movement, such as Cuba in the first half of the twentieth century. Here US occupation in 1898 and investment in sugar plantations not only led to rapid economic development, but also facilitated the separation of church and state, which impeded reform in other countries. For example, as early as 1901 women gained access to free public education, and by 1919 over 60 per cent of the population over 5 was literate, with women and men attaining equal levels of literacy (Stoner, 1991: 132). Educated, middle-class women were at the forefront of a feminist movement that strove for women's rights and contributed to significant reforms in areas such as women's property rights, the right to divorce (granted in 1918), and the elimination of double standards for adultery. The 1940 Cuban Constitution was the most progressive in the Western Hemisphere and granted women the right to vote and hold office, and incorporated an equal rights article recognizing the equality of the sexes. However, most of these reforms were of greatest benefit to the privileged women who promoted them, without attacking directly the deep racial and class stratification of Cuban society (Martinez-Alier, 1974). They facilitated the entrance of élite Cuban women into certain spheres of the public domain, such as education and welfare, thus preserving Hispanic patriarchal values of separate spheres for men and women. Even the institution of a maternity code for working women symbolized feminists' concern for motherhood, for which they now sought the protection of the state rather than relying exclusively on individual men. The reform of Cuban family law is thus an excellent example of how the feminist movement and concern for women's rights helped to shift patriarchy from the private to the public domain, which reduced the power of individual men but made the state the new protector of women. This paved the way for the socialist state to champion women's rights after the Cuban revolution in 1959.

The reform of Cuban family law apparently had little to do with the incorporation of women into the labour force, which remained at the low level of 10.6 per cent from 1899 to the early 1950s (Stoner, 1991: 168), and even in 1959 had only reached 13 per cent, the lowest in Latin America. Though middle-class women began to enter white-collar jobs, particularly in the economic boom of the 1950s, and some women were incorporated into the growing textile industry, the great majority of working women were poor and black and worked as servants and laundresses (Prieto, 1992) Despite clear class and racial differences, the low number reflects the continued ideological separation of men and women into the separate spheres of *casa/calle* (house, street).

The biggest boom to women's labour-force incorporation in Latin America occurred in the post-war period of rapid economic growth. The size of the female labour force increased threefold in Latin America between 1950 and 1980, with overall participation rates rising from almost 18 per cent to over 26 per cent in the same period. Participation rates for women grew faster than those for men, and included all age groups, although single women between the ages of 20 and 29 continued to be the most active (ECLAC, 1988: 15).

This increase in female labour-force participation results from changes in both the supply and demand for female labour. Demographic changes such as declining fertility, higher educational levels, and rapid urbanization have increased the supply of women workers. At the same time, there has been an increased demand for women workers in the expanding service sector, which includes newer white-collar and professional jobs for women. However, domestic servants are still the largest occupational group, averaging around 20 per cent of the economically active female population in the region as a whole (ECLAC, 1988: 22). Domestic service and street vending are traditional jobs in the informal sector, which has increased rapidly in recent years due to the economic crisis. The economic crisis and structural adjustment policies threaten to overturn women's newly won gains, at the same time that they have driven even more women into the labour force. Currency devaluation, rapid increases in inflation and the cost of living, and cuts in government expenditure and subsidies have weakened men's role as economic provider and increased the importance and the visibility of women's contribution to the household economy.

The weakening of the man's role as provider and the growing importance of the woman's contribution is contributing to growing gender consciousness in Latin America and the Caribbean. As in the USA women are beginning to challenge male domination in the home, the work place, and the polity. However, women workers do not have the same legitimacy as male workers, despite their increasing importance as wage earners. As in an earlier period in the USA Latin American women still frame their demands within an ideology of women's separate sphere, which stresses gender differences and complementarity rather than gender equality. This reflects socio-economic factors such as the lower and more recent incorporation of women, particularly married women, into the labour force in Latin America as compared to the USA. It also reflects differences in ideology and gender consciousness, manifest in women's attachment to the family and their domestic role. The ideology of separate spheres maintains patriarchal gender ideologies, and implies that there are ideological as well as structural obstacles to greater gender consciousness in Latin America. As a result, women have greater difficulty in pressing their demands for greater equality in the work place and the state than in the home, which has long been recognized as women's legitimate domain (Safa, 1990). Thus, I argue that in Latin America, women's wage labour has had a greater impact on gender equality in the household than at the level of the work place and the state, where they are still regarded as supplementary wage earners.

In the next section, I shall test the validity of this argument through an empirical analysis of women workers in export manufacturing in the Dominican Republic. I shall examine the impact of women's increased wage labour on gender consciousness by analysing the ways in which women challenge their subordination in the family, in the work place, and in the polity. It is easier to measure such changes in women's consciousness through a case study in which women speak for themselves, rather than inferring such changes through the macro-level analyses I have reviewed thus far. A case study also facilitates the analysis of the structural and ideological factors conditioning the impact of paid employment on women's gender consciousness. The data are drawn from a survey of 231 women workers in the three oldest free-trade zones of the DR, conducted in 1981 by CIPAF,[1] a private Dominican women's research centre, as well as eighteen in-depth interviews with a sub-sample of these women which I conducted in 1986. All of the in-depth interviews are with garment workers, who constituted over 60 per cent of all workers in the Dominican free trade zones in the 1980s (Dauhajre *et al.*, 1989: 189). While comparable studies have been done on women workers in Puerto Rico and Cuba, I shall confine my analysis here to the Dominican Republic, because it is a classic case of rapid export-led industrialization, which has accentuated the incorporation of women into the industrial labour force.

EXPORT-LED INDUSTRIALIZATION AND WOMEN'S WAGE LABOUR IN THE DOMINICAN REPUBLIC

Starting in the 1960s, the Dominican Republic underwent a rapid transformation from an agrarian to an urban, industrial economy supported by the state and heavily financed by US capital. Nevertheless, the Dominican Republic remained dependent on agricultural exports, principally sugar, until the early 1980s, when the US drastically cut its sugar quotas. Initial efforts at industrialization focused largely on import substitution until the massive and rapid expansion of export manufacturing in the 1980s, resulting largely from the reduction in the cost of labour due to the debt crisis and currency devaluation. Industrial exports from the free-trade zones grew in value 307.4 per cent between 1981 and 1988 to US$502.1 million (Dauhajre *et al.*, 1989: 38–9), and made the Dominican Republic the leading source of exports under the CBI in the Caribbean. Total exports grew to US$516.9 million in 1988, 2.6 times more than the total of exports from other CBI countries (ibid.: 97).

This growth in export manufacturing is centred in the free-trade zones, and 63 per cent of the firms in 1992 were direct subsidiaries of US multinationals. The total number of free-trade zones in the Dominican Republic

[1] I am grateful to CIPAF and to its director, Magaly Pineda, for allowing me to use this data. Much of the analysis on the survey of Dominican women workers was carried out by Milagros Ricourt, Quintina Reyes, and Lorraine Catanzaro for their M.A. thesis at the University of Florida, and much of this analysis, including some of Ricourt's tables, have been incorporated here. I also wish to thank Francis Pou, who assisted me in conducting the in-depth interviews in the Dominican Republic, and the Wenner-Gren Foundation, which funded this aspect of my research.

grew from 3 established between 1969 and 1973 to a total of 27 free-trade zones in operation by 1992 in various regions of the country. The number of firms and workers in the free-trade zones rose spectacularly between 1985 and 1992, when there were over 140,000 workers in 404 firms (Consejo Nacional de Zonas Francas, 1993). Sixty per cent of these jobs are held by women, and about half of the workers are still employed in the three original free-trade zones created before 1973, which are the focus of this study.

Export manufacturing in the Dominican Republic has contributed to increased female labour-force participation, which quadrupled from 9.3 per cent in 1960 to 38 per cent in 1990 (Ramirez *et al.*, 1988: 41; Báez, 1991: 13). During this period, the supply of qualified women workers grew through increased educational levels, declining fertility, and migration from rural to urban areas, where most of the jobs available to women were being created in the expanding service sector. The growth of this sector and of export manufacturing also increased demand for women workers. In 1980, more than half (54 per cent) of the economically active women were in the tertiary sector, which includes white-collar workers as well as domestic servants, who still constituted 25 per cent of the female labour force. The percentage of women in manufacturing also grew after 1970, so that by 1981 they constituted 40 per cent of the workers in the non-sugar manufacturing sector, most of them concentrated in the free-trade zones (Duarte *et al.*, 1989: 119, 124). Export processing now constitutes one of the most important sources of urban employment for women, rivalling domestic service. Female labour-force participation rates increased at a much faster rate than male rates, which since 1960 have stabilized at around 72 per cent (Ramírez *et al.*, 1988: 41; Báez, 1991: 13). However, with the onset of the economic crisis and the decline in sugar production and import substitution industrialization in the 1980s, unemployment rates rose and increasing numbers of both sexes are entering the informal sector. The informal sector employs more men than women and is now the principal source of employment for men (Báez, 1991: 19).

The economic crisis which hit the Dominican Republic in 1982 accelerated the erosion of the man's role as primary breadwinner and increased the importance of the woman's contribution. The crisis has contributed to declines in wages, rising unemployment, and increases in the cost of living, all of which increased the need for additional household income, leading even more women to seek paid employment. Unemployment rates in the Dominican Republic are among the highest in all Latin America, and reached 29 per cent in 1986, with under-employment estimated at about 40 per cent. Unemployment rates are higher for women than for men, while wages are lower; in 1983, the average monthly wage for women was DR$165 compared to DR$291 for men (Báez, 1991: 20). Despite several increases in the minimum wage, the real hourly wage declined 62.3 per cent from 1984 to 1990 (Fundapec, 1992: 32). From 1980 to 1987, the weekly cost of a family food-basket more than doubled (Ceara, 1987), due to devaluation, the reduction in state price controls on staples such as rice and sugar, and increasing reliance on food imports. The result has been growing hunger and poorer health, as public health services deteriorated rapidly in the 1980s. Government expenditures on health and education have always been low in the Dominican Republic, which never fully assumed social welfare responsibilities for its citizens, but debt-servicing commitments forced even greater cutbacks. (Deere *et al.*, 1990: 52–60). The burden of these economic hardships at the household level falls primarily on women, who attempt to maximize earnings while they minimize expenditures. Consumption patterns are changing, with increased reliance on cheap sources of food such as rice and root crops, while women's participation in both the formal and informal labour market is increasing.

The exploitation of women's wage labour by capital and the state

Export manufacturers have shown a preference for women workers, because they are cheaper to employ, less likely to unionize, and have greater patience for the tedious, monotonous work employed in assembly operations. In addition, the majority of the export-processing firms in the Dominican Republic are labour-intensive, and even some of the newer high-tech industries such as electronics in the recently established free-trade zone employ primarily women. As of 1988, the free-trade zones employed more workers than domestic industries (excluding sugar), and the latter's percentage of total exports decreased from 97 per cent in 1975 to 63.6 per cent in 1988 (Dauhajre *et al.*, 1989: 43), suggesting a decline in domestic industrial production.

The free-trade zone in La Romana, where the in-depth interviews for this study were conducted, is the oldest of the free-trade zones in the Dominican Republic, established in 1969 by the Gulf and Western Corporation, a major force in the Dominican economy since the 1920s. The free-trade zone along with a large tourist complex was part of the company's attempt to diversify the sugar economy of the south-east region of the country in which La Romana is located, which traditionally employed a large male (and militant) labour force, primarily Dominican in the sugar mill and Haitians as cane cutters. In 1984, Gulf and Western sold all of its holdings in La Romana, including the free-trade zone, to a Cuban American consortium. By 1992, the La Romana export-processing zones (including a new industrial park built in the late 1980s) had a total of thirty-two firms with 14,000 workers, considerably below that of San Pedro de Macoris and Santiago, the other two major free-trade zones, where growth has been much greater.

As in export manufacturing in other parts of the world, most of the women workers in the free-trade zones are young, recent entrants to the industrial labour force, which increases their vulnerability. Nearly three-quarters of the women in our sample are under 30 years of age and two-thirds have no previous job experience, while one-third have been working at their present job for less than one year. Over 78 per cent of these women are migrants, and 60 per cent have been living in the city for ten years or less. On the other hand, educational levels are quite high; over 40 per cent have some secondary education compared to 15 per cent of the general female population, indicating selective recruitment by employers in the free-trade zones. In fact, a 1991 national-level survey of workers in the free-trade zones indicates that women have higher educational levels than men, as they do nationally; in the free-trade zones, 63 per cent of women have completed secondary school compared to 47 per cent of the men. Despite these higher educational levels, women are still primarily confined to unskilled production work, while better-paid administrative, professional, and supervisory jobs are held by men (Fundapec, 1992: 119, 128). Thus, occupational segregation re-establishes gender hierarchies in the free-trade zones, even though most of the workers are women and better educated than men.

Young single women have the highest educational levels in the sample, and many of them take courses after work at night or on weekends to learn English or secretarial skills in hopes of preparing for a better job. Higher educational levels also enable a woman to become more independent, as Lydia, a 25-year-old single woman claims: 'Si tú no tienes nada, pues nada vales. Y por eso yo he dedicado mi tiempo a estudiar. El día que . . . yo me case, es lo que digo yo: "Bueno, tú tienes la puerta para que salgas, mi'jo. Que yo dependo de mí, de mi trabajo."' (If you have nothing, then you are worth nothing. And for that reason I have dedicated my time to studying. The day that I marry, I can tell him, 'Well, there's the door for you to leave, my son. I depend on myself, I depend on my work'.)

In contrast to global patterns, which show a distinct preference for single women in export manufacturing, more than half of the women interviewed in the Dominican free trade zones are married,[2] while one-quarter are divorced or separated. This reflects both the early age of marital unions in the Dominican Republic and the increasing percentage of female heads of household, who constituted nearly one-quarter of all households in 1984 (Gómez, 1990: 27). Two-thirds of our sample have children, but the number of children seldom exceeds four, which is

[2] Unless indicated otherwise, married women includes women in consensual unions, who in our sample are twice as numerous as married women. At the national level as well, the percentage of women in consensual unions is 34.6%, compared to 21.4% in legal marriages (Duarte *et al.*, 1989: 35).

comparable with the average fertility level in the Dominican Republic as a whole in 1980 (Duarte *et al.*, 1989: 21). Some employers in the free-trade zones in the Dominican Republic indicated a preference for women with children because they feel their need to work ensures greater job commitment (Joekes with Moayedi, 1987: 59). However, in order to avoid paying maternity leave, several employers also distribute birth control pills free of charge to their women workers, and a few require a pregnancy test or sterilization certificate before they are hired, illustrating the extent of control over the woman's reproductive as well as productive roles.

Most of the women in the in-depth interviews complained about the wages and working conditions in the free-trade zones, but felt powerless to do anything about it. Juana Santana, for example, is 25 years old with two children from her first consensual union, and at the time of our interview, was on leave expecting her third child from her current partner. They live in one room with no private cooking or bathroom facilities, for which they pay DR$45 a month. She also pays DR$20 weekly to a girl to look after her youngest child, while her mother who lives in another neighbourhood has the older 6-year-old. Her husband drives a taxi (*público*) owned by his family, but does not earn much because he has to buy gasoline and only earns a percentage of his intake, the rest of which goes to his father. Juana receives no financial assistance from the father of the children, who left town to work in another town, and she doesn't know his address. So with her salary of DR$57, and occasional bonuses for exceeding her production quota, she covers all basic expenses, including food, rent, the babysitter, as well as her own transportation, lunches, etc.

Juana has worked for the same garment firm for eight years, and except for a six-month cleaning job, this was her first job at 17 after arriving as a child with her family from a nearby town in the rural area. She thinks it is better to remain where she is than seek another job elsewhere, though she has many complaints. The company often requires them to work overtime until 9.00 p.m. without notice, and if they cannot, they are fired, which is especially difficult for women with young children. They used to fire everyone every five years (perhaps to avoid the accumulation of seniority) and then they only paid about half of the required severance pay, but she claims the current manager has discontinued this practice. Juana has tried to earn a little extra playing *san*, a form of rotating credit association, but the company has a strict policy against any form of business activity in the plant. This company was also among the last to grant workers a government-mandated pay increase after devaluation. Juana wishes they would fire her so she could use her severance pay to set up her own business. With two (and now three) children to support, her husband's unstable income, and the high cost of living, she knows she has to continue working, and plans to be sterilized after this child. Juana notes: 'De todas maneras yo tengo que trabajar, sea en la Zona o por ahí en una casa de familia, de todas maneras, porque es que yo, yo no puedo estar atenía al esposo mío. Porque lo que él gana no me da, para yo ayudar a mi familia y ayudarme en la casa.' (Anyway, I have to work, either in the zone or in a private home [as a domestic], anyway, because, I cannot be dependent on my husband. Because what he earns is not enough, to help my family and to help me here at home.)

Juana's situation is typical of what many women workers in the free-trade zones face—low wages, poor working conditions, lack of child care, limited job alternatives, partners who offer no or limited assistance, and an increasingly high cost of living. Like many of our informants, Juana and her partner are thinking of leaving, he for Puerto Rico and she for St Maarten, where she has a friend working in the tourist industry, 'porque aquí lo que tú trabajas no da pa' la comida' (because here what you earn doesn't even pay for food). Thus, discontent is expressed in turnover or eventual withdrawal, rather than through labour organizing, which Juana does not even want to talk about. It is clear that in the plant where she works, any union activity would be severely punished.

There are no unions operating in the Dominican free-trade zones, although they are not legally prohibited, and acknowledgement of workers' rights to association in free zones is included in the US Generalized System of Preferences and as a criterion of eligibility under the CBI. The level of unionization in the country as a whole never represented more then 10 or 15 per cent of the labour force, and unions have been plagued by fragmentation because of their ties to political parties (Espinal, 1988). Workers are fired and blacklisted with other plants if any union activity is detected. Hilda, for example, was fired several years ago along with sixty other women for trying to organize a union in the same factory where she and Juana work. The women received no support from the Ministry of Labour and Hilda was blacklisted from working in any other factories in the free-trade zone. As the manager told them when they were fired: 'La que se meta en sindicato sabe que va a perder su empleo aquí y no va a trabajar más en Zona Franca, porque ustedes saben que el peje grande come al peje chiquito.' (Whoever gets involved in unions here know she will lose her job and will no longer work in the free-trade zone, because as you know the big fish eats the little fish.) Seventy per cent of the women workers responding to this question in the CIPAF sample[3] indicated they were in favour of unionization, and Hilda thinks unions could bring about many improvements such as better wages, transportation, and cafeterias for workers. After she was fired, Hilda went to work in San Pedro de Macoris, another free-trade zone about one hour's drive from her home, but eventually, she got back her old job because she is such a good worker.

[3] Twenty per cent of the sample refused to answer this question, indicating the degree of intimidation about unions among women workers in the free-trade zones.

Workers are conscious of their exploitation and of the need to organize, but feel helpless to do anything about it. Workers can be dismissed for any reason, and know that there are a lot of other women waiting for their job. Some feel that women are easier to intimidate than men. Dominga claims: 'El hombre es más fuerte que la mujer y cuando existen hombres, la cosa es mejor. Ellos le temen a los hombres. A las mujeres no, porque como las mujeres son tan sencillas, no podemos hacer nada.' (The man is stronger than the women and when there are men, things are better. They are afraid of men. But not of women, because women are so simple, we can't do anything.) These patriarchal notions of male superiority are reinforced by gender hierarchies recreated in the work place, with male managers and supervisors in control of female workers, and weaken women's ability to undertake collective action.

The lack of support women receive from the Ministry of Labour is another factor designed to deter worker militancy. Women who have tried to take complaints of mistreatment or unjust dismissal to the Ministry of Labour have generally been rejected in favour or management. In the survey, 86 per cent of the women in the free-trade zones claim not even to know about this office, and only 12 per cent have ever presented complaints. As Luz, a 26-year-old garment worker stated: 'La Secretaria del Trabajo no se envuelve en defender a una de nosotras. O sea, ellos siempre se van a favor de los gerentes.' (The Secretary of Labour does not defend one of us. That is, they are always in favour of the managers.)

Workers also complain about the quality of health care through the IDSS (Instituto Dominicano de Seguro Social), which is designed to cover all permanent employees through a fund to which employers, employees, and the state are supposed to contribute. However, in 1980 only 41 per cent of the total labour force was actually covered (Ramírez *et al.*, 1988: 102), and these are mostly workers in large, capital-intensive firms, most of whom are men. The government has also not made regular payments to the fund, resulting in a deterioration of health services. In the national-level study of free-trade zones conducted in 1991, three-fourths of the workers were covered by IDSS (Fundapec, 1992: 135). The women in our sample made full use of the maternity hospital of the IDSS, and their 12 weeks of maternity leave, but often go to private doctors for routine care, because of the poor quality and the long delays in treatment. The economic crisis and structural adjustment has led to further reductions in public health expenditure, leading to shortages of medical personnel, medicine, surgical supplies, and vital equipment. It would seem that the notion that governments are responsible for the social reproduction of their citizens has never really taken hold in the Dominican Republic, where corruption and personal aggrandizement and concern over balance of payments and inflation has always taken precedence over public expenditure for social welfare. At the same time, structural adjustment measures such as reductions in state price controls on basic items like rice and sugar have contributed to rising food prices and in the cost of living generally, aggravated by devaluation.

Although there have been several increases in the minimum wage to keep up with inflation, purchasing power has declined, and workers know that their salaries buy less than previously. All workers in the Dominican free-trade zones are paid the minimum wage, which in 1990 stood at DR$.50 an hour, one of the lowest in the Caribbean (Deere and Melendez, 1992: 19). Salaries are so low in the free-trade zones that many workers try to earn extra income through a *san* or *rifa* (raffle) and sell objects ranging from food to jewellery, watches, and cosmetics to their fellow workers in the plant. Some managers prohibit these activities, but many workers still engage in them. Hilda, for example, plays *san*, although she knows that the manager doesn't like it, claiming 'si yo viviera atenida a lo que me pagan en mi fábrica yo no pudiera sostener mi casa. Porque yo tengo cuatro hijos.' (if I lived off what they paid me in the factory, I couldn't support my household. Because I have four children.) In the survey sample, about three-fourths reported income from other sources than their salary, but this was chiefly from other household members who were working, rather than non-wage activities like *sans*. However, it would appear from our in-depth interviews that the level of informal economic activity has increased because of the high cost of living brought on by devaluation and the economic crisis.

Why don't workers protest? Many factors contribute to the lack of worker solidarity in export manufacturing, including the youth and constant turnover among workers, their recent entry into industrial employment, family responsibilities, high unemployment, and the lack of job alternatives. However, the principal obstacle to greater labour solidarity in the Dominican Republic is outright government repression. There have been several strikes in the the free-trade zones, principally over wage increases, and several attempts to set up labour unions, but all have been met by mass firings of the workers involved, as well as blacklisting in other plants, to intimidate other workers.

It could be argued that weak and vulnerable labour is necessary to the success of export manufacturing because cheap wages and a docile labour force are critical components for international competition. This is one reason women are preferred as unskilled production workers in export manufacturing. Nationally, their wage levels are lower than men, and their unemployment levels are higher, creating an abundant, but well-educated labour force. Even within the free-trade zones, the better-paid, more qualified jobs are given to men. Women workers are less able than male workers to press their demands against employers and the state, who continue to treat women as supplementary workers, without the same legitimacy as men. Women workers lack representation in labour unions and political parties, and receive no support from the state for their grievances. They are locked into dead-end, poor-paying jobs and have no opportunity to move into managerial or skilled positions. Thus, these public forms of patriarchy perpetuate the subordination of Dominican women workers.

Women's resistance to male dominance in the family

While they are relatively weak at the level of the work place and the polity, where power must be exercised collectively as workers to confront capital and the state, Dominican women workers in the free-trade zones have begun to assume more authority in the family. Their authority in the home is derived from their increased economic contribution to the household, which has taken on major significance in the light of declining male wages and its debilitating impact on a man's ability to be the sole breadwinner. In short, it is not simply a question of whether women are employed or not, but the importance of their contribution to the household economy, which gives women a basis of resistance to male dominance in the family.

Most women agree that paid employment has given them greater legitimacy to negotiate with their husbands, even if they still consider him the head of the household. In general, more egalitarian relationships seem to be found among couples who are both working, are better educated, have lived in the city longer, have not married very young, and are legally married rather than living in consensual union. For example, Julia was recently married in a civil ceremony at 24 and is expecting her first child. Both she and her husband work in the zone, where she has worked for seven years, and she notes: 'Yo diría que eso me hace sentir más segura, porque ya yo misma manejo mi dinero y sé en que lo voy a gastar y lo que me corresponde.' (I would say that [work] makes me feel more secure, because I manage my own money and I know what I will spend it on and what belongs to me.)

Women are clearly becoming major economic contributors to the household, and in our sample of Dominican women workers in export manufacturing, 38 per cent consider themselves to be the major economic provider. However, there is considerable variation in the importance of the woman's contribution to the household economy by marital status (Table 1), which affects household composition and the number of other contributors to the household economy. In our sample, only 20 per cent of single women are the principle economic providers, because they are likely to share the support of the household with parents, siblings, or other relatives. Some single women live alone, but can seldom afford more than a single room, because housing in La Romana is very expensive. Lydia, for example, has been working in the free-trade zone for five years, after

Table 1 Women workers in the free-trade zones of the Dominican Republic by marital status and principle provider (in percentages)

Principle provider	Marital status			
	Single	Married*	Widows, divorced, and separated	Total
Woman Worker	19.6	26.3	74.2	37.7
Spouse	—	58.4	1.6	30.3
Parent(s)	35.3	.8	11.3	11.2
Other	45.1	14.5	12.9	20.8
Total %	100.0	100.0	100.0	100.0
	(51)	(118)	(62)	(231)

* Includes consensual unions.
Source: Ricourt (1986: 95).

arriving at 17 with her aunt and uncle from the rural area. Her relatives have since returned, and for two years she lived with another women worker whom she met at the night secretarial school she attends. Now Lydia lives alone in a single room with no private bathroom or cooking facilities, but she has asked her sister from the country to join her. She doesn't tell anyone at work that she lives alone, because then men try to take advantage of you. Lydia claims that many young women living alone in La Romana have become pregnant: 'Un hombre porque cree que uno vive sola y decirle a uno "yo voy a quedarme contigo", eso es lo más que le dicen a uno y yo, para mí, lo detesto. Detesto los hombres que solamente quieren burlarse de uno.' (A man thinks because you live alone, all he has to do is say 'I am going to stay with you', that's all they say, and I, I detest that. I detest men who only want to deceive you.)

Female heads of household carry the heaviest financial responsibility, and nearly three-fourths of these households in our sample consider themselves the principal economic provider. Female heads of household constitute 26 per cent of the women in our Dominican sample and are generally older than married or single women, and have more children. While a few are widows or divorced, most are separated from one or more consensual unions, which were often initiated before they were 20. It would appear that increased female employment has enabled some women to become less dependent on men and more prone to leave an unsatisfactory relationship. For example, Teresa is now 38 and lives alone, although she has had eight children in three consensual unions, starting at age 13. The younger children still live with their father, and she did not work while she lived with him. Her ability to leave this marriage was clearly dependent on her

Table 2 Women workers in free-trade zones of the Dominican Republic by marital status and head of household

Head of household	Marital Status					
	Single		Married & consensual unions		Widow, divorced, and separated	
	No.	%	No.	%	No.	%
Herself	5	0.8	14	11.0	40	64.5
Husband	—	—	92	80.0	2	3.2
Both	—	—	7	6.0	—	—
Mother	14	27.5	1	0.9	9	14.5
Father	17	33.3	2	1.6	5	8.1
Other	15	29.4	2	1.6	6	9.7
Total	51	100.0	118	100.0	62	100.0

Source: Ricourt (1986: 96).

finding employment, and she now works as a supervisor in the same plant where she has been working for ten years. She says she would not quit working, even if she found another man, because: 'Son hombres machistas. De que piensan de que si la mujer trabaja se va a gobernar demasiado, porque así es que se usa aquí en Santo Domingo. De que cuando la mujer trabaja entonces ellos ven que es liberal, un poco más liberal, que no pueden hacerle mucha maldad y no pueden abusar . . . Pero muchos hombres cuando la mujer no trabaja, la mujer tiene que esperar obligado, mal pasar, aguantarle al hombre muchas cosas. Pero cuando la mujer trabaja ya ahí cambia, porque estamos trabajando los dos.' (They are *machistas*. They think that if the woman works, she will rule too much, because that's the way it is here in Santo Domingo. That when a woman works, they think she is liberal, a little too liberal, that they can't mistreat or abuse her . . . But many men when the woman isn't working, the woman is obliged to wait, to have a bad time, to put up with many things from a man. But when the woman is working, then things change, because we are both working.) Teresa clearly expresses the dependence which lack of paid employment imposes on Dominican women.

Households with young children to support are in the most critical stage economically, and this is the period when women are the most dependent on men. Eighty per cent of the married women in our sample still consider the man as head of the household (Table 2) and 58 per cent consider him the principal economic provider. The man is expected to pay for the basic expenses like the house and food, but an increasing number of Dominican working women are taking over these expenses as well as paying for clothes, schooling, the babysitter, as well as their own work-related costs. For example, Luz and her partner live in a single room with a makeshift kitchen and a communal bathroom and laundry. Their two young children live with her mother in the rural area, and she only sees them every two or three weeks. Luz's partner has nine children from four previous consensual unions, but has no regular income since he works at occasional jobs in construction or driving a cab, or even fishing. He would like to get married, but Luz is not interested, claiming marriage would give him more rights over her. She notes: 'Ellos cuando son casados tienen como más derechos en uno. "No, porque tú eres la esposa y tú tienes que obedecerme", que sé yo qué . . . Los que sólo están unidos se comportan como mejor, más si las mujeres trabajan, se portan mejor todavía.' (When they [men] are married, they have more rights over you. 'No, because you are my wife and you have to obey me' and so on . . . Those who are only *unidos* [in consensual union] behave better, better yet if the women are working, they behave even better.) While legal marriage confers more status and legal rights on a woman and should be more stable than a consensual union, its rejection may be seen as another form of resistance to male authority.

Women married in consensual unions often carry more financial responsibility for the household than legally married women. Women in consensual unions have no legal right to their partners' social security or property, and may be left to fend for themselves and their children if the union dissolves. In addition, these women are likely to have children from previous unions, for whom their current partner is not expected to assume financial responsibility. Nor are they likely to receive financial assistance from the fathers of these children, so they are left with the primary responsibility of raising these children. Hilda, for example, continued to work after she had two children with her second partner, although he wanted her to quit. Hilda said she felt more secure working, especially since she had two children from a previous union, noting: 'Me sentía bien segura porque sabía si él se va por los menos mis hijos no van a pasar hambre, porque yo los puedo . . .' (I felt very secure because I knew that if he goes my children at least would not go hungry, because I could [support them].) Like Hilda, many women in consensual unions feel insecure in their relationships with men, and have come to depend on themselves for supporting their family.

In our sample, the number of women in consensual unions is twice as high as those legally married, which corresponds to the higher percentage of consensual unions nationally in the Dominican Republic (Báez, 1991: 3). Legal marriages are more stable, and both in our sample, and at the national level, the proportion of women who have had more than one partner is much higher among those living in consensual union than among those legally married. Consensual unions are also linked to lower educational levels and lower socio-economic status, indicating that the type of union may be a less important factor in marital stability than general class characteristics (Duarte *et al.*, 1989: 40–2). In our sample, for example, 49 per cent of those legally married have a secondary education, compared to 23 per cent of those in consensual unions.

The lower educational level of women in consensual unions may help explain their greater receptivity to patriarchal norms. There is a curious contradiction between behavioural norms and ideological beliefs among women in consensual unions in our sample. At the behavioural level, as we have seen, women in consensual unions often assume greater responsibility for the household and are less economically dependent on men than legally married women. In our sample, women in consensual unions are more likely to pay the bills, to make major household purchases, to decide how many children to have and how to educate them, than legally married women. Brown (1975) has argued that the greater authority and responsibility of Dominican women in consensual unions makes them less subordinate to men, and less dependent on them economically. However, our data suggest that women in consensual unions ideologically subscribe to patriarchal norms more than legally married women. For example, in our sample, 58 per cent of the legally married women compared to 39 per cent of women in consensual unions think that the husband should share important domestic decisions with his wife. Women were also asked their opinion (as opposed to their actual behaviour) about matters such as whether women should work outside the home, whether domestic concerns should be left entirely to women, and whether men and women should enjoy equal access to education and equal rights at work. In almost all these questions, women in consensual unions consistently favoured less autonomy and equality for women than women who were legally married, though the majority of women in both cases were in favour of more egalitarian relationships. These attitudes reflect not only the class and educational differences noted earlier, but also suggest the insecurity Dominican women feel in their increasingly fragile relationships with men. By subscribing to patriarchal norms, women in consensual unions may be rejecting their heavy financial responsibilities and voicing their desire to share the responsibility for raising a family with a stable male partner. In order to oblige a man to assume this responsibility, a woman cannot directly challenge his role as head of the household, and thus she is forced to support the maintenance of patriarchal authority patterns. This persistence of traditional gender ideology reflects the constraints women feel in raising a family on their own.

It is difficult for women to support a family on their low wages, particularly since they have no state supports like welfare or unemployment insurance, as in Puerto Rico and advanced industrial countries like the USA. Half of the households in our sample have relatives living in the household, generally siblings who are looking for work and who are expected to contribute to the household once they are employed. The addition of adult working members becomes another way of enlarging the household income, and 30 per cent of the households in our sample report receiving financial assistance from relatives. The majority of those receiving assistance are single women, who are most likely to be living with immediate family or other relatives. However, aid or support from relatives left behind in the rural area has been attenuated because of rapid rural–urban migration and the poverty of the older generation. Older parents are often poor subsistence farmers, who cannot afford to live in the city because of the high cost of living, particularly housing. They also cannot help support their children, although occasionally they send some fresh vegetables or help them build a place to live in the city. The most important assistance they provide is in terms of child rearing. Young children are often left with grandparents in the rural area while their mother or parents work in the free-trade zone. For example, Dolores now lives in La Romana with her two grown sons who work in the free-trade zone of San Pedro de Macoris. They pay their own expenses, including their studies, and contribute what they can to the household. When Dolores separated, she left her four children with her father in the country and the youngest child still lives with his grandfather. She came to work in the free-trade zone of La Romana ten years ago, but sent her children money regularly. She has thought of remarriage, but notes: 'Es muy bueno tener un compañero para ayudarlo en el hogar, uno sentirse con mayor apoyo, de cualquier cosa, cualquier problema fuerte así. Pero fijate, mis hijos son varones todos, ya no son niñitos chiquititos, que ya son hombrecitos. Yo no doy mis hijos por un hombre, y mucho menos por los que aparecen hoy.' (It is good to have a companion, to help you in the house, to feel you have more support, for whatever thing, whatever tough problem. But look, my children are all men, they are no longer little boys, they are little men. I wouldn't give up my sons for a man, and much less for those who are around now.) Despite her reluctance to remarry, however, Dolores still thinks that it is the man '*que manda en la casa*' (who gives the orders in the house).

Resistance to male authority has been heightened by the increasing inability of men to fulfil their role as breadwinner. Male unemployment in the sub-sample of households interviewed in 1986 appears to have increased from the time of the original 1981 survey, when it stood at only 11 per cent compared to 18 per cent nationally. Increased male unemployment reflects the crisis and the subsequent decline in government jobs and employment in the sugar industry, which fell drastically during the early eighties, and is a principal source of male employment in La Romana, where these in-depth interviews were conducted. Most of the men like Luz's partner were *chiriperos*, doing odd jobs in the informal sector like selling cooked food, driving cabs part-time, working at temporary jobs in construction, and participating in *sans* or *rifas*. A few who had the capital to start their own business were doing quite well.

The erosion of the man's role as economic provider has led some men to tighten their control over women. Many Dominican men are threatened by their wives' employment and may even forbid them to continue working. One woman had to stop working because her husband objected so strenuously, and even refused to buy anything for the house. Men may exert economic pressure in this way to keep women dependent on them. Adolfina, who is working, notes the difficulty her employment causes with her husband: 'Ahora a veces como yo trabajo, sucede que a veces me acusa de que yo . . . es decir, que como que me gobierno, que yo hago lo que yo quiero. El me acusa de que yo me gobierno porque yo trabajo y yo hago con ese dinero lo que yo quiero . . . Y hay muchos hombres no les gusta que la mujer trabaje por eso.' (Now that I work, it happens that he accuses me of . . . that is, that I rule myself, that I do what I want. He accuses me of ruling myself because I work and I do with that money what I want . . . And there are many men who don't like a woman to work for that reason.) However, there are also men who wait on Fridays outside the gate of the free-trade zone to collect their wives' or girlfriends' pay check, that is, they live off of women's wages. When I asked if men felt threatened by women working, one of our respondents laughed 'Se aprovechan' (They take advantage of it).

This kind of male irresponsibility is leading some women to reject marriage or remarriage. For example, Josefina is 33 years old and lives with another woman in a nicely furnished house provided by her roommate's relatives in New York. She has no plans to marry, because she thinks men today are too irresponsible, noting: 'ellos ahora no se ocupan de la mujer como se ocupaban antes. Que antes un hombre se llevaba una mujer o se casaba con una mujer y sabía que a esa mujer tenía que comprarle zapatos, vestidos, o sea todo lo que necesitaba. Pero ahora no, ahora ellos, "Ah no, tú trabajas, cómpratelo tú." ' (They [men] don't take responsibility for a woman the way they used to. Before a man took a woman or married a woman and knew that he had to buy that woman shoes, dresses, everything she needed. But now no, now they say 'Oh no, you work, buy it yourself.') In short, increased employment has brought women greater financial responsibility as men abdicate their role as economic provider.

Some younger women have succeeded in negotiating a more egalitarian relationship with their husbands, partly through the independence which paid employment has give them. For example, Eva and her husband both work and have two children after nine years of marriage and they make most decisions jointly: 'El siempre lo ha dicho, "que aquí tanto mando yo como mandas tú". . . . Que él no se siente como esos hombres que dicen, "allí en la casa mando yo". El siempre comparte conmigo, Igual que yo con él.' (He always has said, that 'here I give the orders along with you'. He is not like those men who say, 'here, I give the orders'. He always shares with me, and I with him.)

Fertility is one area where most Dominican women in our sample are clearly challenging male authority. Many women in both legal and consensual unions are now making their own decisions regarding the use of contraception and how many children to have, although an equally high percentage of legally married women share this latter decision with their husbands. Very few women expressed a desire for more than three children, and some have stopped at two. Many of these women came from families with ten or more children, indicating a rapid fertility decline in one generation, as can be seen as well at the national level. Our sample survey reveals that 30 per cent of the women use contraceptives (primarily pills), while 18 per cent have been sterilized. However, our in-depth interviews suggest that sterilization is more frequent, and it is possible that it has increased due to economic pressures during the early eighties. Young children are a burden to working women because paid child care in the free-trade zones is very expensive, and many women complain that their children are not well taken care of. Women who leave their children in the rural area with their parents or other relatives must contribute to their support, and they may not see their children more than once a month or less.

Married women still do most of the housework alone, which again increases the burden of young children, although female relatives or children may help out. Men never do routine domestic tasks except for occasional shopping, although 63 per cent of the women sampled would like men to assume more household responsibilities. Only two men in our sample regularly looked after their children. Men tend to dominate financial matters, like paying the bills or making major household purchases, since this gives them control of the family purse strings, although married women now have a greater say in the family budget.

Several factors inhibit Dominican women workers from asserting more authority in the household. The need to support young children, the increasingly high cost of living, and the inability of extended kin who remain behind in the rural area to provide more support, combined with their low wages and precarious jobs, make it very difficult for Dominican women workers to support a family on their own. Even when both the man and woman are working, they can barely make ends meet, and cannot save to buy a home of their own or to meet an emergency like illness. The high rate of consensual unions and of marital instability coupled with the pressures of the economic crisis heightens the woman's insecurity and her fear of challenging male dominance. The crisis has also threatened the man's role as provider, and made households all the more dependent on the woman's wages. Thus, it is not only increasing female labour-force participation, but the diminished economic role of men that is having an impact on household authority patterns.

CONCLUSIONS

The data on Dominican women workers presented here point up both the validity and the limitations of the general theoretical model outlined earlier for examining the impact of a wage economy on women workers in Third World countries undergoing rapid industrialization. It is clear that paid employment has had an impact on gender inequalities in the Dominican Republic, and that this impact is greater at the level of the household than in the work place or in the polity, where women are still regarded as supplementary wage earners. In part, women's exploitation as workers reflects the weakness of labour generally in the Dominican Republic, due to a long history of labour surplus, fragmentation of the labour movement, and state repression. But women workers receive even less attention than men from political parties and labour unions, at the same time that their wages are lower, their unemployment higher, and they are still responsible for child rearing and domestic tasks. For women workers to gain greater legitimacy in the work place and the polity, they would have to organize collectively, but all attempts to unionize have been suppressed by management and failed to receive substantial government support.

At the household level, however, women have always had more legitimacy and here they are able to negotiate individually. Paid employment, as well as higher educational levels and declining fertility, offer women a basis for exerting greater authority in the family, although many women still cling to the traditional notion of the man as the head of the household. Their modes of resistance to male dominance take several forms, including the rejection of marriage or remarriage, greater control over the budget and a greater share in household decisions, and control over their own fertility. It is clear that Dominican women are conscious of subordination and even exploitation by men, and are attempting to gain as much leverage as possible in household decisions, without totally undermining the man's authority. Most would prefer to maintain a stable conjugal relationship, while they struggle to make it more egalitarian, because they realize the difficulty in maintaining a family on their own. They recognize the increasing burden of children in a wage economy, but are still heavily identified with their mother role, which remains the prime source of female identity in Latin American society. This continued identification with their wife and mother role suggests that Dominican women workers still operate on the basis of separate spheres for men and women, despite the increasing importance of their public role as workers.

The Dominican data also underline the importance of examining the man's role as economic provider in analysing gender inequalities. Dominican women workers are acquiring more authority in the household not just because they are employed, but because of the importance of their economic contribution. As a result of the economic crisis and the collapse of an economy based on sugar and import substitution industrialization, men's capacity to fulfil their role as economic provider has been seriously eroded. Unemployment and under-employment is increasing and many men are seeking refuge in the informal sector, while the rates of female labour-force participation are rising. This pattern holds true for many Third World countries undergoing the economic crisis and global restructuring, and is becoming more relevant as well to advanced industrial countries like the USA. As Safilios-Rothschild (1990: 227) notes: 'When male breadwinning inadequacy becomes chronic and women become co-breadwinners on a permanent basis, men are no longer able to maintain their superior and authoritarian position vis-à-vis their wives.'

However, the degree of dependence on a male provider changes over a woman's life cycle, so that her age and marital status become critical determinants of her capacity to resist male dominance at the household level. This is one reason why female heads of household are often found among older women who do not have young children to support, and who may even be able to call on their children to contribute to the household. However, older women often maintain more traditional gender roles than younger women, who generally have higher levels of education and fewer children. As a result, young, better-educated women are also less likely to subscribe to patriarchal norms and more likely to expect to share responsibility and authority with their conjugal partners than older women, who were raised in an agrarian society in which the man's dominance in the household was unquestioned. Patriarchal norms have eroded in Dominican society as a whole with the move to a wage economy and increasing urbanization and education.

A recent study of rural Dominican women in the agro-industrial zone of Azua confirms that the changes in gender roles documented here are not confined to women workers in the free-trade zones. Comparing women workers in this agro-industrial complex with largely non-employed women in the community, Finlay (1989) concludes that workers had more power and control over resources within the family and were more likely to limit their fertility, which closely parallels our own findings. Among Dominican women immigrants to New York City, their increased employment and the importance of their contribution to the household have also led to a more egalitarian division of labour and distribution of authority, with a greater sharing of household tasks and control over the budget, and women beginning to define themselves as co-partners in heading the household. However, the struggle over domestic authority has also led to marital breakup, and may help account for the rising percentage of female-headed households in the Dominican community in New York City (Grasmuck and Pessar, 1991: 148–56). On the other hand, among Dominican rural women limited to unpaid labour on family farms or to seeking supplementary sources of income through the informal sector, a strong patriarchal gender ideology and dependence on a male breadwinner still prevails (Pou *et al.*, 1987; Jansen and Millan, 1991; Georges, 1990). A national-level study of Dominican rural women conducted in 1983 by CIPAF concludes: 'Está tan interiorizado en la mujer de la zona rural que el hombre es el principal proveedor que, de hecho, concibe su participación en las actividades generadoras de ingreso como transitorias y las justifica mientras perdure la crisis de reproducción de su unidad familiar' (Pou *et al.*, 1987: 204). (The woman in the rural area has so internalized the man as principal breadwinner that she, in fact, conceives her participation in income-generating activities as transitory and justifies them as long as the reproductive crisis in her household lasts.) That is, these rural Dominican women have not even begun to see themselves as permanent wage earners and continue to view men as the principal breadwinners.

In short, our empirical analysis of Dominican women workers in export-led industrialization suggests several additional factors which condition the impact of paid employment on gender subordination. The importance of the woman's contribution to the household economy in itself is partially determined by the number of other contributors to the household, which varies by life cycle and marital status. It is also affected by the level of male employment and wages, which largely determines how well men can carry out their breadwinner role. The woman's age and educational level as well as the type of work women do (permanent wage labour versus unpaid family labour and informal sector) also influence the ability of the women to challenge male domination. Our data suggest that legally married women subscribe less to patriarchal norms than women in consensual unions, which are more subject to marital instability. Women with young children are most dependent on a man's support, and least likely to challenge male dominance, particularly if they have no support from parents or other relatives.

Have Dominican women benefited from their increased wage labour? Here again the results are complex and contradictory. By taking advantage of women's inferior position in the labour market, export-led industrialization may reinforce their subordination through poorly paid, dead-end jobs. On the other hand, women's increased ability to contribute to the family income may challenge traditional patriarchal authority patterns and lead to more egalitarian family structures. This is particularly true where, as in the Dominican Republic, women have become critical contributors to the household economy. This more egalitarian pattern is the result of a gradual process of negotiation, in which women use their earnings and the family's increased dependence on them to bargain for increased authority and sharing of responsibilities within the household (Roldán, 1985: 275). However, the erosion of the man's role as breadwinner may also lead to greater marital instability and an increasing percentage of female-headed households.

Gender consciousness grows as the contradiction between women's increasingly important economic contribution to the household and their subordination in the family, in the work place, and in the polity become more apparent. But the myth of the male breadwinner is preserved by public forms of patriarchy who continue to profit from women's subordinate status. At present these women workers have no adequate vehicles to express their grievances or to transform their sense of exploitation (which is very real) into greater class consciousness. Until women workers are given the same legitimacy as men, and not regarded as supplementary wage earners, they will be more vulnerable as a source of cheap labour.

REFERENCES

ACKER, JOAN (1988), 'Class, Gender, and the Relations of Distribution', *Signs*, 13/3: 473–97.

Alt-WID (Alternative Women in Development) (1992), *Reagonomics and Women: Structural Adjustment US Style: 1980–1992* (Washington, DC).

ARROM, SILVIA M. (1985), *The Women of Mexico City, 1790–1857* (Stanford: Stanford University Press).

BÁEZ, CLARA (1985), *La Subordinación de la Mujer Dominicana en Cifras* (Santo Domingo: Dirección General de la Promoción de la Mujer/INSTRAW).

—— (1991), *Mujer y Desarrollo en la República Dominicana: 1981–1991* (Santo Domingo: unedited report prepared for Inter-American Development Bank).

BARRETT, MICHÈLE (1980), *Women's Oppression Today* (London: Verso).

BROWN, CAROL (1987), 'Mothers, Fathers and Children: From Private to Public Patriarchy', in L. Sargent (ed.), *Women and Revolution* (Boston: South End Press).

BROWN, SUSAN (1975), 'Love Unites Them and Hunger Separates Them: Poor Women in the Dominican Republic', in R. Reiter (ed.), *Toward an Anthropology of Women* (New York: Monthly Review Press).

CEARA, MIGUEL (1987), *Situación Socioeconómica Actual y Su Repercusión en la Situación de la Madre y el Niño* (Santo Domingo: INTEC and UNICEF).

Consejo Nacional de Zonas Francas de Exportación, Secretaría de Estado de Industria y Comercio (1993), Evaluación Zonas Francas Industriales: Sto. Domingo, D.R.

CORNIA, G. R. JOLLY and STEWART, F. (eds.) (1987), *Adjustment with a Human Face*, vol. 1 (New York: UNICEF/Oxford, Clarendon Press).

DAUHAJRE, ANDRÉS, RILEY, E., MENA, R., and GUERRERO, J. A. (1989), *Impacto Económico de las Zonas Francas Industriales de Exportación en la República Dominicana* (Santo Domingo: Fundación Economía y Desarrollo, Inc.).

DEERE, CARMEN DIANA, ANTROBUS, PEGGY, BOLLES, LYNN, MELÉNDEZ, EDWIN, PHILLIPS, PETER, RIVERA, MARCIA, and SAFA, HELEN (1990), *In the Shadows of the Sun: Caribbean Development Alternatives and US Policy* (Boulder, Colo.: Westview Press).

—— and MELÉNDEZ, EDWIN (1992), 'When Export Growth is not Enough: US Trade Policy and Caribbean Basin Economic Recovery', *Caribbean Affairs*, 5/1: 61–70.

DUARTE, ISIS, BÁEZ, CLARA, GÓMEZ, CARMEN J., and ARÍZA, MARINA (1989), *Población y Condición de la Mujer en República Dominicana* (Santo Domingo: Instituto de Estudios de Población y Desarrollo, Estudio no. 6).

Economic Commission for Latin America and the Caribbean (ECLAC) (1988), *Latin American and Caribbean Women: Between Change and Crisis*, LC/L.464 (CRM. 4/2). Santiago, Chile.

ESPINAL, ROSARIO (1988), *Torn between Authoritarianism and Crisis-Prone Democracy: The Dominican Labor Movement* (Notre Dame, Ind.: The Helen Kellogg Institute for International Studies, Working Paper no. 116).

FINLAY, BARBARA (1989), *The Women of Azua: Work and Family in the Rural Dominican Republic* (New York: Praeger).

FOLBRE, NANCY (1991), 'The Unproductive Housewife: Her Evolution in Nineteenth Century Thought', *Signs*, 16/3.

Fundapec (Fundación APEC de Crédito Educative, Inc.) (1992), *Encuesta Nacional de Mano de Obra* (Santo Domingo; Report prepared for Inter-American Development Bank).

GEORGES, EUGENIA (1990), *The Making of a Transnational Community: Migration, Development, and Cultural Change in the Dominican Republic* (New York: Columbia University Press).

GÓMEZ, CARMEN JULIA (1990), *La Problemática de las Jefas del Hogar* (Santo Domingo: CIPAF).

GRASMUCK, SHERRI and PESSAR, PATRICIA (1991), *Between Two Islands: Dominican International Migration* (Berkeley: University of California Press).

HARTMANN, HEIDI (1981), 'The Unhappy Marriage of Marxism and Feminism Towards a More Progressive Union', in L. Sargent (ed.), *Women and Revolution* (Boston: South End Press).

—— (1987), 'Changes in Women's Economic and Family Roles in Post-World War II United States', in L. Beneria and C. Stimpson (eds.), *Women, Households and the Economy* (New Brunswick: Rutgers University Press).

JANSEN, SENAIDA and MILLAN, CECILIA (1991), *Género, Trabajo y Etnia en los Bateyes Dominicanos* (Santo Domingo: Instituto Tecnológico de Santo Domingo, Programa de Estudios de la Mujer).

JOEKES, SUSAN, with MOAYEDI, ROXANA (1987), *Women and Export Manufacturing: A Review of the Issues and AID Policy* (Washington, DC: International Center for Research on Women; prepared for the Office of Women in Development, USAID).

KANDIYOTI, DENIZ (1991), 'Bargaining with Patriarchy', in J. Lorber and S. Farrell (eds.), *The Social Construction of Gender* (Newbury Park, Calif.: Sage).

KESSLER-HARRIS, ALICE (1990), *A Woman's Wage: Historical Meanings and Social Consequences* (Lexington: The University Press of Kentucky).

—— and SACKS, KAREN (1987), 'The Demise of Domesticity in America', in L. Beneria and C. Stimpson (eds.), *Women, Households and the Economy* (New Brunswick: Rutgers University Press).

LAMPHERE, LOUISE (1986), 'From Working Daughters to Working Mothers: Production and Reproduction in an Industrial Community', *American Ethnologist*, 13/1: 118–30.

LIM, LINDA (1990), 'Women's Work in Export Factories: The Politics of a Cause', in I. Tinker (ed.), *Persistent Inequalities: Women and World Development* (New York: Oxford University Press).

MANN, MICHAEL (1986), 'A Crisis in Stratification Theory? Persons, Households/Families, Lineages, Genders, Classes and Nations', in R. Crompton and M. Mann (eds.), *Gender and Stratification* (Cambridge: Polity Press).

MARTINEZ-ALIER, VERENA (1974), *Marriage, Class and Colour in Nineteenth-Century Cuba* (Cambridge: Cambridge University Press).

POU, FRANCIS, MONES, B., HERNÁNDEZ, P., GRANT, L., DOTTIN, M., ARANGO, A., FERNÁNDEZ, B., and ROSADO, T. (1987), *La Mujer Rural Dominicana* (Santo Domingo: CIPAF).

PRIETO, YOLANDA (1992), 'Cuban Women in New Jersey: Gender Relations and Change', in D. Gabaccia (ed.), *Seeking Common Ground: Multidisciplinary Studies of Immigrant Women in the United States* (Westport, Conn.: Greenwood Press).

RAMÍREZ, NELSON, SANTANA, ISIDORO, DE MOYA, FRANCISCO, and TACTUK, PABLO (1988), *República Dominicana: Población y Desarorollo 1950–1985* (San Jose, Costa Rica: Centro Latinoamericano de Demografía (CELADE)).

RICOURT, MILAGROS (1986), *Free Trade Zones, Development and Female Labor Force in the Dominican Republic*. Masters thesis, Center for Latin American Studies, University of Florida.

ROLDÁN, MARTHA (1985), 'Industrial Outworking, Struggles for the Reproduction of Working-Class Families and Gender Subordination', in N. Redclift and E. Mingione (eds.), *Beyond Employment: Household, Gender and Subsistence* (New York: Basil Blackwell Inc.), 248–85.

ROSEN, BERNARD (1982), *The Industrial Connection: Achievement and the Family in Developing Societies* (New York: Aldine Publishing).

SACKS, KAREN B. (1989), 'Toward a Unified Theory of Class, Race, and Gender', *American Ethnologist*, 16/3: 534–50.

SAFA, HELEN I. (1981), 'Runaway Shops and Female Employment: The Search for Cheap Labor', *Signs*, 7/2: 418–33.

—— (1983), 'Women, Production and Reproduction in Industrial Capitalism: A Comparison of Brazilian and US Factory Workers', in J. Nash and M. Patricia Fernandez Kelly (eds.), *Women, Men and the International Division of Labor* (Albany: State University of New York Press).

—— (1990), 'Women and Industrialization in the Caribbean', in S. Stichter and J. Parpart (eds.), *Women, Employment and the Family in the International Division of Labour* (London: Macmillan Press), 72–97.

SAFILIOS-ROTHSCHILD, CONSTANTINA (1990), 'Socio-economic Determinants of the Outcomes of Women's Income-Generation in Developing Countries', in

S. Stichter and J. Parpart (eds.), *Women, Employment and the Family in the International Division of Labour* (London: Macmillan Press), 221–8.

SASSEN, SASKIA and FERNANDEZ-KELLY, M. PATRICIA (1995), 'Recasting Women in the Global Economy: Internationalization and Changing Definitions of Gender', in E. Acosta Belén and C. Bose (eds.), *Women in the Latin American Development Process* (Philadephia: Temple University Press).

STANDING, GUY (1989), 'Global Feminization through Flexible Labor', *World Development*, 17/7: 1077–96.

STONER, K. LYNN (1991), *From the House to the Streets: The Cuban Woman's Movement for Legal Reform, 1898–1940* (Durham, NC: Duke University Press).

TIANO, SUSAN (1986), 'Women and Industrial Development in Latin America', *Latin American Research Review*, 21/3: 157–70.

WALBY, SYLVIA (1986), *Patriarchy at Work* (Cambridge: Polity Press).

—— (1990), *Theorizing Patriarchy* (Oxford: Blackwell).

State, Gender, and the Organization of Business in Rural Taiwan

Rita S. Gallin

An 'economic miracle', Taiwan has been in the forefront of development through export. In contrast to other Third World countries, however, Taiwan's planners did not depend primarily on direct foreign investment to stimulate development. Rather, they relied on capital mobilization within the domestic private sector and an elaborate system of subcontracting to spearhead the growth of manufactured exports. As a result, small- and medium-sized businesses are the mainstay of the island's trading economy, accounting for 65 per cent of exports in the late 1980s (Bello and Rosenfeld, 1990: 241). The purpose of this paper is to discuss the organization of such businesses in a rural area in central Taiwan.

The paper is based on data collected in Hsin Hsing, a village which has changed over the past thirty years from an economic system primarily based on agriculture to one predominantly dependent on off-farm employment.[1] I begin by describing development in Taiwan and the traditional Chinese family to establish the context for the material that follows. Then, I describe development in Hsin Hsing, examine production and reproduction in the village, and discuss how the Chinese family system articulates with state policy and managerial practices to shape patterns of production and reproduction in the local area. In the concluding section, I consider the implications of the Taiwan case within the context of recent analyses of global economic restructuring and employment generation.

DEVELOPMENT IN TAIWAN

When the Nationalist government retreated to Taiwan in 1949, it found the island to be primarily agricultural with conditions not consistently favourable to development. The strategies it adopted to foster economic growth have been documented in detail elsewhere (Ho, 1978; Lin, 1973; Pang, 1987). Here it need only be emphasized that the government initially

[1] The research covers the period from 1957 to 1990. The first field trip, in 1957–8, involved a 17-month residence in the village. This was followed by two separate studies, in 1965–6 and 1969–70, of out-migrants from the area. The more recent research spanned 2 months in 1977, 6 months in 1979, 1 month in 1982, and 8 months in 1989–90. During these visits, my colleague, Bernard Gallin, and I collected data using both anthropological and sociological techniques, including participant observation, in-depth interviews, surveys, and collection of official statistics contained in family, land, school, and economic records.

strengthened agriculture to provide a base for industrialization, pursued a strategy of import substitution for a brief period during the 1950s, and then in the 1960s adopted a policy of industrialization through export.

The latter policy produced dramatic changes in Taiwan's economic structure. The contribution of agriculture to the net domestic product declined from 36 per cent in 1952 to only 7 per cent in 1986, while that of industry rose from 18 to 47 per cent over the same period. Trade expanded greatly, increasing in value from US$303 million in 1952 to US$64 billion in 1986. The contribution of exports to the volume of trade also rose dramatically, from US$116 million (38 per cent) in 1952 to US$40 billion (63 per cent) in 1986 (Lu, 1987: 2).

To achieve this transformation, Taiwan's planners relied on the mobilization of capital within the island's private sector and an intricately woven system of subcontracting to stimulate the production of commodities for export. Indeed, subcontracting is so thoroughly institutionalized on the island that one foreign executive remarked that Taiwan 'is not an exporting nation . . . [but rather] is simply a collection of international subcontractors for the American market' (cited in Sease, 1987: 1). This assessment notwithstanding, Taiwan's industrial structure is based on and sustained by vertically integrated and geographically dispersed small-scale businesses.

As early as 1971, for example, 50 per cent of the industrial and commercial establishments and 55 per cent of the manufacturing firms in Taiwan were located in rural areas (Ho, 1976).[2] Most such businesses are small- and medium-sized operations that produce for domestic and international markets; more than 90 per cent of the island's enterprises each employ fewer than 30 workers (Bello and Rosenfeld, 1990: 219) and, in 1987, these small businesses employed almost three-quarters (74.2 per cent) of Taiwan's labour force (DGBAS, 1988: 116–17).[3]

The predominant form such enterprises take is the family firm. (Greenhalgh (1980: 13) estimates that 97 per cent of all businesses owned by Taiwanese are family organized.) These firms were founded with capital drawn almost exclusively from the informal money market of domestic savings and personal loans. In sum, Taiwan's economy is sustained by a multitude of small- and medium-sized family firms that traverse the island and provide income for the majority of the population—a population in

[2] The dispersal of industry to the countryside has been explained as a product of industry's desire to be near the sources of low-cost labour and raw materials (Ho, 1976). While true, the government encouraged the movement by refraining from protecting agricultural land until the goal of industrialization had been achieved and farm productivity had declined. In November 1975 the government promulgated a law barring the use of certain agricultural land (i.e. grades 1–24) for purposes other than farming. (Before this law, only land grades 1–12 had been so regulated.)

[3] Following Ho (1976: 57), 'small' is defined as fewer than 10 workers, 'medium' as 10 to 99 workers, and 'large' as 100 workers or more. The definition of size varies in the literature on Taiwan. Stites (1982: 248), for example, defines small as 100 or fewer workers, while Gold (1986: 141 n. 16) defines large as more than 300 workers.

which wealth is becoming increasingly unequally distributed (*Free China Journal*, 1988: 2; Hsiao, 1987).

THE TRADITIONAL CHINESE FAMILY

The economic family, the *chia*, is central to these enterprises and is the basic socio-economic unit in China. This family can take one of three forms: conjugal, stem, or joint. The conjugal family consists of a husband, wife, and their unmarried children; the joint family adds two or more married sons and their wives and children to this core group. The stem family—a form that lies somewhere between the conjugal and joint family types—includes parents, their unmarried offspring, and one married son with his wife and children.

Life within the family is shaped by China's patrilineal kinship structure which recognizes only male children as descent-group members with rights to family property. In the past (and to a large extent today) residence was patrilocal; when a woman married she left her natal home to live as a member of her husband's family and severed her formal ties with her father's household. Parents considered daughters a liability: they were household members who drained family resources as children and who withdrew their assets (domestic labour and earning power) when they married. Sons, in contrast, contributed steadily to the family's economic security during its growth and expansion and provided a source of support in old age. Not surprisingly, parents strongly preferred male children.

Traditionally all members of the family lived under one roof, except for a few who worked outside to supplement or diversify the group income. Ideally the family functioned as a single co-operating unit in all activities. Men and women performed different tasks as members of a co-operative enterprise in which all property belonged to the family as a whole, except for the jewellery and cash brought into the household by a woman as part of her dowry. Others in the family had no rights to this 'private property' (*sz fang chien* (Mandarin) or *sai khia* (Taiwanese)), which a woman could augment with any money she might be allowed to retain during her married life.

An authoritarian hierarchy based on gender, generation, and age dominated life within the family. The eldest male had the highest status; a woman's status, although it increased with age and with the birth of sons, was lower than that of any man. Women's desires were subordinated to those of men, just as the wishes of the young were subordinated to those of the old. Even though women's work was necessary for the maintenance of the household, family members took their labour for granted. In short, women had no real control over their own lives; social and economic marginality marked their experience.

Table 1 Population of Hsin Hsing village by period and age

Age	1958		1989	
	No.	%	No.	%
1–15	269	44.2	137	30.0
16–44	235	38.6	194	42.5
45–64	90	14.8	77	16.8
65 and older	15	2.5	49	10.7
Total	609	100.0	457	100.0
Sex ratio (m/100f)	95		93	

Note: Although the sources of data contained in the table differ, correlations with other statistical materials confirmed the accuracy and comparability of the two data sets.
Sources: 1958, Household Record Book, Pu Yen Township Public Office; 1989, Field Survey.

DEVELOPMENT IN HSIN HSING

Hsin Hsing, the research site, is a nucleated village approximately 125 miles south-west of Taipei, Taiwan's capital city, and is located beside a road that runs between two market towns, Lukang and Ch'i-hu. Its people, like most in the area, are Hokkien (Minnan) speakers whose ancestors migrated from Fukien, China, several hundred years ago.

In 1958, the registered population of the village was 609 people in 99 households or economic families. About four-fifths of the population was between the ages of 1 and 44 years, and slightly less than half was male (see Table 1). Conjugal families predominated, accounting for 66 per cent of village families (56 per cent of the population). In contrast, only five per cent of households (10 per cent of the population) was of the joint type, while the remaining 29 per cent of households (35 per cent of the population) was of the stem form.

During the 1950s, when no significant industries or job opportunities existed locally, land was the primary means of production. Almost all families derived most of their livelihood from two crops of rice, marketable vegetables grown in the third crop, and, in some cases, wages from farm labour.[4] Men worked in the fields while women managed the house and children, worked as an auxiliary farm labour force, and, in their 'spare time', wove fibre hats at home to supplement the family income.

[4] Despite implementation of the Land Reform Programme and changes in the tenancy/ownership ratio, most families cultivated small farms: 45% of village families cultivated below 0.5 hectare, and 84% cultivated below 1.0 hectare. (Approximately one hectare (0.97) equals 2.4 acres or 1.0 *chia*.) See B. Gallin (1966) for a detailed description.

The village began to change in the mid-1950s and early 1960s, as the growing population pressure on the land created problems of under-employment and farms too small to support family members. Increasing numbers of men began to migrate to the larger cities of the province to seek jobs and supplemental income (Gallin and Gallin, 1974). The stream continued throughout the 1960s and labour shortages became acute, farm profits dropped, and agricultural production declined. (In Taiwan as a whole, production levelled off and varied by only a small amount from year to year in the late 1960s (CEPD, 1979: 59).) The stream of migration and the decline in production might well have continued in Hsin Hsing but for certain national and international developments in the 1970s.

The government's policy of export-oriented industrialization had brought about rapid urbanization and migration from rural areas to cities during the 1960s. Large segments of the rural population had been absorbed by urban industry, and the value of a farmer's production in 1972 was only one-fifth that of an off-farm worker's (Huang, 1981: 3). To stem the stagnation of agriculture, in 1973 the government instituted a guaranteed rice price and established the Accelerated Rural Development Programme (Yu, 1977). The implementation of these policies created a climate in which farmers believed they could derive profits from the cultivation of their land, and it accelerated the move of industry—which had begun in the 1960s—to the countryside.

These attempts to invigorate agriculture were followed by the oil crisis of 1974 and the world recession and inflation of 1974–5. The pace of industrialization in Taiwan's cities slowed (CEPD, 1979: 78), and more than 200,000 urban workers lost their jobs (Huang, 1981: 163) when some factories shut down and others cut back production. The city began to lose the aura of opportunity as the countryside began to acquire one of promise.

A comparison of the structure of the village population in 1989 with the population in 1958 suggests one of the outcomes of these developments. By 1989 only 457 people in 76 households were members of Hsin Hsing. Fully three-quarters (75.1 per cent) of the population was 46 years of age or younger and the proportion of men had increased to 52 per cent (see Table 1). This increase in part reflected a decline in male emigration and a rise in the migration of unmarried women to urban areas. In part, it also reflected the return of male out-migrants to the village in search of business opportunities and work.

Further examination of the data suggests another way in which the villagers responded to change in the macro-environment. By 1989, conjugal households no longer predominated in Hsin Hsing; only 38 per cent of families (29 per cent of the population) was of the simple type. Fully 12 per cent of households (16 per cent of the population) was of the joint type, while the remaining 50 per cent of families was of the stem form.

The reasons for this increase in complex families have been described in detail elsewhere (Gallin and Gallin, 1982*a*, 1982*b*; R. S. Gallin, 1984, 1986, 1991). Suffice it to say that the villagers believed that this form of family organization provided a mechanism for socio-economic success in a changing world. A family that included many potential off-farm workers, as well as other members who could manage the household, supervise children, and care for the land, had a better chance of diversifying economically than did a family of small size.

The success of this strategy could be seen throughout the local area. Labour-intensive factories, service shops, retail stores, and construction companies pervaded the local terrain. By 1989, 47 enterprises had been established in the village, and resident families derived 85 per cent of their income from off-farm employment. Nevertheless, fully 84 per cent of village households continued to farm, and families engaged in both farming and off-farm work were by far the most common.[5]

The transformation of the village economy altered the class structure of the community. Whereas in 1958 all but ten of village families were owner-farmers, by 1989 the community was economically differentiated. It included members of the proletariat who were protected by government labour codes and received wages determined by contract, and members of the sub-proletariat who, not benefiting from government legislation, received casual rather than protected wages. The community also included members of the petty bourgeoisie and bourgeoisie (owner-farmers, small shopkeepers, workshop owners, and subcontractors) who owned the means of production but who were distinguished by the fact that the first did not hire waged labour whereas the second had control over labour power. While the diversity of reasons for a family's location in this hierarchy defy easy generalization, women's and men's roles in production and reproduction were integral to its formation.

PRODUCTION AND REPRODUCTION IN HSIN HSING

One travels by bus from Lukang to Hsin Hsing on a cement road flanked by clusters of village houses, farmland, and more than fifty factories. These labour-intensive companies produce for domestic and foreign markets: they include large establishments that manufacture mirrors and venetian

[5] The change in the villagers' mode of production was not simply a response to rural industrialization. Despite implementation of new policies, agriculture remained an unprofitable venture; on the average, Hsin Hsing farmers realized less than NT$2,000 (US$50) from the rice they grew on one *chia* of land in 1989. Nevertheless, they continued to cultivate the land because: (1) it was a source of food (rice), (2) the mechanization and chemicalization of agriculture obviated the need for either a large or a physically strong labour force, and (3) the decreased size of family farms—in 1989 the average acreage tilled per farming household was 0.63 *chia*—required less labour. (For Taiwan as a whole, the average acreage tilled was 0.79 *chia* (*Free China Journal*, 1990: 3).)

blinds, medium-sized enterprises that produce furniture and clothing, and small factories and family workshops that either operate as subcontractors for larger firms or produce directly for the domestic market. In addition to the factories situated along the road, the area is dotted with other establishments that also produce commodities for domestic and foreign consumption. Many are located in or next to their owners' homes.

This was the case for eleven factories, two workshops, and seventeen sales and service shops owned by Hsin Hsing villagers.[6] The diversity of these enterprises can be seen in Table 2, as can their tendency to be controlled on the basis of gender. Fully four-fifths of the village enterprises were owned by men. Moreover, men tended to operate businesses which were larger in scale and more well capitalized than were those of women. Only one woman, the producer of sport-shoe tongues, owned a firm of a calibre comparable to men's.

Ten of the factory owners produced for export. Nine were subcontractors, whose production represented a sub-process in the creation of a final product for export, while one, the toy and novelty manufacturer, produced a complete product which he exported with the help of a trading partner. Seven factory owners employed wage workers, and one was the woman who produced sport-shoe tongues. All of these employers paid their male workers monthly wages and their female workers by the piece. 'Women's hours are uncertain', one male employer explained. 'Sometimes they arrive late and leave early to take care of housework.' Four of the factory owners also employed outworkers, supplying them with raw materials and paying them on a piece-rate basis at levels lower than the minimum wage.

Regardless of whether or not men employed outsiders, most were assisted in their businesses by family members, primarily by their wives. Indeed, only ten (25.6 per cent) of the men operating businesses did so without wage or non-wage workers. Five of these men (the three itinerant vegetable sellers, the juice vendor, and the farm-labour broker) worked outside the village, while four others were involved in gambling ventures. In one case, this latter undertaking was so successful that the man's wife had retired from her factory job to become a housekeeper. The only other man who worked alone owned a grocery store, and his wife was a full-time factory labourer. Women entrepreneurs, in contrast, tended to manage their businesses single-handedly. Six (75 per cent) of the eight women owning businesses operated small-scale enterprises which they managed by themselves.

Because village enterprises tended to be owned by men, it was not surprising to find that over one-quarter (28.4 per cent) of the married men in the village identified themselves as entrepreneurs (and farm marketers)

[6] Two businesses, the fried chicken and juice vending undertakings, were operated outside the village, as was the construction and masonry enterprise.

Table 2 Enterprises operated by Hsin Hsing villagers, 1989–90

Type of enterprise	Number	Type of enterprise	Number
Factories and workshops		*Sales and services*	
Toys and novelties[b,c]	1	Grocery stores[a]	4
Auto mirrors[b,c]	1	Barber shop[a]	1
Auto oil seals[b,c]	1	Beauty parlour[a]	1
Decorative pillows	1	Motorcycle repair and sales	2
Umbrella frames[b,c]	1	Tailor shop	1
Nylon athletic rope finishing[b]	1	Chinese medicine shop	1
		Pinball parlour[a]	1
Suitcase construction	1	Pesticide shop	1
Sport shoe tongues[a,b,c]	1	Betel nut vending[a]	3
Metal finishing[b,c]	2	Taxi service	1
Custom iron springs[b,c]	1	Interior design and decoration[a]	1
Wire sealing[b]	1	Fried chicken vending[a]	1
Puffed rice candy and cereal	1	Juice vending	1
Per cent of total	13 (27.7%)	Per cent of total	19 (40.4%)
Agriculture-related		*Other*	
Itinerant vegetable sales	3	Construction and masonry[c]	1
Rice mill	1	Gambling (numbers games)	4
Grape farms	2		
Pig farm	1		
Duck farm	1		
Duck farm	1		
Vegetable farm	1		
Farm-labour brokerage	1		
Per cent of total	10 (21.3%)	Per cent of total	5 (10.6%)

Total number 47; total per cent 100.0.

[a] With the exception of three grocery stores operated by men, these enterprises were operated by women.

[b] The owners of these factories produced for export. With the exception of the man producing toys and novelties, all were subcontractors.

[c] With the exception of one metal finisher, the owners of these enterprises hired waged labour.

in comparison to less than one-tenth (6.7 per cent) of the married women (see Table 3).[7] Similarly, it was not surprising to find that married women were four times more likely than men to be workers in a family business and to report that they were working without wages.

[7] The number of entrepreneurs in Table 3 and enterprises in Table 2 do not correspond because several men operated more than one enterprise. For example, one man who was involved in gambling also operated one of the grocery stores and the Chinese medicine shop. Another was a subcontractor for both the umbrella-frames and nylon athletic-rope finishing operations.

Table 3 Primary occupation of married Hsin Hsing villagers by gender, 1989–90

Primary occupation	Gender					
	Male		Female		Row totals	
	No.	%	No.	%	No.	%
Wage worker	39 (35.8%)	40.6	57 (47.5%)	59.4	96	41.9
Entrepreneur	25 (23.8%)	76.5	8 (6.7%)	23.5	34	14.8
Worker in family business	5 (4.6%)	19.2	21 (17.5%)	80.8	26	11.4
Farmer/marketer	5 (4.6%)	100.0	—	—	5	2.2
Farmer	27 (24.8%)	71.1	11 (9.2%)	28.9	38	16.6
Soldier	2 (1.8%)	100.0	—	—	2	0.9
Housekeeper	—	—	13 (10.8%)	100.0	13	5.7
Retiree	5 (4.6%)	33.3	10 (8.3%)	66.7	15	6.5
Column totals	109	47.6	120	52.4	229	100.0

Note: In addition to married villagers, the figures include 5 widowed men and 21 separated women and widows.
Source: Field survey.

Only two (10.5 per cent) of the nineteen women working in family businesses were paid for their efforts; both were newly married women who worked for their fathers-in-law; each received NT$3,000 (US$75) a month for her labour. Three (60 per cent) of the five men working in family businesses, in contrast, were paid for their efforts: one was an unmarried son who, his father reported, 'needed money for entertainment'; the other two were married men who were partners in a business with their married-out sister. Because she was no longer a member of their family—having married and severed formal ties with her father's household—the three divided their profits and paid themselves salaries.

Women who worked without wages were dissatisfied with the arrangement. For some, this dissatisfaction was rooted in the knowledge that others were paid for performing similar work and, often, worked for fewer hours. As one woman said:

I work eight hours a day and if we're busy I . . . might work until 1:00 or 2:00 in the morning. When you export, you must meet deadlines. The only difference between me and the workers is that I don't get a wage. (47-year-old woman)

Other women were dissatisfied because they felt their husbands were withholding a resource which, they believed, gave a woman a degree of control over her life and a measure of self-respect. These functions of a wage are illustrated in the following quotes.

When a woman has *sai khia* [private money], she can have her own opinion. She can speak louder. If she wants something, she can say, 'I'm using my own money.' I would rather work for others than work for my husband. If I worked for others, I would get paid and then I would have my own money. (34-year-old woman)

If you have *sai khia* you don't have to ask your husband for money. You can have self-esteem. You don't have to be raised—like a child—by your husband. (29-year-old woman)

Still other women resented the inequitable division of labour the arrangement imposed. As one 36-year-old women reported, 'Women have two jobs—work and housework. A husband only has one job. Its not fair.'

While this woman's analysis of the gender division of labour in the village was correct, few married women identified themselves as housekeepers. Indeed, only one-fifth (22.5 per cent) reported that housework was something they did.[8] This was so because most women had entered what traditionally was considered men's sphere of production—the agricultural and industrial sectors. Men and women, however, tended to occupy different economic spaces in these sectors.

For example, married women were less likely than their male counterparts to report that they were farmers; rather they identified themselves as auxiliary farm workers.[9] Women, however, were one and one-half times more likely than men to say that they worked for others. (If one included women who were workers without wages in family firms, the ratio would increase to two to one.) Moreover, the type of jobs men and women held were different (see Table 4).

Twenty-six women identified themselves as domestic-based outworkers in comparison to only one man, a widower without adult children in the village. More women than men also held jobs that were classified as unskilled. For example, men were four times as likely as women to be

[8] In addition to the 13 women who identified housekeeping as their primary activity, 14 others reported it as their second activity. To determine the occupation of villagers, we asked two questions: What do you do most of the time?; What else do you do?

[9] All of the farmers were, with one exception, over 50 years of age. The one exception was the 34-year-old man who was involved in a numbers game and whose wife identified herself as a housekeeper. Farming is the work of older villagers because young people, as one woman reported, 'don't like to work in the fields. Therefore, they must do it. Their daughters-in-law are busy with their work and so they must do it.' Farming was the only occupation which correlated with age.

Table 4 Type of off-farm employment of married Hsin Hsing villagers working for wages by gender[a]; 1989–90

Type of employment	Gender					
	Male		Female		Row totals	
	No.	%	No.	%	No.	%
Factory	19 (48.7%)	42.2	26 (45.6%)	57.8	45	46.9
Other blue collar[b]	11 (28.2%)	78.6	3 (5.3%)	21.4	14	14.6
White collar[c]	8 (20.5%)	80.0	2 (3.5%)	20.0	10	10.4
Homework	1 (2.6%)	3.7	26 (45.6%)	96.3	27	28.1
Column totals	39	40.6	57	59.4	96	100.0

[a] Includes 5 widowed men and 21 separated women and widows.
[b] Other blue collar includes construction workers, artisans, and line supervisors in factories.
[c] White collar includes practical nurses, clerical workers, and minor officials in banking and government.
Source: Field surveys.

white-collar workers and more than three times as likely to be skilled blue-collar workers. Further, although three women worked in construction, as did four men, the men were, as one woman explained, 'masters' (*shih fu*) (bricklayers and plasterers) while the women were 'helpers' (brick and sand carriers).

This difference in classification may, in part, explain why women were paid less than men. 'They make less money,' in the words of a 46-year-old factory worker, 'because they do lighter work. If more strength is needed to do the job, then the worker will get more pay.' While she did not complete her syllogism, its logical conclusion was that strong men, accordingly, made more money than weak women. This explanation, however, side-steps the context in which village men and women were embedded.

PRODUCTION AND REPRODUCTION IN POLITICAL, SOCIAL, AND ECONOMIC CONTEXTS

Because the political economy of Taiwan is inextricably linked to the world capitalist system, it depends heavily on foreign trade and is extremely vulnerable to international market fluctuations. Accordingly, the government has pursued two courses to ensure its advantage in the world economy: support of domestic-based subcontracting to stimulate manufactured exports, and maintenance of a favourable investment climate to attract foreign investors. Both policies have had profound effects on the political, social, and economic contexts in which villagers work.

Political context

To attract foreign investors to the island, the Taiwan government has maintained a favourable investment climate, including political stability and low wage rates, to ensure that capital does not seek a cheap labour force elsewhere.[10] Since its arrival on the island, the government has passed a series of laws to restrict workers' rights.[11] The Labour Union Law, for example, includes provisions that limit severely the right to organize and to bargain collectively; the Labour Dispute Law prohibits strikes. The Labour Standards Law, in contrast, guarantees workers rights such as minimum wages, pensions, benefits, pay equity, and occupational safety and health. But this law covers only a small proportion of the island's workers, primarily because it exempts work places with fewer than 30 employees. Moreover, passage of the law in 1984 did little to improve workers' conditions. The minimum wage it mandates—NT$8,000 (US$290) per month—is less than the amount needed to maintain a minimally adequate standard of living; the benefits it guarantees apply only to workers and not to dependents.[12]

Provisions for pay equity and pensions included in the Labour Standards Law are rarely enforced. The government relies on management's voluntary compliance, imposing only extremely light fines for infractions of the law. Moreover, the government grants industry considerable latitude in choosing strategies that will encourage productivity and discourage labour unrest (R. S. Gallin, 1990). In combination, government regulations and

[10] Wages have been rising in Taiwan and many local manufacturers have 'gone offshore' to decrease their wage bill. The increase in wage rates, however, has not slowed foreign investment in the island. Presumably the population's high levels of education, relative to other countries in Asia, have been more important to capital than its cost. The government was well aware of the links between education and development when it made junior high school free and 'compulsory' in 1969.

[11] Until 15 July 1987, Taiwan was under martial law on the grounds that the province was engaged in civil war. The lifting of 'emergency controls' and changes in labour laws, however, have not changed 'the basic pattern of industrial relations' (Cohen, 1988: 128). Additional information on government policy and its impact on workers can be found in Cohen (1988: 127–38), the source of the material that follows on the laws governing workers.

[12] In contrast to most developing nations, the government of Taiwan has not intervened to any real extent in the determination of wages. Although a minimum wage rate has been in effect since 1956, the minimum has always been lower than actual rates of pay.

guidelines erect powerful barriers to equitable labour relations, thereby creating an attractive environment for investment.

Other laws and policies enhance the attractiveness of this environment by affirming the ideological precepts of traditional Chinese culture. Equal rights for women are incorporated in the constitution, but family law places women at a decided disadvantage (Chiang and Ku, 1985: 12–21). Women's rights are subordinated to those of men, and a woman has no legal claim to a share in family decisions. This subordination is reinforced through the ideological messages delivered by the educational system and the media. Public discourse defines women's primary roles as wife and mother and men's as husband and worker. The law and the government's ideological apparatus, in short, create the conditions necessary for the family to shape women and men into the kind of workforce that the political economy requires.

Social context

The small- and medium-sized enterprises that constitute the mainstay of the subcontracting industry in Taiwan take one predominant form—the family firm. According to Greenhalgh (1989: 375),

> The family firm is a business firm . . . whose major decision-making positions are occupied by individuals related by blood, marriage, or adoption. . . . As a small-scale unit of production, the family generally owns all the productive resources and holds all the managerial and worker positions. As it expands, it must bring in outside capital and personnel. Both are usually obtained through personal networks of kin, friends, and others associated through common schooling, locality, and the like. Even when the firm becomes very large, its core family tends to own the largest bloc of shares and to keep the most important decision-making positions for trusted members of the inner circle.

This description focuses on the organizational characteristics of the family firm and emphasizes the way the family system is used to ensure 'a core of dedicated and trustworthy managers and workers . . . [and] a relatively smooth flow of authority within the company' (1989: 377). What Greenhalgh neglects to point out, however, is the nature of the family system in Taiwan and the way *this system* is used to organize the social division of labour and forces of production in the island's family firms.

Based on hierarchical male principles, the family system grants legitimate 'authority' to men. As a result, in the family firm, normally 'productive resources' are vested in male hands, 'decision-making' and 'managerial positions' are allocated to men, and women are relegated to the category 'worker'. The use of the family system as an organizing principle in small firms is so prevalent in Taiwan that their personnel tend to be divided into two classes: male entrepreneurs who organize labour, and women workers who provide labour with or without wages.

In 1986, for example, men were almost five times as likely as women to own firms employing fewer than 30 workers, while women were two and a half times more likely than men to be workers without wages in such firms (DGBAS, 1987: 173–4). Further, although women constituted slightly less than two-fifths (38.1 per cent) of paid workers in small firms (ibid.), they were, and continue to be, the backbone of the end-of-the-line labour force—domestic-based outworkers (see Beneria and Roldan, 1987; Boris and Daniels, 1989).

How can we account for this gendered division of labour? I submit that it is rooted in women's and men's different access to three resources crucial to the establishment and maintenance of a business firm: education, capital, and connections. First, women's education in Taiwan is limited relative to men's. While 9 years of education has been free and 'compulsory' since 1969, parents systematically discriminate against their daughters and educational investments vary by gender. In 1986, for example, the ratio of female to male graduates was 0.85 at the junior high-school level, 0.83 at the senior high-school level, and 0.74 at the college level (DGBAS, 1987: 132–3) (see Table 5).[13]

Second, most women in Taiwan lack control of the means of production. Laws have been enacted to alter traditional patterns of inheritance and provide women institutionalized access to family property. Customary law, however, continues to be applied in practice, and women seldom claim their inheritance. Rather, they accept their dowries—to which they themselves make substantial contributions—as their patrimony. Nevertheless, although married women 'own' their *sai khia* (husbands have no rights to their wives' private money), most use it either for family living or to provide venture capital for their husbands', rather than their own, enterprises.[14]

Third, women's personal networks are more circumscribed than are men's in Taiwan. Military service, education, employment, and membership in fictive kinship groups all provide men with opportunities to acquire friends who may be potential fonts of business advice and assistance. Based in their home villages, they cultivate these friendships, frequently transforming them into lucrative business relationships. Although women have some of these same opportunities while they are single, upon marriage they move to their husbands' homes, where they are soon immersed in work and children. Preoccupied with these responsibilities, they inevitably lose contact with their earlier friends, schoolmates, and workmates.

[13] The figures for Hsin Hsing were stark. Older women were two times as likely as older men to be illiterate (see Table 5). Further, although younger villagers were more educated than their older counterparts, women's educational levels continued to lag behind men's; married women were one and one-half times less likely than their husbands to have continued their education beyond primary school.

[14] Only two of the women entrepreneurs, the owner of the beauty parlour and the woman who produced sport shoe tongues, had used their *sai khia* to establish their businesses. In the latter case, the woman's father-in law bought the land on which she erected her factory.

Table 5 Education of married Hsin Hsing villagers by age and gender, 1989–90

Education Level	Age							
	20–39		40–59		60 and older		Total	
	No.	%	No.	%	No.	%	No.	%
None								
Male	—	—	6	28.6	15	71.4	21	9.2
Female	1	1.9	21	40.4	30	57.7	52	22.7
1–6 years								
Male	11	25.0	21	47.4	12	27.3	44	19.2
Female	21	45.6	19	41.3	6	14.0	46	20.1
7–9 years								
Male	20	71.4	8	28.6	—	—	28	12.2
Female	13	92.9	1	7.4	—	—	14	6.1
10–12 years								
Male	6	54.5	5	45.5	—	—	11	4.8
Female	7	100.0	—	—	—	—	7	3.1
13–16 years								
Male	5	100.0	—	—	—	—	5	2.2
Female	1	100.0	—	—	—	—	1	0.4
Total	85	37.1	81	35.4	63	27.5	229	100

Note: In addition to married villagers, the figures include 5 widowed men and 21 separated women and widows.

In sum, family firms are predominately owned by men in Taiwan because they are built on a pre-existing social form—the family system. Permeated with deeply ingrained prejudices and practices, this system allows men to exploit women's labour and to appropriate what they create. Yet, while the precepts of the family system may be a necessary condition to explain the organization of business in Taiwan, they are not a sufficient condition to explain either men's and women's assignment to different positions in the labour force or their different wage rates. Other forces are implicated. In Hsin Hsing, one of these was poverty.

Because the rural economy was highly commoditized, cash was required to maintain a family. The money which entered the household in the form of a husband's income, however, often was not adequate to pay for the wide range of expenditures incurred monthly by village families. Some women, therefore, had to work to secure a basic standard of living for the family, as a 50-year-old factory worker trenchantly described.

If I retired where will we get money? I have to bear it [low pay and poor working conditions] because I have to earn money. It would make no difference if it was a man, if the man also needed to work.

Men as well as women, then, entered the wage labour force and accepted low wages if they were poor. The forces that induced women to accept wages lower than men's, however, were more complex. The data suggest that the socialization process, along with its psychological repercussions, also were implicated in women's acquiescence—because in the village (and in most of Taiwan) this process and its repercussions varied by gender.

Village parents expected children of both sexes to work, but girls had many more responsibilities than boys. From an early age, they helped with the myriad tasks their mothers performed, while their brothers experienced much greater freedom.[15] This different treatment was intentional. In preparation for a woman's move to another family at marriage, a mother socialized her to be an able worker, obedient wife, and good mother. Male socialization, in contrast, encouraged the construction of bonds of sentiment between mothers and their sons, who would stay in the family and provide for parents in their old age.

Village men and women had internalized these norms, as their definitions of proper 'womanhood' illustrate. Domestic work was women's work and men were unwilling to accept responsibility for housework. Rather, they identified productive labour as their primary role, as one 28-year-old married man confirmed.

Men aren't willing to do housework. If you asked ten men, you wouldn't find three willing to do housework. I wouldn't do it. I don't have the patience to do it. [Why?] In the old days, the men farmed and the women took care of the house. If I stayed in the house, I would think I was inferior. Women have to do housework. Its the traditional way. Its *natural* for a man to earn money. I would not stay home.

Domestic work was also women's work because villagers believed that society was constructed in ways such that housework was a 'natural' counterpart to female existence. Nevertheless, although reproduction was an integral part of the wife and mother roles, women did not disassociate these roles from the work role. Working was central to the wife/mother role, and a good wife:

helps her husband with whatever he needs. If a husband can't do something, then the wife has to help. [Help?] Work and make money. Everyone agrees that you should make money. Women don't have to ask their husbands when they go out to work. If they have small children, they do piece work at home to earn money.

[15] Daughters also received less education than their brothers. In 1989–90, half of all school-age children were attending primary and middle school. Fully two-thirds of those continuing on to senior high school and or technical schools, however, were young men; their female counterparts were working in the industrial sector.

There's no need to discuss going to work since you work to make money. The money is for family living. (29-year-old factory worker)

Working off-farm, then, both fell within the definition of proper 'wifehood' and was necessary, legitimate, and an integral part of caring for the family.

These ingrained understandings about appropriate male/female roles were carried by women and men to the work place. In addition, they brought with them very different personality traits that gave men but not women a decided advantage in their dealings with employers. A 62-year-old factory worker illustrated this difference well. I had visited the mirror factory where she was employed and had seen her and a man working together to transfer very large and heavy mirrors from the floor to a hoist. When I visited with her later, she offered the following explanation for men's and women's different wage rates.

Men get more money because they ask for more money. If they didn't get more money, they would change their jobs. Men are stronger and therefore can move things [countering what I had seen earlier]. There's a division of labour: men do big jobs; women do small jobs. There's no way [to change the division of labour]. Its useless to ask for a raise. They won't pay attention if I ask for a raise. Also [and she smiled], it saves money to let women do certain work.

This woman explicated well how the socialization process plays itself out in adult behaviour, and how capital benefits from women's low-cost labour. In addition, she suggested yet another reason why women's wages may be lower than men's. By indicating that employers meet the demands of men and ignore those of women, she proposed a strategy—'gender logic'—that employers used to suppress women's wages relative to men.

Economic context

'Gender logic' refers to the tactics managers use to promote hierarchy in the work place (Hossfeld, 1990: 157), thereby controlling and dividing workers. Local managers were maestros of this strategy. They consistently invoked and reinforced existing ideas about women's roles and subordinate position encoded in public discourse and family practices to explain the organization of business in the area. For example, they used villagers' understandings of men's and women's capacities to assign them different responsibilities. 'Women are weaker than men and can't do big and heavy jobs', one manager offered in explanation for job segregation in the factory.[16] Another reported that 'women are better than men at jobs which require patience', an ability critical to the successful completion of work in the venetian blind factory which he managed.

[16] Workers sometimes use this logic to obtain release from a task they do not want to do. 'We say [one women reported] "You can't ask us to do this. We're too weak to do this".'

Managers, however, paid women who had this skill less than they paid men who did not. On the one hand, they paid women less than men because they believed that 'men have to raise families' and, thus, require higher wages than women. On the other, they paid women less than men because they regarded women's primary roles to be those of wife and mother, even when women were full-time workers. Accordingly, managers assumed that women worked to supplement their husbands' incomes, and they used this presumption to pay, and to justify paying, women low wages.

Managers were also able to hire women at low wages because they played upon women's own consciousness as wives and mothers. Women entered the off-farm labour force with the ideology of domesticity thoroughly internalized, as they and the village factory owner quoted earlier demonstrated. Citing the demands of women's domestic responsibilities as a rationale to pay them on the basis of the piece, he showed how women's understanding of the gender division of labour was implicated in their acceptance of disparate wage rates. While the women of Hsin Hsing invariably spoke to the unfairness of this disparity, they accepted it as their fate. They did not expect that, as women, they would be paid men's high wages.

In sum, managers 'gendered' the work place through job segregation and different wage rates. They used existing gender ideology to counterpoise women as 'weak' and tractable and men as 'strong' and demanding, thereby legitimizing the organization of work and its different rewards. Women and men workers rarely challenged these ideas: men benefited from them, and women expected to be treated differently because they are women. Different, however, meant lower pay for women and higher pay for men.

SUMMARY AND CONCLUSIONS

The focus of this paper has been the organization of business in Hsin Hsing and its environs. We saw that women and men were incorporated into the labour process in different and unequal ways. We also saw that the gender division of labour masked important aspects of the relations of production and that these relations were 'engendered' on the basis of crucial assumptions about women and men. I have argued that the articulation of the Chinese family system with state policy and managerial practices systematically have confined women's and expanded men's options.

Nevertheless, there are strands in the excerpts from interviews I have quoted which suggest that the incorporation of women into the labour process also brings with it the possibility of change. Money can be a mechanism that imposes and reproduces hierarchical structures. Money, however, can also be a mechanism that modifies gender relations within the family. While only a few women—and they are primarily young women—controlled their earnings in the village, their access to an income provided them with an extremely important base from which to alter a dimension of the conjugal relationship they judged oppressive—absolute financial dependence on husbands. Women's control of their earnings thus has the potential to erode traditional norms of behaviour and to provide them with the resources necessary to create an autonomous space.

Is it possible to generalize from the Taiwan case presented here? Unique historical and cultural factors were responsible for the Taiwan 'miracle'. Nevertheless, recent analyses of global economic restructuring and employment generation (MacEwan and Tabb, 1989; Redclift and Mingione, 1985) resonate with images of the Taiwan experience.

> There is a global trend to reduced reliance on full-time wage and salary workers earning fixed wages and fringe benefits. . . . [The quest for] flexible low-cost labour has encouraged industrial enterprises everywhere to reduce their fixed wage labour force, make payment systems more flexible and use more contract workers, temporary labour and out-sourcing through use of homeworking or subcontracting to small informal enterprises that are not covered by labour or other regulations. (Standing, 1989: 1079)

Informalization (Portes *et al.*, 1989; Connolly, 1985) and fragmentation of the labour process (Beneria, 1989), in both industrialized and industrializing nations, have spurred the rapid growth of low-wage female employment (Standing, 1989). And, as the Taiwan case shows, the incorporation of women into divisions of production that lack the capacity for the development of skills and the accumulation of capital is not accidental.

The feminization of labour reflects the desire to have a more disposable or flexible labour force with lower fixed costs. Women have very specific characteristics that make them vulnerable and that allow companies and intermediaries to enforce their demands. Women's compliance with these demands is generated through complex processes in which they learn to accept an image of themselves as less important than men. This image, reproduced within the family and imposed by state institutions and managerial practices, is an effective form of control that is difficult, but not impossible, to contest.

REFERENCES

Bello, Walden and Rosenfeld, Stephanie (1990), *Dragons in Distress: Asia's Miracle Economies in Crisis* (San Francisco: The Institute for Food and Development).

BENERIA, LOURDES (1989), 'Subcontracting and Employment Dynamics in Mexico City', in Alejandro Portes, Manuel Castells, and Lauren A. Benton (eds.), *The Informal Economy* (Baltimore: Johns Hopkins University Press), 173–88.

—— and ROLDAN, MARTHA (1987), *The Crossroads of Class and Gender* (Chicago: University of Chicago Press).

BORIS, EILEEN and DANIELS, CYNTHIA R. (1989), *Homework: Historical and Contemporary Perspectives on Paid Labor at Home* (Urbana: University of Illinois Press).

CEPD (Council for Economic Planning and Development) (1979), *Taiwan Statistical Data Book* (Taipei, Taiwan: Council for Economic Planning and Development, Executive Yuan).

CHIANG, LAN-HUNG NORA and KU, YENLIN (1985), 'Past and Current Status of Women in Taiwan', Women's Research Programme Monograph no. 1 (Taipei: Population Studies Centre, National Taiwan University).

COHEN, MARC J. (1988), *Taiwan at the Crossroads* (Washington, DC: Asia Resource Center).

CONNOLLY, PRISCILLA (1985), 'The Politics of the Informal Sector: A Critique', in Nanneke Redclift and Enzo Mingione (eds.), *Beyond Employment: Household, Gender and Subsistence* (Oxford: Blackwell), 55–91.

DGBAS (Directorate-General of Budget, Accounting and Statistics) (1987), *Yearbook of Labour Statistics, Republic of China* (Taipei, Taiwan: Executive Yuan).

—— (1988), *Yearbook of Manpower Statistics, Taiwan Area, Republic of China* (Taipei, Taiwan: Executive Yuan).

The Free China Journal (1988), 'Hard to Slow a Rich Man Down in the ROC', 11/3 (Aug.).

—— (1990), 'As Taiwan Modernizes Agriculture's Face Wrinkles', 9/3 (Aug.).

GALLIN, BERNARD (1966), *Hsin Hsing, Taiwan: A Chinese Village in Change* (Berkeley, Calif.: University of California Press).

—— and GALLIN, RITA S. (1974), 'The Integration of Village Migrants in Taiwan', in Mark Elvin and G. William Skinner (eds.), *The Chinese City Between Two Worlds* (Stanford: Stanford University Press), 331–58.

—— —— (1982*a*), 'Socioeconomic Life in Rural Taiwan: Twenty Years of Development and Change', *Modern China*, 8: 205–46.

—— —— (1982*b*), 'The Chinese Joint Family in Changing Rural Taiwan', in Sidney L. Greenblatt, Richard W. Wilson, and Amy Auerbacher Wilson (eds.), *Social Interaction in Chinese Society* (New York: Praeger), 142–58.

GALLIN, RITA S. (1984), 'The Entry of Chinese Women into the Rural Labor Force: A Case Study from Taiwan', *Signs*, 9: 383–98.

—— (1986), 'Mothers-in-law and Daughters-in-law: Intergenerational Relations in the Chinese Family in Taiwan', *Journal of Cross-Cultural Gerontology*, 1: 31–49.

—— (1990), 'Women and the Export Industry in Taiwan: The Muting of Class Consciousness', in K. Ward (ed.), *Women Workers and Global Restructuring* (Ithaca: ILR Press).

—— (1991), 'Dowry and Family in Changing Rural Taiwan', *Journal of Women and Gender Studies*, 2: 67–86.

GOLD, THOMAS (1986), *State and Society in the Taiwan Miracle* (New York: M. E. Sharpe).

GREENHALGH, SUSAN (1980), 'Microsocial Processes in the Distribution of Income', paper presented at the Taiwan Political Economy Workshop, East Asia Institute, Columbia University, New York, NY, Dec. 18–20.

—— (1989), 'Social Causes and Consequences of Taiwan's Postwar Economic Development', in Kuang-chou Li *et al.* (eds.), *Anthropological Studies of the Taiwan Area: Accomplishments and Prospects* (Taipei: Department of Anthropology, National Taiwan University), 351–90.

Ho, Samuel P. S. (1976), 'The Rural Non-farm Sector in Taiwan', *Studies in Employment and Rural Development*, 32 (Washington: International Bank for Reconstruction and Development).

—— (1978), *Economic Development of Taiwan, 1860–1970* (New Haven: Yale University Press).

Hossfeld, Karen J. (1990), 'Their Logic Against Them: Contradictions in Sex, Race, and Class in Silicon Valley', in K. Ward (ed.), *Women Workers and Global Restructuring* (Ithaca: ILR Press).

Hsiao, Wey (1987), 'Changes in Class Structure and Rewards Distribution in Postwar Taiwan', in R. V. Robinson (ed.), *Research in Social Stratification and Mobility*, vol. 6 (Greenwich, Conn.: JAI Press), 257–78.

Huang, Shu-min (1981), *Agricultural Degradation: Changing Community Systems in Rural Taiwan* (Washington, DC: University Press of America, Inc.).

Lin, Ching-yuan (1973), *Industrialization in Taiwan, 1946–1970* (New York: Praeger).

Lu, Min-jen (1987), 'Promotion of Constitutional Democracy Government's Goal', *The Free China Journal*, 5/2 (Oct.).

MacEwan, Arthur and Tabb, William K. (eds.) (1989), *Instability and Change in the World Economy* (New York: Monthly Review Press).

Pang, Chien-Kuo (1987), *The State and Economic Transformation: The Taiwan Case* (Unpublished Ph.D. Dissertation, Department of Sociology, Brown University).

Portes, Alejandro, Castells, Manuel, and Benton, Lauren (eds.) (1989), *The Informal Economy: Studies in Advanced and Less Developed Countries* (Baltimore: The Johns Hopkins University Press).

Redclift, Nanneke and Mingione, Enzo (eds.) (1985), *Beyond Employment: Household, Gender and Subsistence* (Oxford: Blackwell).

Sease, Douglas (1987), 'US Firms Fuel Taiwan's Trade Surplus', *Asian Wall Street Journal*, 8/1 (June).

Standing, Guy (1989), 'Global Feminization through Flexible Labor', *World Development*, 17/7: 1077–95.

Stites, Richard (1982), 'Small-Scale Industry in Yingge, Taiwan', *Modern China*, 8: 147–79.

Wu, Rong-I (1990), 'The Distinctive Features of Taiwan's Development', in Peter L. Berger and Hsin-Huang Michael Hsiao (eds.), *In Search of an East Asian Development Model* (New Brunswick: Transaction Publishers), 179–96.

Yu, Terry Y. H. (1977), 'The Accelerated Rural Development Programme in Taiwan', in *Industry of Free China* (Taipei, Taiwan: Council of Economic Planning and Development, Executive Yuan), 2–16.

Development Strategies, State Policies, and the Status of Women: A Comparative Assessment of Iran, Turkey, and Tunisia

Valentine M. Moghadam

Compared with other regions of the developing world, the Middle East and north Africa is only just beginning to receive the attention it deserves from a gender-and-development perspective. In the past, the preponderance of a culturalist approach and the presumption that cultural and religious variables explain more than do economic and political ones have precluded an application of standard theoretical frameworks towards an explanation of women's roles and status in Arab-Islamic countries. Yet the Middle East and north Africa is an area rich in theoretical potential. In particular, it is a region where contending propositions pertaining to the relationship between development and patriarchy may fruitfully be explored (see Moghadam, 1993: esp. ch. 4). Has the development process broken down the traditional patriarchal system of gender relations, with its features of gender segregation, family and male control over female mobility, and early marriage? In what ways have women been integrated in the development process? How do specific economic and social policies of the state affect women's social positions and economic status? This chapter will address these questions through a comparative assessment of development strategies, state policies, and their differential impact on women in three countries of the Middle East and north Africa. The emphasis will be on women's labour-force participation and access to employment.

Iran, Turkey, and Tunisia share a common Islamic culture but otherwise differ ethnically and linguistically, as well as in the official status and application of Islamic laws. Turkey and Tunisia are secular republics with comprehensive civil codes, while Iran has been an Islamic Republic since 1979 and has built a legal system that combines the Code Napoleon with Islamic canon law (the Sharia). Although in all three countries a majority of the population are self-defined Muslims, only in Iran does the state define itself and its legal system as Islamic. In the 1960s and 1970s all three countries shared a Western orientation in their governments' foreign policies, but after 1979 the Islamic Republic of Iran assumed a staunchly pro-Third World and anti-imperialist stance in its external relations, which only began to wane in the early 1990s. Turkey is a member of NATO and the OECD and is keen to join the European Community as a full member, but recently it has also become oriented toward the newly independent

Turkic republics of the former Soviet Union. Tunisians have a three-pronged orientation towards Europe, the Maghreb, and Africa (Tunisia is a member of the United Nations Economic Commission for Africa); furthermore, Tunis has been host to Arab organizations such as the secretariat of the PLO.

In terms of economic policy, Iran, Tunisia, and Turkey shared what some analysts have called a nationalist development strategy, that is, one based on import substitution industrialization (ISI), the promotion and protection of domestic industries, and a preponderant role for the state in economic development (see Seddon, 1993; Richards and Waterbury, 1990). But there have been important differences among the three, particularly since 1980. Iran's economy has always been, and remains, primarily oil-based, in that most of its exports and revenues are derived from oil income. After the Iranian Revolution of 1979, ISI policy was strengthened, and it was not until the late 1980s that the government adopted a more outward-oriented strategy for growth and development, as outlined in the Islamic Republic's First Five-Year Plan, 1990–5. Tunisia has had a relatively open economy since the 1970s, but it was not until the mid-1980s that extensive economic liberalization was implemented under IMF guidance. In 1987, the textile sector accounted for 29 per cent of total export earnings, and by 1990 it had increased to 35 per cent, with a concomitant increase in non-agricultural employment, especially for women. Turkey's economic policy was also largely statist until the economic crises of the 1970s. In 1980, the Turkish authorities embarked upon an extended stabilization and reform programme, began to privatize state economic enterprises, and adopted a policy of export-led industrialization (ELI). Turkey is the most industrialized of the three countries, and its industrial products are important export earners; in 1990 textiles accounted for 37 per cent of total exports. Table 1 illustrates differences in the three countries' export strategies. Note Iran's almost exclusive reliance on the oil sector for export earnings.

In world-system terms, all three countries are part of the semi-periphery, which means that they combine labour-intensive, low-wage, low-technology production (characteristic of peripheral countries) and capital-intensive, high-wage, high-technology production (characteristic of core countries). However, unlike the newly industrialized economies, they enjoy neither the extent of foreign direct investment nor the level of manufactured exports of the NIEs. This would suggest that a relatively large part of their rural and urban labouring classes are self-employed or engaged in economic activities in the informal sector, rather than being full proletarians. Semi-periphery location further suggests that a sizeable part of the female population in Iran, Turkey, and Tunisia is under-endowed or under-utilized. This is indeed the case.

Of the three countries, Turkey enjoys the most foreign direct investment but Tunisia has the largest proportion of women in the manufacturing

Table 1 Structure of merchandise exports

	Percentage share of merchandise exports									
	Fuels, minerals, and metals		Other primary commodities		Machinery and transport equipment		Other manufactures		Textiles and clothing	
	1965	1990	1965	1990	1965	1990	1965	1990	1965	1990
Tunisia	31	19	51	12	0	8	19	61	2	35
Turkey	9	7	89	25	0	7	2	61	1	37
Iran, Islamic Rep.	88	98	8	1	0	0	4	1	4	0

Source: *World Development Report 1992*, table 16, pp. 248–9.

workforce, concentrated in the textiles and garments industries. Despite the fact that Turkey is more industrialized, urbanized, and literate, it also has a large peasant-based agricultural sector and pronounced urban–rural and male–female disparities. Iran in 1986 reported the largest self-employed workforce. In all three countries, women constitute a relatively small proportion of the salaried labour force, suggesting that large numbers of women are unpaid family workers or engage in 'disguised employment' in the urban informal sector. The socio-economic similarities and differences in the three countries are highlighted in Table 2, which provides descriptive data on basic population indicators, and Table 3, which focuses on indicators pertaining to women.

This chapter begins with a general discussion of development, state, and gender in the Middle East and North Africa (MENA) region, followed by a survey of women's economic and social positions in each of the three countries under consideration. The elaboration of national development strategies and state policies is not meant to dismiss the importance of cultural understandings in the shaping of women's roles. Rather, it follows from the theoretical premise that gender inequality is a universal phenomenon which varies historically, cross-culturally, and cross-nationally according to the system of production and distribution, the class and social structure, the orientation of political élites, and women's own mobilization.

DEVELOPMENT, STATE, AND WOMEN IN THE MIDDLE EAST: AN OVERVIEW

Through most of the 1960s and into the 1970s, and notwithstanding the social-democratic and populist features of Turkish and Tunisian politics, the three states under consideration could be characterized broadly in terms of 'state capitalism', in which the role of the state was to protect and nurture private capital accumulation while also acquiring property itself. Richards and Waterbury have suggested that this 'handmaiden' role was in operation in Turkey since 1950, in Iran between 1963 and 1979, and in Tunisia since 1969 (Richards and Waterbury, 1990: 214–18). For these states, the preferred strategy for economic and social development was essentially that of nationalist development based on ISI. There was also a public commitment to social development and social welfare, even if the benefits of increasing public expenditure and the growth of the state apparatus were by no means equally distributed (Seddon, 1993: 92).

In all three countries, and elsewhere in the region, the nationalist development strategy, combined with the oil boom in the Middle East, led to educational and employment opportunities favourable to women in the Middle East. A massive investment programme by the oil-producing countries affected the structure of the labour force not only within the relevant

Table 2 Basic population indicators, *c.* late 1980s

	Population (millions) 1990	Population growth rate (annual %) 1960–88	Urban population as a % of total population 1990	Adult literacy rate 1990	% labour force in manufacturing (1984–6)	% labour force in agriculture	% labour force in salaried employment	% labour force self-employed
Iran	55.8	3.5	57.0	54.0	13.2	29.0	41.4	42.7
Turkey	56.1	2.4	61.0	80.7	10.1	56.2	33.3	22.3
Tunisia	8.1	2.2	54.0	65.3	15.6	23.4	60.8	22.4

Sources: *World Development Report*, 1992; *Human Development Report*, 1993; Moghadam, 1993, table 2.4; ILO, *Yearbook of Labour Statistics, Retrospective Edition on Population Censuses 1945–1989*, table 2A.

Table 3 Indicators on the status of women

	Tunisia	Turkey	Iran
Life expectancy at birth (years) 1990	67.5	67.0	66.6
Maternal mortality rate (per 100,000 live births) 1988	200	200	250
Average age at first marriage (years) 1980–5	24.3	20.6	19.7
Women currently married (%) aged 25+	58	70	72
Total fertility rate	3.6	3.5	6.2
Married women of child-bearing age using contraception (%)	50	63	n.a.
Literacy rate (age 15–24 only) 1980–9	63	75	42
Enrolment ratio: Primary (net) 1988–90	91	—	90
Enrolment ratio: Secondary (gross) 1988–90	40	42	45
Enrolment ratio: Tertiary (gross) 1988–90	7	10	4
Tertiary science and engineering enrolment (% female) 1987–8	24	26	10
Women in labour force (% of total) 1990	21.0	32.7	9.0
Female share of salaried labour force	16.8	16.7	9.4
Administrative and managerial staff (% female) 1980–9	—	3	—
Parliament (% of seats occupied by women) 1991	4	1	2
State signatory to UN Women's Convention	Yes	Yes	No

Sources: *Human development Report*, 1993, table 8, p. 150; *The World's Women 1970–1990: Trends and Statistics*, various tables; Moghadam, 1993, table 2.4, p. 46.

countries, but throughout the region, as a result of labour migration, creating what Owen (1985) has called a regional oil economy. The structure of the labour force changed from a predominantly agricultural population to a workforce oriented to manufacturing and professional services. With the growth of non-agricultural employment the urban areas began to see an expansion of the female labour force, as women occupied paid positions in factories and offices, as workers, administrators, and professionals. Increases in female labour-force participation continued during the 1980s, especially in the non-oil economies such as Tunisia, Morocco, Syria, and Egypt (ILO/INSTRAW, 1985; see also Moghadam, 1993: ch. 2). In most countries, government agencies and state-owned enterprises absorbed much of the female labour force. In Tunisia and Morocco, much of the increase in the female labour force was in the industrial sector.

Throughout the world both the supply of and demand for female labour have been growing. Table 4 provides a list of some relevant supply and demand factors. Three interrelated forces condition and structure the position of women in the labour market: (*i*) supply factors that influence

Table 4 Factors in female labour supply and demand

Supply factors (includes changes in individual attributes)	Demand factors (availability of opportunities)
• demographic factors, including size of female population of working age; educated women; fewer children; divorced, single women; shortage of male labour (via warfare or migration); higher life expectancy • changing aspirations • improvements in home technology easing burden of domestic labour • inflation and housing costs • economic need or poverty • household survival strategy	• evolution of new types of resource-generating work roles • economic expansion or wartime economy • industrial development • deskilling (of industrial work) • technological change (e.g. computer revolution) • export manufacturing • 'woman-friendly' social policies

whether the women are available for wage labour outside the household; (*ii*) the specific structure of the economy, which conditions the demand for workers in the labour market; (*iii*) the implicit and explicit policies regarding the inclusion/exclusion of women in the labour market as reflected in hiring practices, segregation of jobs by sex, earnings/wage structure, and so on. These three forces imply class, gender, technical, and institutional determinants, all of which operate in dynamic way. Coventional labour-market analyses, including the few studies that exist on the Middle Eastern or Arab female labour force, tend to stress supply-side factors as the most significant determinants of female labour-force participation. Hijab (1988), for example, cites need and ability, as well as opportunity, as the three relevant factors in female labour-force participation. Pissrides (1992) emphasizes the growth in the supply of highly educated women, whose preferred employment destination is usually public service. Although I have also emphasized the importance of the supply of educated women in the expansion of the female labour force in the Middle East (Moghadam, 1993), I agree with those who argue that the demand for female labour conditions the supply; supply factors are more responsive to demand than vice versa (see e.g. Chafetz, 1990: 123). For example, women choose to have fewer children when they are employed outside the home; women's entry into the workforce is facilitated by woman-friendly social policies.

In tandem with the dramatic entry of women into the public sphere, feminist concerns and women's movements also emerged, and by 1980 most MENA countries had women's organizations dealing with issues of literacy, education, employment, the law, and so on. These social changes have had a positive effect in reducing traditional sex segregation and female seclusion, in introducing changes in the structure of the Middle Eastern family, and in producing a generation of middle-class women not dependent on family or marriage for survival and status. Increased educational attainment and a trend towards labour-force attachment of some women has created a stratum of highly visible and increasingly vocal women in the public sphere (see Moghadam, 1993: chs. 2 and 4).

I have said above that the nationalist development strategy, including state-sponsored education and state-directed investment, created educational and employment opportunities for women. Yet this is true only up to a point, for the MENA region still has the smallest labour force of any region in the world, and an especially small female share of the salaried labour force. Why is this the case? Many analysts have attributed this to conservative Muslim culture and the patriarchal gender attitudes of state managers. While this is certainly a factor, the emphasis on 'Islamic patriarchy' has tended to preclude a consideration of other relevant factors—such as development strategy, type and extent of industrialization, overall size of the employee class, and government social policies. In some MENA countries, conservative state managers have done little to promote female employment or even mass literacy, as gender equality and female empowerment rank low in their priorities. In other countries, state policies have facilitated female integration into public life. For example, with respect to the three countries under consideration, Tunisia and Turkey are state-parties to the UN Convention on the Elimination of All Forms of Discrimination Against Women, but the Islamic Republic of Iran is not. Another reason has to do with the nature of ISI and especially of oil-based economies. WID specialists have noted that during the period of ISI in Latin America and south-east Asia, the bulk of the workforce, particularly in capital-intensive sectors such as steel, shipbuilding, and heavy industry, was male (see Pearson, 1992: 223). The significant rise in female employment occurred with the shift from ISI to ELI—a pattern of industrialization that allowed Third World economies to compete in Western consumer-goods markets, and which was largely based on the availability of productive labour at cheap cost. This shift has only recently been made in the Middle East and north Africa—1980 in the case of Turkey and 1990 in the case of Iran.

The size of the female labour force should also be seen in the context of limited industrialization in the region. As argued by Mabro (1988) and Richards and Waterbury (1990), industrialization in the Middle East, in contrast to Latin America and south-east Asia, has been fairly limited in the region. Countries that have relied on oil wealth are less likely to have diversified economies and be export-oriented. Moreover, because of the conflict with Israel, many Middle Eastern countries have invested heavily in armaments, imported from Western countries and the Soviet bloc. This has diverted resources from investments in dynamic industrialization. These are some of the reasons why, unlike Latin America, ISI in the Middle East did not evolve into manufacturing for export. Because of oil revenues, governments chose to extend the import substitution process, moving into capital-intensive sectors involving sophisticated technology (Mabro, 1988: 692). As mentioned above, capital-intensive industries and technologies tend to favour male labour.

Notwithstanding the limitations imposed upon female employment derived from the region's political economy and conservative state managers, there *was* a secular trend toward altering and improving women's work and women's lives. But this trend seems to have encountered an impasse in the 1980s, in the context of a global economic crisis and a regional crisis of political legitimacy.

During the 1970s and 1980s, global recessions and international restructuring affected the states of the Middle East and north Africa. At the same time, government policies of adjustment and austerity adopted to respond to the deepening economic crisis themselves generated new contradictions and conflicts (for a full discussion, see Seddon, 1993). As Seddon explains, in countries where revenues from oil exports did not exist, or were insufficient to provide a cushion against the growing tensions in economy and society, 'governments were faced during the second half of the 1970s with the stark choice between attempting to maintain the nationalist development strategy by further external borrowing, or implementing austerity measures as part of a programme aimed at liberalizing and internationalizing the economy'. The second alternative risked domestic unrest in response to rising prices and declining real incomes and to the evident withdrawal of the state from its previous commitment to safeguard the citizen's basic economic and social welfare, but was increasingly being 'pressed on governments by the international financial institutions as a precondition for further lending or for debt rescheduling' (Seddon, 1993: 94). Government measures to promote economic reform, often adopted under the auspices of the IMF and World Bank, began to be implemented during the second half of the 1970s, although they were often less stringent than reforms in Latin America. At the same time, the global oil market became very unstable, leading to fluctuating and declining prices, and the near-collapse of prices in 1986 (from US$28 per barrel to US$7 per barrel). During the 1980s the most active Arab borrowers from the World Bank—Algeria, Egypt, Jordan, Morocco, Syria, Tunisia, Turkey—had to impose austerities on their populations as a result of World Bank and IMF structural adjustment policy packages, and several experienced 'IMF riots' (Niblock, 1993; Seddon, 1993; Önis, 1991).

The Iraqi invasion of Kuwait in August 1990 raised the price of oil again, but the damage had already been done. Another problem is that while MENA countries are committed to liberalizing trade, opening their domestic markets, and withdrawing support and protection for their indigenous industries, they face trade restrictions imposed by the advanced industrialized countries on imports of petrochemicals, iron, ready-to-wear clothing, and various agricultural products (Marzouq, 1994: 48–50).

Tough economic reforms, along with poverty, unemployment, and debt servicing—as well as political repression—have served to delegitimize 'Western-style' systems and revive questions of cultural identity, including renewed calls for greater control over female mobility. It is in this context of economic failures and political delegitimation that Islamist movements are presenting themselves as alternatives. The combination of Islamist movements and economic failures has distinct implications for women's legal status and employment opportunities (see Moghadam, 1993: ch. 5). Various governments have sought to placate the Islamist opposition by conceding to them control over family law, some educational institutions, and some mass media. Examples are Jordan, Egypt, and Algeria in the 1980s. Other governments, notably Tunisia and Turkey, have generally resisted Islamist political and cultural demands.

WOMEN, STATE, AND DEVELOPMENT IN TURKEY

In Turkey, from 1923 onwards, political independence was succeeded by far-reaching economic and social change, constituting what has often been referred to as 'a revolution from above' (Trimberger, 1977). In April 1931, Mustapha Kemal 'Ataturk', former military leader and nationalist and now head of state, issued a manifesto containing six principles that were to provide the basis for the 1937 Constitution of the Republic: the Turkish state would be republican, nationalist, populist, secular, étatist, and revolutionary. He declared: 'We desire to have the government take an active interest, especially in the economic field, and to operate as far as possible in manners that lend themselves to the safeguarding of vital and general interests, or, in short, that the government ensure the welfare of the nation and the prosperity of the state' (Hershlag, cit. Seddon, 1993: 91). While supporting private enterprise the ruling Republican People's Party prescribed state intervention in agriculture, industry, public works, commerce, health, and education; and Turkey became one of the first developing countries to conduct an experiment in planned development, with its first five-year plan in 1934. Turkey was also one of the first Muslim countries in which the emancipation of women was an explicit priority. Ataturk took a personal interest in the question of women and declared that Turkey could not modernize itself if its female population remained subordinated (see Moghadam, 1993: ch. 3).

Since 1980, Turkey has been transformed from a state-dominated to an export-led economy. Prior to that, the strategy of import substitution industrialization, which began in 1961, was based on a leading role for state economic enterprises (SEEs). But even in the early 1970s the private sector accounted for nearly one-half of industrial output and its rate of capital investment had become almost equal to public-sector investment (Seddon, 1989: 868). An economic and political crisis in the late 1970s led to a military coup and a shift in economic policy. A structural adjustment programme was introduced in 1980, and in May 1987 the government announced plans for privatization of the SEEs.

Government emphasis on export-led growth has increased the manufacturing labour force. And yet, according to the 1985 census, the manufacturing sector employs only 386,000 women (a female share of about 17 per cent) out of a total manufacturing workforce of 2.3 million. In 1991, of the 6.5 million women counted as economically active, only 441,562 were in manufacturing, and even so, 30 per cent of them were not regular salaried employees.[1] It may very well be that large numbers of women in small, unregistered workshops, or those who work at home, are not being enumerated. Based on findings from survey research in Istanbul, Cinar argues that a large part of unreported or 'disguised' female employment takes place at home, where the woman, besides domestic duties, produces marketable goods by taking in piece work at home (Cinar, 1991). Indeed, annual manufacturing survey data covers only large establishments with 10 or more workers (Cagatay and Berik, 1990: 123). In the formal sector, a woman on maternity leave is given the right to return to the job she held before childbirth. But for the majority of Turkish women, wage work is elusive.

The textile and clothing industry is Turkey's largest, accounting for about one-third of manufacturing employment and contributing about 20 per cent of manufacturing output, and it is here that the female labour force is found. In both public and private manufacturing, apparel, textiles, tobacco, and pottery remain the most 'female-intensive' industries, with little change over time (Cagatay and Berik, 1990: 126). Tourism, too, is one of Turkey's fastest growing industries. Although nearly two million people are involved in trade, restaurants, and hotels, the female share of that workforce is only about 5 per cent (86,000). It remains to be seen whether privatization of state-owned tourism-related industries will increase the demand for female employees, and whether more women will open their own businesses, such as restaurants and *pensions*.

Thus far in Turkey, women have been excluded from formal-sector manufacturing, but this may change as privatization and ELI proceed. Citing the results of the 1985–6 Manpower Training and Requirements

[1] Sources of statistics are ILO *Yearbook of Labour Statistics 1993*, table 2A, and previous years; 'Turkey Women in Statistics: Population', State Ministry, Directorate General on the Status and Problems of Women (Ankara, n.d., but statistics pertain to Oct. 1993); DISK Institute of Research, *Turkish Working Class in 1990s: Social and Economic Indicators* (Istanbul, 1992).

Survey, Cagatay and Berik explain that: 'while in private manufacturing 38.43 per cent of the demand for labour was for women, in public manufacturing this figure was only 8.18 per cent' (1990: 124). Cinar writes that in the formal industrial sector in general, the demand for unskilled females is predominantly for young, single females, whose work horizon is limited, who do not require severance pay, and who are willing to take on entry-level positions. The demand for unskilled females in subcontracting arrangements in informal labour markets is similarly based on a cheap-labour calculation: payment per satisfactory piece produced is less than hiring workers at minimum wage and paying the worker's social security (Cinar, 1991: 9).

Will this demand for cheap female labour eventually confirm the Standing thesis of feminization of labour? Cagatay and Berik assert that 'one could talk of a defeminization in public manufacturing and a feminization of employment in the private sector' with the switch to export-led industrialization. Still, they conclude with the well-known observation, discussed also by Standing, that women have higher representation when an industry is more export-oriented, more labour-intensive, and has a high ratio of non-skilled to skilled production workers. And of course, 'we cannot rule out the possibility that gender composition of overall manufacturing employment may have changed in favour of women under the export-led regime through the use of flexible labour supplied by women outside the large manufacturing establishments' (Cagatay and Berik, 1990: 125, 128, 130). This accords well with Cinar's findings that employers 'preferred farming work out to homes because this gave them a lower wage bill, lower overhead costs and flexible production to cope with fluctuating market demand. The types of labour-intensive output they sold, such as hand-knit sweaters for the export market, could only compete in international markets when they were produced by home work' (Cinar, 1991: 22–3).

The surprisingly small percentage of women in the formal-sector workforce certainly does suggest that a large percentage of the female economically active population is engaged elsewhere: agriculture and the urban informal sector. Yet another explanatory factor must lie in the persistence of patriarchal gender relations in Turkey, for in both the informal and formal sectors there exists 'a very important supply restriction in the unskilled female labour market. . . . Permission of the male household head is a necessary condition before any attempt can be made to search for jobs in the market.' The survey conducted by Cinar and her colleagues found that 'the presence of children at home is definitely of lesser importance, when compared to lack of permission'. Further investigation reveals other factors at work in limiting the supply of female labour: mainly, sexual harassment prevalent in jobs open to them in the formal sector, especially as shop clerks and factory workers (Cinar, 1991: 17, 22).

Although Turkey's recent high growth rates have been industry-led, the economy still relies heavily on agriculture. In 1988 the agricultural sector contributed nearly 17 per cent of GNP, while industry contributed over 32 per cent of GDP. Most of the farms are small and the average size of a family farm is only 8 hectares. The principal agricultural exports are cotton, tobacco, wheat, fruit, and nuts (Seddon, 1989: 865). As seen in Table 2, more than half the labour force works on the land. This is also where the vast majority of Turkey's economically active female population is located. About 80 per cent are found in agriculture, where their economic status is that of unpaid family worker. Cagatay and Berik (1990: 123) point out that relative to the distribution of women across economic sectors, a lower proportion of men are in agriculture (43.2 per cent in 1985) and a higher proportion of men are in manufacturing (14.2 per cent in 1985).

In the agricultural sector unpaid female family workers are under the legal authority of the male household head. The latter dominates access to capital (land and the instruments of production) and organizes the production process. 'The authority of the household head is reinforced by the prominence he is given by external agencies such as State marketing boards and credit institutions, who for official purposes deal with him alone' (Morvaridi, 1993: 6). According to the 1985 Turkish census, 96.8 per cent of household heads—'a person who is responsible for the earnings and expenditures of the household and who actually manages the household'—are male. In rural areas only 5.1 per cent of household are said to be female-maintained (ibid. 8). Many studies have revealed the extensive tasks that rural women undertake and their disproportionate share in the overall workload (Kandiyoti, 1984; Berik, 1987).

As part of state plans to transform Turkey from a closed to an open economy, many family farms in the 1980s were encouraged to commercialize their farming, assisted by subsidies and credit facilities provided by government agencies. But structural adjustment subsequently led to reductions in subsidies to farmers, and the price of agricultural inputs has fluctuated even above the price of the main crops (Morvaridi, 1992: 577–8). Government programmes make little or no mention of the impact on women's work and welfare. Morvaridi (1993) discusses the intra-household consequences of macro-economic transformation and concludes that by encouraging small farms to adapt to a more intensive cropping system, state policy-makers—and male household heads—have increased the workload and labour time of peasant women. Cuts in subsidies to farmers intensifies women's workloads even further.

Morvaridi notes that although women from all households—landless, smallholder, largeholder, and sharecropping—perform the same farm work, the intensity of their labour differs. Women from the richer, larger households are the least active in the production process, working mainly in peak periods when female paid labourers are scarce. In contrast, women from small and middle-sized households have to work from early morning to evening. 'The employment of wage labour is seen as a last resort, particularly by the smaller farmers, who will push their female household labour to work long hours' (Morvaridi, 1992: 574).

Morvaridi writes that 'men are willing to encourage women to work in the fields as long as it assists household income, but do not consider them suited for responsibility or agricultural management'. This is in contrast to changes in gender relations that occur when women engage in formal-sector employment. One study of Turkish women factory workers showed that 'married women factory workers in Bursa have gained a considerable degree of power over decision-making in their families as a result of their employment. Over half the married women who were interviewed reported that they and their husbands took decisions together and often consulted each other' (Ecevit, 1991: 77). One can only concur with Morvaridi that 'the low status of women as unpaid family labour is perpetuated by social relations within the household, intensified under cash crop production' (Morvaridi, 1992: 585).

State economic policy seems to collude with patriarchal gender relations, especially in the countryside, to impede women's advancement and gender equality. One area where the Turkish state has been deficient is in the provision of literacy and education, especially for girls. Between 1975 and 1985 the illiterate female population declined from 49 per cent to 32 per cent, but the reduction of male illiteracy was much steeper, from 24 per cent to 13 per cent. In 1985, women constituted fully 70 per cent of the illiterate population. These illiteracy figures may help to explain the large number of Turkish women in agriculture. Is there a link between the persistence of rural female illiteracy and the development strategy of export-led agriculture?

Kandiyoti's research in the 1970s comparing the status of Turkish women in nomadic tribes, peasant villages, rural towns, and cities reveals that the influence of the patrilineal extended household—where the father dominates younger men and all women, and there is a hierarchy by age among the women—is pervasive in all sectors, but is less so in the towns and cities because of neolocal residence and the diminished importance of elders. It is true that compared to peasant and nomadic women, urban women play a sharply reduced role in the productive process, even though they are more likely to head their own households. But peasant and nomadic women do not receive recognition for their own labour, not even for their offspring, as these belong to the patrilineal extended family (Kandiyoti, 1984). In many parts of rural Turkey, women have been traditionally called the 'enemy of the spoon', referring to the fact that they will share the food on the table without contributing economically to the household (Berik, 1985). Berik's study of carpet weavers in rural Central Anatolia reveals that the labour power of the female weavers, and the wages that accrue to them, are controlled by male kin.

The development process is supposed to break down such patriarchal gender relations. But development strategies and state policies that rely on peasant farming and on unpaid family labour reinforce rather than diminish patriarchy.

WOMEN, DEVELOPMENT, AND THE STATE IN TUNISIA

Tunisia has had a social-democratic form of government since independence, and liberal social policies. As in Turkey in the 1930s, President Habib Bourguiba's enlightened views on women led in the 1950s to a secular civil code in which women's rights are greatly strengthened in the areas of marriage, divorce, and child custody. Government policy since independence has prioritized women's emancipation and integration into the economy, and the constitution and civil code have reflected and reinforced that position. Staunchly secular, President Bourguiba made the participation of women in public life a major policy goal. The constitution ensured all citizens the same rights and obligations. Polygamy and male repudiation were outlawed, allowing women the right to petition for divorce and custody of their children. Such legal reform has made Tunisia the most liberal country in the Arab world.

Though economic policies tended towards the socialistic in the 1960s, government policy shifted in the 1970s towards encouragement of foreign investment for export-oriented projects. Tunisia's development record in the 1970s was fairly impressive, with GDP, measured in current prices, increasing from US$4.3 million ($773 per head) in 1975 to 8.7 million ($1,356 per head) in 1980. In the early 1980s, however, the economy entered a period of turbulence following a decline in the price of oil, a series of droughts that affected the agricultural sector, and a balance-of-payments deficit. In 1987 the IMF encouraged Tunisia to adopt a radical economic programme based on an increase in exports of agricultural and manufactured goods, a rise in revenues from tourism, and severe reductions in the government's investment budget (Harris, 1989: 832).

Tunisia's industrial sector ranges from the traditional artisan activities, such as textiles and leather, to 'downstream' industries based on the country's phosphate reserves. More than one-half of Tunisia's industry is located in Tunis. In the past, manufacturing tended to concentrate on processing raw materials, especially foodstuffs, and was aimed at meeting local demand. In an attempt to attract foreign investment and to promote exports, the government ratified a new industrial investment code in 1987, and exports became the driving force behind GDP growth. Thus, in 1988 manufactures constituted 47 per cent of total exports and were 56 per cent higher than in 1986 (World Bank, 1991: 539).

Compared with other states in the Middle East and north Africa, Tunisia has had fairly liberal policies pertaining to the labour movement. Following a series of strikes during 1976, a social contract was agreed between the government, union leaders, and industrialists, to run for the duration of the 1977–81 Plan, involving wage rises in all sectors, including agriculture, and a general 33 per cent rise in the minimum wages. In 1985–6, however, and in the context of economic reforms, the authorities took measures to restrict the power of the trade union movement, and it was announced that, in future, wage rises would be linked to improvements in productivity (Harris, 1989: 836).

Unemployment and under-employment remain a problem in Tunisia especially for women and young men. Women's unemployment could worsen if the government further stalled recruitment in the public sector (especially public administration), which employs many women. The Eighth Plan, 1992–6 aims to create 320,000 new jobs and cut unemployment from 15 per cent 13 per cent of the workforce. It also continues its vigorous industrial export drive, encouragement of private investment, and assistance to small and medium-sized enterprises (ILR, 1993: 8).

In the 1980s the distribution of the female labour force was more balanced in Tunisia than in many other Middle Eastern countries: 26 per cent in agriculture, 48 per cent in manufacturing, 21 per cent in services. The female share of government employment was 24.5 per cent in 1987; of the country's magistrates, 13.5 per cent were women; of medical personnel, 20.6 per cent; of paramedical personnel, 48 per cent; of the country's teachers, 31.5 per cent. Women's participation in formal politics matched the trends in employment. In 1981 there were 7 female deputies in Parliament; in 1983 there were 50,000 female members of the ruling social-democratic Neo-Destour Party and 57,000 members of the National Union of Tunisian Women; and in 1985 some 492 women were voted municipal councillors around the country (UNFT, 1987). Like Turkey but unlike most other Muslim countries, Tunisia not only has women lawyers but women judges as well.

Employed women enjoy fairly generous entitlements. In 1960 a law gave the minority of women who are members of the social insurance service (mainly those employed in industry, handicrafts, and services, with the exception of housework) the right to pregnancy leave—6 weeks before delivery and 6 weeks afterward. During this period 50 per cent of monthly wages were to be paid. More recently the length of maternity leave has been set at 30 days, as part of government policy to lower the birth rate. Public employees are also entitled to child-care leaves. In an effort to stabilize population growth, the government has reduced maternity leave and family allowances. Since 1 January 1989 the social security fund (CNSS) limits family allowances to three children, and not four as in the past. Law No. 81-6 of 12 February 1981, introduced a social security scheme for wage-earning agricultural workers and those engaged in co-operative undertakings. The following year this scheme was extended to cover small farmers and the self-employed. Since so few women are considered wage-earning agricultural workers, however (15,600 according to the 1989 labour-force sample survey, compared with 166,600 men), small farmers (9,700 compared with 180,800 men), or self-employed (83,500 compared with 412,700 men), the extension of social security to women may be very limited indeed.[2]

The textiles and garments sector is one of Tunisia's leading non-oil industries, accounting for 26 per cent of total export earnings in 1990. While exports of petroleum and derivatives earned 418.3 million dinars in 1987, exports of clothing and accessories earned 354.7 million dinars (Harris, 1989: 842). In US dollar terms, in 1990 crude oil exports earned Tunisia some 527.3 million dollars, while exports of clothing amounted to 922.1 million dollars (UNCTAD, 1992: table 4.3). There are about 1,100 companies registered in the sector, of which 450 are wholly or partly export-oriented. Another major sector of manufacturing industry is food, which usually accounts for about one-quarter of industrial production. In order of importance, the other leading sectors are: construction materials, mechanical and electro-mechanical, chemicals, and paper and wood. Tunisia also manufactures glass, furniture, batteries, paint and varnish, leather goods and shoes, and rubber goods (Harris, 1989: 835).

Manufacturing is by far the most female-intensive sector of the Tunisian economy and labour force. In 1985, of the 318,000 workers in this sector, fully 55 per cent were female, though this declined to 43.2 in 1989. This decline suggests either that women have been losing jobs with restructuring, or that new entrants are not accepting industrial jobs at current pay levels. Women are also heavily represented (43 per cent) in the sector of finance, insurance, real estate, and business services (ILO, 1993: table 2A). On the other hand, women's role in agriculture is not as prominent as it is in Turkey: a 20 per cent female share, or 21 per cent of the female labour force. Perhaps for this reason, agricultural extension in Tunisia has tended to bypass women. An Agricultural Research and Extension Project for Tunisia was implemented by the World Bank in 1990, with a provision for a pilot extension scheme in which two female extension agents would focus on the needs of female farmers, male farmers' spouses and daughters, and female farm workers (World Bank, 1990: 20).

Until 1976 tourism was Tunisia's principal source of foreign currency, after which it was overtaken by petroleum, whose earnings reached a peak in 1980. Although current Tunisian economic policy is to promote tourism as a foreign exchange earner (Proirier and Wright, 1993), it remains a heavily male-dominated sector. As in Turkey, women in Tunisia comprise

[2] Data from ILO *Yearbook of Labour Statistics 1993*, table 2A.

a very small percentage (6 per cent) of workers in trade, restaurants, and hotels. This may or may not be a function of undercounting.

Various aspects of Tunisia's performance have earned it kudos from outside observers. A UNDP publication stresses the advances made in 'human development': a healthy and educated population providing an efficient workforce.

> Tunisia has made more progress in this respect than many other (generally wealthier) Arab states. . . . Adult literacy is now 65 per cent. Tunisia's women have made significant progress. The women's literacy rate in the average Arab state is only 63 per cent of the male rate while in Tunisia the figure is 76 per cent—and rising. . . . Tunisia's export record in the 1980s has been impressive: not so much in volume as in composition. The balance has shifted from raw materials to manufactured goods—a change of direction that profited greatly from earlier investments in human development. (UNDP, 1992: 73)

A World Bank publication, too, stresses Tunisia's 'long-term emphasis on developing human resources and maintaining macroeconomic stability' (World Bank, 1991: 537). The Tunisian government intends to pursue the path of export promotion and is keen to create new labour-intensive outlets to combat the growing problem of unemployment. But will this development strategy lead to employment generation for women and opportunities for advancement?

WOMEN, STATE, AND DEVELOPMENT IN IRAN

The late Shah's programme for the modernization of Iran included land reform, commercialization of agriculture, and rapid industrialization. The Islamic government chose another strategy. The results for women have been mixed.

In the 1920s, Colonel Reza Khan of the Persian Cossacks took over the Iranian state. His original plan had been to proclaim a republic, establish himself as president, and build a modern state along the lines of Ataturk's project in Turkey. Under pressure from the Shi'ite clergy, however, he proclaimed himself Reza Shah Pahlavi in 1928. The 1930s were a period of modern state building and some economic development. In the period between Reza Shah's forced abdication (in 1941) and the *coup d'état* (in 1953) that restored his son, Mohammad Reza Pahlavi, to monarchical power, successive nationalist governments ruled, the first national plan was launched in 1944, and the Anglo-Iranian Oil Company was nationalized. After 1953, Mohammad Reza Pahlavi consolidated the state's control over the direction of economic development. Strong state intervention in key areas of the economy was combined with a professed economic liberalism and commitment to the promotion of capitalist development. The objective, as in Turkey, was a revolution from above; indeed, in Iran it was called the White Revolution. During this period, the emancipation of women was not considered a priority issue as it had been in Turkey or was in Tunisia, but women from the élite families assumed important and visible roles in charitable foundations and similar social functions, while increased educational attainment by women of the middle class allowed them to occupy positions within the government bureaucracy and the media. At the same time, women from working-class and lower middle-class families found job opportunities in the expanding modern factory sector.

In the first stage of the Iranian land reform programme (1961–3), the majority of peasants received very small, fragmented plots of land and lacked appropriate technology and financial means to afford machinery. Their reliance on intensive family labour consequently increased. Partial mechanization of labour often occurred in the share of the work traditionally assigned to male peasants, increasing the female share of the work rather than reducing it. For instance, better ploughed and irrigated land needs more frequent weeding, the task traditionally assigned to women in the peasant division of labour (Tohidi, 1994: 116). Some studies on women's specific role in the post-revolutionary Iranian rural economy document the same pattern of a greater contribution by women's labour to both agricultural production and the income generated from the produce. 'Hossein Nayer's study of a village in Khorasan, north-east Iran, showed that women's share in production comprised 68 per cent of the entire agricultural and pastoral work versus 32 per cent of men's. The monetary output of women's work was over twice that of men's' (Tohidi, 1994: 116).

The inefficiency of small plots of land and the increasing need for cash income forced large numbers of men to migrate to the cities in search of a job in construction or industry, leaving most of the agricultural work and the household responsibilities to women. In the case of large-scale commercialization and mechanization of land allocated for the growing of cash crops for exports, the tradition was to employ men as seasonal farm labourers, depriving women of paid agricultural work. The growth of the market for Iranian carpets led to a great increase in the number of carpet weavers, 90 per cent of whom were rural female, and 40 per cent of them under the age of fifteen. But the majority of female rural carpet weavers are unpaid family workers, as payments are usually under the control of male kin.

Where agricultural inefficiency of small plots forced peasants to abandon village life and migrate to the cities, they usually worked as seasonal labourers, peddlers, or small traders and resided in slums. Unsurprisingly, they became fervent supporters of Ayatollah Ruhollah Khomeini in the anti-Shah movement. Most of the female migrants to cities like Tehran 'found themselves relegated to the limited role of a housewife with no recognized productive role, with increased economic dependence on men, and with restricted social conditions' (Tohidi, 1994: 118).

Meanwhile, industrialization increased income and the stock of capital, raising the demand for labour of all kinds, including female workers. 'The gradual upward trend in the participation of women in market activities, together with improved facilities for female education, generated a greater incentive for families to invest in the education of their female children' (Mirani, 1983: 72). At the same time, the government introduced certain measures to enhance the position of women in society, and in the family. These measures increased the range of opportunities open to middle-class women, but they had little effect on the status of the majority of women in Iran. The first of these measures was the Family Protection Law, enacted in 1967 and amended in 1973. This law was designed to reduce the dominance of men in divorce, child custody, and polygamy. Men who wished to divorce their wives now had to obtain court permission; until this time, men had been permitted to divorce their wives at will and with no judicial proceeding. The new law allowed women wider grounds for divorce, and made it possible for women to attain custody of their children. Furthermore, men who sought additional wives were required to obtain the consent of their existing wives or of the courts.

Manpower and census data of the 1970s reveal that the majority of active women were employed in manufacturing, while agriculture and services accounted for 46.2 per cent of female employment. The high rate of female employment in manufacturing is due to the inclusion of cottage industries in this sector; in 1971 more than half of the economically active women in rural areas worked in small textile workshops (Mirani, 1983: 78). The majority of these were carpet-weaving workshops; the rest comprised such crafts as spinning, knitting, and rug weaving. Although more and more women filled white-collar positions in the growing public and private sectors, the majority of women in the workforce were unpaid workers in small workshops or on family farms. Accordingly, in 1976, only 55 per cent of urban women, and 30 per cent of rural women, were literate.

The Shah's rule came to an end with the Iranian Revolution. The revolutionary government that followed the Shah's downfall revised nearly all Iran's economic and social strategies. The new leaders announced that priority would be given to low growth rates, a concentration on small-scale projects in industry, emphasis on traditional agriculture, and stringent control of petroleum exports. In 1979 the Islamic Republic of Iran nationalized all banks, insurance companies, and large industries, and took over foreign trade. Throughout the 1980s, the Islamic Republic of Iran lacked a coherent development strategy, relying instead on *ad hoc* economic measures, generous subsidies to consumers and small-scale producers, and a fairly extensive social welfare programme. The war with Iraq and loss of forecast petroleum revenues led to a deteriorating economic situation. Political conflicts and confusion over the management of the economy aggravated these problems and resulted in contradictions in policy and economic mismanagement. In the late 1980s, a deteriorating economic situation forced the government to reassess its populist economic and social policies and institute economic liberalization under President Rafsanjani.

Ten years after the Revolution, the Iranian economy was still oil-based, with exports of crude petroleum or oil products accounting for most of the country's export revenues. No clear policy had been formulated for the industrial sector. Steel, petrochemicals, and copper remain the country's three basic industries, and these are capital-intensive, male-intensive industries. Traditional exports include cotton, carpets, pistachio nuts, fresh and dried fruits, hides, and caviar. 'New' industrial products include knitwear, textiles, clothes, metal ores, pharmaceuticals, chemicals, soaps, detergents, and shoes. Of the modern manufacturing plants that were established under the Shah's regime, those which remained in production (estimated at only 20 per cent of the total by value of output) encountered serious difficulties. At the end of 1988 it was reported that most factories were operating at less than 50 per cent of their capacity, owing to shortages of raw materials from abroad (Fischer, 1989: 440). As a result of the stated policies of the revolutionary government favouring small-scale, traditional or bazaar-related enterprises, this type of private-sector economic activity grew during the 1980s. Self-employment also grew between the 1976 and 1986 population censuses, reflecting growth of the traditional, small-scale private sector. At the same time, women's industrial employment declined dramatically between the two censuses.

Women continued to work in the large industrial establishments, but their participation in modern-sector industrial activity was almost insignificant. Data in the 1976 Census indicate that women earning wages and salaries in public- and private-sector manufacturing and mining/quarrying made up about 20 per cent of the total. The 40,000 female wage and salary earners in urban factory employment reported 1983 represented 6 per cent of total employment here. Clearly there had been a sharp decline in female factory employment. By the mid-1980s there was a further decline in industrial work by women, although the Statistical Yearbook 1364 [1985–6] showed a decrease in industrial employment for both men and women, indicating the weakness of this sector of the economy. In 1986, the participation of women in the formal industrial sector was still limited, indeed, almost marginal. Most of the measured female labour force was to be found in services. The largest number of enumerated women were in private and public services; agriculture ranked second, with about 263,000 women, and industry third, with a mere 216,000 women employees. Clearly vast numbers of women were not being counted in the agricultural sector; the figure for men in agriculture was nearly 3 million.

According to the census data, some 990,000 women were classified as employed, which is 6 per cent of the female population aged 10 and over, and 9 per cent of the total employed population. Female civil service employees—that is, employees of ministries and state agencies—numbered about 420,000 (as against over a million men), comprising 28 per cent of the total number of government employees, and 41 per cent of the total employed female population.[3] The largest numbers of female government employees were in the Ministries of Education and Health. The same is true of male state employees, and this concentration obtained in pre-revolutionary Iran as well. Women's share of total public-sector employment, however, was only 14 per cent, because of men's far higher participation in the steel works, oil fields, and other state-owned industrial and service-sector enterprises, where women were barely represented. In terms of distribution over occupational groups, women were found in: (*a*) professional, technical, and related workers (35 per cent of employed women), (*b*) agricultural, animal husbandry, forestry, fishing, and hunting workers (26.6 per cent of employed women), and (*c*) production and transport workers (23.4 per cent of employed women). Women were still under-represented in managerial, administrative, clerical, and sales work.

Among the most significant characteristics of the employed female population during the 1980s that may be discerned from the 1986 census are: (*a*) the female share of the total labour force was very small, at under 10 per cent; (*b*) the majority of women employees were teachers and health workers; (*c*) apart from carpet-weaving and traditional craftwork, women's role in modern industrial production was limited—only 14 per cent of the manufacturing labour force, and mostly unwaged; and (*d*) large numbers of 'employed' women in the private sector were not receiving a wage for their work. Indeed, the proportion of women in the private sector receiving a wage or salary was only 19 per cent—which does not bode well for future economic policies emphasizing growth of the private sector.

For the small percentage of women in the formal sector, government employment provides many advantages. Nearly all women who are waged and salaried are in government employment or the public sector, where they enjoy insurance, pensions, and other benefits. Labour legislation enacted in 1990 provides women with 90 days of maternity leave, at least half of which must be taken after childbirth. There is also a job-back guarantee with no loss of seniority and a half-hour break every three hours for breast-feeding, with a crèche or child-care centre provided at the

[3] In 1991 the female share of civil service employment was 30 per cent, according to a personal communication from M. Changizi, senior statistican, Central Statistical Office, Tehran, May 1994. See also Statistical Yearbook 1370 [1991], p. 79, which shows that out of 1.6 million civil servants, there were 511,818 females.

workplace.[4] But in the private sector, most women are likely to be 'self-employed' or unpaid family workers in agriculture or rug-weaving workshops, where they have no benefits at all.

The Islamic Republic's first Five-Year Plan, which went into effect on 21 March 1990, was intended to decrease the size of the public sector and encourage the growth of the private sector.[5] The government adopted a policy of privatizing a notable proportion of state-owned enterprises, which are to be gradually returned to either their previous owners or to the public (Karshenas and Mazarei, 1991). As the government has 'recognized the necessity of reintegration in the world economy' (ibid.), the Plan also called for a shift from the earlier reliance on the agricultural sector to the expansion of manufacturing for export. Since 1990 the government has extended invitations to foreign investors, along with generous taxation and operations incentives. Joint ventures are encouraged in numerous areas, particularly in the fields of petroleum and petrochemicals. An impediment to realization of the plan is the scarcity of managerial and skilled resources; thus the government is actively encouraging expatriate entrepreneurs, technicians, and engineers to return to the country.

These changes in economic policy reflect a modification of ideological considerations and have implications for women and the gender system. Some restrictive barriers to women's achievement have been removed, such as limiting female enrolment in a number of fields of study.[6] The state has also altered its population policy from pro-natalist to pro-family-planning. In June 1989 the government formally lifted the ban on contraceptives at state hospitals and clinics, in the interests of population stabilization. The goal is to reduce the population growth rate to 2.3 per cent. In July 1991 the government approved a proposal by the Ministry of Health whereby family entitlements end with the third child. Family planning clinics throughout the country distribute contraceptives and family planning advice, frequently free of charge.[7]

Another shift in gender policy lies in the area of women and law. Immediately after the revolution, women in the legal profession, notably all judges, were purged from their positions due to 'lack of commitment to the principles of the Islamic Republic', suspended, or appointed to clerical positions in the Ministry of Justice. Furthermore, women were discouraged from studying law, although they defied this official opprobrium and

[4] During a research trip to Iran in May 1994, I visited child-care centres at Moghaddam Textile Factory in Qazvin and the Daroupakhsh Pharmaceutical Firm in Karadj. Both enterprises had large numbers of female employees.

[5] For a detailed discussion of the Five-Year Plan, see Ghasimi (1992).

[6] For an elaboration of these quotas and the Islamic state's educational policy, see Moghadam (1993: ch. 6).

[7] This aggressive policy has won the admiration of the UNFPA's Director, Dr Nafis Sadik, although she notes that the target is women, not men. See interview with Dr Sadik in Kayhan International, 23 Sept. 1993, p. 5.

continued to enter law school, albeit in small numbers. Toward the end of the 1980s, the field of law became more open to women. Unless they were designated anti-revolutionary, even those women who had been purged in the early 1980s were asked to come back to work, though not necessarily to their previous positions. Former judges could now work in as inspectors in the equivalent of a district attorney's office.[8] Thus, after a decade of discouraging women from entering the legal profession, the Iranian state reversed itself and deemed it advantageous to draw on women with legal experience and education, including women who had acquired their expertise in the period before the Revolution. According to one report, in April 1993 there were 2,661 registered lawyers in Iran, including 185 women (Lawyers Committee, 1993: 44).

A final example of a shift in gender policy pertains to women and agriculture. In addition to a serious undercount of rural economically active women, there were hardly any female agricultural extension agents in post-revolutionary Iran. This derived in part from discriminatory educational and training policies that barred women from studying such fields as veterinary science, animal science, and agrarian affairs. But by late 1991, the Minister of Agriculture, Issa Kalantari, recognized the fallacy of denying women a role in the agricultural sector, and announced that agricultural training centres for women would be established 'to better utilize the female work force in the sector'. The Ministry of Agriculture had apparently counted more women in agriculture than the Statistical Centre of Iran had, for the minister said that 40 per cent of the farm work in Iran is performed by women. According to a newspaper account, he 'regretted that there still exist restrictions preventing women from enrolling in certain academic fields, and that there were certain difficulties in training female farmers'. But he said that arrangements would be made to train women alongside men in agricultural fields. Interestingly, he also called on other government agencies to 'further employ women and trust them with more key posts' (cit. Moghadam, 1993: 202).

These significant changes should be understood in the context of the government's new attention to economic issues, in a shift from its earlier focus on cultural, political, and moral issues. Apparently, there are voices throughout the bureaucracy with a new message: economic growth and national development cannot take place in a situation of unbridled population growth and the under-utilization of the female resource base.

Female parliamentarians, the advisor to the President on women's issues, and other prominent women, particularly those working in various state agencies, seem to be taking advantage of the emerging new environment and the new economic imperatives to push for legislative changes in favour of women's rights.

[8] Personal communication from Professor Shahin Gerami.

CONCLUSIONS

This chapter has shown that the development process broadly speaking has had contradictory effects on women's positions in MENA countries. The effects of the development process are variable by social class, with the main beneficiaries being middle-class women (and men) in the professions. As the main agent of development, the state plays a central role in the determination of women's legal and economic status through its social and economic policies. In this regard, the Tunisian state compares favourably to the Turkish and especially the Iranian state.

Throughout the Third World, manufacturing for export, increased trade, and foreign investment have tended to encourage female employment. In Tunisia, Morocco, and Turkey, export-oriented garment industries contributed to the growth of the female labour force during the 1980s. But much of this employment is home-based or in small unregistered workshops where wages are low and social security non-existent. Although public education has expanded the ranks of employment-seeking women, educational attainment remains low and the demand for female labour is limited, especially in the modern industrial sector. Tunisia has the largest female manufacturing workforce, but it is located mainly in the informal sector. The vast majority of Turkey's economically active women are still in the agricultural sector, and recent policies geared to the intensification of crop production seem to have added to rural women's workloads. And in Iran, an oil-based economy, state policies, conservative attitudes, and continuing high female illiteracy have constrained both the supply of and demand for female labour. Economic liberalization may raise the demand for (relatively cheap) female labour, but not necessarily in ways conducive to women's welfare.

Given the favourable employment conditions for women workers in government employment and the public sector, the implications of privatization and cuts in public spending, such as are recommended by structural adjustment packages, are grim. The severity of adverse effects depends on the extent and sectoral location of cuts put into effect. A weakening of government commitment to labour standards and women-friendly social benefits and a shrinking public sector may reverse the favourable conditions for women workers in public enterprises. Recent studies show that the rate of unemployment is higher among women than among men (see Al-Qudsi *et al.*, 1993), especially in Jordan, Egypt, Algeria, and Iran, where educated women experience higher rates of unemployment than do educated men, and where working-class men are still favoured for industrial jobs over working-class women. This is clearly a result of gender discrimination, whereby at a time of slack in the labour market employers discriminate by preferring to hire males who are seen as the breadwinners of the household. Women may also be seen as more expensive labour because of labour legislation requiring child-care and maternity leave, especially in the public sector and in large private enterprises. This situation will need to be monitored so that women are not the principal losers in the restructuring of the economies and labour markets in the Middle East and north Africa.

REFERENCES

AL-QUDSI, SULAYMAN, ASSAAD, RAGUI, and SHABAN, RADWAN (1993), 'Labor Markets in the Arab Countries: A Survey', prepared for the Initiative to Encourage Economic Research in the Middle East and North Africa, First Annual Conference on Development Economics, Cairo (4–6 June).

BERIK, GÜNSELI (1985), 'From "Enemy of the Spoon" to "Factory": Women's Labor in the Carpet-Weaving Industry in Rural Turkey', paper presented at the Middle East Studies Association annual meetings, New Orleans (Nov.).

—— (1987), *Women Carpet Weavers in Rural Turkey: Patterns of Employment, Earnings and Status* (Geneva: ILO, Women, Work and Development Series, no. 15).

CAGATAY, NILUFER and BERIK, GÜNSELI (1990), 'Transition to Export-Led Growth in Turkey: Is There a Feminization of Employment?' *Review of Radical Political Economics*, 22/1: 115–34.

CHAFETZ, JANET SALTZMAN (1990), *Gender Equity: An Integrated Theory of Stability and Change* (Newbury Park, Calif.: Sage Publications).

CINAR, E. MINE (1991), *Labor Opportunities for Adult Females and Home-Working Women in Istanbul, Turkey* (the G. E. von Grunebaum Center for Near Eastern Studies, University of California, LA, Working Paper no. 2).

ECEVIT, YILDIZ (1991), 'The Ideological Construction of Turkish Women Factory Workers', in Nanneke Redclift and M. Thea Sinclair (eds.), *Working Women: International Perspectives on Labour and Gender Ideology* (London and New York: Routledge), 56–78.

FISCHER, W. B. (1989), 'Iran', in *The Middle East and North Africa 1990* (London: Europa Publishers (36th edn.), 416–59.

GHASIMI, MOHAMMAD REZA (1992), 'The Iranian Economy After the Revolution: An Economic Appraisal of the Five-Year Plan', *International Journal of Middle East Studies*, 24/4 (Nov.): 599–614.

HARRIS, D. R. (1989), 'Tunisia', in *The Middle East and North Africa 1990* (London: Europa Publishers (36th edn.), 820–49.

HIJAB, NADIA (1988), *Womenpower: The Arab Debate on Women and Work* (Cambridge: Cambridge University Press).

ILO (International Labour Organization) (1990), *World Labour Report 1989* (Geneva: ILO).

International Labour Review (1993/1), News Briefs (Geneva: ILO).

ILO/INSTRAW (1985), *Women in Economic Activity: A Global Statistical Survey*

1950–2000 (Geneva: International Labour Office, and Santo Domingo: UN Training and Research Institute for the Advancement of Women).

Islamic Republic of Iran (1985–6), *Statistical Yearbook 1364* (Tehran: Plan and Budget Organization, Statistical Centre of Iran).

—— (1990), *Statistical Yearbook 1367* (Mar. 1988–Mar. 1989) (Tehran: Plan and Budget Organization, Statistical Centre of Iran).

KANDIYOTI, DENIZ (1984), 'Rural Transformation in Turkey and its Implications for Women's Status', in UNESCO, *Women on the Move: Contemporary Changes in Family and Society* (Paris: UNESCO), 17–30.

KARSHENAS, MASSOUD and MAZAREI, JR., ADNAN (1991), 'Medium-Term Prospects of the Iranian Economy', in *Iran and the Arabian Peninsula: Economic Structure and Analysis* (London: The Economist Intelligence Unit), 19–24.

Lawyers Committee for Human Rights (1993), *The Justice System of the Islamic Republic of Iran* (New York: Lawyers Committee for Human Rights).

MABRO, ROBERT (1988), 'Industrialization', in Michael Adams (ed.), *The Middle East* (New York: Facts-on-File), 687–96.

MARKS, JON (1993), 'Tunisia', in Tim Niblock and Emma Murphy (eds.), *Economic and Political Liberalization in the Middle East* (London: The Academic Press), 166–76.

MARZOUQ, NABIL (1994), 'The Arab States: Workers Facing an Uncertain Future', *The World of Work* (75th Anniversary Issue of the ILO), no. 8.

MIRANI, KAVEH (1983), 'Social and Economic Change in the Role of Women, 1956–1978', in Guity Nashat (ed.), *Women and Revolution in Iran* (Boulder, Colo.: Westview Press), 69–86.

MOGHADAM, VALENTINE M. (1993), *Modernizing Women: Gender and Social Change in the Middle East* (Boulder, Colo.: Lynne Rienner Publishers).

MORVARIDI, BEHROOZ (1992), 'Gender Relations in Agriculture: Women in Turkey', *Economic Development and Cultural Change*, 40/3: 567–86.

—— (1993), 'Impact of Macro Economic Policies on Gender Relations: The Study of Farming Households', paper presented at the Conference on 'Engendering Wealth and Well Being', University of California, San Diego (Feb. 17–20).

NIBLOCK, TIM (1993), 'International and Domestic Factors in the Economic Liberalization Process in Arab Countries', in Tim Niblock and Emma Murphy (eds.), *Economic and Political Liberalization in the Middle East* (London: The Academic Press), 55–87.

ÖNIS, ZIYA (1991), 'The Evaluation of Privatization in Turkey: The Institutional Context of Public-Enterprise Reform', *International Journal of Middle East Studies*, 23/2 (May): 163–76.

OWEN, ROGER (1985), 'The Arab Oil Economy: Present Structure and Future Prospects', in Samih Farsoun (ed.), *Arab Society: Continuity and Change* (London: Croom Helm), 16–33.

PEARSON, RUTH (1992), 'Gender Issues in Industrialisation', in Tom Hewitt, Hazel Johnson, and David Wield (eds.), *Industrialisation and Development* (Oxford: Oxford University Press), 222–47.

PISSARIDES, CHRISTOPHER A. (1992), 'Labor Markets in the Middle East and North Africa', mimeo.

PROIRIER, ROBERT A. and WRIGHT, STEPHEN (1993), 'The Political Economy of Tourism in Tunisia', *The Journal of Modern African Studies*, 31/1 (1993): 149–62.

RICHARDS, ALAN and WATERBURY, JOHN (1990), *A Political Economy of the Middle East* (Boulder, Colo.: Westview Press).

SEDDON, DAVID (1989), 'Economy' [of Turkey], in *The Middle East and North Africa 1990* (London: Europa Publishers (36th edn.)), 865–75.

—— (1993), 'Austerity Protests in Response to Economic Liberalization in the Middle East', in Tim Niblock and Emma Murphy (eds.), *Economic and Political Liberalization in the Middle East* (London: The Academic Press), 88–113.

TOHIDI, NAYEREH (1994), 'Modernity, Islamization, and The Woman Question in Iran', in V. M. Moghadam (ed.), *Gender and National Identity: Women and Politics in Muslim Societies* (London: Zed Books).

TRIMBERGER, ELLEN KAY (1977), *Revolutions from Above* (New Brunswick, NJ: Transaction Books).

UNCTAD (1992), *Handbook of International Trade and Statistics 1992* (Geneva: UNCTAD).

UNDP (1992), *Human Development Report 1992* (New York: Oxford University Press).

UNFT [Union Nationale des Femmes Tunisiennes] (1987), *La Femme au Travail en Chiffres* (Tunis: UNFT).

World Bank (1990), 'Republic of Tunisia: Agricultural Research and Extension Project', Staff Appraisal Report (May 8).

—— (1991), *Trends in Developing Economies 1990* (Washington, DC: The World Bank).

Cumulative Disadvantage? Women Industrial Workers in Malaysia and the Philippines

Guy Standing

INTRODUCTION

In every society some pattern of labour-force stratification occurs, usually with certain demographic, ethnic or religious groups being relegated to low-paid, low-status jobs with little prospect for upward socio-economic mobility. Stratification is contrary to principles of equity and has adverse efficiency consequences. Reducing its prevalence is therefore always desirable. The problem is that to formulate the most appropriate policies to combat it we need to know not only the nature of the segregation and stratification, as well as their socio-cultural roots, but the causes of the stratification within the labour market. In particular, it is important to know where the main points of discrimination occur—recruitment, job allocation, training, initial wages, other forms of payment and benefit entitlement, employment security, and so on.

Women workers are usually presumed to face discriminatory barriers at all stages. Whether or not that is true is an empirical matter, and in any case it is most likely that in different countries, sectors and types of organization the relative importance of specific factors will vary. This chapter compares the situation of women workers in industrial employment in Malaysia and the Philippines, and is based on two almost identical surveys carried out in 1988 and 1990 respectively. These were the Malaysian Labour Flexibility Survey (MLFS) and the Philippines Labour Flexibility Survey (PLFS), the former covering 3,100 manufacturing establishments, the latter 1,311 industrial firms, most of which were in manufacturing.[1]

Both countries had experienced some form of structural adjustment programme in the 1980s, in which there had been concerted attempts to shift towards more export-oriented industrialization. Both had also experienced periods of recession just prior to the respective surveys, and their governments were intent on making the labour market more flexible through reform of regulations and/or tightening controls over union activities. Both have been strongly influenced by multinational investment.

There are also major differences that should be borne in mind. In *Malaysia*, economic growth over the decade of the 1980s was spectacularly

[1] One difference was that the PLFS covered construction and trade as well as manufacturing, though most establishments were in manufacturing.

better. However, there was a sharp recession in 1985–6, which prompted some rethinking about development strategy and, *inter alia*, stimulated public debates about the role of women workers. The earlier phases of export-led industrialization had been based on the massive employment of young women, hired from the countryside as cheap labour for two or three years and then replaced from similar sources. For well over a decade, the image of women industrial workers had been the familiar one of 'nimble fingers', 'docility', and 'beaverish productivity', with an eventual return to the kampong as mothers and wives.[2] Although that was always an over-simplification, the basic question in 1985–6 and thereafter was whether or not women would be treated as a labour reserve, to be laid off in large numbers. Coupled with that was the question whether women would be displaced in the anticipated labour-displacing phases of industrialization, eased out of manual jobs as automation and capital–labour substitution occurred.[3] Against that, one could hypothesize that after more than a decade of export-led industrialization women might have been absorbed into the industrial workforce to the point where many barriers to their continued employment would have crumbled. In effect, young women workers in the urban-industrial areas could have severed links with their rural kampongs and have learned the basic 'skill' of being industrial wage labour. So, the overriding question is: Were women a labour reserve or was feminization of employment continuing?

A related hypothesis is that the increasing globalization of production, coupled with the pursuit of flexible forms of labour to retain or increase competitiveness, as well as changing job structures in industrial enterprises, favour the feminization of employment, such that women would gain an increasing share of many levels of job.[4]

In the *Philippines*, the Labour Code gives a measure of protection to women. Under article 130, nightwork is prohibited for women, regardless of age, and under Section 1 of the Republic Act 6725 (approved on 12 May 1989), amending article 135 of the Labour Code, 'it shall be unlawful for any employer to discriminate against any woman employee with respect

[2] Numerous studies have highlighted the characteristics of factory girls in the mid-1970s and early 1980s. See, for instance, F. Daud, *Minah Karan: The Truth about Malaysian Factory Girls* (Kuala Lumpur: Berita Publishing Co., 1985); B. K. Tan, 'Women Workers in the Electronics Industry', in A. Y. Hing and R. Talikb (eds.), *Women and Employment in Malaysia* (Kuala Lumpur: Department of Anthropology and Sociology, University of Malaysia, 1986), 17–32; K. Salih, M. L. Young, L. H. Chan, K. W. Loh, and C. K. Chan, *Young Workers and Urban Services: A Case Study of Penang, Malaysia: Final Report* (Penang: University Sains Malaysia, Participatory Urban Services Project, 1985).

[3] This is a popular international hypothesis. See e.g. S. Joekes. 'Gender and Macroeconomic Policy', *AWID Occasional Paper*, no. 4 (Washington, DC, Sept. 1989), 19. See also D. Elson and R. Pearson (eds.), *Women's Employment and Multinationals in Europe* (Basingstoke: Macmillan, 1989).

[4] G. Standing, 'Global Feminization through Flexible Labour', *World Development*, 17/7 (July 1989), 1077–95.

to terms and conditions of employment solely on account of her sex'. The Code defines as an act of discrimination: (*a*) payment of a lower wage, salary or other form of remuneration and fringe benefit, for work of equal value; (*b*) favouring a male employee over a female with respect to promotion, training opportunities, study and scholarship grants solely on account of their sexes.

That is the context of this chapter, which considers ways by which discriminatory barriers intensify sexual stratification and segregation, and how the relative significance of such barriers differs in the two countries—Malaysia, with a rapidly industrializing economy in which ethnic pluralism has been the outstanding characteristic, and the Philippines, where industrial growth had been much less successful and where a structural adjustment programme had been pursued far more assiduously for most of the past decade.

SEGREGATION BY ENTRY: DISCRIMINATORY RECRUITMENT

It is often assumed that the main form of discrimination by which labour segregation occurs is through the hiring process. This covers two aspects—whether a particular type of person is recruited at all, and whether certain groups are recruited for particular types of job. A problem of interpretation arises in that women might not apply for jobs, either in general or for specific types of job, whether because they believe they will not obtain any employment or the type of job in question, *or* because they do not wish to do so. We will not deal with those issues, important though they are in the discrimination story.

In a sense, we control for that factor in that in the two surveys on which this analysis is based the section on the pattern of hiring began by asking separate sets of questions on employers' recruitment *preferences* for clerical and production workers separately, and for the Philippines for professional and technical workers as well.

Discrimination is a notoriously complex process. An employer may discriminate against a woman or an ethnic or minority group or an age category directly, simply by stating a preference, or may discriminate indirectly, by stipulating characteristics desired in workers that a certain group does not possess or possesses to a lesser extent, even though those characteristics were not essential for the employment or set of tasks in question.[5] This indirect form of discrimination is hard to identify but should be borne in mind in interpreting employer attitudes and revealed behaviour.

[5] This brings to mind an experience in the pilot of the Malaysian Labour Flexibility Survey. A Chinese owner of a furniture-making factory, when asked if he had a preference for any ethnic group when he was recruiting, said, 'No, no, I have no preference. I don't discriminate—just as long as they speak Mandarin.'

All employers—personnel directors in large-scale firms, owner-managers in small-scale—were asked identical questions about worker characteristics that might have been used as screening devices in the recruitment process, and before turning to the perceived significance of gender we will note the pattern displayed on other factors. The first aspect examined in the two countries was the age at which firms preferred to hire workers. Employers might state that they prefer to recruit at a certain age because that is perceived as indicative of expected short-run or long-run productivity; others might have such a preference from a mix of cultural norms and prejudice. It is best to be eclectic on such matters, since a combination of motives is probably usually involved.

In response to the age-preference question, as far as clerical workers were concerned, some firms gave specific ages, others gave an age range. In both Malaysia and the Philippines most employers preferred to recruit clerical workers aged between 21 and 25, but in Malaysia many more preferred to recruit teenagers (Table 1). In the Philippines many more employers said they had no age preference.

For production workers, in Malaysia the electronics industry was conspicuous for preferring to hire very young workers, as has been the pattern since its early days in the 1970s. In the Philippines that was less pervasive, as Table 2 shows. In general, in both Malaysia and the Philippines large firms preferred to recruit at a younger age (Table 3), implying that most smaller firms did not practice ageism. Although this may seem a trivial point, if large formal enterprises prefer to recruit very young workers, whereas small-scale informal enterprises were less inclined to do so, it would be irrational and even impractical for young workers to enter the latter while waiting for opportunities in the formal firms, a pattern commonly *presumed* to apply to urban industrializing labour markets.[6]

Firms were also asked about their schooling preferences. Most recruited clerical workers on the basis of level of schooling, but as expected, that was less important in the case of production workers (Tables 4 and 5). Small firms put much less emphasis on credentialism than did large establishments, both for clerical and production workers (Table 6). That, of course, does not imply that the schooling was any more necessary for the work in large firms.

Employers were also asked to identify what they regarded as the *most important factor* when recruiting. For clerical workers, while most firms expressed a preference for some particular age and schooling level, a

[6] The queuing hypothesis is associated with variants of the Todaro model of labour migration and with the widespread belief that urban unemployment can be explained by reference to workers preferring to wait for 'formal sector' jobs rather than enter small 'informal' units. See e.g. L. A. Riveros, *Equity Impact and Effectiveness of Adjustment Policies with Segmented Labour Markets: The Case of the Philippines* (Washington, DC: The World Bank, 1989, mimeo).

Table 1 Employers' age preference for recruitment of clerical workers, by industry, Malaysia, 1988 and the Philippines, 1990 (per cent distribution of establishments in each industry)

Industry	Malaysia							Philippines						
	Age preferred					Any age under 45	No age preferred	Age preferred					Any age under 45	No age preferred
	16–20	21–5	16–25	26–35	36–45			16–20	21–5	16–25	26–35	36–45		
Food, etc.	3.6	52.7	15.6	9.7	0.2	11.1	7.1	—	49.4	13.0	13.0	—	5.2	19.5
Textiles, etc.	4.8	55.9	22.3	5.2	—	7.4	4.4	—	56.2	19.8	9.1	—	3.3	11.6
Wood products	4.1	50.6	22.1	8.8	0.3	8.5	5.6	2.0	52.0	6.0	10.0	2.0	4.0	24.0
Paper products	3.0	57.6	18.2	7.3	0.6	6.7	6.7	—	51.5	9.1	18.2	-	3.0	18.2
Chemicals, etc.	2.5	60.7	15.6	7.0	0.2	8.3	5.5	—	56.4	6.4	14.9	1.1	2.1	19.1
Non-metallic minerals	3.2	51.6	21.0	11.5	0.6	7.0	5.1	—	47.8	30.4	17.4	—	—	4.3
Basic metals	4.0	50.0	14.9	14.9	1.3	8.1	6.8	—	47.2	13.9	16.7	2.8	—	19.4
Fabricated metal	3.9	60.2	16.8	6.2	0.2	8.0	4.7	—	59.7	6.9	9.7	—	5.6	18.1
Electronics	—	44.8	41.4	6.9	—	5.2	1.7	5.4	51.4	10.8	18.9	—	2.7	10.8
Other manufacturing	8.7	52.2	19.6	6.5	—	4.3	8.7	—	60.0	7.5	25.0	—	—	7.5
Construction	—	—	—	—	—	—	—	1.3	43.0	7.6	16.5	—	2.5	29.1
Trade	—	—	—	—	—	—	—	—	50.0	7.7	22.5	1.4	1.4	16.9
Total	3.6	55.4	18.5	8.0	0.3	8.4	5.7	0.5	52.3	10.8	15.7	0.6	2.7	17.4

Table 2 Employer's age preference for recruitment of production workers, by industry, Malaysia, 1988 and the Philippines, 1990 (per cent distribution of establishments)

Industry	Malaysia							Philippines						
	Age preferred					Any age under 45	No age preferred	Age preferred					Any age under 45	No age preferred
	16–20	21–25	16–35	26–35	36+			16–20	21–5	16–25	26–35	36+		
Food, etc.	8.6	29.0	20.5	12.2	1.5	17.9	10.2	2.6	28.6	29.9	10.4	2.6	6.5	19.5
Textiles, etc.	16.4	22.7	34.9	6.3	0.4	10.9	8.4	2.5	35.8	35.0	6.7	—	6.7	
Wood products	4.3	25.8	15.1	15.6	3.5	23.8	11.9	4.2	27.1	8.3	10.4	—	12.5	37.5
Paper products	13.0	34.6	27.8	10.5	0.6	9.9	3.7	—	50.0	14.1	15.6	—	1.6	18.8
Chemicals, etc.	10.5	33.8	24.5	8.1	0.2	15.4	7.3	2.2	33.3	25.6	11.1	1.1	2.2	24.4
Non-metallic minerals	3.1	33.1	18.7	14.4	0.6	21.2	8.7	4.3	39.1	14.1	17.4	—	—	17.4
Basic metals	5.2	33.8	20.8	15.6	—	15.6	9.1	—	37.1	22.9	14.3	2.9	—	22.9
Fabricated metal	8.0	35.0	22.6	10.8	1.2	14.4	8.0	4.3	38.6	20.0	10.0	4.3	8.6	17.1
Electronics	22.4	15.5	51.7	—	—	5.2	5.2	5.6	27.8	41.7	5.6	1.4	5.6	11.1
Other manufacturing	26.0	26.0	30.0	2.0	—	8.0	8.0	2.6	39.5	23.7	18.4	—	—	15.8
Construction	—	—	—	—	—	—	—	2.6	24.7	13.0	22.1	3.9	2.6	31.2
Trade	—	—	—	—	—	—	—	4.0	38.9	19.0	13.5	1.6	3.2	19.8
Total	9.4	30.3	23.4	10.9	1.2	16.1	8.6	2.9	35.1	22.8	12.4	1.4	3.9	23.6

Table 3 Employer's age preference for recruiting clerical and production workers, by employment size of establishment, Malaysia, 1988 and Philippines, 1990 (per cent distribution for each size category)

Age preference	Malaysia							Philippines							
	Employment size							Employment size							
	1–4	5–20	21–50	51–100	101–500	501–1000	1001+	1–20	21–50	51–100	101–250	251–500	501–1000	1000+
Clerical workers														
16–20	—	3.3	3.3	3.9	3.9	3.4	4.7	—	—	0.7	0.9	—	1.7	—
21–5	46.7	54.9	56.7	54.0	56.8	57.9	53.1	53.6	44.1	50.7	53.4	58.9	63.3	51.1
16–25	26.7	16.0	16.0	19.3	19.2	26.1	35.9	8.7	10.2	14.3	9.5	6.3	10.1	23.4
26–35	6.7	9.0	8.1	8.3	8.2	4.5	3.1	11.6	16.9	16.4	16.8	18.8	10.0	8.5
36–45	—	1.0	0.2	—	0.3	—	—	1.4	—	—	0.9	—	—	—
Under 45	20.0	9.0	9.4	7.9	8.3	6.8	1.0	—	2.3	2.9	4.3	1.8	3.3	2.1
No age preference	—	9.5	6.3	6.6	3.3	1.1	1.6	23.3	26.6	15.0	13.8	14.3	11.7	14.9
Production workers														
16–20	12.9	7.8	7.2	8.3	10.6	22.7	18.7	3.0	3.6	1.5	1.8	1.8	4.9	8.7
21–5	29.0	29.3	31.0	30.7	31.6	27.3	18.7	27.3	33.9	38.6	31.7	40.9	42.6	32.6
16–25	12.9	17.2	20.4	22.2	27.4	36.4	54.7	13.6	14.9	23.5	26.7	27.3	26.2	28.3
26–35	6.5	13.4	12.9	10.7	9.0	2.3	3.1	18.2	13.7	9.8	28.0	9.1	13.1	13.0
36–45	3.2	2.1	1.5	0.9	0.7	—	—	3.0	1.2	0.8	0.9	—	—	2.2
46+	—	—	0.5	—	—	—	—	1.5	—	0.8	—	0.9	—	—
Under 45	19.4	18.9	17.5	16.9	14.5	9.1	3.1	4.5	3.0	6.8	6.3	4.5	—	6.5
No age preference	16.1	11.3	9.1	10.2	6.3	2.3	1.6	28.2	29.8	18.2	19.9	15.5	13.1	8.7

Note: 'Under 45' means any age under 45.

Table 4 Employers' schooling-level preference for clerical workers, by industry, Malaysia, 1988 and Philippines, 1990 (per cent distribution of establishments for each job category)

Industry	Malaysia				Philippines					
	Lower secondary	Upper secondary	Any	Other	Elementary	Secondary	Vocational	College	Any	Other
Food, etc.	4.2	89.1	4.8	1.2	—	3.6	0.9	93.7	1.8	—
Textiles, etc.	3.9	92.1	0.9	3.1	—	2.7	2.0	91.9	2.0	1.3
Wood products	5.0	90.9	2.9	1.2		2.4	2.4	90.2	4.9	—
Paper products	3.0	92.7	2.4	1.8	—	1.0	3.1	92.7	1.0	2.1
Chemicals, etc.	2.5	94.5	1.8	1.0	—	2.6	2.6	91.5	2.6	0.9
Non-metallic minerals	1.3	91.7	3.8	1.9	—	2.6	7.7	84.6	5.1	—
Basic metals	5.4	87.8	2.7	2.7	—	7.3	—	89.1	3.6	—
Fab. metal	1.4	93.4	2.5	2.7	1.0	2.0	3.0	93.1	2.0	—
Electronics	3.4	87.9	—	8.6	—	4.8	—	95.2	—	—
Other manufacturing	2.2	93.5	4.3	—	—	—	—	98.3	1.7	—
Construction	n/a	n/a	n/a	n/a	—	2.3	4.6	89.7	2.3	1.1
Trade					—	2.3	1.4	93.5	2.9	—
Total	3.5	91.8	2.8	1.9	−0.1	2.6	2.2	92.3	2.4	0.5

Table 5 Employers' schooling-level preference for production workers, by industry, Malaysia, 1988 and Philippines, 1990 (per cent distribution of establishments for each job category)

Industry	Malaysia					Philippines					
	Complete primary	Lower secondary	Upper secondary	Any	Other	Elementary	Secondary	Vocational	College	Any	Other
Food	24.7	20.9	5.9	43.6	5.0	2.9	58.8	5.1	5.9	25.8	1.5
Textiles	32.3	24.8	3.4	34.4	5.0	4.4	62.1	8.2	0.5	23.6	1.1
Wood products	19.9	14.2	2.6	57.8	5.5	4.0	45.5	5.0	1.0	44.5	—
Paper products	18.4	38.0	12.9	25.1	4.9	1.0	56.4	12.9	5.9	23.8	
Chemicals, etc.	20.6	30.0	10.1	36.4	4.7	1.6	67.2	6.6	4.9	19.7	—
Non-metallic minerals	20.6	15.0	8.7	50.0	5.6	4.0	54.0	8.0	—	34.0	—
Basic metals	20.8	24.7	13.0	36.4	5.2	1.6	46.9	14.1	1.6	36.0	—
Fab. metal	16.0	34.5	9.0	36.3	4.2	3.8	49.5	21.0	1.9	23.8	—
Electronics	10.3	51.7	34.5	3.4	—	—	66.7	–7.1	14.3	11.9	—
Other manufacturing	28.0	30.0	4.0	30.0	8.0	3.0	48.5	9.1	4.5	34.9	—
Construction	n/a	n/a	n/a	n/a	n/a	1.2	32.9	12.9	3.5	49.4	—
Trade	n/a	n/a	n/a	n/a	n/a	1.6	47.4	7.9	26.3	14.8	2.1
Total	21.4	26.1	7.9	39.7	4.8	2.6	53.5	9.5	7.0	26.9	0.6

Table 6 Employers' school-level preference for clerical and production workers, by employment size of establishment, Malaysia, 1988 and Philippines, 1990 (per cent distribution for each size category)

	Malaysia						Philippines						
	Complete primary	Lower secondary	Upper secondary	Any	Other		No schooling	Elementary	Secondary	Vocational	College	Any	Other
Employment size		*Clerical workers*				*Employment size*			*Clerical workers*				
1–4	n/a	13.3	73.3	13.3	—	1–20	1.3	—	5.3	4.6	82.2	5.9	−0.7
5–20	n/a	6.5	86.2	8.5	1.2	21–50	0.3	0.3	2.7	2.0	92.7	2.0	—
21–50	n/a	3.3	90.7	3.8	2.1	51–100	—	—	1.1	2.7	93.1	1.6	1.6
51–100	n/a	4.1	92.6	1.3	2.0	101–250	—	—	3.0	1.1	93.6	1.9	−0.4
101–500	n/a	1.9	96.0	0.3	1.8	251–500	—	—	0.8	1.6	96.9	0.8	—
501–1000	n/a	1.1	95.4	—	3.4	501–1000	—	—	2.0	—	95.9	—	2.0
1001+	n/a	1.6	95.3	—	3.1	1001+	—	—	2.0	—	95.9	—	2.0
		Production workers							*Production workers*				
1–4	19.4	16.1	6.5	45.2	12.9	1–20	10.1	4.3	42.2	8.9	7.4	26.0	1.2
5–20	21.4	15.3	3.6	52.2	7.5	21–50	2.3	2.9	52.3	9.2	7.5	25.5	−0.3
21–50	22.4	21.6	4.7	46.3	4.9	51–100	2.8	2.2	52.2	11.8	6.7	23.6	−0.6
51–100	22.8	25.6	6.9	40.8	3.9	101–250	2.3	1.2	54.2	10.4	8.1	23.5	−0.4
101–500	19.7	33.7	12.2	30.1	4.3	251–500	1.6	3.2	60.8	8.0	8.0	16.8	1.6
501–1000	23.9	15.4	18.2	11.4	1.1	501–1000	1.5	—	70.6	10.3	1.5	16.2	—
1001+	17.2	53.1	21.9	7.8	—	1001+	—	2.0	77.6	4.1	2.0	14.3	—

majority in all sectors except electronics said that the most important factor was previous work experience (Table 7). This was also the factor most often cited in the case of production workers (Table 8), in all industries except electronics in Malaysia, in which formal schooling was regarded as the most important, followed by personal characteristics and contacts with existing workers, classified as 'other' in the tables.

For both clerical and production workers, small firms were more likely to regard past work experience as the most important factor, whereas large firms gave more weight to formal schooling. This further suggests that small units were not necessarily an easy entry point for workers. For production workers, lager firms were more likely to state that the gender of the applicant was of primary importance (Table 9). They were also more inclined to cite the primary importance of age and schooling, whereas small firms overwhelmingly gave past work experience. Remarkably few firms—less than one in ten—cited 'past training' as the most important, suggesting that for most clerical and production jobs the necessary training could be conveyed to new workers fairly easily and with little cost.

So, what about overt sex discrimination? Consider first the recruitment of *clerical workers*. Whereas a majority of Malaysian firms stated that they preferred to recruit women for clerical jobs, in the Philippines a majority said they were equally willing to hire either men or women (Table 10). Indeed, in both Malaysia and the Philippines, the larger the firm, the more likely the preference for *either* male *or* female clerical or production workers (Table 11).

As for *production workers*, there were major industrial differences. In Malaysia, although a majority of firms overall (51.2 per cent) preferred men, this varied widely by industry, with electronics and textiles-and-garments firms overwhelmingly preferring women (Table 10). Men were preferred in a large majority of firms in the basic metals, non-metallic mineral products, wood products, and fabricated metal products sectors. Only in the paper and chemicals industries could one suggest that there was no sex segregation via recruitment.

In the Philippines, firms in the two industries in which women were preferred in Malaysia were also most inclined to recruit women (Table 10). However, a larger proportion of firms in all industries (56.7 per cent) preferred to recruit men, although a high proportion reported that they had no preference. These differences in preferences may be linked to cultural or legislative differences, and deserve future sociological analysis.

In the Philippines's survey, though not in the earlier MLFS, we also asked employers whether they preferred to recruit men or women as professional or technical workers. Though nearly two-thirds reported that they had no preference, discrimination against women was widespread (Table 12). It may have been slightly stronger in small firms, as with clerical and production workers, which was only partly due to the industrial

Table 7 Most important factor in recruiting clerical workers by industry, Malaysia, 1988 and Philippines, 1990 (per cent distribution for each industry group)

Industry	Malaysia						Philippines					
	Gender	Age	Schooling	Experience	Trained	Other	Gender	Age	Schooling	Experience	Training	Other
Food, etc.	3.8	0.6	20.8	61.3	4.2	9.4	1.8	—	14.5	71.8	6.4	5.4
Textiles, etc.	3.5	0.4	15.7	73.8	3.5	3.1	1.3	—	22.0	64.7	8.0	3.4
Wood products	4.7	1.2	13.8	73.0	2.0	5.3	—	—	17.7	67.1	8.9	6.3
Paper products	2.4	1.2	17.0	69.7	1.2	8.5	—	—	17.9	74.7	5.3	2.2
Chemicals, etc.	3.0	1.3	16.2	67.7	2.3	9.6	—	—	19.3	66.7	7.0	7.1
Non-metallic minerals	3.2	1.3	13.4	73.2	0.6	8.3	—	—	15.8	73.7	2.6	7.8
Basic metals	1.3	1.3	16.2	78.4	—	2.7	—	—	23.6	65.5	7.3	7.1
Fab. metal	2.5	1.0	11.1	77.2	1.8	6.4	1.0	—	34.0	58.0	5.0	2.0
Electronics	1.7	—	24.1	48.3	3.4	22.4	2.4	—	24.4	61.0	9.8	2.4
Other manufacturing	4.3	6.5	8.7	71.7	2.2	6.5	—	1.6	19.7	68.9	8.2	1.6
Construction	n/a	n/a	n/a	n/a	n/a	n/a	—	—	22.6	64.3	9.5	3.6
Trade	n/a	n/a	n/a	n/a	n/a	n/a	—	0.5	20.7	64.4	7.7	6.8
Total	3.3	1.1	15.6	70.0	2.4	7.6	0.5	0.2	21.1	63.3	7.2	4.8

Table 8 Most important factor in recruiting production workers, by industry, Malaysia, 1988 and Philippines, 1990 (per cent distribution for each industry group)

Industry	Malaysia							Philippines					
	Gender	Age	Schooling	Experience	Trained	Other	None	Gender	Age	Schooling	Experience	Trained	Other
Food	9.3	7.4	5.7	40.1	8.4	25.2	3.9	0.8	2.3	6.0	69.9	8.3	11.9
Textiles	13.3	5.0	5.4	51.4	10.8	12.4	1.7	0.5	—	5.4	79.3	7.1	7.6
Wood products	6.6	3.8	1.6	59.6	6.6	16.5	5.2	—	—	1.0	77.2	10.9	11.0
Paper products	5.9	4.1	7.1	51.5	11.8	15.4	4.1	1.0	—	2.0	80.2	10.9	6.7
Chemicals, etc.	7.5	7.5	7.7	36.8	10.4	27.6	2.4	3.3	—	11.6	66.1	9.1	13.2
Non-metallic minerals	11.3	4.2	3.0	43.4	10.7	22.6	4.8	—	—	2.0	77.6	10.2	6.1
Basic metals	7.6	7.6	6.3	45.6	11.4	19.0	2.5	1.5	—	4.6	72.3	9.2	13.4
Fab. metal	7.5	5.7	6.9	54.6	8.7	14.0	2.6	0.9	1.9	5.7	74.5	12.3	8.5
Electronics	15.5	17.2	25.9	15.5	1.7	24.1	—	2.4	2.4	9.5	61.9	11.9	—
Other manufacturing	5.9	15.7	5.9	41.2	11.8	17.6	2.0	3.2	—	4.8	66.7	15.9	12.4
Construction	n/a	n/a	n/a	n/a	n/a	n/a	n/a	1.2	—	—	72.8	13.6	12.6
Trade	n/a	n/a	n/a	n/a	n/a	n/a	n/a	2.2	1.1	6.6	62.8	9.8	14.6
Total	21.4	26.1	7.9	39.7	4.8		3.3	1.4	.7	5.2	71.9	10.2	10.7

Table 9 Most important factor in recruiting clerical and production workers, by employment size of establishment, Malaysia, 1988 and Philippines, 1990 (per cent distribution for each size category)

Factor	Malaysia, employment size							Philippines, employment size						
	1–4	5–20	21–50	51–100	101–500	501–1000	1001+	1–20	21–50	51–100	101–250	251–500	501–1000	1000+
	Clerical workers							*Clerical workers*						
Gender	—	5	4.2	2.6	2.2	1.1	4.7	—	1.7	—	—	0.8	—	—
Age	6.7	1	1.5	1.5	0.1	2.3	1.6	0.7	0.3	—	—	—	—	—
Schooling	6.7	10.9	3.3	90.7	3.8	2.1	23.4	12.1	16.3	24.2	24.6	20.5	29.2	36.7
Experience	86.7	73.2	74.3	71.5	65.2	63.6	53.1	74.5	69.8	58.1	65.2	67.7	64.6	57.1
Trained	—	2.1	2.3	1.8	3.1	3.4	3.1	6.7	7.1	11.3	6.8	7.1	1.5	4.1
Other	—	7.8	5.2	7.7	8.9	9.1	14.1	5.4	5.4	6.4	3.5	4	4.6	2
	Production workers							*Production workers*						
Gender	6.5	9.1	7.8	8.3	8.2	17	21.9	1.1	1.3	1.1	2	1.6	—	2.1
Age	—	4.8	5.8	6	7.5	14.8	10.9	1.9	—	—	0.4	—	1.6	2.1
Schooling	—	2.1	3.6	5.1	9.9	15.9	25	0.4	4.3	4	6.6	9.7	10.9	14.9
Experience	80.6	57.7	53.6	47.6	42.1	23.9	12.5	75.9	74.8	68.2	71.5	69.4	8.9	10.5
Trained	3.2	7.1	11.1	9	10.7	6.8	7.8	8.4	9.6	14.8	10.2	8.9	12.5	6.4
Other	9.7	19.1	18	24.1	21.7	21.6	21.9	12.3	10	12	9.4	10.5	11	8.5

Table 10 Gender preference in recruitment of clerical and production workers, by industry, Malaysia, 1988 and Philippines, 1990 (per cent distribution of preference in sector)

Industry	Malaysia						Philippines					
	Clerical workers			Production workers			Clerical workers			Production workers		
	Male	Female	Either	Male	Female	Either	Male	Female	Either	Male	Female	Either
Food, etc.	15.7	46.0	38.3	56.1	21.9	22.0	4.5	36.0	59.5	59.9	6.6	33.6
Textiles	3.1	70.3	26.6	10.1	73.1	16.8	1.3	36.7	62.0	15.8	27.2	57.1
Wood, etc.	8.5	61.0	30.5	69.1	11.6	19.4	3.7	47.6	48.8	66.0	3.0	31.0
Paper, etc.	3.0	49.7	47.3	42.6	19.1	38.3	2.1	46.3	51.6	63.7	2.9	33.3
Chemicals, etc.	12.1	49.6	38.3	40.9	24.7	34.3	—	41.0	59.0	57.7	4.9	37.4
Non-metallic minerals	10.2	61.1	28.7	70.6	8.7	20.6	2.6	41.0	56.4	76.0	4.0	20.0
Basic metals	5.4	63.5	31.1	75.3	6.5	18.2	1.8	38.2	60.0	93.8	—	6.2
Fabricated metals	3.1	67.1	29.8	62.0	19.4	18.6	4.0	51.0	45.0	92.4	1.0	6.7
Electronics	3.4	48.3	48.3	8.6	87.9	3.4	—	38.1	61.9	45.2	26.2	28.6
Other manufacturing	4.3	67.4	28.3	22.0	52.0	26.0	1.7	46.7	51.7	39.4	18.2	42.4
Trade	n.a.	n.a.	n.a.	n.a.	n.a.	n.a.	1.4	46.7	51.9	41.1	26.3	32.6
Construction	n.a.	n.a.	n.a.	n.a.	n.a.	n.a.	4.6	44.8	50.6	89.4	—	10.6
Total	n.a.	n.a.	n.a.	n.a.	n.a.	n.a.	2.3	43.1	54.6	56.7	11.8	31.5

Note: n.a. = data not available.

Table 11 Gender preference in recruitment of clerical and production workers, by employment size of establishment, Malaysia, 1988, and Philippines, 1990 (per cent distribution of preference)

Size	Clerical workers			Production workers		
	Male	Female	Either	Male	Female	Either
			Malaysia			
1–4	26.7	60.0	13.3	67.7	22.6	9.7
5–20	9.5	67.8	22.7	60.6	19.1	20.3
21–50	9.1	66.4	24.5	54.3	20.6	25.1
51–100	8.5	55.6	35.9	49.1	25.7	25.2
101–500	7.6	46.8	45.6	49.5	26.2	24.3
501–1000	5.7	51.1	43.2	21.6	64.8	13.6
1001+	1.6	42.2	56.2	14.1	76.6	9.4
			Philippines			
1–20	4.0	54.3	41.7	68.3	9.5	22.1
21–50	3.0	43.0	54.0	62.1	8.8	29.1
51–100	1.1	47.9	51.1	54.5	10.1	35.4
101–250	2.2	40.4	57.3	55.5	8.8	35.8
251–500	1.6	38.0	60.5	42.9	24.6	32.5
501–1000	—	39.7	60.3	42.6	14.7	42.6
1001+	2.0	24.5	73.5	30.6	26.5	42.9

composition of the sample of large and small firms. Of those preferring men as production workers, most (76.7 per cent) claimed that it was because men had more appropriate skills for the work, whereas among those preferring women for production work, 83.6 per cent gave that reason.

Many firms with a preference for men as production workers did not have such a preference for professional or technical workers. The most common situation was a preference for men as production workers combined with an apparently non-discriminatory policy towards professional and technical workers.[7] Even so, given the widespread sex discrimination admitted for both manual and non-manual jobs, those in the Philippines concerned with overcoming sex discrimination have a major challenge at higher job levels as well as at the lower levels.

[7] This raises a more general point. One senses that a disproportionate amount of attention has been directed at 'middle-class' discrimination against women. It is at the manual-worker level that most discrimination surely occurs. These data in a timeous way support that view.

Table 12 Gender preference in recruitment of professional and technical workers, by industry, and by establishment size, Philippines, 1990 (per cent distribution of preference in sector)

	Male	Female	Either
Industry			
Food, etc.	27.3	5.0	67.5
Textiles	16.0	12.0	72.0
Wood, etc.	22.6	11.3	66.0
Paper, etc.	23.9	11.9	64.2
Chemicals	21.2	6.1	72.7
Non-metallic minerals	22.2	3.7	74.1
Basic metals	33.3	—	66.7
Fabricated metals	41.1	2.7	56.2
Electronics	36.8	—	63.2
Other manufacturing	27.5	20.0	52.5
Trade	20.1	16.1	63.8
Construction	53.1	3.1	43.2
Total	27.3	8.8	63.8
Employment size			
1–20	29.4	10.6	60.0
21–50	28.8	9.8	61.4
51–100	28.2	12.0	59.9
101–250	29.4	7.7	63.0
251–500	23.7	8.8	67.5
501–1000	20.3	7.8	71.9
1001+	23.4	—	76.6

GENDER SEGREGATION BY SECTOR

Women's employment shares

Explicitly stated preferences may not correspond to actual outcomes or revealed preference. In terms of employment, in both countries, about 3 per cent of all manufacturing firms had no women workers. And in both, the electronics and textiles sectors had the most firms in which women comprised a majority of all workers (Table 13). However, in Malaysia in both those industries women comprised over 75 per cent of total employment in a majority of establishments, which was far more than in the Philippines. Probably, the industrial structure of firms partly explained the strong positive correlation between employment size and the share of women, a point to which we will return. But the basic tabulations raise the

Table 13 Female Share of employment, by industry, Malaysia, 1988, and Philippines, 1990 (per cent distribution within sector)

Industry	Per cent of employment female						
	0	0.01–10	10.01–25	25.01–50	50.01–75	75.01+	Total
				Malaysia			
Food, etc.	5.6	18.7	23.2	27.8	22.0	2.7	100.0
Textiles	2.1	0.8	3.7	12.1	23.3	57.9	100.0
Wood, etc.	6.1	25.7	31.8	22.6	11.9	1.9	100.0
Paper, etc.	—	3.0	15.1	55.1	23.0	3.6	100.0
Chem., etc.	2.2	8.3	21.4	33.6	27.0	7.5	100.0
Non-metallic metals	2.4	26.2	30.9	30.9	9.5	—	100.0
Basic metals	3.8	32.9	40.5	16.5	5.1	1.3	100.0
Fabricated metals	4.5	20.4	31.2	23.1	13.2	7.5	100.0
Electronics	—	—	—	13.8	20.7	65.5	100.0
Other manufacturing	3.8	1.9	7.7	26.9	30.8	28.8	100.0
Total	3.8	16.2	23.5	26.8	18.7	11.0	100.0
				Philippines			
Food, etc.	3.5	16.3	26.2	29.1	20.6	4.3	100.0
Textiles	1.6	3.8	4.8	29.6	26.3	33.9	100.0
Wood products	2.9	23.1	41.3	26.9	4.8	1.0	100.0
Paper products	3.9	6.9	47.1	32.4	7.8	2.0	100.0
Chemicals	1.6	20.5	29.1	35.4	10.2	3.1	100.0
Non-metallic minerals	8.0	36.0	34.0	20.0	2.0	—	100.0
Basic metals	6.2	63.1	21.5	7.7	—	1.5	100.0
Fabricated metals	7.4	55.6	26.9	8.3	0.9	0.9	100.0
Electronics	—	11.4	36.4	15.9	11.4	25.0	100.0
Other manufacturing	1.5	16.2	19.1	33.8	11.8	17.6	100.0
Trade	1.3	8.8	25.9	25.0	21.1	18.0	100.0
Construction	—	65.9	23.9	8.0	1.1	1.1	100.0
				[illegible]	12.8	10.9	100.0

Table 14 Female share of employment, by export orientation of establishment, Malaysia, 1988, and Philippines, 1990 (per cent distribution of female share for each export-orientation category)

Per cent exported	Per cent of employment female					
	0	0.01–10	10.01–25	25.01–50	50.01–75	75.01+
				Malaysia		
0	6.7	18.8	26.5	26.2	16.3	5.5
1–10	0.9	8.9	22.5	31.7	27.4	8.6
11–25	1.1	18.3	22.2	32.2	18.9	7.2
26–50	1.6	16.8	24.2	26.3	22.1	8.9
51–75	1.3	27.3	23.3	26.7	15.3	6.0
76+	0.2	7.1	15.5	23.3	19.1	34.8
				Philippines		
0	3.3	24.8	27.9	23.8	12.0	8.1
1–10	—	25.0	32.7	32.7	7.7	1.9
11–25	—	16.0	32.0	32.0	20.0	—
26–50	—	40.7	18.5	22.2	11.1	7.4
51–75	—	14.8	18.5	25.9	14.8	25.9
76+	—	11.8	12.4	27.1	19.4	29.4

possibility that the internationally popular policy of boosting small enterprises relative to large-scale could harm women's employment chances.

The relationship between export-orientation and female employment, about which so mush has been written, is brought out fairly conclusively in Table 14. It applied to both countries. By contrast, most firms oriented to the domestic market employed small percentages of women. This suggests that a structural adjustment programme involving a shift to export-led growth would promote female employment, rather than male.

To unravel the determinants of the female share of employment, a multiple regression model was tested with the female per cent of total employment being the dependent variable. For Malaysia, we found a strong positive relationship between employment size of establishment and female share, only disrupted for the size group having between 100 and 250 workers. Perhaps this non-linearity reflects the changing occupational structure as a firm goes from small to medium; as it goes beyond the size of a foundry or family business, clerical and administrative staff are hired, mainly women; then beyond a certain size, the share of production operatives rises, and in many medium-sized, craft-oriented factories men comprise the majority. It may be that such craft work, rather than processing–assembly work, predominates in medium-sized firms, whereas in large-scale firms a majority of workers are engaged in processing, which is typically assigned to women. What is clear is that beyond a workforce of about 250, the female share started to rise quite substantially, controlling for the influence of industry and other factors.

Also, as expected, the greater the degree of labour casualization, the higher the women's share of total employment. By contrast, establishments with high shares of contract labour had fewer women, a pattern consistent with the nature of contract labour in Malaysian manufacturing, in which quasi-independent male craftsmen are common in the wood products and fabricated metal foundries.

The observed influence of the industry variables (employment size and industry branch) were as expected. And even controlling for the influence of industry and establishment size, the more export-oriented the factory the higher women's share of employment.

For the Philippines, a comparable function showed a positive relationship between establishment size and female share, although less strong than in Malaysia. However, the strong positive relationship between export orientation and female share was similar to that found in Malaysia.

Changes in female employment share

As for changes in female employment, the countries differed. In Malaysia, since large export-oriented firms were those that grew most in the preceding three years, as shown in the report of the survey's main findings,[8] it was expected that female employment in manufacturing would have increased as well. That was the case.[9] In most industries, those establishments that expanded overall employment between 1985 and 1988 typically had much higher female employment shares than those that had cut employment or that had maintained their 1985 level.

In the Philippines, there was no apparent relation between recent employment change and women's employment share. However, in the PLFS (regrettably not in the MLFS) we also asked for employment by gender for two years prior to the time of the survey, allowing direct examination of changes. Overall, this showed there had been no strong net change in either direction, although in most firms the proportion had changed in one direction or another. In the electronics sector, the female share certainly had increased, and in construction it had fallen sharply. Some of the other industrial changes were slightly more surprising, but in most cases the

[8] G. Standing, *Structural Adjustment in Malaysian Manufacturing* (Geneva and Kuala Lumpur: ILO and EPU, 1991).

[9] A World Bank analysis argued that in Malaysia women industrial workers 'lost ground' in the recession before 1988. These data do not support that claim. S. Horton, R. Kanbar, and D. Mazumdar, *Labour Markets in an Era of Adjustment* (Washington, DC: World Bank, 1991), 51.

Table 15 Expected change in women's employment share in next two years, by ownership, Malaysia, 1988 (per cent distribution within ownership categories)

	Increase	Decrease	No change	Don't know
Foreign	24.7	2.6	70.6	2.1
Chinese Malaysian	16.3	2.8	76.8	4.0
Other Malaysian	12.3	6.3	76.4	5.0
Total	16.4	3.7	75.7	4.1

changes were small in either direction. An OLS regression model was estimated to explain the change in per cent female in the past two years. Although results indicated a rather poor fit, necessitating further work, they suggest that the female share fell in firms with above-average female shares and that there was an inverse relationship between the extent of casual labour and women workers, an issue to which we will return.

Expected change in women's employment

Now let us briefly turn to the employers' future intentions. In Malaysia, not only had the female share of employment risen in more firms than in which it had fallen, but many more expected the female share to rise. This was particularly so in foreign-owned firms (Table 15). The main reason given for expecting the share to rise was that women were more suitable for the type of work being generated, although many cited lower wage costs or women's apparently greater adaptability to work demands (Table 16). Within each industry, firms *expecting* overall employment to rise were also more likely to have a *preference* for women as production workers. All this suggests a continuing growth of one form of feminization of employment.

Does this imply that industrial sex segregation was declining? One way of considering this is to compare recruitment-level discrimination in growing and shrinking firms. Our data suggest that in the food processing, wood products, paper products, and chemicals sectors, sex segregation was weakening, since the firms expecting employment to grow were far more likely than those expecting to cut employment to have no overt discriminatory recruitment practice. By contrast, in the garments and textile industry segregation was likely to strengthen even more, since firms expecting to expand were those already practising discrimination in favour of women. By contrast, discrimination in favour of men in non-metallic minerals, basic metals, and fabricated metals industries could be expected to increase.

Table 16 Main reason for expecting to employ relatively more women in next two years, Philippines, 1990, and Malaysia, 1988 (per cent distribution of reasons)

Main reason	Philippines	Malaysia
More suitable for work	—	48.5
Business growth	73.0	26.9
New techniques/products/work reorganization	7.8	3.7
Business uncertainty	1.4	—
Lower wages	—	7.1
More adaptable	—	6.4
Other	7.1	5.3

In the Philippines, most firms said they expected a constant female share over the next two years, but whereas 11 per cent expected the share to rise, only 1.9 per cent expected it to fall. As more of the larger firms expected women's employment to grow, the overall increase in feminization would probably be much greater than the bare numbers suggest. And not only did more firms expect women's share to rise whether they preferred men or women as production workers, but whereas only 7 per cent of firms preferring men as production workers expected the female share to rise, 22 per cent of those that preferred women expected their share to rise.

SEX SEGREGATION BY LABOUR STATUS: EXTERNAL LABOUR FLEXIBILITY

There are reasons for believing that a general feminization of employment is associated with a growth of external labour flexibility, that is, a shift to non-regular forms of labour.[10] In Malaysia, those firms that had resorted more to temporary or casual labour were relatively likely to prefer women as production workers. However, as overall women were *less* likely to be classified as temporary labour, and as they were also less likely to be contract labour, women comprised a *smaller* proportion of non-regular workers generally (Table 17). This may seem a minor point, but it is a clue to the nature of the labour process.

In the Philippines, women were more likely to be in temporary labour statuses than in Malaysia, but the industrial pattern was similar (Table 18). As a share of total female employment, non-regular employment was substantially higher than in Malaysia, with particularly high percentages in garments and textiles, wood products, and food processing (Table 19).

[10] Standing, 'Global Feminization'.

Table 17 Per cent non-regular, by sex, by employment size, Malaysia, 1988 (per cent of each gender in non-regular work statuses)

Emp. size	Per cent men in non-regular				Per cent women in non-regular			
	0	0.01<10	10–25	Over 25	0	0.01<10	10–25	Over 25
1–20	43.9	3.7	16.4	36.1	67.2	0.8	6.1	25.8
21–50	54.9	8.8	9.7	26.6	73.2	3.9	5.6	17.1
51–100	61.5	9.2	6.5	22.7	73.7	4.5	6.3	15.2
101–250	59.2	11.5	9.0	20.3	72.4	5.5	7.7	14.3
251–500	58.3	16.6	13.9	11.2	63.6	14.4	9.6	12.3
501+	67.3	17.3	8.7	6.7	66.0	18.7	6.7	8.7

Table 18 Per cent of female employment temporary, by industry, Philippines, 1990 (per cent with temporary shares in sector)

Industry	Per cent temporary		
	0	0.01–20	Over 20
Food, etc.	76.3	8.9	14.8
Textiles, etc.	76.0	10.4	13.7
Wood products	88.1	1.0	10.9
Paper products	84.7	5.1	10.2
Chemicals, etc.	89.6	6.4	4.0
Non-metallic minerals	80.4	13.0	6.5
Basic metals	95.1	1.6	3.3
Fabricated metals	92.9	4.0	3.0
Electronics	74.4	14.0	11.6
Other manufacturing	83.6	4.5	11.9
Trade	70.0	9.9	20.2
Construction	87.4	3.4	9.2
Total	81.5	7.1	11.4

In Malaysia, for both men and women, non-regular forms of labour were more prevalent in smaller establishments, and in this respect only in very large concerns were women *relatively* disadvantaged. In the Philippines, non-regular labour was greater for men in large-scale firms, but this was probably not so for women (Table 20).

As there was also no evidence that firms with high percentages of non-regular workers had high female shares, perhaps in the Philippines as well, women's employment has been an implicit substitute for non-regular labour.

Table 19 Per cent of female employment non-regular, by industry, Philippines, 1990 (per cent distribution of firms in each sector)

Industry	Per cent non-regular			
	0	0.01<10	10<25	Over 25
Food, etc.	47.8	10.3	11.8	30.1
Textiles, etc.	37.2	25.7	14.8	22.4
Wood products	50.5	3.0	7.9	38.6
Paper products	58.2	8.2	6.1	27.6
Chemicals	73.4	9.7	8.1	8.9
Non-metallic minerals	58.7	8.7	10.9	21.9
Basic metals	75.4	6.6	3.3	14.8
Fabricated metals	76.0	5.0	7.0	12.0
Electronics	61.4	13.6	11.4	13.6
Other manufacturing	50.7	10.4	11.9	26.9
Trade	50.7	12.9	12.4	24.0
Construction	65.9	3.4	9.1	21.6
Total	56.1	11.2	10.2	22.5

There is another labour status issue that is too rarely captured by published statistics. Within the broad category of wage workers, one should distinguish sub-categories according to the basis on which they are paid, since those receiving monthly salaries, for example, have more income security than those paid on a daily or piece-rate basis. Most labour analysts agree that piece-rate workers are the most easily 'sweated'—in the time-honoured jargon—and most insecure.

In that regard, in Malaysia women were more likely to be paid on a piece-rate or hourly basis, whereas many more men were paid on a monthly basis (Table 21). As can be seen, the differences were less marked in the Philippines, further evidence that women's labour-market position in Malaysia was more disadvantaged.

SEGREGATION BY TRAINING

In the Philippines, but not in Malaysia, we also asked employers whether they were more likely to provide training to men or to women. This form of discrimination has received surprisingly little empirical study. Given a normal tendency for respondents to wish to appear 'good employers', any evidence of such overt discrimination must be treated as an understatement of its real extent.

Table 20 Per cent of employment non-regular, by employment size, by sex, Philippines, 1990 (per cent distribution of firms in each size category)

Employment size	Per cent men non-regular				Per cent women non-regular			
	0	0.01<10	10–25	Over 25	0	0.01<10	10–25	Over 25
1–20	46.3	5.5	13.2	34.9	59.1	1.2	7.1	32.5
21–50	49.8	16.1	11.1	22.9	61.7	7.0	11.7	19.6
51–100	38.1	19.6	20.6	21.7	63.7	10.0	13.7	12.6
101–250	34.1	23.2	14.6	28.1	55.1	16.5	12.0	16.5
251–500	34.6	20.0	10.0	35.4	49.2	16.2	14.6	20.0
501–1000	17.6	22.1	14.7	45.6	31.9	26.1	11.6	30.4
1001+	18.4	24.5	24.5	45.6	32.7	30.6	18.4	18.4

Table 21 Regular wage workers' basis by which paid, by skill and by sex, Malaysia, 1988, and Philippines, 1990

	Malaysia				Philippines			
	Skilled		Unskilled		Skilled		Unskilled	
	Male	Female	Male	Female	Male	Female	Male	Female
Hourly, daily	30.8	36.9	52.7	58.1	36.3	36.9	43.3	43.3
Monthly, weekly	66.9	53.8	46.0	39.6	59.9	57.2	54.9	51.8
Piece rate	2.1	8.7	1.1	2.2	2.6	4.8	1.4	4.0
Other	0.2	0.6	0.2	0.1	1.2	1.1	0.4	0.9

Note: In Malaysia, only a very few firms paid regular workers on a weekly basis.

There are two forms of structural disadvantage that women could experience in this respect—they could face discrimination within any given firm or they could find themselves concentrated in firms that provide little or no training. On the first, we found that one in every five firms admitted to giving a preference to men while 4 per cent said they gave a preference to women, the latter mainly because of the sex-stereotyping of jobs in garments and textiles and in electronics. Most firms reported that the main reason for preferring men (or women) was 'type of work'—that is, classic discrimination—and those firms that stated a preference for recruiting men for production jobs were also most likely to report that training was more likely to be provided to men. Such preference discrimination was greater in small firms, and was more common in Filipino private sector firms than in either public or foreign firms.

However, firms with high shares of women in total employment were, if anything, more likely to provide training and retraining generally—at the recruitment level, to improve job performance, or to shift workers between jobs at the same level and to enable them to be upgraded. Whereas none of the firms without women workers provided all three forms of training, over 24 per cent of those in which more than three-quarters of their workers were women provided all three forms. So, the structural distribution of employment and the training pattern tended to correct, to some extent, the subjective discrimination by individual employers.

SEX SEGREGATION BY OCCUPATIONAL CROWDING

One potential cause of women's labour-market disadvantage is what has been described as 'crowding' into a smaller range of jobs than are available to men. This hypothesis was first presented by Edgeworth in 1922, though many incorrectly attribute it to Bergmann.[11] Although the crowding hypothesis does not explain the persistence of occupational segregation, which has been attributed to various forms of discrimination that need not be reviewed here, it is important to identify whether it does exist and if so in what form.

If there were overcrowding of some disadvantaged group, such as women, into a narrower range of jobs than were open for other groups, wages of all workers in those jobs would be reduced (presuming wages respond to demand and supply), *and* the wages of women in those occupations would fall, which would also be likely to lower women's reservation wages and aspiration wages generally.[12]

It is difficult to assess the pattern of job segregation, and one should feel uncomfortable with all conventional concepts in this sphere.[13] We can only stress that, while more finely disaggregated analyses and data are required, it is hoped that the following gives a reasonable sketch of the industrial pattern of job segregation. Our survey found that for the Philippines, women comprised a far higher proportion of higher-level jobs than of manual positions, a fairly unusual pattern. Although for each occupational level, there were wide inter-industry and intra-industry differences, the mean female share was as follows: 32.3 per cent managerial and administrative; 39.1 per cent professional and technical; 76.6 per cent clerical; 28 per cent sales and service workers; 22.8 per cent supervisors; 18.9 per cent skilled workers; 22.5 per cent semi-skilled workers; 20.3 per cent unskilled workers. And whereas women comprised a larger proportion of managerial, administrative, and clerical jobs in small firms than in large-scale establishments, the reverse was the pattern for manual jobs, including supervisory levels.

In the previous two years, the female share of managerial, administrative,

[11] F. Y. Edgeworth, 'Equal Pay to Men and Women', *Economic Journal*, 32 (Dec. 1922), 431–57. Its roots can be found in E. J. Rathbone, 'The Remuneration of Women's Services', *Economic Journal*, 27 (1917), 55–68. Bergmann is the author most often cited as having originated the crowding hypothesis. B. R. Bergmann, 'Occupational Segregation, Wages and Profits when Employers Discriminate by Race and Sex', *Eastern Economic Journal*, 1 (April–July 1974), 103–10.

[12] O. Duncan and B. Duncan, 'A Methodological Analysis of Segregation Indices', *American Sociological Review*, 20 (1955), 210–17. The Duncan index has been widely used, but also widely critiqued in recent years. See e.g. Z. Tzannatos, 'Employment Segregation: Can We Measure It and What Does the Measure Mean?', *British Journal of Industrial Relations*, 28 (1990), 105–11. It is clearly correct that the greater the disaggregation of occupations, the greater the degree of job segregation that is likely to be observed. W. T. Bielby and J. N. Baron, 'Men and Women at Work: Sex Segregation and Statistical Discrimination', *American Journal of Sociology*, 91/4 (1986), 759–99.

[13] This applies in particular to the notions of 'skill', 'occupation', and 'job', all of which are multi-dimensional and open to a variety of definitions, some of which are gender biased. On these issues, see G. Standing, 'A Labour Status Approach to Labour Statistics' (Geneva: ILO, 1983); on skill *per se*, see S. Horrel, J. Rubery, and B. Burchell, 'Gender and Skills', *Work, Employment and Society*, 4/2 (June 1990), 189–216.

professional, technical, and clerical jobs had slightly increased. Although their share of sales and service jobs had fallen, it had also risen among semi-skilled jobs. In sum, the data suggest that although there was occupational segregation in Filipino industry, it was not rigid; there had been some upgrading of women's occupational status. And those firms that in 1988 had a high per cent of women in total employment were relatively more likely to have increased their female share of management, professional, and technical employees and to have cut their share of manual workers.

Multiple regression analysis indicated a strong positive correlation between the extent of feminization of production-worker employment, as measured by the per cent of manual occupations taken by women, and feminization of higher-level, white-collar categories.[14]

Regression analysis also showed that larger firms had proportionately fewer women in higher-level occupations, and that foreign firms tended to employ fewer women in managerial, administrative positions. Among shop-floor workers, the relationships differed, with, for example, the female share of supervisors and foremen rising with size of workforce, except in the very largest category.

SEGREGATION BY WAGES

What then of the role of wages in the process of stratification and discrimination? We cannot treat all aspects of this, bearing in mind that there are supply-side (human capital) explanations of wage differentials that have been extensively examined over the past two decades. The following tries to highlight basic demand-side factors linked to the pattern of women's disadvantage in the industrial labour market. The statistical associations relate primarily to the hypothesis that women's earnings are depressed by women's 'overcrowding' into a narrow range of jobs.[15]

Studies elsewhere have found an inverse relationship between feminization of employment and the earning of both men and women.[16] A priori, however, there is no reason to presume that occupational or industrial

[14] The regression function controlled for the influence of industry, employment size, ownership of firm, and export orientation. The results and estimates of an occupational crowding index are presented in a longer version of this paper. G. Standing, 'Cumulative Disadvantage?' (Geneva: ILO, 1992).

[15] Edgeworth, 'Equal Pay to Men and Women'; Bergmann, 'Occupational Segregation'.

[16] See e.g. M. Tienda, S. A. Smith, and V. Ortiz, 'Industrial Restructuring, Gender Segregation and Sex Differences in Earnings', *American Sociological Review*, 52/2 (Apr. 1987); F. Bettio, 'Secular Decrease of Sex-linked Wage Differentials: A Case of Non-union Competition', *Economia e Lavoro*, 19/3 (July–Sept. 1985); F. D. Blau and A. H. Beller, 'Trends in Earnings Differentials by Gender, 1971–81', *Industrial and Labour Relations Review*, 41/4 (July, 1988). For a dissenting view, see OECD, 'Women's Activity, Employment and Earnings: A Review of Recent Developments', in *Employment Outlook 1988* (Paris: OECD, 1988).

Table 22 Average monthly wages and earnings, by female share of employment, Malaysia, 1988 (Malaysian ringgit) (mean wage/earnings in each female-share category)

	Per cent female						
	0	0.1–5	5.1–10	10.1–25	25.1–50	50.1–75	75.+
Mean wage	442.8	469.6	505.3	474.5	388.3	327.1	308.1
Mean earnings	511.6	560.8	616.8	557.3	457.4	386.5	370.9

crowding, or segregation, would be linked to overall earnings. Indeed, in the USA, one study reported that once industry differences were taken into account, being employed in a female-dominated occupation only lowered earnings by a small amount.[17] A crucial point is that if there is a crowding effect on wages, then a policy of comparable worth would be justified.

The following sections cover average earnings, average wages of men and women separately, average wages of occupational groups, and gender-related wage differentials.

Average earnings

It is clear that in Malaysia, beyond a minimal level, the larger the female share of total employment the lower the overall *average* wage of regular workers (Table 22). One might suppose that this reflected both lower wage rates paid to women and a tendency for women to be in the lower-wage jobs, issues to which we turn shortly. However, the level of *average earnings* varied enormously in firms with different female shares of employment. Table 23 is reproduced to stress that many of the plants in which women comprised the bulk of the workforce were paying very low wages and benefits, barely sufficient to meet subsistence needs.

Estimates of earnings functions, in which the dependent variable was the logarithm of average hourly wages or the logarithm of average monthly earnings, showed that for Malaysian industry, even controlling for skill composition, industry, size of firm, ownership, extent of casualization, past employment growth, and unionization, establishments with high shares of women workers were relatively low paying.[18] The causal relationship may be debatable, but the association is disquieting.

[17] G. Johnson and G. Solon, 'Estimates of the Direct Effects of Comparable Worth Policy', *American Economic Review*, 76/5 (1986), 1117–25.
[18] The full results are presented in Standing, 'Cumulative Disadvantage?'

Table 23 Distribution of average earnings, by per cent female, Malaysia, 1988 (Malaysian ringgit) (per cent distribution in each female-share category)

Per cent female	Average monthly earnings					
	0–300	301–400	401–500	501–600	601–800	801+
0	20.4	20.4	16.8	13.2	20.5	8.4
0.1–10	5.6	9.7	23.3	23.1	22.8	15.5
10.01–25	8.0	15.1	22.4	17.4	24.8	12.1
25.01–50	19.6	25.6	23.9	12.8	12.1	6.0
50.01–75	30.3	31.1	20.0	11.0	5.5	2.1
75.01+	28.9	29.9	27.2	8.7	4.9	0.3

Comparable earnings functions were estimated for the Philippines. Although there were differences with respect to some of the other variables, there was a similarly strong inverse relationship between feminization of employment and average earnings. Interestingly, if we omit the proxy variable for 'labour intensiveness', the inverse relationship emerged more strongly.

Average wages by gender

For the Philippines, regression functions for male and female wages were also estimated separately. Average wages seemed higher in firms with less segregated workforces, that is, those that were not either mainly male or mainly female.

Among the main points from the male and female wage functions are that the industrial sectors in which men earned relatively high (or low) wages were also those in which women earned relatively high (or low) wages compared to women workers in other firms. Both men and women earned relatively high wages in foreign-owned firms. However, the higher the women's share of total employment the lower women's wages, controlling for other influences; for men, the coefficient was not statistically significant, although it was also negative.

Wage differentials by gender

The next stage in the discrimination or disadvantage process is the wage differential between men and women. Wage discrimination may take many complementary *or* compensating forms—different starting wages, smaller or fewer increments, fewer fringe payments, and so on. Moreover, average wages are not ideal proxies for identifying discrimination, since they combine

Table 24 Average monthly wage of occupational groups, by sex, by establishment size, Philippines, 1990 (monthly, in pesos)

Emp. size	Skilled			Unskilled			Prof./Tech.		
	Male	Female	M/F	Male	Female	M/F	Male	Female	M/F
1–20	2274	2117	1.07	2110	1603	1.32	3786	3863	0.98
21–50	2733	2526	1.08	2242	2127	1.05	4883	4085	1.20
51–100	2897	2860	1.01	2497	2348	1.06	5135	4493	1.14
101–250	3111	2786	1.12	2646	2556	1.04	5380	4907	1.10
251–500	3117	2846	1.10	2627	2600	1.01	5260	4974	1.06
501–1000	3289	3241	1.01	2610	2548	1.02	5423	5270	1.03
1001+	3571	3465	1.03	2937	3106	0.95	5745	5251	1.09
Total	2897	2803	1.03	2484	2464	1.01	5171	4732	1.09

supply-side behavioural factors as well as demand-side discriminatory influences. So, differentials in average wages are slightly ambiguous indices of discrimination. With that proviso, basic patterns can be discerned, although one might quibble about the exact meaning of the data.

First, in both Malaysia and the Philippines, in a small minority of firms women's average wages were actually higher than men's for broadly equivalent skill levels. Second, the distribution of firms by the ratio of male to female wages was far more bunched around equality in the Philippines than in Malaysia. Third, in Malaysia, the wage ratio for skilled workers indicated that in many firms men received over 50 per cent more than their female colleagues. The exception was the electronics industry, where in one in every five firms women received more than men. In the Philippines, in that sector, wage equality for skilled workers seemed remarkably close.

For semi-skilled workers, more firms in both countries had women's average wages higher than men's, but again the differentials were larger in Malaysia. Only for unskilled workers did more firms in Malaysia pay women higher wages. A possible reason is that more firms there *classified* more women's jobs as unskilled. Even so, the proportion of firms paying much higher wages to men was far greater in Malaysia.

In both countries, gender-based wage differentials were greater in small firms, for skilled, semi-skilled, and unskilled workers. For all occupational groups, there was a fairly linear relation between firm size and level of average wage, for both men and women, as illustrated for the Philippines in Table 24. Indeed this table suggests that much of the differential wage between men and women could be explained by firm size.

The higher the occupational level, the higher the probability that men were earning higher wages than women.[19] And in both countries, for unskilled workers (although not for other groups), the higher the share of employment taken by women the lower women's relative wage. Direct correlations also suggest that in Malaysia, although not in the Philippines, the more women relative to men in a plant the lower female *and* male wages.[20]

Gender wage differentials were apparently smaller in Malaysian-owned firms than in multinationals, for all skill levels. The final relation that deserves to be stressed is that in Malaysia the presence of a trades union was associated with a narrower gender wage differential among skilled, semi-skilled, and unskilled categories.[21]

For Malaysia, we can also say a little about *changes* in relative wages. Controlling for the gender composition of employment, in nearly 27 per cent of all establishments wages of female skilled workers had risen in the previous year, whereas wages of male skilled workers had risen in fewer than 22 per cent of all firms. Moreover, women's wages were more likely to have risen, regardless of the change in total employment over the previous two years.

CONCLUSIONS

In Malaysia, female labour-force participation and the female share of manufacturing employment rose in the 1980s, as they did in many countries.[22] The MLFS data show that in the industrial labour market, feminization of employment was sustained through the serious recession of the mid-1980s and that it could be expected to continue. The continuing trend to greater export-oriented production was promoting this, a pattern that one would expect in the many other countries that have been shifting to

[19] Others have also reported an absence of gender-related wage differentials in the Malaysian electronics industry. For instance, the Ministry of Labour's 1983 Occupational Wage Survey reported that the average daily wage rates of female material handlers was M$13.3, whereas the male average was only M$10.5.

[20] In industrialized countries, the tendency for earnings differentials to increase with the level of the occupational hierarchy has been widely reported, though not universally. Thus it has been observed in France, where it has been attributed to the effect of minimum-wage legislation, but not in (West) Germany, where there is no minimum wage. D. Depardieu and J. F. Payeu, 'Disparités des salaires dans l'industrie en France et en Allemagne: Des ressemblances frappantes', *Economie et Statistiques*, 188 (May 1986).

[21] For details see G. Standing, 'Do Unions Impede or Accelerate Structural Adjustment? Industrial versus Company Unions in an Industrialising Labour Market', *Cambridge Journal of Economics*, 16 (Sept. 1992), 327–54.

[22] For trends in Malaysian labour-force participation, see A. Cheshire, *Labour Force Participation in Malaysia* (Report prepared for the ILO-EPU Human Resource Development Project, 1989, mimeo); for international trends on participation and manufacturing employment, see Standing, 'Global Feminization', esp. tables 3 and 5.

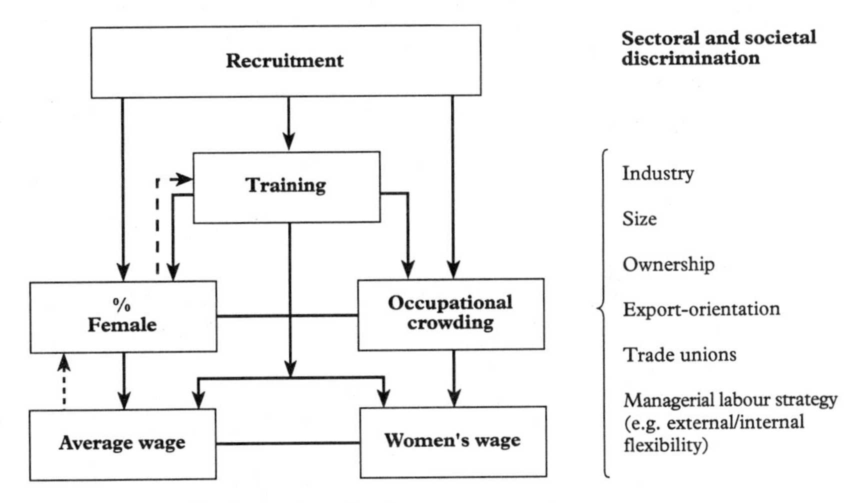

Figure 1 The discrimination disadvantage process

export-led industrialization strategies.[23] Moreover, while women's wage earnings remained below those of their male counterparts, there is evidence that job segregation was declining and that women's relative wages were rising. But one should not be too sanguine. Feminization of employment in Malaysia was also associated with more precarious labour relations.

In the Philippines, discrimination against women in terms of recruitment, training, and wages was persisting in the context of recently strengthened legislative commitment to sexual equality in the labour market, including a national plan for women and a Dutch-funded technical assistance project, 'Women in New Trades', designed to help promote women's access to a wide range of occupations.

This chapter has attempted to create building blocks for a systematic analysis of the process of discrimination, segregation, and cumulative disadvantage. Figure 1 illustrates, somewhat crudely, the implicit theoretical model that we have postulated. The solid arrows and lines indicate the main hypotheses, as supported by the statistical analysis, and the dotted arrows indicate possible links that would modify or accentuate the strength of those statistical findings. Thus, discrimination at the hiring stage influences the share of employment taken by women, and this influences the average wage, the wage of women workers, and the male–female wage ratios. An intervening variable is training. The data for the Philippines show pervasive discrimination against women in that sphere, and that must influence the share of jobs taken by women as well as their share of

[23] However, if should be noted that some observers question the trend towards feminization of manufacturing employment, as hypothesized here and elsewhere.

higher-level jobs and their relative wages. But there is also the likelihood of feedback effects, some strengthening segregation, some potentially weakening it. Thus, if a high female share of employment lowers female wages *more than* male wages, then one might expect employers to adjust their recruitment to employ more women. By contrast, if discriminatory hiring reduces the female share of employment to a low level, that might accentuate discriminatory hiring practices *and* deter women from applying to such firms.

In sum, the approach this research tries to follow is one based on the view that discrimination and labour-market disadvantage take multiple, cumulative forms, and should not be depicted in simple terms of one or other barrier to equal opportunity.

The Nordic Model of Gender Equality: The Welfare State, Patriarchy, and Unfinished Emancipation

Tuovi Allén

INTRODUCTION

What effects have the economic and social development processes had on gender relations in Nordic welfare states? How has the Nordic model of gender equality in the labour market affected patriarchy? Has patriarchy been undermined or has it been strengthened in new forms? What has been the effect of mass employment of women and state intervention in the economy and in social reproduction? Has it changed the public–private split of the society, or has there only been a change from private to public patriarchy? These are among the important questions raised by the research on the status of women in Nordic economies.

Nordic (or Scandinavian) societies have often been regarded as more progressive than other Western societies, as well as socially committed to justice and equality. Sometimes Nordic countries have even been regarded as ideals of gender equality or at least 'women-friendly societies'. Many researchers have still recognized several backlashes of the Nordic model, the problems which are discussed in this paper. The most pressing current question is, will the Nordic model survive after the deep recession of the early 1990s?

The special features of Nordic (or Scandinavian) economies have recently been studied from various different viewpoints.[1] Among industrialized countries the Nordic countries have been found to represent a particular model of (1) distributional policies and welfare state (Alestalo and Uusitalo, 1986; Kosonen, 1987; Ringen and Uusitalo, 1991), (2) general macro-

An earlier draft of this chapter was presented to the Fourth Annual International Conference of The Society for the Advancement of Socio-Economics (SASE), at the University of California, Irvine, March 1992. The revised version was presented at the UNU/WIDER conference on 'Trajectories of Development and Patriarchy', July 1992. The comments of the participants of both conferences are gratefully acknowledged. I owe my special thanks to Valentine Moghadam for many stimulating discussions and encouraging support of my work.

[1] Sweden, Norway, Denmark, and Iceland are called Scandinavian countries. Nordic countries are Sweden, Norway, Denmark, and Finland. Because the data concerning Iceland is not always available, Iceland is not considered here. It is worth mentioning that Denmark is an EC country bur here it is not included in EC averages unless specified.

economic policies (Mjoeset, 1986; Pekkarinen, 1990), as well as (3) labour-market institutions, wage setting, and collective bargaining (Pekkarinen, 1990; Pekkarinen, Pohjola, and Rowthorn, 1992). These characteristics have often been labelled as (1) universal welfare state, (2) Keynesian interventionism, and (3) social corporatism. Last but not least, all these characteristics have been argued to have advanced the economic success of Nordic countries during the last three decades or longer.

In macro-economic policies—until the economic recession of the 1990s—the Nordic countries have succeeded in combining stable and high economic growth and labour-market stability with greater social and economic equality within the population than in other Western countries. These three shared aspects of Nordic economies permit a discussion of the 'Nordic Model'.

The main interest of this chapter is to consider the development process of Nordic economies especially from the point of view of gender equality in the Nordic labour market. The aim of this chapter is to (1) outline the general characteristics of the Nordic model of gender equality, and (2) characterize the national differences between individual countries. Only Denmark, Finland, Norway, and Sweden are considered, but comparisons to EC countries and other industrialized countries are occasionally made to emphasize the distinctive features of the Nordic model.

Although equal-opportunity policies have often been assumed to have affected the promotion of gender equality in these societies, I will argue that the impact of general economic policies—including welfare state and corporatism—has been even more important. This is crucial because the effects of economic policies may have been rather controversial in the Nordic area from the point of view of gender equality. On the one hand, differences (e.g. segregation) between women and men may have increased. On the other hand, gender divisions (e.g. pay differentials) may have narrowed. The important question then arises: what kind of effects have economic policies had on gender relations and patriarchy in general?

In this chapter I begin by describing the Nordic model of economic policy, and then I consider the legislative actions and equal-opportunity policies of different Nordic countries. The main part of the chapter examines the labour-market performance and labour-market structures in Nordic countries from the point of view of gender divisions. Finally, the Nordic model of gender equality is evaluated. How complete is it? Can it ever be complete in patriarchal society, or is there a profound trade-off between one kind of equality and one kind of inequality? Is it correct to characterize the Nordic model as 'unfinished emancipation', where private patriarchy has been undermined while public patriarchy has been strengthened? Are Nordic women only choosing between two imperfect situations without having full citizenship?

ECONOMIC POLICY—WELFARE STATE AND CORPORATISM

Development strategies

In less than a hundred years, the Nordic societies were transformed from less developed and agricultural economies into some of the world's most prosperous economies, with ambitious distribution programmes that permit the benefits of economic progress to be enjoyed by all citizens, women and men equally. It should be noted that the Nordic countries were, in fact, among the poorest in Europe a century ago: agriculture dominated the economy and much of the land was owned by a few people.[2]

During the nineteenth century these countries were in many respects comparable to developing countries of today (for example, the Latin American countries; see Blomström and Meller, 1991). A unique feature of Nordic societies is that economic development was based on a free-peasant economy rather than feudal serfdom. Agrarian society in Nordic countries was founded on a high share of female labour, as well as a distinct division of work by gender. If agricultural labour—waged or not—is accounted for, about 65 per cent of all women of working age in Finland have been economically active since the 1860s. Until the mid-1980s there has not been any further increase in the female participation rates, but instead a transformation of female labour from agriculture to industrial and service sectors (Allén, 1991).[3]

Nordic countries are often regarded as early and advanced 'social-market economies' combining predominantly private ownership in a competitive market setting with activist government policies aimed at (1) egalitarian distribution of income, (2) providing insurance against loss of income, and (3) removing negative 'externalities' of the market economy. These policies were of limited importance before the Second World War but expanded rapidly thereafter, first in Sweden and Denmark and more recently in Norway and Finland. Finland especially has been lagging behind the other Nordic countries both in industrialization and welfare-state policies (e.g. Kosonen, 1987).

[2] The economic transformation from agricultural to industrial society was not concurrent in all Nordic countries. Sweden was already a highly industrialized economy between the world wars, but more than 80% of the Finnish population earned their living from agriculture until the Second World War. Since then the process of industrialization and economic growth has been most rapid in Finland.

[3] In Finland in 1860 more than 85% of the economically active population and 58% of all women of working age were employed in the agricultural sector. During the 1930s these shares were 70% and 40% respectively. In 1987 only 10% of the economically active population and 6% of women of working age were employed in agriculture. About 45% of married women were in the labour market in the 1950s (Allén, 1991). There are no comparative statistics from other Nordic countries, but it can be expected that the shares and trends have been rather similar to those of Finland.

The period from the mid-nineteenth century until the Second World War can be denoted the 'development phase', while the period thereafter can be called the 'welfare phase' (Wihlborg, 1992). For example, at the beginning of the welfare phase the per capita income in Sweden was at the level of Taiwan today. From the development point of view we can easily find some similarities between the Nordic countries during the development phase and developing countries of today (e.g. NICs of Asia). During the period of 1870–1970 the average per capita growth rate of GDP in Sweden was higher than in any other country except Japan. During the period of 1960–90 Finland took the top position—after Japan.

An interesting question is, how have the welfare state and high female participation rates contributed to the rapid economic growth rate and accumulation of capital in Nordic countries? There is some evidence that economic growth has continued and even accelerated during the welfare phase (Wihlborg, 1992). One explanation for this phenomenon can be that the government sector has been a net saver during the welfare phase in Nordic economies, especially in Finland (e.g. Kosonen, 1989). Another explanation may be that government policies accepted the private ownership of industry and financial institutions while recognizing the need for mobility of labour and structural change with minimum social conflict.

The foundations for the development and growth strategies were laid during the nineteenth century and early twentieth century. Wihlborg (1992) has pointed out the important background to the early and rapid development process in these countries: (1) educational reforms, (2) deregulatory policies and free trade, (3) infrastructural investments (railroads), (4) large stocks of raw materials (timber, iron), (5) technological innovations (paper and pulp during the 1930s), (6) migration and urbanization, (7) unregulated financial system (commercial banks), and (8) homogeneous population (no numerous ethnic minorities). According to Wihlborg these prerequisites have supported democratic development and early citizenship rights, political pluralism, and strong civil society in Nordic countries.

It has often been argued that the cultural and ethnic homogeneity have contributed to making the Nordic countries 'consensus-seeking' societies and made it possible to build up a large public sector and uncorrupt class of civil servants, most of whom are women. Such factors may also explain to some extent both the conflict-free economic development and the acceptability of the relatively heavy tax burden.

Behind the different national development strategies of Nordic economies can also be found some historical facts. Sweden and Denmark—both traditional monarchies—are examples of countries were institutions balancing diverse interests have developed over a long time. In contrast Finland is an example of a country that was colonized for a long time: by Sweden until 1810, and by Russia until 1917. This explains the delayed institutional reforms and industrialization in Finland.

Economic policy models

The Nordic economies have many characteristics in common which make them interesting from the point of view of general economic policies. Although there are profound similarities in policies and economic performance, there are still several national differences. The main difference between individual countries after the Second World War has been the national priorities of economic policy targets: accumulation of capital, full employment, or equal distribution of income (Mjoeset, 1986; Kosonen, 1987). The national priorities of course depend upon the background conditions of these economies: investments required by the export sector, the share of wage earners and farmers of the population, or the proportional strength of different political groups (e.g. social-democratic, bourgeois, or agrarian parties) in the society concerned.

All Nordic countries are small, open economies with rather one-sided industrial structure.[4] The *Swedish model* of economic policy has been characterized by the goal of full employment, stable and solidaristic wage formation, egalitarian distribution, and active state intervention by means of fiscal policies. The Swedish model is often characterized as 'social democratic' because of the primacy of redistributional targets. The *Norwegian model* comes rather close to the Swedish one, but it is more 'pragmatic' and oriented to supporting industrialization, accumulation, and the growth of investments.[5]

The *Finnish model* of economic policy can be characterized as growth oriented: the prior target has been the competitiveness of export industries (paper and pulp). Social reforms and redistribution of income have been secondary goals in the Finnish model, and therefore it has often been called 'bourgeois' when compared to other Nordic countries. The *Danish model* can be characterized as 'liberal' and oriented to growth and modernization. Denmark has also been an EC member since 1973, while other Nordic countries only applied for membership in the early 1990s. The detailed characterization of Nordic economic policy models have been developed by Mjoeset (1986) and Kosonen (1987).

[4] The Nordic countries have been—and still are—strongly dependent on foreign trade: (1) the exports of raw materials or intermediate products, and (2) the imports of consumer durables and/or energy. Finland has been exporting paper and pulp and importing energy. Norway has earlier exported mainly fishery products but later also energy and raw oil. The Danish economy relies heavily on agricultural exports to EC markets. The industrial structure of Sweden is more modern, relying on production and exports of high technology (e.g. cars, telecommunication, investment products).

[5] Direct financial support from the government budget to private industrial enterprises has been the crucial means of active economic policies in Norway, but not in other Nordic countries. In Finland the government has instead supported export industries by means of tax deductions and exchange-rate policies (i.e. devaluation of the currency in case of declining price competitiveness of export industries).

Welfare state

The Nordic model of welfare-state and redistribution policies has been called universal in opposition to the marginal (or means-tested) policies typical of many central European countries and North America (Alestalo and Uusitalo, 1986; Kosonen, 1987; Uusitalo, 1988). Universal welfare states are founded on the principle of equal opportunities of citizens, extensive welfare services, and transfer programmes. The universal policies and high public spending on welfare purposes have promoted more equal distribution of income and higher economic standards of living (Uusitalo, 1988). The Nordic welfare programmes cover the total population—irrespective of waged work—aiming at both vertically and horizontally equal distribution.

Although the gender aspect has not been at the forefront of the redistribution policies, the welfare state has resulted in a rather preferential status of women compared to other European countries. The idea of social welfare based on equal citizenship rights has not only advanced democracy, but it has also resulted in the greater equality of opportunity between women and men in the labour market (Hernes, 1988; Siim, 1991). Since the 1960s the public sector—especially the welfare state—has been the most important employer of women in all Nordic countries. Most of the traditional tasks of the household (e.g. caring for and nurturing of children, aged, and handicapped) have been transformed to 'market goods' produced by female waged labour in the public sector. Private supply of welfare services has actually been of marginal importance in Nordic countries during the welfare phase. This kind of welfare policies (e.g. transfer payments, public child-care services) have supported the economic emancipation and employment of women outside households.

Corporatism

An important ingredient of national development strategies in Nordic countries has been corporatism. During the period 1920–50 the participants of corporatist policies were the capital and the state: the government policies were targeted at promoting capital accumulation of private (export) sector. After the Second World War working-class movements became stronger and the third party of corporatist policies rose during the 1960s: labour, represented by confederations of trade unions. This has often been called a 'class compromise' between capital, state, and labour.

Nordic countries—Sweden, Norway, Denmark, and Finland—have kept to a particular form of collective bargaining and negotiating labour relations since the 1960s. The corporatist labour-market model includes strong, centralized confederations of employers and employees negotiating wages, other work-related benefits, as well as many important welfare programmes provided by the state. In Finland the state has been an active party in the bargaining system, while the state has played a minor role in other Nordic countries.

Union membership has been exceptionally high in all Nordic countries, ranging nowadays from 62 per cent in Norway to almost 90 per cent in Sweden (Fletcher and Gill, 1992). The union density of women is about the same as that of men, while in other European countries women are lagging far behind men. In Finland the majority (53 per cent) of union members have been women since the early 1980s, while in North America women's share of union members is below 30 per cent. In Nordic countries women's share of union membership grew rapidly during the 1970s (apart from Norway), but women's share of union leadership has not grown as rapidly as union density: top positions are still occupied by men.

During the 1970s and 1980s the Nordic model of centralized corporatism helped to sustain a faster and more stable rate of economic growth, higher level of employment, and smaller average wage differentials than the economies with more decentralized, or market-based, bargaining systems (Pekkarinen, Pohjola, and Rowthorn, 1992). During this period the Nordic model of corporatism succeeded in combining the targets of equality and economic efficiency in a way that has maintained good economic performance and preserved the cohesion of the existing institutions (see Rowthorn, 1989; Pekkarinen, 1990). There is also some weak empirical evidence that corporatism has been rather beneficial to women: the higher the union density of women the larger the relative growth of women's wages (Fletcher and Gill, 1992).

As far as the institutions bearing on industrial relations are concerned, all Nordic countries rank relatively highly on various scales that are used to indicate the degree of corporatism: union density, centralization of wage bargaining, involvement of interest organizations in economic and social policy design, and low number of strikes (Calmfors and Driffill, 1988). During the 1970s and 1980s these countries (except Denmark) achieved high employment and unemployment rates remained low, while real wages have been rather flexible. In Nordic countries there has not been any remarkable difference between the male and female unemployment rate. The wage dispersion across industries was relatively small and tended to narrow until the late 1980s. This was a result of heavy reliance on progressive income taxation as a revenue source for the public sector. This fact can be expected to have contributed to narrowing the gender gap in the economy during the welfare phase.

One pertinent question is whether the corporatist system has advanced gender equality. It could also be asked whether the economic policy model rather than equal opportunities policies have been the key factors behind the advancement of women's status in the labour market.

Most studies on Nordic economies have touched upon equality in the labour market and economy: none of them has considered gender equality *as such*. According to various measures, gender equality has been achieved more fully in Nordic economies than in other industrialized countries. This kind of argumentation rests on some stylized facts on labour-market performance rather than any deeper analysis of the role of different kinds of policies. Moreover, national differences in the achievement of gender equality have received minor attention even though the national models are rather different.

EQUAL PAY AND EQUAL EMPLOYMENT OPPORTUNITIES POLICIES

It has often been argued that cultural and political factors have contributed to making the Nordic economies consensus-seeking and rather conflict free. The political culture of the Nordic countries has placed a high value on the principles of social equality as a route to democracy (Siim, 1991). One original feature of Nordic countries is that their citizens apparently have a different attitude towards the government from most other Western countries: in Nordic countries the state is rather seen as a tool to be used, not something to be feared, or respected, or worshipped (Siim, 1991). For example, government interventions in social reproduction (and family) have been regarded as beneficial: from the viewpoint of both national economic policy strategies and emancipation of women. This attitude towards the state has had important and positive implications for gender equality, and it contrasts strongly with the Anglo-Saxon idea that the individual and the family should be protected against state involvement.

However, the tradition of state regulation of gender equality—often called 'state feminism' (Siim, 1991)—is remarkably long in Nordic countries. This does not mean that Nordic countries had been the pioneers of equal-opportunity policies as such: actually they have been lagging behind. Instead state regulation by means of welfare policies and corporatism has, in fact, laid a strong foundation for the early emergence of women's employment, early transformation of women's employment from agriculture to industries and services, and massive integration of women into productive activities outside the household. Table 1 shows some historical milestones in the process towards gender equality in Nordic countries.

The United States has been the pioneer of equal-rights legislation during the 1960s. In EC countries equal pay has in principle been regulated since the EEC Treaty in 1957, and the special directives of equal pay and equal employment opportunities were implemented in 1975–6. Compared to EC countries the legislation on equality was adopted rather late in Nordic countries: following the EEC Treaty many EC countries had already passed their national legislation on gender equality before the Nordic countries,

Table 1 Milestones of gender equality in Nordic countries: equal rights for women

Women's right to	Denmark	Finland	Iceland	Norway	Sweden
Equal inheritance	1857	always	1850	1854	1845
Majority					
unmarried women	1857	1864	1861	1863	1858
married women	1988	1930	1900	1888	1921
Suffrage					
municipal	1908	1918	1909	1910	1919
parliament	1915	1906	1915	1913	1919
Academic degree	1875	1901	1911	1884	1873
State office	1921	1926	1911	1938	1925
Priesthood	1947	1988	1911	1952	1958
Equal pay in[a]					
public sector	1919	1962	1945	1959	1947
private sector	1973	1962	1961	1961	1960
Equality in[b]					
labour market	1978	—	1973	—	1980
general	—	1987	1976	1978	—
Equal parental leave[c]	1984	1978	1980	1978	1974

[a] Date refers to the abolition of gender-specific wage schedules, or implementation of collective agreements of corporatist parties or separate legislation.
[b] Date refers to the equality act and its scope (if the law covers only labour-market issues or if it is general).
[c] Date refers to special legislation giving mother and father an equal right to parental leave. Before this date only mothers had the right.
Source: *Women and Men in the Nordic Countries: Facts on Equal Opportunities* (Nordic Council of Ministers, 1988).

and also before the EEC Council Directives on equal pay and equal employment opportunities were implemented.

However, it is easier to understand the timing if one looks at the motives of EC equality policies. The main motivation for the EC norms concerning gender equality has not been gender equality as such, but instead the requirements to 'fair' competition and efficient functioning of the common market (Landau, 1986). On the one hand, the Equal Pay Act of the EEC treaty was needed to prevent the dumping of labour costs, for example, by means of transforming production from high-wage economies to the member countries with excess supply of low-paid female labour. On the other hand, the equality policies were designed to function as economic incentives to increase female labour-force participation when the supply of labour was deficient in the EC area.

Instead of special equality policies, the early realization of equal citizenship rights has often been argued to be the most important underlying factor for economic equality between women and men in Nordic countries during the first half of this century. Several factors contributed to changes in women's citizenship and economic status after the Second World War in these countries. The rapid economic growth and high demand for labour caused a massive entry of women (from households and agriculture) to the labour market. This means that since the 1950s and 1960s Nordic women have become increasingly dependent on their own paid work, and the husband's role as an economic provider has been reduced. However, the European model of family wage and the male provider has never been dominant in the Nordic labour market: the male-breadwinner model has always been rather weak in the Nordic agrarian society.

The emergence of female employment in Nordic countries has been rapid and seemingly irreversible: many important sectors of the economy are dependent on female labour. Since the late 1960s the welfare state came to substitute husbands as economic providers and started to take over the female role of caring. Women accepted the dual role of the welfare state, as it allowed them to become wage labourers in the public sector as well as major clients of the social-service system (e.g. child care and education).

However, it is important to note that the policies of the Nordic welfare state did not intend to create equality between women and men in the family, economy, or society. The emergence of gender equality and economic emancipation of women were rather by-products of the modernization process of Nordic market economies. This means that growing markets created excess demand for labour, and the growth of female labour supply raised in turn an increasing need for specific policies of equal employment opportunities.

In Nordic countries this process has been rather adverse compared to EC countries. At first, women entered the non-agricultural labour market during the 1950s and 1960s, and after that equality policies were activated during the 1970s and 1980s to abolish labour market discrimination. Nordic equality policies derived from a kind of 'fine-tuning' of labour relations, and from the principles of social ethics and the Nordic approach to democracy—not from any feminist motives or the power of a feminist movement.

If the equality policy of the European Community lacks feminist origins, so does the Nordic equality policy. In these countries—especially in Finland—the question of economic emancipation of women was linked to a wider social vision of a better future for all citizens—not only for women. In Nordic countries there was a strong belief that the exploitation of women could be abolished in conjunction with wider social and political reforms (e.g. universal social security, labour protection, class organizations). This kind of thinking was parallel to the reformist policies of social democrats in Nordic governments since the early 1960s.

GENDER, EQUALITY, AND LABOUR-MARKET PERFORMANCE

The economic status of Nordic and other Western women differs in many important respects. In the following sections labour-market performance is considered from the point of view of gender divisions. First, the labour-force participation of women as well as the age profiles of female labour-force participation are considered. Second, unemployment and emergence of atypical forms of employment among women are discussed. Third, degree of occupational segregation and wage gender gap are considered. Finally, all these labour-market structures are held up against the degree of government involvement and corporatism to find out the impact of economic policy stategies on gender equality.

Labour-force participation of women

Cross-country differences in women's integration in the labour market is often described by the labour-force participation rate of women in the working age (15–64 years old). In Nordic countries the share of women in the total labour force is almost half: in Sweden 47.9, in Finland 47.1, in Norway 44.4, and in Denmark 45.7 per cent. In EC countries the share of women in the total labour force is between 30.7 per cent (Ireland) and 42.8 per cent (France). The average activity rate of women in EC countries was 41.2 per cent and women counted 38 per cent of the total employment in 1988 (CEC, 1990).[6] (See Table 2.)

The labour-force participation rates are remarkably higher in Nordic countries (including Denmark) than in the rest of the OECD area. Among industrialized counties the lowest female participation rates are found in EC countries. However, it is noteworthy that the labour-force participation rates of Nordic women were already higher in 1973 than in most EC countries in 1990. The relative labour-market activity (measured by the labour-force participation rate of women to men) of Nordic women has also been remarkably higher than in the rest of the Western world. For example, the labour input of Swedish women is 95 per cent of the input of men, while in EC countries this figure is only 60 per cent on average.

When comparing female labour-market activity among OECD countries, four factors behind the Nordic figures must be noticed. First, the education standard of women is higher and the average duration of

[6] CEC is a shorthand for The Comission of the European Communities, and here refers to a publication of the EC.

Table 2 The labour-force participation rate of women (%) and women/men ratio in Nordic countries, EC countries, and other OECD countries, 1973 and 1990

	Rate of Women		Rate of Women/ Men
	1973	1990	1990
Nordic countries	59.7	75.7	0.89
Finland	63.6	72.9	0.90
Norway	50.6	71.2	0.84
Sweden	62.6	81.5	0.95
Denmark	61.9	77.3	0.86
EC countries (excluding Denmark)	38.2	50.1	0.63
Other OECD	48.8	62.2	0.72
Total OECD	48.2	60.0	0.72

Source: *OECD Employment Outlook 1991.*

schooling is longer in Nordic countries than in the OECD area on average. This means that the younger age cohorts of women tend to enter the labour market later. Second, the proportion of women of working age engaged in full-time housework is remarkably low in all Nordic countries.[7] This means that promoting female labour supply is not a policy issue in Nordic countries nowadays. Third, the variation of annual working hours of women is great among Nordic countries, depending on the popularity of part-time work. If the labour input of women were compared in terms of annual working-hours, that of Finnish women would be the highest since the standard form of female employment in Finland is full-time work (Allén, 1992). Fourth, the high share of public spending of GDP has supported the creation of employment opportunities for women in the welfare state.

From a long-term, historical perspective, the rapid growth of female labour-force participation rates (i.e. waged labour) appears to be a relatively recent phenomenon all over the world. In the long run the female labour-force participation has been growing fastest in Nordic countries, which have also started from higher levels of female economic activity after the Second World War (OECD, 1988: 130). The most rapid growth in female labour-force participation from 1967 until 1990 has taken place

[7] Towards the end of the 1980s the proportion of women (age 25–54 years) engaged in full-time housework was about 17% in Norway, 13% in Iceland, 8% in Denmark, 7% in Finland, and 5% in Sweden (Nordic Council of Ministers, 1988).

in Norway, but the increase in Sweden, Denmark, and Finland has also been in a class of their own. The growth of female labour-force participation has also been more rapid in non-European OECD countries (e.g. the USA and Canada) than in EC countries (except Portugal).

The population dynamics and fertility behaviour of women also direct the labour-force participation of women. The age profiles of female participation usually have two distinctive features in Western countries. First, they differ from the profiles of men both in their levels and shapes. Second, the female age profiles have usually either one peak in younger age groups, or two peaks the one of which is located in the youngest and the other in elderly age groups. When considering the age profiles of female labour-force participation, the curve of an inverted U-shape or plateau, is now characteristic for the countries with the highest participation rates (e.g. Finland, Sweden, Norway, and the USA in the 1980s (OECD, 1988)). These kinds of female age profile are almost identical to those of men in all Nordic countries, but especially in Sweden and Finland.

The gradual upward movement of the female age profiles during the 1970s and 1980s in many countries (e.g. Canada, France, and Italy) means that the youngest age-cohorts of women are not withdrawing from the labour market when they have passed their child-bearing years. This means that the previously peaked or mountain-with-valley-shaped age profiles may be transforming to plateaus or inverted U-shaped participation profiles in most Western countries. Still, in many EC countries the labour-force participation rates decline striking in the most fertile female age groups (e.g. Germany, the Netherlands, and Ireland), evidently because of the lack of child-care services.

In many industrialized countries female labour-market activity is strongly dependent on the marital status and the number of small children, but also on the changes in the volume of GDP. In the countries where the participation rates of women are low and mainly due to the activity of unmarried women, female labour is typically secondary and women form a flexible labour reserve. In Nordic countries—especially in Sweden and Finland—the relationship between the changes of female labour-force participation and economic fluctuations broke down during the 1970s: since then Nordic women have belonged to the primary labour force. This phenomenon has often been explained by the development of the welfare state and the increase of the service sector (both public and private) which have permanently maintained high demand for female labour.

Atypical employment and unemployment by gender

Opportunities to work outside the home means for some women reluctant acceptance of non-standard or atypical employment. Main forms of atypical employment are part-time and temporary work. During the 1980s

Table 3 The share of part-time work in women's employment (1) and the share of women in part-time labour (2) in Nordic countries, EC countries, and other OECD countries, 1979 and 1990 (%)

	(1) 1979	(1) 1990	(2) 1990
Nordic countries	41.6	35.1	78.2
Finland	12.5	10.2	67.8
Sweden	45.9	40.5	83.7
Norway	63.3	48.2	81.8
Denmark			
EC countries (excluding Denmark)	21.5	23.7	76.9
Other OECD	28.6	29.5	75.8
Total OECD	27.4	27.5	76.8

Source: *OECD Employment Outlook 1991.*

women's part-time employment has been increasing in EC countries but declining in Nordic countries and in some non-European OECD countries (Table 3). Both of these atypical forms of employment are more often involuntary than free choices (CEC, 1990). Many temporary jobs are also part time, which means that women's employment is still more precarious than men's unemployment.

The volume and incidence of atypical employment varies a lot among industrialized countries, but still the Nordic countries are in a class of their own. In Table 3 the share of part-time work in women's employment and the share of women in part-time labour are shown. Women's share of part-time labour is on average 77 per cent in the OECD area and slightly more, 78 per cent, in Nordic countries. If Finland were excluded from the Nordic averages, the level of part-time work among women in Nordic countries would be even higher.

The evidence concerning atypical employment of women shows that the higher the labour-force participation rate of women the higher the share of atypical employment of women (apart from Finland). This phenomenon does not always imply the inferior status of women in the labour market. In Nordic countries the labour-market status of women is stronger than in EC countries irrespective of the more frequent atypical employment: the work-related rights and benefits do not usually differ between full-time and part-time work, and the working-hours in part-time work come very close to that of full-time work (e.g. Sweden and Finland).

In Nordic countries (excepting Denmark) the total unemployment rate was very low until the 1990s, and the unemployment rate of women was systematically lower than the rate of men. In the recent recession unemployment rates have been rising and unemployment in Finland has already exceeded the EC average. Nevertheless, it is men rather than women who have been hardest hit by unemployment in the early 1990s.

In EC countries the unemployment rate increased rapidly after the economic recession of the late 1970s, and the unemployment rate of women almost doubled with respect to the rate of men. The risk of unemployment has been higher among men in Nordic countries and the long-term unemployment has been primarily a male problem (OECD, 1991). In most EC countries the reverse is true: women's labour-market status is more unstable than that of men or that of women in Nordic countries.

Labour-market segregation and gender gap in wages

The rapid increase of labour-force participation of Nordic women is partly due to market pressures (i.e. the good economic performance after the world wars), but also due to active policies (i.e. the welfare state). During the 1960s and 1970s the major social reforms were implemented (e.g public schools for youths up to 16–18 years old, national health care, child-care centres, etc.), the public sector increased in size, and plenty of jobs were generated for women. Most of these jobs have been based on full-time work; in Sweden and Norway also on part-time work. While generating employment opportunities for women, this kind of reform has also strengthened the gender division in Nordic labour markets.

In all industrialized countries the labour markets are highly segregated by gender. Figure 1 combined with other available information—presented above—gives some evidence on the relationship between the rate of segregation and other labour-market structures. We may enumerate the following: (1) the higher the share of women of total labour force, the more segregated the labour market both according to occupations and branches of industry (including the public sector); (2) the lower the female unemployment rate or the relative unemployment rate of women to men, the higher the rate of segregation; and (3) the higher the share of part-time work of women's employment, the higher the rate of segregation. During the 1980s Nordic countries appeared to be in a class of their own with high segregation but ales high labour-force participation rate of women, low female unemployment, and high share of part-time work in women's employment.

In some countries, such as the USA, there has been a slight fall in labour-market segregation (Rubery, 1988), but in many countries segregation has even increased: there is no universal trend over time in labour-market segregation. This is probably because the increase of female labour-force participation has not taken place at the same time in all

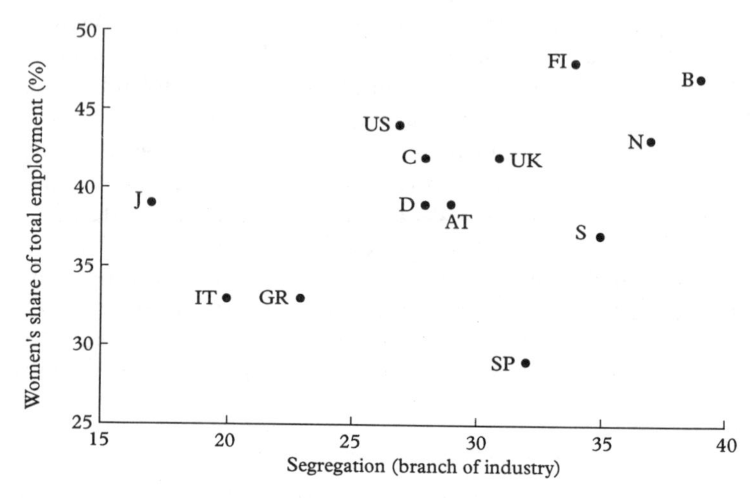

Figure 1 Women's share of total labour force and segregation according to branches of industry in OECD countries during the late 1980s

Note: The statistics on labour-force participation rate are from 1986/7. Segregation is measured by an index taking value (0, 100). If women's employment, relative to its size, were distributed across the major branches of industry in a similar fashion to men, the index would take the value of (0). If men and women were never found in same branches of industry, the index takes the value of (100). The value of segregation index refers to the latest year available, usually 1985 or 1986. FI = Finland, S = Sweden, N = Norway, DK = Denmark, B = Belgium, F = France, LUX = Luxemburg, GR = Greece, IR = Ireland, IT = Italy, N = Netherlands, P = Portugal, SP = Spain, UK = United Kingdom, G = Germany, AT = Australia, A = Austria, C = Canada, J = Japan, US = United States, NZ = New Zealand, SW = Switzerland.

Source: *OECD Employment Outlook, 1988.*

industrialized countries. Still, the growth of female labour and the growth of the service sector have been rather parallel in Nordic countries: a high proportion of new jobs have been taken by women.

The statistical evidence on segregation also shows that the labour markets are more highly segregated across occupations than branches of industry (OECD, 1988). Is this good or bad for women's economic emancipation? From the normative point of view, segregation of the labour market—at least to some degree—has been rather favourable to women. At least the Nordic experience shows that segregation has been parallel to the growth and stability of women's employment. This might be argued even if it is well known that segregation has something to do with the gender gap in earnings.

The most evident and most frequently studied inequality in the labour market is the gender gap in wages and salaries. It has been estimated that the wage differential in the USA in 1987 was from 34 per cent (on median annual income) to 24 per cent (on hourly adjusted income) (Goldin,

1990: 61). It has also been found that the wage differential between women and men is greater in all occupations than in manufacturing. In all Nordic countries the gender gap in wages has been smaller in the 1950s than in the OECD area on average. In Nordic countries (apart from Finland) the wage differentials have also narrowed very rapidly during the 1970s, although there was a slight increase during the late 1980s (OECD, 1988, 1991).

The smallest wage differential in manufacturing among OECD countries in 1989 was in Sweden (10.5 per cent) and the greatest wage differential among Nordic countries was in Finland (23.2 per cent), which coincides with the EC average. However, this phenomenon is worthy of interest since the labour-force participation rate of Finnish women is even higher (when measured by total working hours) and the labour-market status has been more stable than in other Nordic countries.

The gender gap in wages and salaries has often been explained by segregation and the fact that women are crowded in to the occupations of the lowest status in the labour market. Recent research on Finland shows that the gender gap in wages and salaries exists irrespective of gender segregation: also, the occupations highly dominated by women (99 per cent) are lower paid for women than men (Allén *et al.*, 1992). However, there is also evidence that the more men in an occupation, the higher the wages and salaries and the greater the gender gap. There is also empirical evidence that the wage differentials in Finland have increased because of gender discrimination during the period 1975–85 (Brunila, 1990). According to these studies about 25 to 30 per cent of wage differentials can be explained by gender discrimination.

Sweden has been the leading country in the Nordic area both in narrowing the gender gap and in government interventions in the economy. Other Nordic countries have been following the Swedish way—for better or worse. Are the great wage differentials the price that Finnish women have had to pay for the high activity in the labour market? What is the role of government involvement and corporatist policies in labour-market regulation?

ECONOMIC POLICY AND GENDER EQUALITY: THE NORDIC MODEL

The questions asked above can be answered by considering the role of economic policy in the advancement of the labour-market status of Nordic women. Naturally there is no direct evidence about the effects of economic policy on gender equality, but certain observations support this relationship. There are two interesting characteristics in the Nordic economic policy model: (1) the high share of public spending on welfare

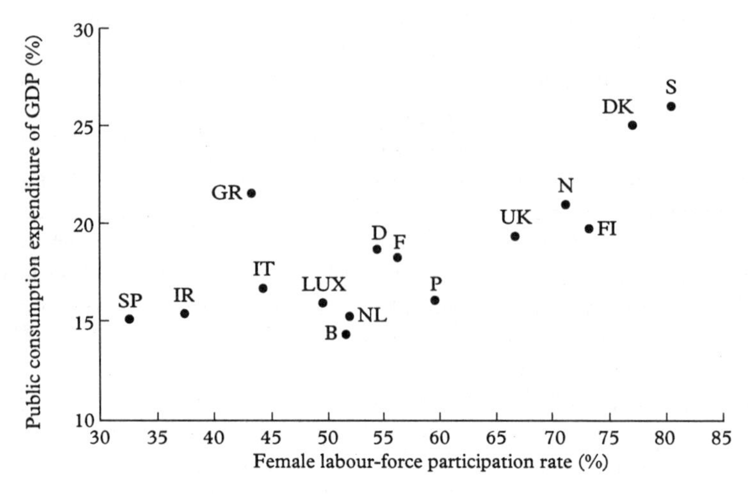

Figure 2 The labour-force participation rate of women and the share of public consumption expenditures of GDP in Nordic countries and EC countries 1989 (%)

Note: See the note for Figure 1 for a list of abbreviations.

Source: *OECD Employment Outlook, 1990.*

expenditures and public-sector employment of GDP, and (2) the high degree of centralization of labour-market regulation and wage bargaining.

Public employment and the welfare state

Figure 2 shows the positive correlation between government intervention into the economy and the economic activity of women. The degree of government regulation or involvement is measured by the share of public consumption expenditures of GDP. That is a proxy for the extent of public employment and the scope of production of welfare services in the economy.

The share of the public sector in women's employment is about 30 per cent and the female share of public sector total labour force is about 60–70 per cent in all Nordic countries. These figures are remarkably lower in other OECD countries, although they have been increasing during the 1980s. Figure 2 gives rather strong evidence that the higher the share of public spending of GDP, the higher women's labour-market activity. The same relationship can be expressed also such that, the higher the government involvement, the more stable the labour-market status of women in a country concerned. There are mainly two explanations behind this argument: (1) the public sector has created employment opportunities for women (i.e the demand for female labour), and (2) the public sector has provided social services (e.g. child care) to encourage women's employment (i.e. the supply of female labour).

Corporatism, segregation, and the gender gap in wages

The term corporatism has many meanings, but here it will be used to denote market economies in which there are strong and relatively centralized employers' and workers' organizations regulating labour relations and bargaining for wages. The economies which readily fit this description are Nordic countries: workers and employers are organized into a small number of centralized confederations, which are able to exert a significant degree of control and power over the whole economy. In this paper the degree of corporatism is measured by a numerical index developed by Calmfors and Driffill (1988; see also Rowthorn, 1989). On the scale of corporatism, the lower the score of the country, the higher the degree of corporatism in the economy concerned.[8]

Since 1973 many OECD countries have experienced a meaningful reduction in wage dispersion across branches of industry. In most Nordic countries, solidaristic wage bargaining has been used to squeeze wage differentials, but a significant reduction, has also occurred in some more decentralized economies (Rowthorn, 1989: 15). Likewise, at all levels of centralization, there are economies where wage dispersion has remained roughly constant or even increased (e.g. in highly centralized Austria). So there does not seem to be any universal link between general wage equality and corporatism.

The relationship between corporatism and the level of employment was even more complex in 1973 and in 1985. Both highly centralized and highly decentralized economies have above-average levels of employment: this means that the relationship is not linear correlation but rather U-shaped. Rowthorn (1989) explains the U-shape of the employment–corporatism relationship with different micro- and macro-mechanisms in wage bargaining (e.g. wage flexibility and labour-market segmentation) which impinge on total employment.

Figure 3 shows the positive relationship between the gender gap of hourly earnings and centralization of wage bargaining for Nordic countries and some OECD countries: the higher the degree of corporatism and union density, the smaller the gender gap in wages and salaries. Figure 4 shows in turn the relationship between the gender division of the labour market and centralization of wage bargaining in OECD countries: the higher the degree of corporatism, the higher the degree of segregation.

[8] The Calmfors–Driffill index was constructed for seventeen OECD countries and the ranking from the highest to the lowest degree of corporatism is as follows: Austria, Norway, Sweden, Denmark, Finland, Germany, the Netherlands, Belgium, New Zealand, Australia, France, United Kingdom, Italy, Japan, Switzerland, USA, and Canada.

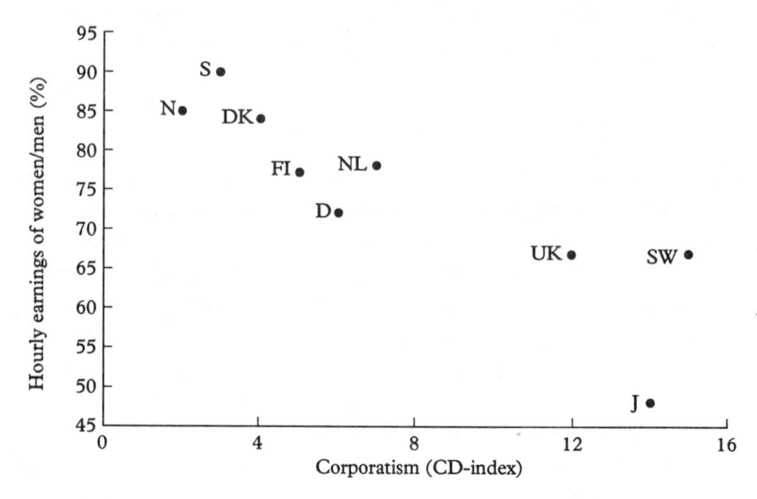

Figure 3 The degree of corporatism (CD-index) and the share of women's to men's hourly earnings in manufacturing 1985

Note: Figures 3 and 4 do not include all OECD countries because the statistics concerning segregation and the wage gap are inaccurate or not available for every country. See the note for Figure 1 for a list of abbreviations.

Source: *OECD Employment Outlook, 1988*; Rowthorn (1989).

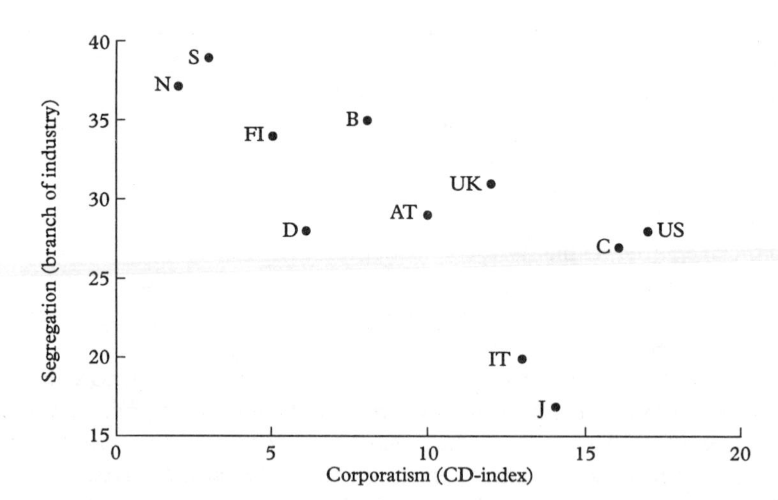

Figure 4 The degree of corporatism (CD-index) and the degree of segregation by branches of industry, 1985

Note: See the note for Figure 1 for a list of abbreviations.

Source: *OECD Employment Outlook 1988*; Rowthorn (1989).

In other studies it has been shown that women make more progress towards wage equality in countries with strong trade-union traditions, high union density in general, and greater union participation of women (Fletcher and Gill, 1992). Women represented by unions are closer to wage equality than women in the countries of more decentralized wage bargaining. This means that although women do not have power in trade unions, they still may have benefited from corporatist policies. This is even more crucial in economies where corporatist wage bargaining and welfare-state policies are linked together, like in Nordic countries.

THE NORDIC MODEL—UNFINISHED EMANCIPATION?

The Nordic model of gender division in the labour market looks rather different from that in other industrialized countries. Nordic countries are modern social-market economies as well as highly centralized in labour-market policies. In Nordic countries the strategy of advancing gender equality can be argued to be in relation to the 'national strategies of economic policies'—that of the welfare state and social corporatism. However, the special policies targeted at equal pay and equal employment opportunities have been of minor importance. The explanations for this kind of development can be found from the early development in these countries of the civil society and democracy which supported gender equality.

Having reviewed the empirical evidence, the question is: Can the Nordic experience be called a model of 'gender equality' or a model of the 'gender gap'? The four Nordic countries—Sweden, Norway, Finland, and Denmark—represent a quite unusual tradition of women's economic activity: (1) early integration into the labour market, (2) high participation rates and high union density, (3) low unemployment, (4) high segregation, (5) frequent but 'safe' atypical employment, and (6) relatively small wage differentials. And finally: most of the stability of women's employment in Nordic countries seems to have been achieved by means of general economic policies rather than by policies targeted at gender equality as such, either equal pay or equal employment opportunities policies.

The Nordic model of gender equality in the labour market was supported by the combination of (1) growth-oriented economic policy, (2) which has maintained high demand for labour, and (3) has been supported by solidaristic welfare-state policies and (4) the class compromise based on corporatism and strong trade-union traditions. Strictly speaking, gender equality in Nordic labour markets has been a by-product of policies targeted at comprehensive citizenship rights and democracy, as well as the promotion of the general standard of living in these countries. It can also be said that the model of the welfare state and that of corporatism have been parallel to the model of 'state feminism' in Nordic countries.

Although Nordic countries have succeeded in achieving gender equality in the labour market—in a fuller sense than other industrialized countries—there still exist many deficiencies: (1) the Nordic model has supported or even strengthened segregation and gender division of work; (2) it has made women increasingly dependent on the state instead of husbands: the private patriarchy has been transformed to the public patriarchy; and (3) it has made women the objects of public policy rather than subjects: Nordic women have been emancipated as wage labourers but they do not have greater economic power than women in other Western countries. In other words, it has become popular to say that, when women enter the scene, the power 'withers away'. This means that women may advance but they usually enter into 'shrinking institutions'.

When comparing the labour-market status of women in Nordic countries and other EC or OECD countries, there seems to be a trade-off between the economic policy model and gender equality. Rather than gender equality, this relationship can be called unfinished emancipation: Nordic women are both worker-citizens and mother-citizens, but not yet full citizens to the same extent as Nordic men, in the economy and institutions of economic policy and power. This means that although private patriarchy has been undermined in Nordic countries, public patriarchy has been strengthening during the welfare phase.

Although this may seem a paradox, we can argue that although the women-friendly state in the form of welfare state has been advancing the economic emancipation of women in Nordic countries, the 'hard core' of the economy has remained the men's estate. The current recession in Nordic countries—and especially in Finland—may also change the institutions of corporatism and the welfare state. What will happen to the Nordic model of the women-friendly state? Will it survive after the present recession, or will we witness the resurgence of patriarchy in Nordic countries in a few years time?

REFERENCES

ALESTALO, M. and UUSITALO, H. (1986), 'Finland', in P. Flora (ed.), *Growth to Limits: The Western European Welfare States since World War II* (Berlin: European University Institute, Series C, Walter de Gruyter).

ALLÉN, T. (1991), 'Kotitaloustuotanto ja naisten palkkatyö—muuttuuko näkymätön näkyväksi markkinoilla?' (Household Production and Female Waged Work—Has Invisible Changed to Visible in the Market?), *Review of Labour Institute for Economic Research*, 4.

—— (1992), 'Economic Development and the Feminization of Poverty', in N. Folbre, B. Bergmann, B. Agarwal, and M. Floro (eds.), *Issues in Contemporary*

Economics, vol. 4, *Women's Work in the World Economy* (London: Macmillan/IEA).

—— ILMAKUNNAS, S., LAAKSONEN, S., and KEINÄNEN, P. (1992), *Wage from Work and Gender: A Study on Wage Differentials in Finland in 1985, Central Statistical Office of Finland Studies*, 190.

BLOMSTRÖM, M. and MELLER, P. (1991), *Diverging Paths: Comparing a Century of Scandinavian and Latin American Economic Development* (Washington, DC: Inter-American Development Bank/Johns Hopkins University Press).

BRUNILA, A. (1990), *Naisten ja miesten palkkaerot vuosina 1975 ja 1985* (*The Wage Differentials between Women and Men in 1975 and 1985*) (Helsinki: Labour Institute for Economic Research, Research Reports 30).

CALMFORS, L. and DRIFFILL, J. (1988), 'Bargaining Structure, Corporatism and Macro-economic Performance', *Economic Policy*, 6.

CEC (1990), *Employment in Europe* (Brussels: Comission of the European Communities).

FLETCHER, J. and GILL, S. (1992), 'Union Density and Women's Relative Wage Gains', in N. Folbre, B. Bergmann, B. Agarwal, and M. Floro (eds.), *Issues in Contemporary Economic*, vol. 4, *Women's Work in the World Economy* (London: Macmillan/IEA).

GOLDIN, C. (1990), *Understanding the Gender Gap: An Economic History of American Women* (New York: Oxford University Press).

HERNES, H. (1988), 'The Welfare State Citizenship of Scandinavian Women', in A. G. Jonasdottir and K. B. Jones (eds.), *The Political Interests of Gender: Developing Theory and Research with a Feminist Face* (London: Sage).

KOSONEN, K. (1989), 'Saving and Economic Growth from a Nordic Perspective' (Helsinki: Labour Institute for Economic Research, Discussion Papers 88).

KOSONEN, P. (1987), *Hyvinvointivaltion haasteet ja pohjoismaiset mallit* (*Challenges of the Welfare State and the Nordic Models*) (Tampere, Finland: Vastapaino).

LANDAU, E. (1986), *The Rights of Working Women in the European Community* (Brussels: CEC).

MJOESET, L. (ed.) (1986), *Norden dagen derpå. De nordiske okonomisk-politiske modellene og deres problemer på 70- og 80-tallet* (*Nordic Countries a Day After: Nordic Economic Policy Models and their Problems during the 1970s and 1980s*) (Oslo: Universitetsforlaget).

Nordic Council of Ministers (1988), *Women and Men in the Nordic Countries: Facts on Equal Opportunities* (Copenhagen and Oslo: The Nordic Council).

OECD (1988, 1990, 1991), *OECD Employment Outlook* (Paris: OECD).

PEKKARINEN, J. (1990), 'Corporatism and Economic Performance in Sweden, Norway and Finland' (Helsinki: Labour Institute for Economic Research, Discussion Papers 97).

PEKKARINEN, J., POHJOLA, M., and ROWTHORN, B. (1992), *Social Corporatism: A Superior Economic System?* (Oxford: Clarendon Press).

RINGEN, S. and UUSITALO, H. (1991), 'Income Distribution in the Nordic Welfare States', in J. E. Kolberg (ed.), *Comparing Welfare States and Labour Markets* (New York: M. E. Sharpe).

ROWTHORN, B. (1989), 'Corporatism and Labour Market Performance' (Helsinki: Labour Institute for Economic Research, Discussion Papers, 93).

RUBERY, J. (ed.) (1988), *Women and Recession* (London: Routledge & Kegan Paul).

Siim, B. (1991), 'Welfare State, Gender Politics and Equality Policies: Women's Citizenship in the Scandinavian Welfare State', in E. Meehan and S. Sevenhuijsen (eds.), *Equality Politics and Gender* (London: Sage).

Uusitalo, H. (1988), *Muuttuva tulonjako. Hyvinvointivaltion ja yhteiskunnan rakennemuutosten vaikutukset tulonjakoon 1966–1985* (*The Changing Income Distribution: The Impact of the Welfare State and Structural Changes of Society on Income Distribution 1966–1985*) (Helsinki: Central Statistical Office of Finland Studies, 148).

Wihlborg, C. (1992), *The Scandinavian Models for Development and Welfare* (Stockholm: The Institute for Economic and Social Research).

Patriarchy and Post-communism: Eastern Europe and the Former Soviet Union

Valentine M. Moghadam

INTRODUCTION

The immediate consequences of the political revolutions in Eastern Europe and the former Soviet Union raise fundamental questions central to the focus of this book. To the surprise of many observers, the dismantling of communism and the transition to a market economy did not lead to a significant improvement in women's position but rather reversed women's gains in employment and political participation. Market reforms have led to high levels of unemployment among women and an apparent trend towards appropriation by men of now-lucrative occupations such as banking and accounting which were previously female-dominated. The first democratic elections resulted in a dramatic decline in female parliamentary participation, from an average of 30 per cent to shares as low as three per cent. Cultural and media images of women began to change, allowing employers to openly advertise to recruit young and pretty women. With the end of government subsidies and the proliferation of new and independent presses engaged in a fierce battle for survival, many newspapers began to adorn their articles with nudity. Another disturbing trend is the burgeoning traffic in women, including migration of sexual workers to places like Helsinki and Istanbul (from the Baltics and Russia) and Amsterdam and Berlin (from Central and Eastern Europe), for hard currency.[1]

In the former Soviet Union, women of the highly educated and intellectual groups initially welcomed *glasnost* and *perestroika* but eventually viewed these developments and their consequences with alarm and dismay. *Glasnost* allowed Soviet citizens to voice patriarchal prejudices once banned as bourgeois or counter-revolutionary. The news media frequently blamed 'over-emancipated, masculinized women' for social ills from juvenile delinquency to divorce to declining birthrates. Mikhail Gorbachev's ambivalent positions on the role of women in political and economic life, along with the social policies proposed by the Communist Party and

I wish to thank Renata Siemienska and Barbara Einhorn for comments on the first draft of this chapter. The analysis and any deficiencies are mine.

[1] In Istanbul, Russian prostitutes are known as 'Natasha'. Author's observations, Istanbul, June 1994. On the growth of prostitution see *Time*, 21 June 1993. For a sociological analysis of the growth of prostitution and a discussion of media and policy attention to it, see Sanjian (1991).

the Congress of People's Deputies in early 1990, further strengthened the view that only women are responsible for children and housework. In the immediate post-communist period, women's maternal, domestic, and family roles began to be exalted, and there was a fierce battle over reproductive rights. In Poland, Hungary, and unified Germany, the issue of abortion assumed a paramount position in the new discourses and policies, and parliamentarians spent long hours debating ways of criminalizing abortion. The resurgence of patriarchal discourses and policies was a striking feature of post-communist Central and Eastern Europe and the former Soviet Union, where the new leaders and élites stressed 'liberation from work' and a return to the joys of domesticity (Einhorn, 1993*a*; Posadskaya, 1993; Wolchik, 1993). Women were unprepared to challenge these changes. The official, communist-era women's organizations lost status and legitimacy, and the women's groups that were formed during the transition lacked the organizational unity and resources to successfully contest policies inimical to women's gender interests, and to effectively influence the direction of change.

These recent developments in a part of the world characterized by high levels of educational attainment and full labour-force attachment of women—as well as decades of official socialist ideology regarding equality and women's emancipation—offer an opportunity to interrogate and elaborate two sets of propositions. One pertains to the relationship between development and patriarchy, specifically, the assumption that the more economically developed (that is, industrialized, urbanized, proletarianized) a society, the less gender inequality and subordination of women. Events in the post-communist world appear to refute any simplistic association between economic development and gender equality, and to suggest that there were systemic deficiencies—which perhaps pervaded the realms of the economy, polity, and culture, and which were manifested in the gender system itself—that allowed the resurfacing of patriarchal practices following the end of official communism.

The implications for women of the end of communism and the politico-economic transformations underway permit the elaboration of a second set of propositions. These pertain to the dynamics of social change and the centrality of gender to constructions of the 'ideal society'. It appears that during periods of social change, transition, and political upheaval, when questions of political and cultural identity come to the fore, there tends to be a high premium placed on the family and on traditional roles for women. As gender roles become politicized, questions of personal life and reproductive rights are fiercely contested. Religious revitalization, an emphasis on the needs or survival of 'the nation', restrictions on fertility control and sex education, exhortations of domesticity, an end to publicly financed child care, polemics surrounding 'appropriate' and 'inappropriate' occupations for women—these are some of the gender dynamics of periods of social change or periods when a new national identity is being forged.[2]

Why has there been a resurgence of patriarchy in the former state-socialist countries? The answer requires an historical overview and a critical assessment of past policies and discourses on women, work, and family under state socialism, and the ways in which women were integrated into the spheres of production and reproduction in the socialist economy and society.

MARXISM, SOCIALISM, AND THE WOMAN QUESTION

At the level of ideology and discourse, gender relations and the position of women under state socialism were broadly shaped by: (1) the Marxist view of labour and the nature of the socialist economy, and (2) Marxism's contradictory view of the family and women's role within it. For Marx, the maintenance and reproduction of material life is the prime human need. As Engels put it, the determining factor in history is the production of the means of subsistence, and the production of human beings themselves. He asserted, but did not develop, the interesting theoretical proposition that social institutions in different historical periods are shaped by 'the development of labour and of the family'.[3]

As sociologist David Lane has shown, labour and the work process is a fundamental component of Marxist theory:

> The work process . . . is human action with a view to the production of use-values, appropriation of natural substances to human requirements; it is the necessary condition for effecting exchanges of matter between man and nature; it is the everlasting nature-imposed condition of human existence, and therefore is independent of every social phase of that existence, or rather, is common to every such phase. (cit. Lane, 1986: 3)

Work has two aspects: (1) it fulfils a social need on the part of the worker—it uses humanity's creative power, and as such is the antidote to alienation, and (2) goods and services are produced which are consumed. As a result, Marxists have always adopted a more positive attitude toward the necessity for people to work. Indeed, Lane dubbed Soviet Marxism with regard to labour the 'Protestant ethic of socialism' (Lane, 1986: 7). For Lenin work was not only perceived as the fulfilment of humanity's 'species being' but was bound up with the development of the productive forces. Under Stalin work as human need and creativity was subordinated

[2] For an elaboration of constructions of gender and national identity, see Yuval-Davis and Anthias (1989); Kandiyoti (1991); Moghadam (1993*a*; 1993*b*; 1993*c*; 1994).

[3] Engels, 1883 preface to *The Origin of the Family, Private Property, and the State* (1972 [1884]).

to an emphasis on the duty to labour. The 1936 Constitution declared that 'work in the USSR is a duty, a matter of honour for every able-bodied citizen—He who does not work shall not eat' (ibid. 9).[4]

The specific character of the socialist or centrally planned economy also shaped women's status and women's lives. Full employment was an integral aspect of socialist economies. Other salient characteristics were state ownership of the means of production, the role of the central plan, and a centralized direction of all the factors of production, macro- and micro-investment decisions, the allocation of resources, foreign trade, and the distribution of the surplus. In theory labour in a centrally planned economy is comparatively immobile, although Turgeon and MacIntyre (1990) argue that 'the very high mobility rates since the Second World War indicate that there has been a seller's market for labor'. Almost by definition, state employees enjoyed complete job security.[5] The Marxist stance towards work, the commitment to equality, and the developmentalist nature of the socialist state underpinned the full employment policies implemented in all state-socialist countries. The result is that right through the 1980s the state-socialist countries not only had the highest rates of female labour-force participation, but the most equitable male–female ratios in full-time paid employment.

The second crucial factor affecting women's social positions in socialist societies were the Marxist and socialist views on the family. Landes (1989) notes two versions of the relationship between capitalism and family life in the writings of Marx, Engels, and other early socialists. On the one hand, family life is depicted as an undesirable and unhealthy institution, a product of class society that will disappear in the socialist future. On the other hand, the family, and especially the working-class family, has been adversely affected by capitalism and should flourish instead. In this regard, Landes observes, Engels' scathing attack in *The Condition of the Working Class in England* was a passionate outcry against the industrial conditions that produced dissolution in family life among the workers. She further notes that the substitution of female for male labour was treated as emblematic of the absolute degradation of human labour by capital, and that in *Capital*, Marx commented upon capital's ability to depress wages by exploiting women and children. These two rather different views on the family help to explain the contradictory trends in women and the family in state-socialist countries.

The Marxist and socialist position on women and work followed from

[4] In the 1977 Constitution citizens were not only given the right to work but also the choice of a trade or profession.

[5] An unintended consequence, however, was that the central planners could not raise productivity without undermining the commitment to full employment. This suggests a trade-off between a full-employment, low-wage economy and a high-wage system with job insecurity, a problem currently facing the OECD market economies. See Lane (1987), and Gaffikin and Morissey (1992).

the critique of capitalism, but recognized the specificity of women's oppression within patriarchy and the family. Marx and Engels argued that the sexual division of labour in agricultural and pre-industrial societies gives way to a capitalist form of the social division of labour, which is an improvement for women in that it permits their organization and development of class and social consciousness. Patriarchy, like 'all fixed, fast frozen relations, with their train of ancient prejudices and opinions [is] swept away', to be supplanted in the socialist future by new forms of human association. Modern industry overturns the economic foundation of the traditional family and its corresponding form of female labour, thereby 'loosen[ing] all traditional ties'.[6] In the socialist future, family life would be replaced by new forms of human association. For the present, women's entry into the public workforce was deemed to be a necessary condition for the emancipation of women, and the working class as a whole (Landes, 1989).

Soviet Russia constituted the first socialist experiment, and there, 'principle and practicality' (Molyneux, 1982) combined to shape gender roles and women's status. Goldman (1989) explains that with the onset of World War I, women had entered production in greater numbers, and by 1917 one-third of Petrograd's factory workers were women. The Bolsheviks published a paper for women workers, *Rabotnitsa*, encouraged women to join factory committees and unions, and considered a policy of separate organizations for them. 'Support for the Bolsheviks, in turn, grew among laundresses, domestic servants, restaurant and textile workers, and soldiers' wives. Although the party was theoretically opposed to separate organizations for women, in practice *Rabotnitsa*'s success resulted in the organization of the Petrograd Conference of Working Women in November 1917 and the formation of the Zhenotdel, or women's department, within the party in 1919' (Goldman, 1989: 60–1).

Under Alexandra Kollantai, people's commissar for social welfare, labour legislation was passed to give women an eight-hour day, social insurance, pregnancy leave for two months before and after childbirth, and time at work to breast-feed. It also prohibited child labour and night work for women. Goldman (1989) shows how the early moths of the revolution also saw legislation to establish equality between husband and wife, civil registration of marriage, easy divorce, abolition of illegitimacy, and the wife's right not to take her husband's name share his domicile, or give up her property or earnings. 'In a remarkable ruling, the Supreme Court acknowledged that housework, as well as waged work, constituted a form of socially necessary labour' (Goldman, 1989: 62). In Central Asia the Zhenotdel organized mass unveilings of Muslim women and ran literacy classes. These activities followed from the view that the emancipation of

[6] Quotes from Marx and Engels, *The Communist Manifesto* (1969).

women was an essential part of the socialist revolution, something to be accomplished through 'the participation of women in general productive labour' and the socialization of domestic duties. The Bolsheviks also stressed the need for political participation of women, as the following quote from Lenin reveals: 'We want women workers to achieve equality with men workers not only in law, but in life as well. For this, it is essential that women workers take an ever-increasing part in the administration of public enterprises and in the administration of the state.'[7]

The Bolsheviks took the initiative in calling the First Communist Women's Conference in 1920, and prepared the position paper for the occasion, *Theses of the Communist Women's Movement.* Elizabeth Waters (1989) shows that, apart from its commitment to the political equality of women and the guarantee of their social rights, the *Theses* included an attack on housewifery and 'the domestic hearth'. The document reflected the Engelsian view that female emancipation would be a twofold process, incorporating both the entry of women into the national labour force and the socializtion of domestic labour. The document also reflected the views of the outstanding Communist women who contributed to its formulation, among them Alexandra Kollantai, Inessa Armand, and Clara Zetkin.

Goldman (1989) has described the process by which the Soviet Land Code, ratified in 1922, combined peasant customary law with a new, revolutionary insistence on gender equality which undermined patriarchal authority in the countryside. It abolished private ownership and granted all citizens, 'regardless of sex, religion, or nationality', rights to the land. Women had the right to full participation in the commune. Unlike customary law, in which a woman's rights depended on the presence of her husband or sons, the Land Code ensured that a woman entering a household by marriage had the right to an equal share. If the household split, land and property were divided among all household members, not only the adult males. Goldman describes the opposition and resistance from many sectors of the population to the new laws.

The liberation of peasant women could only come about through a massive change in the mode of production, as well as a revolutionary transformation of social values and practices. The implementation in the 1920s of the Land Code and the Family Code—with their emphasis on individual rights and freedoms, including women's rights to land and for maintenance—was an extremely audacious act that challenged centuries of patriarchal control. It also undermined the collective principle of the household, the very basis of peasant production, and was thus strongly resisted. There was also resistance to the Bolshevik strategy for transformation in Central Asia. In the absence of an industrial working class, the

[7] Lenin cited in *The Woman Question: Selections from the Writings of Karl Marx, Frederick Engels, V. I. Lenin, Joseph Stalin* (New York: Interational Publishers, 1977), 61.

Bolsheviks directed their campaigns at women because they were considered the most oppressed social category, as Gregory Massell (1974) described in his seminal book. It seems clear that the Bolshevik commitment to women's liberation throughout the 1920s was not only genuine, 'it was doggedly persistent in the face of huge obstacles' (Goldman, 1989: 75). In 1927 the All-Union Congress of Working and Peasant Women—attended by 'working-class and peasant women from every corner of the USSR' (Goldman, 1989: 59) convened in Moscow to discuss women's liberation.

The major blow to rural patriarchal authority came in the 1930s under Stalin's leadership, as a result of the massive but ruthless drive to collectivize agriculture and industrialize the economy. At the same time, economic, political, and ideological factors converged to undermine the early libertarian views. The consolidation of the power of Stalin and his associates ushered in a more culturally conservative era, disbanded the Zhenotdel, ended open discussions of women's liberation, and resurrected the family. The earlier critique of the family was replaced by a strong emphasis on the 'socialist family' as the proper model of gender relations. Family responsibilities were extolled for men and women alike.

In Eastern Europe communist parties came to power after World War II in a manner rather different from the path taken in the Soviet Union. But the implementation of the socialist model of development resulted in some similar outcomes. In many of the countries, economies were greatly modernized. The modernization took place as a result of the mobilization of previously under-utilized resources, especially in agriculture and among women generally. Large numbers of relatively unproductive ex-peasants and women were transformed into productive contributors to a modern industrial base. As a result of generous expenditures for education and public health, there was the growth of an educated and well-informed population. In Eastern Europe, the gains from industrialization were distributed in a manner whereby the former 'have-nots' gained relative to the former 'haves' in what had been a nascent bourgeois society. Among those gaining most were women and children generally. In many places, government-sponsored child care liberated women from child-rearing tasks, allowing them to take employment in the state or co-operative sector. Residents of agricultural areas, particularly women, gained relative to industrial workers as large economies of scale in collectivized agriculture (similar to those achieved in the West through corporate farming) replaced labour-intensive small family farms. As in the USSR, the status and income of miners was upgraded in eastern Europe. Slovaks were subject to affirmative action within post-war Czechoslovakia, and even east European Gypsies upgraded their lives in exchange for giving up much of their traditional mobility (Turgeon, 1990).

Relative losers during the socialist era were members of various professions. The legal profession lost status—partly due to the decline in crime rates—as did doctors, who became entitled to only average pay in a socialized medical system. There was some loss of power by religious organizations in the first part of the post-war period, but during the second half, religion recovered somewhat, resulting in the construction of new churches in some of the eastern European countries, especially Poland, Hungary, and the GDR (Turgeon, 1990).[8]

Rapid economic development and the acceleration of social change toward a centralized, secular, more egalitarian society were fundamental aims of socialist countries, achieved by an active, interventionist, and welfarist state and the mobilization of an adequate supply of labour. Within this context, as Molyneux (1982) has pointed out, the emancipation of women can be seen to have played a double role. First, it was a principle to which socialist states were committed as part of their overall support for more egalitarian social order, the legacy of Marxist and socialist thought; and second, it was an integral part of the wider developmental goals of socialist states.

WOMEN, WORK, AND FAMILY UNDER STATE SOCIALISM

One of the development goals of the state-socialist countries was to raise fertility rates in a context of labour shortage. Throughout the 1980s, female labour-force participation rates in the socialist countries were extremely high by world standards, with women making up half the labour force or more. Fertility rates declined, a consequence of both the full employment of women and couples' desire to raise their standard of living by having fewer children.[9] Generous maternity benefits were, therefore, intended in part to raise the birth-rate.

The number of women in the economically active population in the USSR and in the socialist countries of Europe grew very rapidly in the post-World War II period. Data from censuses carried out in these countries indicate an increase of 83 per cent in the economically active female population; for example, in Hungary between 1949 and 1980, 47 per cent; in Poland between 1950 and 1978, 78 per cent; in Czechoslovakia between 1947 and 1980, 21 per cent; and 19 per cent in the USSR between 1959 and 1979. According to ILO estimates, in 1980 'the highest female participation rates for ages 15 and 24 are found in the USSR (about 60 per cent), and in other European centrally planned economies (about 57 per cent)' (cit. ILO/INSTRAW, 1985: 136). The proportion of women of working age (women aged 16 to 54) carrying out an economic

[8] Renata Siemienska notes that the Church played 'an incomparably stronger role' in Poland than in Hungary and the GDR, and for a much longer time. Personal communication, 12 Nov. 1993.

[9] Personal commmunication from Renata Siemienska, 12 Nov. 1993.

activity ranged from 70 to 90 per cent. The growth in general of female employment was the direct result of the growth of the socialist economy. Indeed, the female labour force grew faster than the male labour force engaged in the socialist sector. The proportion of women in the total of workers and employees also increased (ibid. 138).

In an ILO study on female employment and fertility in socialist countries (Bodrova and Anker, 1985), Richard Anker noted that along with the nearly complete integration of women into socialist economies, women were found in virtually all occupations and industries except mining and heavy transport. He also found that the sexual division of labour in the work place in socialist countries was significantly more equal than in market economy countries in similar stages of development (Anker, 1985: 6). A global survey of working women found that in 1983, for eastern Europe as a whole, 30 per cent of all women workers were in industry, with large percentages in the engineering field. In the USSR, 40 per cent of all industrial engineers and 43 per cent of engineers and architects employed in construction were women. In 1982 in the USSR, the number of women with specialized training accounted for half of all workers engaged in agriculture. Around 30 per cent of agronomists, 55 per cent of experts in animal husbandry, and 37.5 per cent of veterinary surgeons working in state farms and kolkhozes were women (ILO/INSTRAW, 1985: 140–5). More women were concentrated in industry than in agriculture.

According to Anker, 'The social and population programmes in the socialist countries considered here are in many ways extraordinary—and many are specifically designed to reduce the conflict for women between their roles as mother and workers. Thus, over 2.5 per cent of national income is given in the form of family allowances for children in Bulgaria, Czechoslovakia and Hungary. In these same countries, cumulative family allowances for the second child amount to approximately 12, 18, and 21 per cent, respectively, of the average wage in manufacturing, and to 34, 53 and 37 per cent, respectively, for the third child' (Anker, 1985: 16). Policy measures for working mothers included paid maternity leave which could range from two months in the Uzbek SSR to six months in Czechoslovakia and one year in the GDR. Mothers were allowed to take extended periods of unpaid child-care leave when their child was young, as well as sick leave to care for a sick child; allowances paid to mothers on extended unpaid child-care leave were substantial in Bulgaria, Czechoslovakia, and Hungary. While on extended child-care leave, women usually continued to accumulate their rights to social benefits (such as pensions) as well as additional years of seniority (ibid. 18).

In the section below, we examine social policies and patterns of women's employment in three former communist countries. The discussion highlights some of the negative as well as positive trends during the state-socialist era, as a way of helping to explain the post-communist outcomes for women.

Hungary

Hungary's female labour-force participation rates were generally above those of other advanced capitalist countries, including Austria, West Germany, and Switzerland. But in 1975, female labour-force participation rates were lower than those for the Scandinavian countries, excluding Norway; ten years later they were below all four Scandinavian countries, as well as the United States.

It is believed that the Hungarian special maternity allowances had a significant impact on Hungarian female labour-force participation rates. Hungary was the pioneer country paying women to stay at home taking care of their infants and small children under three beginning in 1967, and until 1989 was still the most generous country in this respect, even though it was replicated to a certain extent in Nordic countries. Turgeon suggests that the main reason for this generosity was the precipitous decline in the Hungarian fertility rates following the legalization of abortion in 1956. Hungarian abortions were exceeding live births and the net reproduction rate was less than that required to reproduce the Hungarian population. The second important factor mentioned by Turgeon is the uncertainty of what would happen when centralized planning would be replaced by the New Economic Mechanism (NEM) in 1968. The Yugoslav experience with decentralized planning was already producing significantly more unemployment domestically and pressure to export 'guest workers' to West Germany and elsewhere. A further complication for Hungarian manpower planners was the fact that the baby boomers of the early 1950s—the so-called Ratko babies—were about to enter the labour force.[10]

A 1981 law allowed Hungarian mothers who used up their six months full-salary maternity pay to remain at home until the child reached the age of three, while their employment status and all social insurance rights remained uninterrupted. Beginning in 1985, mothers were receiving 75 per cent of their former earnings or the equivalence of sick pay until the child reached the age of 18 months.[11] While these child-bearing years had an adverse effect on women's lifetime earnings, they were counterbalanced to some extent by the fact that Hungarian men were required to submit to the draft—earlier in their life cycle so careers were not disturbed—where they received very low wages for one and a half years. Furthermore, women were eligible for pensions five years earlier than men, as was the case in other countries.

[10] Ms Ratko, the Minister of Health during the Rakosi era, strictly opposed abortion, thereby producing a baby boom before 1956. See Turgeon (1989).

[11] The allowance was for a minimum of 2,500 forints per month and a maximum of 4,500 forints per month, compared to an average mothly wage of 5,800 forints, according to Turgeon (1989).

Turgeon notes that the emergence of a thriving second economy during the 1980s may have meant more income for many Hungarian families, but the share of housework done by women probably rose since risk-preferring men were predominantly the participants in the second economy. The reduction of the official Hungarian work week to five days and 40–2 hours led to more activity within the second economy on the part of Hungarian males and may have led to a greater share of housework for Hungarian women.

The German Democratic Republic

According to Einhorn, 'The German Democratic Republic had a policy of combating sex discrimination, indeed, of positive discrimination toward women, since its foundation in 1949.' She has also argued that 'The economic, legal, and social status of women in the GDR as workers, as mothers and as individuals was undeniably far in advance of that enjoyed by their sisters in West Germany and many other Western capitalist countries and even that in the other state socialist countries' (Einhorn, 1989: 282, 283–4). Redhead, Shaffer, and Turgeon (1989) note that GDR women had the highest labour-force participation rates in the world (with Sweden as a close second). In 1988, 83.2 per cent of all women of working age in the GDR were employed outside the home, as compared with 55 per cent of West German women (Einhorn, 1993*b*: table 4.2). Female membership in the trade unions as a whole accounted for 53 per cent of the total, as compared with only 23 per cent in West Germany, and 48 per cent of shop stewards were women. Women were well represented in positions of public responsibility. Einhorn reports that in 1989, women comprised 25 per cent of local mayors; 47 per cent of residential and arbitration commissions; 40 per cent of county, district, and borough councils. At the national level, there were 161 women in the GDR parliament, holding 32.2 per cent of the total 500 seats. (This compared with 5 per cent in the US House of Representatives and 2 per cent in the US Senate.) The ruling party, the SED, had a 35 per cent female membership. At the highest levels there was less female participation: 23 per cent representation on the Central Committee and no full members on the Politburo.

Women 'made substantial advances in formerly male-dominated professions', accounting for 45 per cent of judges and 30 per cent of lawyers in 1977–9, and 57 per cent of dentists and 52 per cent of doctors in 1983 (Einhorn, 1989: 289). The comparison with OECD countries is instructive: 'According to 1987 statistics, only 4 per cent of lawyers and 16 per cent of doctors were women in the United Kingdom; 15 per cent of judges and 14 per cent of lawyers were women in West Germany, as were 23 per cent of doctors and 20 per cent of dentists; and only 8 per cent of lawyers, 6 per cent of dentists, and 17 per cent of doctors were women in United States' (Einhorn, 1989: 289–90).

Benefits for working mothers connected with pregnancy and childbirth included 6 weeks maternity leave before childbirth and 20 weeks thereafter. During these 26-week periods, women's maternity allowances matched their latest average net earnings. After the termination of maternity leave, women were entitled to an additional leave up to the child's first birthday. During that period they received monthly child-care allowances equivalent to sick pay, or 60–90 per cent of their salary. The minimum child-care allowance was 250 marks for one child and 300 marks for two children. In certain cases, father or grandmothers could take advantage of the allowance, a practice that was pioneered in Bulgaria (Redhead *et al.*, 1989: 19).

According to an official GDR pamphlet, in 1986, 73 per cent of GDR children between the ages of one and three were looked after in crèches compared with 32 per cent in 1971. After 1979, all children aged three to six were able to attend kindergarten. In 1981, places became available in after-school centres for all children in grades one to four, or until they were at least ten years old. Attendance was free, with only token payments covering the cost of meals. Beginning in 1984, and in an effort to stimulate the birth-rate, government policy gave families with three or more children preferential housing, special health care, preferential allocation of crèche places, preferential allocation of holiday trips, and financial support to pay for meals in pre-school facilities. Mothers of larger families also had slightly shorter work weeks—40 hours rather than the standard 43.75 hours. There were also special dispensations for children from single-parent households.[12]

The Soviet Union

The Soviet Union produced the first woman ambassador, Alexandra Kollantai, and the first woman in space, Valentina Tereshkova. In the 1980s it contained the largest number of women professionals and specialists on the globe, and close to 90 per cent of its female population was in the workforce. The Soviet experience demonstrates the degree to which women's mobility into industrial employment can be accelerated and channelled through the deliberate use of public policy, which also provided special benefits to working mothers. The only area in the Soviet Union with an under-utilized female labour force was in the Central Asian and Transcaucasian republics where female participation rates outside agriculture—particularly among the local nationalities—were much lower than the national average. Since the recruitment of native women into

[12] See *Equal Rights in Practice: Women in the GDR* (Berlin, DDR: First-Hand Information Department, 1986), 38–41.

industry encountered great difficulties in these regions, a high proportion of women workers and employees in central Asia were Russian and Ukrainian (Lapidus, 1985: 14).

As we have seen, early Soviet legislation sought to secure full economic and social equality for women. But the socialization of housework never took place. In 1977, Party Chairman Leonid Brezhnev admitted in a speech to the Trade Union Congress: 'We men . . . have thus far done far from all we could to ease the dual burden that [women] bear both at home and in production' (Lapidus, 1985: 14). In 1986, the Communist Party programme included a statement that 'favourable conditions will be created that will enable women to combine motherhood with active participation in work and social activities'. It was not until April 1990, however, that the Supreme Soviet pass a resolution which for the first time allows 'fathers, grandfathers, or other family members' the right to take unpaid child-care leave. By 1990, and in the context of glasnost and perestroika, many Soviet women expressed yearning for a traditional female role centred around the family and the home. They were apparently exhausted by years of a double burden made more difficult by consumer shortages. Yet national polls showed that only 20 per cent of Soviet women would quit their jobs even if they could afford to (Vanden Heuvel, 1990).

In the 1980s, demographic trends such as lower rates of marriage, later marriage age, rising rates of divorce, and declining birth rates became the focus of anxious discussion. For the first time since the 1920s, Soviet writers began to suggest that female liberation and family stability may be incompatible. Lower fertility rates in the European parts of the country relative to the higher fertility rates in the central Asian republics seemed to trigger a pro-natalist mood. Lapidus notes that as economic stagnation worsened, a growing array of studies by Soviet scholars, as well as numerous Soviet novels and films, documented the conflicting demands of women's dual role, the constraints it places on occupational mobility, and its harmful effects on the health of women workers and the well-being of their families (Lapidus, 1993). The contradictory gender attitudes characteristic of the Soviet Union in the 1980s can also be found in Gorbachev's book *Perestroika* where he wrote:

> Today it is imperative for the country to more actively involve women in the management of the economy, in cultural development and public life. For this purpose women's councils have been set up throughout the country. (Gorbachev, 1988: 116)

Yet he also wrote that the breakdown of family life was to blame for an array of Soviet social problems, and stressed the goal of 'what we should do to make it possible for women to return to their purely womanly mission' (ibid. 117–18).

A critical assessment

Clearly state-socialist countries had gender-related problems, including inequalities and biases, that intensified as economic stagnation set in after the mid-1970s and were exacerbated in the 1980s. For one thing, state-socialist policies had generally changed from those of the 1950s and 1960s, and in some countries women's labour-force participation began to decline. Funk notes that Yugoslavia, with its high unemployment, had introduced measures, as did Hungary, which made it possible for women to stay out of the workforce for three years in Hungary and five in the former Yugoslavia while raising children. This became a way for the state to maintain supposed full employment. Hungary had already decided prior to 1989 that women staying home with young children was a cheaper investment than developing an adequate daycare system (Funk, 1993: 31).

There were inequalities in educational tracking, access to training, location in the occupational structure, and income levels. Notwithstanding their high educational attainment—indeed, Siemienska (1993) and Bialecki and Heyns (1993) have argued that in Poland women were the educational superiors—women were rarely found at the highest levels of management, authority, and decision-making. Despite a pattern of occupational distribution that was less segregated than in many Western and developing countries, women tended to be concentrated in the lower-paid jobs in industry and the services sector. Although gender-based wage differentials were smaller than in Western countries, they existed and were at odds with the official ideology of equality.[13] Some authors have stressed the unhealthy work conditions women suffered. According to one account, women in Czechoslovakia between the ages of 30 and 74 had an 11–18 per cent higher rate of health problems than men (Funk, 1993: 31). In the Soviet Union, about one-third of the women working for industry received special benefits for unhealthy working conditions (Rimachevskaya, 1993). Nevertheless, it should be noted that in all former communist countries, women's life expectancy exceeded men's by several years, and in the former Soviet Union by as much as ten years.

Turgeon estimated that Hungarian women's wages were between 70 and 75 per cent of men's with a slight tendency for the discrimination gap to close. Likewise, in agriculture, women's wages seemed to approximate 70 per cent of men's wages on average. Lapidus estimated that Soviet women made 65–70 per cent of male earnings. In comparison with advanced capitalist countries, such as Japan, the United States, Canada, and Great Britain, this discrimination gap was smaller. It was about the same as the gap in Austria, Belgium, West Germany, France, and

[13] These contradictions are discussed in detail in various contributions in Moghadam (1993*c*), esp. chs. by Einhorn, Paukert, and Fong and Paull.

Holland. But the gap was larger than in Australia and in the Scandinavian countries.

One reason for the earnings gap is that as in the USSR, Hungarian women were excluded from underground coal mining, the highest-paid occupation in both countries. In Hungary, average wages of mining (principally coal mining) in 1984 were 8,096 forints per month, or 44 per cent higher than the average wage generally (Turgeon, 1989). Another explanation for the male–female income differentials was offered by Anker, who speculated that women were not as committed to the labour force as men. Women frequently saw themselves as secondary earners, often withdrawing from the labour force for extended period of time in order to raise their children. This applied to a significantly lesser degree to professional married women (Anker, 1985). Yet, in state-socialist countries, where the society gradually lost the 'Protestant work ethic of socialism', women were considered less reliable workers. They used sick leave extensively to take care of sick children; and given that children were often sick, women were frequently absent.

Notwithstanding the earnings gap between men and women, and in the absence of precise data, it is possible that women's total lifetime earnings were on average higher than men's because of (*a*) benefits and allowances for childbirth and childcare, and (*b*) pensions that began earlier for women than men and lasted longer because of women's longevity. It is perhaps due to these factors, and especially because of the generous social policies of the socialist era and women's extensive use of maternity and family benefits, that women are perceived in the post-communist era as constituting 'expensive labour', rather than the cheap labour usually sought after by capital. This rendered them vulnerable to lay-offs and discriminatory hiring practices during the transition. From a market point of view, the social costs of female labour would have to be lowered before the demand for female labour rose again.

THE LEGACY OF THE DOUBLE BURDEN

It appears that, although decades of communism eliminated the traditional forms of patriarchy, female disadvantage remained, pervaded the spheres of production and reproduction alike, and was manifested in gender inequalities in economic life, in political power, and even in attitudes towards 'feminine' and 'masculine'. The new post-communist leaderships in eastern Europe were therefore able to draw on a repertoire of patriarchal attitudes and practices to try to initiate the marginalization of women from the sphere of production and their re-attachment to domestic life and reproductive roles.

It is interesting to note that in 1918, at the first All-Russian Women's Congress, Lenin had strong words to say about women and housework, and admonished his party comrades to do something about it:

> Notwithstanding all the liberating laws that have been passed, woman continues to be a domestic slave, because petty housework crushes, strangles, stultifies and degrades her, chains her to the kitchen and the nursery, and wastes her labour on barbarously unproductive, petty, nerve-wracking drudgery. The real emancipation of women, real communism, will begin only when a mass struggle (led by the proletariat in power) is started against this petty domestic economy . . . Do we devote sufficient attention to this question which, theoretically, is indisputable for every communist? Of course not . . .[14]

Unfortunately sufficient attention was not devoted to this question in later decades. In a comprehensive and fascinating book on Soviet women written in the early 1970s, Mandel included a discussion of the problems associated with women's dual burden, adding that Soviet men 'did not understand that the solution lies in men's fully sharing the homemaking role' (Mandel, 1975: 221). And we have seen that in 1977, Soviet leader Leonid Brezhnev admitted to the unequal gender division of labour in the spheres of production and reproduction.

Although the status of women in the GDR was considered to be the highest, some observers noted gender-related problems. A sociological study found that 'traditional women's and men's spheres of activity in the household have been maintained', especially, in 'working-class and farming families' (Meier, 1989: 41). In a perceptive and prescient commentary on contradictions of women's work and family roles in the GDR, Susan Bassnett wrote that 'the need for women to enter the labour force outside the home has led to the development of childcare services and systems of benefits, but at the same time little or nothing seems to have been done to tackle the whole question of whether the housework holds the same status as paid work outside the home'. She also noted the automatic association of *Familie* with *Frau* in the GDR: 'when on occasion I queried this and suggested that this terminological link-up had sexist implications, the responses varied from bewilderment to hostility. Clearly, the argument went, the link-up was primarily between women and the family, because the women gave birth to the children' (Bassnett, 1986: 70).

Another important observation on Bassnett's part was that while East German women seemed to be achieving so much in material terms, some had already begun to ask more fundamental questions, such as whether women's needs and desires are not fundamentally different from those of men. She observes that Christa Wolf, one of the GDR's leading writers, asked whether women ought to aspire 'to take roles that have done such

[14] Cited in *The Woman Question: Selections from the Writings of Karl Marx, Frederick Engels, V. I. Lenin, Joseph Stalin* (New York: International Publishers, 1977), 56.

damage to men throughout the ages' (cit. Bassnett, 1986: 70). Bassnett's reflections are worth reviewing:

> The material position of the average East German woman is undeniably better than that of the average woman in capitalist countries, and the women's movement in many countries is still struggling to achieve tiny gains in areas that East German women have ceased even to consider problematic. The difficulties arise with the simultaneous emphasis on women's right to work and on the special relationship between woman and the family. . . .
>
> . . . Socialism offers a rethinking of property and labour relations, but has not come up with a rethinking of sex relations . . . (ibid. 81).

This 'unfinished business of socialism' may help to explain why, in the wake of the political and economic changes in Eastern Europe and the Soviet Union in 1989–90, there was much talk of women's *relief* at no longer having to be employed, and the importance of *choice* under the new arrangements. However, since women's only experience was of full employment and of jobs awaiting them after extended child-care leave, 'women initially had no way of knowing that exercising choice in a decision to "stay at home with the children for a few years" might result in their becoming long-term unemployed' (Einhorn, 1993*a*: 58).

FACING THE NEW LABOUR MARKETS

In the immediate post-communist, transition period, women had to face new problems: growing unemployment, competition with men for jobs, the closure of child-care centres at work places or the introduction of relatively high fees for daycare facilities, and many kinds of gender bias. Economic recession has further entailed inflation, the collapse of household incomes, and increasing poverty. In 1993 available evidence suggested that as in earlier years, the majority of the unemployed were female in all countries but Hungary and Slovenia (see Table 1 below). In the former USSR, the share of women among those who lost employment in the period 1989–91 was 60 per cent. When the state bureaucracy was streamlined in the period 1985–7, more than 80 per cent of those laid off in the industrial sector were women. More than half of all unemployed women had higher education. In general, there were fewer chances for women to find a new job (United Nations, 1993: 206). Unwillingness of some firms to hire women because of the possible extra costs due to maternity leave may have been a factor in reducing these possibilities. In 1993 in Russia, 50 million people, a third of the Russian population, were living below the poverty line, and more than half of the households headed by women fell into poverty. According to a recent analysis of unemployment and poverty:

Table 1 Unemployment rates by gender, selected CEE countries, 1990–1993, as percentages

	1990	1991	1992	1993
Bulgaria				
Total	1.7	11.1	14.1	16.4
Male			13.7	
Female			14.5	
Croatia				
Total	8	14	15	
Male	6	11	12	
Female	11	16	18	
Czech Republic				
Total	1.0	4.1	2.6	3.5
Male	0.9	3.5	2.2	3.0
Female	1.0	4.8	3.0	4.1
Germany (former GDR)				
Total		10.3	14.8	15.0
Male		8.5	10.5	11.0
Female		12.3	19.6	21.0
Hungary				
Total	1.7	8.5	12.3	12.1
Male	1.8	9.2	14.0	14.2
Female	1.4	7.6	10.5	10.1
Poland				
Total	3.5	9.7	13.3	15.7
Male	3.2	7.9	11.8	14.3
Female	3.8	11.4	14.9	17.3
Romania				
Total	.	3.2	8.4	10.1
Male	.	2.2	6.2	8.1
Female	.	4.0	10.7	12.6
Slovakia				
Total		6.6	11.4	12.7
Male		6.3	11.1	12.5
Female		6.9	11.7	12.9
Slovenia				
Total	4.7	8.2	11.5	14.4
Male	4.5	8.5	12.1	15.3
Female	4.8	7.9	10.8	13.5

Source: ILO, *Yearbook of Labour Statistics 1994*, table 9A; UN, *World Economic and Social Survey 1994*, table VI.12.

Women constitute more than 70 per cent of the unemployed in Russia. The majority of them were previously employed in factory management and the scientific and technical subdivisions of enterprises of the state sector. Discrimination against women occurs both during the mass release of personnel and the taking on of new workers. (Tchernina, 1993: 10)

According to a 1986 official report, 59 per cent of all GDR women in employment had completed vocational training. There had been considerable progress in the textiles, clothing, and leather industries, which employed mostly women. These were also industries in which women were heavily represented in supervisory categories: 'the proportion of female supervisors in that area went up from 33 to almost 44 per cent between 1976 and 1984'.[15] Typically, one found a female engineer in a cotton-spinning factory, active in the trade union movement, and the chair of her factory's works council. Kindergartens and leisure activities for children were also frequently organized by the enterprises. Following unification, however, there was a tremendous decline in the textile industry in eastern Germany, where three quarters of the industry's workforce were women. Most vulnerable were older and middle-aged women with no training or experience relevant to the restructured economy and new technology. As enterprises closed down, so did the child-care facilities. Unsurprisingly, a poll carried out in Brandenburg, a textile-producing state in the east, found that 82 per cent of women surveyed believed that for them, things were worse than they had been before unification. In the former GDR, single mothers enjoyed shorter hours, longer vacations, special protection against layoffs, and comprehensive child-care in daycare centres, kindergartens, and after-school programmes. Following unification and the onset of serious economic problems, more and more of these parents began to live on unemployment or welfare.[16]

In 1989, the number of employed people in the GDR—with employment still being guaranteed by the State—was 9.8 million. Within the space of three years, roughly 40 per cent of these jobs (more than 4 million) disappeared (Wiedemeyer *et al.*, 1993). Approximately 600,000 people—mainly young skilled workers—migrated westwards, where the majority have since found employment, and more than 400,000 workers (mostly men) commute daily or weekly from eastern to western Germany to jobs not available at home. A 1993 study found that although the official unemployment rate in eastern Germany had reached 15 per cent, the figure rose appreciably when the numbers engaged in labour-market policy programmes and in early-retirement schemes were taken into account. The same study found women's employment to be considerably worse than men's:

[15] *Equal Rights in Practice*, 17.

[16] See *World Press Review*, April 1992.

As long-term unemployment worsens, a growing number of disillusioned claimants are losing their entitlement to unemployment benefits and simply leaving the labour force. There is also a marked trend towards sex-related labour market segmentation, and women now account for two-thirds of the jobless; in the former GDR 84 per cent of women of working age were in the labour force (compared with 53 per cent in the west). Now standing at over 20 per cent, official unemployment among women in the new federal states (i.e. eastern Germany), is almost double that of men. Women are also proportionally under-represented in labour market programmes. (Wiedemeyer *et al.*, 1993: 606–7)

Gender stereotypes presume that unemployment is less traumatic for women than for men, and that many women in the former state-socialist countries welcomed the opportunity to withdraw from the labour force. Yet surveys carried out in Bulgaria, Hungary, Poland, and Russia have disproved these notions. Referring to Bulgaria, Kostova states that 'unemployment has a very strong effect on women's position in society, on family relations and women's life satisfaction. To women, who for decades have considered their job as one of their most important roles in society, the loss of paid employment leads to serious distress' (Kostova, 1994: 14). Bodrova reports that according to a poll she supervised in May 1994, 'in the opinion of 86 per cent of working women, their greatest concern was a fear of losing their jobs' (Bodrova, 1994: 8). Paukert (1994) reports on an ILO survey conducted in the Czech and Slovak Republics which revealed that the majority of women would want to continue working, even if the income of their husband or partner increased substantially. Paukert (1994: 2) concludes that the labour-force attachment of women in east and central Europe remains intact.

There is some evidence that male employment has been rising faster than female employment in some 'women-dominated' service branches such as banking and insurance. Siemienska points that in the 1980s 'finance and insurance were highly feminized (83 per cent of those employed were women)' but that at present 'in the newly created sector of "financial consultants" women form a very small group (28 per cent of the total employed)' (Siemienska, 1994: 10). ILO surveys of manufacturing establishments carried out in Bulgaria, Hungary, and the Czech and Slovak Republics between 1991 and 1993 showed that at the recruitment stage, and for the majority of occupations, managers mostly preferred men. 'The surveys revealed undeniable gender bias among managers in recruitment, but also in retrenchment, the highest amount of gender bias existing in the Czech Republic and the lowest one in Hungary' (Paukert, 1994: 3). The current economic climate, and neoliberal economic policies in general, favour expansion of self-employment, and some women have been responding by trying to open up their own businesses such as restaurants, cafés, shops, and guest-houses, as Siemienska (1994) reports for Poland. But many women face such difficulties as lack of training in business-related skills and a shortage of credit on affordable terms (Fong and Paull, 1993: 237).

POLITICAL DISEMPOWERMENT

Studies of gender and revolution have documented the frequent exclusion of women from the new political institutions, in such cases as France, Mexico, Iran, and Algeria (Moghadam, 1993*a*, 1995; Tétreault, 1994). Women's exclusion from political power has been based on notions of sexual difference and justified in terms of natural or divine law. A similar development occurred in the former state-socialist countries. In the immediate post-communist period, feminist commentators noted that democratization in eastern Europe had acquired a 'male' face, and this despite the importance of women's active involvement in the opposition movements, especially in Poland and Czechoslovakia. The first democratic elections resulted in a dramatic decline in the presence of women in formal political institutions, particularly the new parliaments. Before 1989, women held a third of all Romanian parliamentary seats; after the new elections, they held 3.5 per cent. Similar drops were registered in Czechoslovakia (from 29.5 to 6 per cent), and in Hungary (from 21 to 7 per cent). In Bulgaria in 1991, women won only 34 seats out of 400; but fully 24 of the female parliamentarians were with the Socialist Party (Inter-Parliamentary Union, 1992: 69). In the former Soviet Union, multi-candidate elections in 1989, the freest since 1917, produced a Congress of People's Deputies in which fewer than 15 per cent of the deputies were women, as compared with 33 per cent under previous governments. And in the local elections to the Russian Republic's Parliament (held in spring 1990), the proportion of women elected dropped from 35.3 per cent before the quotas were removed to 5.4 per cent afterward (see Moghadam, 1990: 25–8). A pre-election poll in *Argumenti i Fakti* in 1989 showed that voters considered 'being a man' one of the most important qualities in a candidate (Vanden Heuvel, 1990: 778).

In 1990, Zsuzsa Berés, 38, a Hungarian translator and editor, a single mother of two children, and a founding member of the Hungarian Green Party, was quoted as saying: 'Ours is the only newly emerged party that addresses women's needs. The Democratic Forum, the Christian Democratic People's Party, the peasants party, and the Alliance of Free Democrats—all speak only of family. I am afraid our political situation is very much reminiscent of the period before World War II—open anti-Semitism, racism, no job security, an economy in ruins, pornography flooding our streets. I ask myself, what did the past two years of democracy bring us?' (Drakulic, 1990) It did not bring many women members of parliament: 28 out of 386, the lowest ratio of women in four decades.

Not only did women's parliamentary representation decrease, but the official women's organizations lost their prestige and influence, not to mention funding. In response to a questionnaire from the Inter-Parliamentary Union in 1991, Poland offered the following information: 'Only a few institutions in the Republic of Poland deal specifically with the problems of women. The most popular and the best-known of these is the Women's League, created in 1945, a mass organization, member of the World Democratic Women's Federation. Its objectives are: educational work with women, organizing help in the daily life of women and families, activization of women in the economic, cultural, and social life of the country. Owing to the recent political and social transformations in Poland, the importance of this organization has decreased considerably' (Inter-Parliamentary Union, 1992: 43).

What can explain women's political disempowerment? According to Wolchik (1993), women's prior participation in political structures had been more formal than real, and parliaments themselves were formal bodies, while real power existed in the highest levels of the Party. Women were excluded when parliaments became sites of real political power. She also argues that 'the effort to mobilize women by means of official women's organizations, and the willingness of the leaders of those organizations to follow the party line in most cases' further 'fuelled the backlash against women's political involvement' (Wolchik, 1993: 35). In contrast, Einhorn asserts that women were genuinely involved in political activities, especially at the local and grassroots levels, and that these are the forms of participation that could endure (Einhorn, 1993*b*: 164). Still, she notes an 'allergy to feminism' and a widespread view of high politics as masculine and unfeminine (ibid. 168–72). This is confirmed by information provided by the Inter-Parliamentary Union, which carried out a survey among 150 national parliaments in October 1991. In response to a question about images of male and female politicians, Hungary responded thus: 'In Hungary, the image of a politician is essentially masculine. There is no special image for women politicians. The media and the political parties do nothing in this respect' (Inter-Parliamentary Union, 1992: 168). The response from Poland was that 'some parties and organizations of Christian orientation tend to perceive a woman more as the traditional mother-type, unfit not only for public office, but even for speaking out on important social problems'. The response also noted that the image portrayed by the mass media 'depreciates women and their potential as politicians and activists' (Inter-Parliamentary Union, 1992: 171).

In the early 1990s some women began to respond to the new political climate by forming activist and self-help goups. Polish, German, and Hungarian feminists have publicly protested discourses and policies unfavourable to women, while Russian feminists have sought to influence parliamentary decisions on child care, parental leave, and other aspects of family policy. Since then academic women have established women's studies centres in Budapest, Prague, Warsaw, and throughout Russia, where advocacy is combined with research on women's changing positions and on economic and social policies. All these feminists have tapped into international women's networks, and resulting alliances could prove effective in the future.

CONCLUSIONS

Early Soviet Marxism and socialist thought predicted that patriarchy would wither away with the entry of women in the sphere of production. As Marx and Engels put it in the *Communist Manifesto*, 'all fixed, fast frozen relations, with their train of ancient prejudices and opinions are swept away'. Yet it appears that 'the traditions of the dead generations weigh heavily on the minds of the living', to quote from Marx's *Eighteenth Brumaire*. One reason may have been the ambivalence towards fundamental change in family relations. Nevertheless, the unexpected resurgence of patriarchy in the former state-socialist countries now undergoing the transition to a market economy raises fundamental questions about the relationship between patriarchy and development, and the relationship between gender and social transformation.

At least two lessons, theoretical and political, may be gleaned from the experience of patriarchy and post-communism. One pertains to the centrality of gender in processes of social, political, and economic change. There can be no doubt that gender is at least as important as class in the course and consequences of change processes, and that economic and political restructuring has gender-specific effects and profound implications for women's status and welfare. Not only must gender be integrated into socio-economic analysis, but new policies must take into account the effects of economic and political transformations on women and on gender relations.

The second lesson is that the full integration of women in the sphere of production is not a sufficient condition for the emancipation of women, the elimination of patriarchy, and the achievement of gender equality. Although full and equitable participation of women in economic life is a necessary condition for equity, empowerment, and autonomy, it must be combined with transformations in the sphere of reproduction, especially the attainment of a more equitable gender division of labour. Without radical changes in the arenas of child care, care for relatives, shopping, cleaning, cooking, and other aspects of household management, women will continue to be exhausted by their double burden, while cultural images of women and popular perceptions will continue to link women to domesticity and family. The current situation of women in eastern Europe and the former Soviet Union provides compelling evidence that the elimination of patriarchy requires equity and empowerment in the spheres of both production and reproduction, and political organization to effectively counter backlashes.

REFERENCES

ANKER, RICHARD (1985), 'Comparative Survey', in Valentina Bodrova and Richard Anker (eds.), *Working Women in Socialist Countries: The Fertility Connection* (Geneva: ILO), 1–20.

BASSNETT, SUSAN (1986), *Feminist Experiences: The Women's Movement in Four Cultures* (London: Allen and Unwin).

BIALECKI, IRENEUSZ and BARBARA HEYNS (1993). 'Educational Attainment, the Status of Women, and the Private School Movement in Poland', in Valentine M. Moghdam (ed.), *Democratic Reform and the Position of Women in Transitional Economies* (Oxford: Clarendon Press).

BODROVA, VALENTINA (1994), 'Economic Restructuring, New Social Policies, and Working Women in Russia: Tendency and Behaviour', paper prepared for UNU/WIDER, Helsinki.

—— and ANKER, RICHARD (eds.) (1985), *Working Women in Socialist Countries: The Fertility Connection* (Geneva: ILO).

DRAKULIC, SLAVENKA (1990), 'In Their Own Words: Women of Eastern Europe', MS, July–Aug., pp. 36–47.

EINHORN, BARBARA (1989), 'Socialist Emancipation: The Women's Movement in the German Democratic Republic', in Sonia Kruks, Rayna Rapp, and Marilyn B. Young (eds.), *Promissory Notes: Women in the Transition to Socialism* (New York: Monthly Review), 282–305.

—— (1993*a*), 'Democratization and Women's Movements in Central and Eastern Europe: Concepts of Women's Rights', in Valentine Moghadam (ed.), *Democratic Reform and the Position of Women in Transitional Economies* (Oxford: Clarendon Press).

—— (1993*b*), *Cinderella Goes to Market: Citizenship, Gender and Women's Movements in East Central Europe* (London: Verso).

ENGELS, FREDRICK (1972 [1884]), *The Origin of the Family, Private Property, and the State*, introduction by Evelyn Reed (New York: Pathfinder Press).

FONG, MONICA and PAULL, GILLIAN (1993), 'Women's Economic Status in the Restructuring of Eastern Europe', in Valentine Moghadam (ed.), *Democratic Reform and the Position of Women in Transitional Economies* (Oxford: Clarendon Press).

FUNK, NANETTE (1993), 'Women Under Post-Communism', *Against the Current* (May/June).

GAFFIKIN, FRANK and MORISSEY, MIKE (1992), *The New Unemployed: Joblessness and Poverty in the Market Economy* (London: Zed Books).

GOLDMAN, WENDY (1989), 'Women, the Family, and the New Revolutionary Order in the Soviet Union', in S. Kruks, R. Rapp, and M. Young (eds.), *Promissory Notes: Women in the Transition to Socialism* (New York: Monthly Review Press).

GORBACHEV, MIKHAIL (1988), *Perestroika* (new edn.) (London: Fontana).

ILO (1993), *Yearbook of Labour Statistics 1993* (Geneva: ILO).

ILO/INSTRAW (1985), *Women in Economic Activity: A Global Statistical Survey 1950–2000* (Geneva: International Labour Organization; Santo Domingo: United Nations Institute for Training and Research on Women).

Inter-Parliamentary Union (1992), Women and Political Power: Survey Carried Out Among the 150 National Parliaments Existing as of 31 October 1991. Series 'Reports & Documents', No. 19 (Geneva: Inter-Parliamentary Union).

KANDIYOTI, DENIZ (ed.) (1991), *Women, Islam and the State* (London: Macmillan).

KOSTOVA, DOBRINKA (1994), 'Economic Restructuring, Social Policy and Women Workers in Bulgaria', paper prepared for UNU/WIDER, Helsinki.

LANDES, JOAN (1989), 'Marxism and the "The Woman Question"', in S. Kruks, R. Rapp, and M. Young (eds.), *Promissory Notes: Women in the Transition to Socialism* (New York: Monthly Review Press).

LANE, DAVID (ed.) (1986), *Labour and Employment in the USSR* (New York: New York University Press).

—— (1987), *Soviet Labour and the Ethic of Communism: Full Employment and the Labour Process in the USSR* (Brighton, UK: Wheatsheaf Books).

LAPIDUS, GAIL (1985), 'The Soviet Union', in Jennie Farley (ed.), *Women Workers in 15 Countries* (Ithaca, NY: ILR/Cornell University Press), 13–32.

—— (1993), 'Gender and Restructuring: The Impact of Perestroika and Its Aftermath on Soviet Women', in Valentine Moghadam (ed.), *Democratic Reform and the Position of Women in Transitional Economies* (Oxford: Clarendon Press).

MANDEL, WILLIAM M. (1975), *Soviet Women* (Garden City, NY: Anchor Books).

MARX, KARL and ENGELS, FREDERICK (1969), *Selected Works*, vol. 1 (Moscow: Progress Publishers).

MASSELL, GREGORY (1974), *The Surrogate Proletariat: Moslem Women and Revolutionary Strategies in Soviet Central Asia, 1919–1929* (Princeton, NJ: Princeton University Press).

MEIER, UTA (1989), 'Equality without Limits? Women's Work in the Socialist Society of the German Democratic Republic', *International Sociology*, 4/1: 37–49.

MOGHADAM, VALENTINE M. (1990), 'Gender and Restructuring: Perestroika, the 1989 Revolutions, and Women', WIDER Working Paper no. 87 (Nov.).

—— (1993*a*), *Modernizing Women: Gender and Social Change in the Middle East* (Boulder, Colo.: Lynne Rienner Publishers).

—— (ed.) (1993*b*), *Identity Politics and Women: Cultural Reassertions and Feminisms in International Perspective* (Boulder, Colo.: Westview Press).

—— (ed.) (1993*c*), *Democratic Reform and the Position of Women in Transitional Economies* (Oxford: Clarendon Press).

—— (ed.) (1994), *Gender and National Identity: Women and Politics in Muslim Societies* (London: Zed Books).

—— (1995), 'Gender and Revolutions', in John Foran (ed.), *Theorizing Revolutions* (New York: Routledge).

MOLYNEUX, MAXINE (1982), 'Socialist Societies Old and New: Progress Toward Women's Emancipation?', *Monthly Review* (July–Aug.): 65–100.

PAUKERT, LIBA (1993), 'The Changing Economic Status of Women in the Period of Transition to a Market Economy System: The Case of the Czech and Slovak Republics after 1989', in Valentine M. Moghadam (ed.), *Democratic Reform and the Position of Women in Transitional Economies* (Oxford: Clarendon Press).

—— (1994), 'Gender and Change in Central and Eastern Europe', paper prepared for the International Forum on Equality for Women in the World of Work: Challenges for the Future, Geneva, 1–3 June.

POSADSKAYA, ANASTASIA (1993), 'Changes in Gender Discourses in the Former Soviet Union', in Valentine M. Moghadam (ed.), *Democratic Reform and the Position of Women in Transitional Economies* (Oxford: Clarendon Press).

REDHEAD, SCOTT, SHAFFER, HARRY G., and TURGEON, LYNN (1989), 'GDR Women in a Comparative Perspective', mimeo, Department of Economics, Hofstra University, Hempstead, Long Island, NY.

RIMACHEVSKAYA, NATALIA (1993), 'Socio-Economic Changes and the Position of Women in the Union of Soviet Socialist Republics', in Liisa Rantalaiho (ed.), *Social Changes and the Status of Women: The Experience of Finland and the USSR* (University of Tampere Research Institute for Social Sciences, Centre for Women's Studies and Gender Relations), 42–74.

SANJIAN, ANDREA STEVENSON (1991), 'Prostitution, the Press, and Agenda-Building in the Soviet Policy Process', in Anthony Jones, Walter D. Connor and David E. Powell (eds.), *Soviet Social Problems* (Boulder, Colo.: Westview Press).

SIEMIENSKA, RENATA (1993), 'Gender as a Factor Differentiating Social Position in Transition to a Market Economy in Poland', paper prepared for delivery at the annual meeting of the American Sociological Association, Miami Beach, Florida, 13–17 Aug.

—— (1994), 'Economic Restructuring, Social Policies, and Women Workers in Poland', paper prepared for UNU/WIDER, Helsinki.

TCHERNINA, NATALIA (1993), 'Employment Deprivation and Poverty: The Ways in which Poverty is Emerging in the Course of Economic Reform in Russia' (Geneva: International Institute for Labour Studies, Discussion Paper no. 60).

TÉTREAULT, MARY ANN (ed.) (1994), *Women and Revolution in Africa, Asia, and the New World* (Columbia, SC: University of South Carolina Press).

TURGEON, LYNN (1989), 'Hungarian Women in a Comparative Perspective', mimeo.

—— (1990), 'What's To Become of Socialism in Eastern Europe?' Paper delivered at Southern Oregon State College, Ashland, Jan. 11.

TURGEON, LYNN and MACINTYRE, ROBERT (1990), 'Comments on "Perestroika and the Future Socialism"', *Monthly Review* (Sept.): 50–1.

United Nations (1993), *1993 Report on the World Social Situation* (advance copy) (New York: United Nations).

—— (1994), *World Economic and Social Survey 1994* (New York: United Nations).

VANDEN HEUVEL, KATRINA (1990), 'Glasnost for Women?' *The Nation* (4 June): 773–9.

WATERS, ELIZABETH (1989), 'In the Shadow of the Comintern: The Communist Women's Movement, 1920–43', in Sonia Kruks, Rayna Rapp, and Marilyn B. Young (eds.), *Promissory Notes: Women in the Transition to Socialism* (New York: Monthly Review Press).

WIEDEMEYER, MICHAEL, BEYWL, WOLFGANG, and HELMSTADTER, WOLFGANG (1993),

'Employment Promotion Companies in Eastern Germany: Emergency Measures or a Basis for Structural Reform?' *International Labour Review*, 132/5–6.

WOLCHIK, SHARON (1993), 'Women and the Politics of Transition in Central and Eastern Europe', in Valentine Moghadam (ed.), *Democratic Reform and the Position of Women in Transitional Economies* (Oxford: Clarendon Press).

World Press Review (1992) (Apr.).

YUVAL-DAVIS, NIRA and ANTHIAS, FLOYA (eds.) (1989), *Women-Nation-State* (London: Macmillan).

APPENDIX

Women's Positions at Century's End: Cross-national Trends and Comparisons in Socio-economic Indicators

Table A1 Demographic profile, selected developing and industrial countries

	Estimated Population (millions)			Annual population growth rate (%)		Total fertility rate 1991	Contraceptive prevalence rate (%) 1985–90
	1960	1991	2000	1960–91	1991–2000		
DEVELOPING COUNTRIES							
Brazil	72.6	151.6	172.8	2.4	1.5	2.9	66
Cuba	7.0	10.7	11.5	1.4	0.8	1.9	70
Dominican Republic	3.2	7.3	8.6	2.6	1.8	3.5	50
India	442.3	862.7	1,018.7	2.2	1.8	4.0	43
Iran, Islamic Republic of	21.6	59.9	77.9	3.3	2.9	6.1	—
Korea, Republic of	25.0	43.8	46.9	1.8	0.8	1.7	77
Malaysia	8.1	18.4	22.3	2.6	2.1	3.7	51
Mexico	36.5	86.3	102.6	2.8	1.9	3.3	53
Nicaragua	1.5	3.8	5.2	3.0	3.4	5.2	27
Philippines	27.6	63.8	76.1	2.7	2.0	4.0	44
Thailand	26.4	55.4	61.2	2.4	1.1	2.3	66
Tunisia	4.2	8.2	9.8	2.2	1.9	3.6	50
Turkey	27.5	57.2	68.2	2.4	2.0	3.6	63
Yemen	5.2	12.1	16.4	2.7	3.4	7.3	—
Zimbabwe	3.8	10.3	13.2	3.2	2.8	5.5	43

INDUSTRIAL COUNTRIES							
Bulgaria	7.9	9.0	8.9	0.4	–0.1	1.9	76
Czechoslovakia	13.7	15.7	16.3	0.4	0.4	2.0	95
Denmark	4.6	5.1	5.2	0.4	0.2	1.7	63
Finland	4.4	5.0	5.1	0.4	0.3	1.8	80
Hungary	10.0	10.5	10.5	0.2	–0.0	1.8	73
Norway	3.6	4.3	4.5	0.6	0.6	1.9	71
Poland	29.6	38.3	39.5	0.8	0.3	2.1	75
Romania	18.4	23.3	24.0	0.8	0.4	2.2	58
Russian Federation	118.8	148.7	155.2	0.7	0.5	2.0	22

Source: *Human Development Report 1993*.

Table A2 Status of women

	Life expectancy at birth (years) 1990	Maternal mortality rate (per 100,000 live births) 1988	Average age at first marriage (years) 1980–5	Literacy rate (age 15–24 only) 1980–9	Enrolment ratio			Tertiary science and engineering enrolment (% female) 1987–8	Women in labour force (% of total) 1990	Administrative and managerial staff (% female) 1980–9	Parliament (% of seats occupied by women) 1991
					Primary (net) 1988–90	Secondary (gross) 1988–90	Tertiary (gross) 1988–90				
DEVELOPING COUNTRIES											
Brazil	68.4	230	22.6	85	—	—	12	—	35	—	6
Cuba	77.3	54	19.9	99	95	94	25	39	32	—	34
Dominican Rep.	68.9	200	20.5	—	73	—	—	—	15	21	—
India	59.3	550	18.7	40	—	33	4	22	26	2	7
Iran	66.6	250	19.7	42	90	45	4	10	10	18	2
Korea (South)	73.1	80	24.1	—	100	86	28	13	34	3	2
Malaysia	72.3	120	23.5	83	—	58	7	29	31	8	5
Mexico	73.0	150	20.6	91	—	53	12	—	31	15	12
Nicaragua	66.2	200	—	—	77	44	9	48	—	34	16
Philippines	66.2	250	22.4	92	98	75	—	—	37	25	9
Thailand	68.1	180	22.7	96	—	32	—	—	47	21	4
Tunisia	67.5	200	24.3	63	91	40	7	24	23	—	4
Turkey	67.0	200	20.6	75	—	42	10	26	33	3	1
Yemen	52.0	800	17.8	—	—	10	—	—	13	—	3
Zimbabwe	61.4	330	20.4	—	—	46	2	—	35	15	12

INDUSTRIAL COUNTRIES												
Bulgaria	75.6	40	20.8			—	—	44	—	29	9
Czechoslovakia	75.5	14	21.6			—	—	26	43	—	9
Denmark	78.7	4	26.1			—	33	23	40	14	33
Finland	79.2	15	24.6			—	42	24	44	19	39
Hungary	74.6	21	21.0			—	—	19	42	—	7
Norway	80.5	4	24.0			97	31	30	43	22	36
Poland	75.8	15	22.5			—	—	29	—	—	14
Romania	73.6	210	21.1			—	—	—	—	—	4
Russian Fed.	74.4	49	—			—	—	—	—	—	—

Note: Literacy rate and primary enrolment ratio for developing countries only. [— indicates data not available]
Source: Human Development Report 1993.

Table A3 Indicators on women's work, labour force by status in employment, 1980/7

	Employers/own account		Employees		Unpaid family	
	% of total	% female	% of total	% female	% of total	% female
India	9	9	17	12	4	23
Iran	31	5	48	12	10	49
Korea, Republic of	30	30	54	36	13	83
Malaysia	29	29	54	31	10	54
Philippines	36	29	40	37	15	52
Tunisia	22	26	58	14	6	77
Turkey	23	7	32	15	41	70

Source: United Nations, *The World's Women* (New York: UN), 1991.

Table A4 Laws and regulations governing maternity protection, 1989

	Maternity leave	% of wages paid during leave
DEVELOPING COUNTRIES		
Algeria	12 weeks	50
Brazil	12 weeks	100
Cuba	18 weeks	100
Dominican Republic	12 weeks	50
Egypt	90–100 days	50
India	12 weeks	100
Iran, Islamic Rep. of	12 weeks	two-thirds
Mexico	82 days	100
Morocco	12 weeks	50
Nicaragua	12 weeks	60
Philippines	45 days	100
Taiwan	n.a.	*
Thailand	none	none
Tunisia	30 days	two-thirds
Turkey	12 weeks	two-thirds
Zimbabwe	90 days	75
INDUSTRIAL COUNTRIES		
Bulgaria	4–6 months	100
Czechoslovakia	28 weeks	90
Denmark	28 weeks	90
Finland	263 days	80
GDR	26 weeks	100
Germany	12 weeks	100
Hungary	24 weeks	100
Norway	120 days	100
Poland	16 weeks	100
US	none	none
USSR	16 weeks	100

* maternity grant equal to two months' earnings
n.a. = information not available
Note: ILO conventions call for at least 12 weeks' maternity leave at two-thirds salary.
Source: Social Security Administration, *Social Security Programs Throughout the World—1989* (Washington, DC, GPO, 1990).

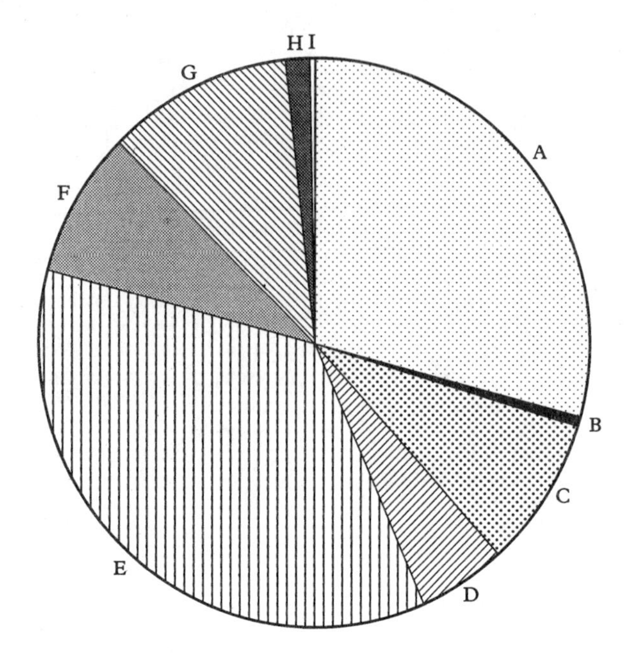

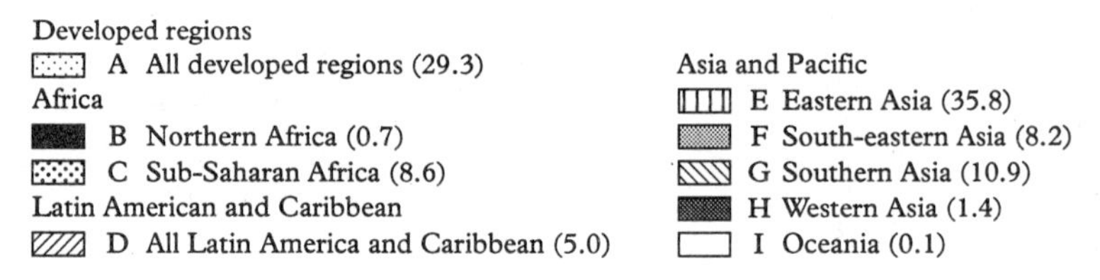

Figure A1 Percentage distribution of the world's female labour force, 1990

Source: UN, *The World's Women: Trends and Statistics 1970–1990*, 83.

INDEX